A LIFE OF JESUS

A LIFE OF JESUS

A Devotional Study

by

MELVA PURKIS

THE CHRISTADELPHIAN
404 Shaftmoor Lane
Birmingham B28 8SZ

2005

First Published 1953

Reprinted 1964, 1973, 1980

Second Edition 1987

Third Edition 2005

ISBN 0 85189 040 7

Printed and bound in England by
WILLIAM CLOWES LTD
Beccles
Suffolk
NR34 7TL

FOREWORD

WRITERS of biographies usually find that they are helped by the shadows cast by their subjects rather than by any nobility of character radiating from them. Weaknesses reveal more than excellences; so many apparent virtues are counterfeits.

But Jesus cast no shadows. He stands irradiated by the light of Heaven, beloved of God. Those who abide with him glow in his light, and even the wrath of his enemies is transmuted into the glory of love when it falls upon him. He is altogether lovely.

It is impossible to write a biography of Jesus for another reason. We become conscious as we write that we are not approaching a subject but a living person. And as our pen writes of his earthly life, we become more and more aware that we are writing in his presence. And then become convinced that his life should be written upon our knees, and exercised in our lives.

My purpose has been to present a simple picture of Jesus, so that the reader may be encouraged to look even more reverently at the Man who can be confused with no other man, and meditate more frequently upon the words that could have fallen from no other lips. To undertake so much is to feel a sense of presumption which is only tempered by the knowledge that God's strength is made perfect in weakness, and He is sometimes pleased to make use of an imperfect vessel to further His eternal purposes.

One or two observations seem necessary in introducing this work to its readers. It is essentially a devotional and not a theological book. It is designed to help in the work of feeding the flock, rather than in the equally necessary task of casting forth the nets. It may not do much towards clarifying the understanding, but it is our prayer that it may help to warm the heart.

This self imposed limitation has meant that some important and interesting matters have been passed over without critical examination. Points such as the date of Christ's birth, the historicity of Luke, the genealogies of Matthew and Luke, the use of prophecy in Matthew's Gospel, have not been discussed. Abundant evidence awaits the student on these subjects, and to have paused to examine them would have clouded the purpose for which this book was written.

The chronology of the Gospels is not an easy problem to resolve, and in this I have been generally guided by the order of events in Mark. Where it was not possible to follow that Gospel, I have in the majority of cases yielded to the reasoning of Samuel Andrews in his *Bible Student's Life of our Lord*.

The parables recorded in the Gospels have been fully dealt with by John Carter in *Parables of the Messiah*; the discourses of Jesus recorded by John, in the same writer's *The Gospel of John*. These two subjects have therefore been only cursorily covered here. It is an arrangement not altogether without advantage since it allows a greater emphasis upon the LIFE of Jesus, as distinct from his teaching.

Our knowledge of Jesus in its deepest sense can never be something we read about him in a book, or even in the Gospels themselves. It must always be a sacred communion with him in the sanctuary of our own devoted hearts.

It is with the earnest prayer that it will help us to love and serve him that we dedicate this humble work to him.

MELVA PURKIS

NOTE TO THE 2005 EDITION

For nearly fifty years Melva Purkis' study of the Master has given instruction, insight and joy to countless readers. After five impressions a further printing has become necessary. The text is unchanged but a number of new colour plates have been included. These are from transparencies kindly supplied by Leen Ritmeyer. Other acknowledgements are for the plates facing pages 180 and 276 (Alan Clarke and Cyril Cooper respectively).

TABLE OF CONTENTS

BOOK FOUR: THE GALILEAN MINISTRY

BOOK FIVE: LESSONS IN DISCIPLESHIP

BOOK EIGHT: THE PRINCE OF LIFE

PROLOGUE

THE redemption of the world by Jesus of Nazareth is the entrance of the eternal purpose of God into this temporal sphere where man lives his human life, records his history, and returns to his dust.

For thirty-three years that purpose was worked out day by day in the life of One who lived in a small country on the outposts of the Roman Empire, and died on a plot of ground outside the walls of Jerusalem, when Pontius Pilate was Procurator of Judea.

History shows us a garden tomb, a military guard, frightened disciples and anxious rulers. With this background there was wrought out the eternal purpose of redemption. We see nothing of that outworking. We see only its evidence in an earthquake, a stone rolled away, an empty sepulchre. That is history.

Forty days later on the Mount of Olives we see a band of disciples looking steadfastly into the heavens. That is history. As a cloud receives their Lord out of their sight, history merges into eternity.

It is in this setting that the pages which follow find their true perspective.

Book One

THE FULNESS OF TIME

1

THE BIRTH OF JESUS

JOSEPH and Mary were nearing the end of their long journey to Bethlehem.

It seemed to Mary more than a few short months since the Angel Gabriel had come to her with his breathtaking message. She still could scarcely believe that the fulness of time had come and God was about to fulfil the promise He had made through the prophets to send the Messiah to redeem Israel and bring salvation to the ends of the earth. As the time drew nearer she had felt again and again a surge of wonder that she should have found favour with God, that she was destined to be the virgin through whom God's purpose was to be revealed. "Behold the handmaid of the Lord", she had said as she had looked into the face of her heavenly visitor, "be it unto me according to thy word."

Gabriel had departed leaving her alone with tumultuous thoughts. The life of Nazareth had gone on as usual; nothing seemed to have happened to disturb its normal course, yet Mary knew that nothing would ever be the same again. For the first time she had understood the literal significance of the message of the Lord to Ahaz nearly eight hundred years before. "Therefore the Lord himself shall give you a sign: Behold, a virgin shall conceive and bear a son, and shall call his name Emmanuel."

With the growing realization of the honour and responsibility had come an intense desire to place herself unreservedly in the hand of God, to live in His presence in a state of constant prayer. It had also awakened a natural desire to confide in some understanding heart. But to whom could she go? She had been far too wise to share her dread and glorious secret with any ordinary acquaintance: a sweet modesty and apprehension had sealed her lips when she met Joseph.

1

There was only one to whom she could go. Elisabeth her elderly cousin was intimately associated with the angel's message. She was rejoicing in the prospect of bearing a promised son long after she had given up all hope of motherhood. So Mary had departed hastily to the hill country of Judea, and there in affectionate companionship preparations had been made for the birth of the messenger and the Saviour. The atmosphere of love and reverence in which these months had been passed can be sensed from the salutation of Elisabeth and the responsive cry of Mary. They had been months of joy and exaltation, and the spirit of both women was a perfect preparation for the lives that were about to be manifested.

Mary had returned to Nazareth before John was born; she was no longer the simple, carefree Israelitish maiden. The events of the past months had brought her to womanhood, the long hours of exalted communion had strengthened her for the trials and bitterness that lay before her. Indeed, a severe trial had awaited her at Nazareth, for her condition could no longer be concealed. The innuendos, the whisperings and the subtle persecutions of her neighbours could be endured, but with what horror she had watched the doubt and pain clearly discerned on Joseph's honest face. Torn between a sense of honour which could not contemplate further association, and a love which would not expose her to public disgrace, he had finally decided to put her from him privately, when the solution had come from the only possible source. His troubled sleep had been invaded by a heavenly visitor: "Joseph thou son of David, fear not to take unto thee Mary thy wife, for that which is conceived in her is of the Holy Spirit". The divine message would do more than restore harmony and love, it would call forth a profound reverence from Joseph and bring out all his manly instincts to help and protect her in the difficult days ahead.

The decree of Caesar Augustus that a census should be taken in Israel with a view to future taxation had set the whole country in motion. The decree required that everyone should go to his ancestral home for registration. Thus Joseph and Mary were faced with a long and perilous journey at a critical time. Mary would almost certainly know, as the scribes knew, that the Messiah was to be born in Bethlehem. This prophecy of Micah may well have bewildered her, and even taxed her faith until one day the news was brought of the necessity to go to Bethlehem at the precise time that she should give birth to her son. In that event her journey would be in conscious obedience to the will of God.

The long journey south was slow and arduous. Mary was conscious of the nearness of the great event which had occupied her thoughts and prayers constantly during the past months. Joseph, looking frequently and searchingly into her tired brave face, would view the domes of Bethlehem with unconcealed relief, and quicken the pace of the donkey to climb the hill upon which it stood. But a disappointment awaited them. Many travellers whose progress had been faster and whose journey had been shorter had come to register in the city of David. With growing consternation Joseph would watch the jostling crowds in the narrow streets. There was no room in the inn. It was a dark symbol of the advent of the Messiah who "came to his own, and his own received him not". Although Mary's condition must have been obvious to many residents in Bethlehem no friendly home opened its doors to receive her, and there was no motherly arm to minister to her need. At last Mary sank down exhausted in the straw of the stable with Joseph watching anxiously over her as the shadows grew deeper.*

There in the darkness of the night a tiny cry mingled with the noises of the asses and the camels. In the city in which God had chosen to anoint David King of Israel, David's greater Son was born.

There can be no more conclusive evidence than this that God has chosen the weak things of the world to confound the things which are mighty, and the base things of the world, and the things which are despised, to bring to nought the things that are.

The advent of the Son of God to bring light and life to a dark and perishing world, heralded by God's prophets, foreshadowed by His law, was the most momentous event in the earth's history. Human ingenuity would have been baffled by the task of preparing a fitting occasion for introducing him to the children of men. The everlasting Father takes us, infinitely wondering, to a rude stable, and to a simple, pure Israelitish maid lying among the animals with a bundle of life clasped to her breast. Learning the lesson of the stable we

---

*There would be only one large room at the inn; approximately half of this was raised a foot or more to provide a sleeping space for the guests, whilst the lower half formed the stable for their beasts. The manger was hollowed out along the top edge of the raised part.

progress far in our knowledge of the ways of God, and cry with the apostle Paul, "O the depth of the riches both of the wisdom and knowledge of God!"

As God chose the base things so He chose the poor of this world, rich in faith, to receive the glad tidings of salvation. The angel passed over the city of Jerusalem; there Herod and his courtly nobles held their drunken carousals, and there the religious rulers of the Jews were preoccupied with secular ambitions. The glory of his presence lit up the hills of Bethlehem where David had tended the flocks and learned confidence in God. Watching shepherds fell back in fear, until strong, clear words had reassured them. No angel of judgment stood before them. "Fear not! I bring you good tidings of great joy which shall be to all people. For unto you is born this day in the city of David a Saviour which is MESSIAH The Lord."

Suddenly the heavens were filled with the exultant throng of angels ascribing glory to the God of Heaven and acclaiming the deliverance He had brought to the earth.

Though naturally slow and silent men, the shepherds immediately left their flocks and came with haste to find and worship the newborn Saviour. They returned glorifying the God of Israel, and praising His Name.

Next morning the sun rose over the hills of Moab bringing another day. The people of Bethlehem busied themselves with their daily tasks, the registration continued, little bands of travellers left the town for their homes—oblivious of the events of the most momentous night the world had known.

Eight days passed and then the babe was circumcised according to the Jewish law and received the name the Angel had pronounced before his birth. JESUS was a name which already had an illustrious significance in Israel. In its Hebrew form Joshua, it described one who had continued the work of Moses, and by a series of remarkable conquests had brought the children of God into the land of promise. It is a name which means "Jehovah is salvation", and was destined to become sacred far beyond the confines of Palestine and the few thousands of men and women who saw him for a short period of years. Christ, the Messiah, is his title as the anointed of God. Jesus is the personal name of him who loved us and gave himself for us. To us he is precious when we dedicate ourselves to his service in baptism, and with the passing years he becomes more precious. In our own bitter struggle against environment and temperament we learn the greatness of his conquests, and feel the need for his presence; we are conscious of the fellowship of his sufferings in our victories, and the strength of his inspiration in our defeats. Our knowledge of him is no longer confined to the revelation of Scripture. He becomes a living reality in our lives, leading us to realize in ourselves that "he ever liveth to make intercession" for us.

The records of Matthew and Luke do not linger upon the incidents which describe the birth of our Saviour, they quickly pass to the development of his character and his work. But it is well that our minds return to a contemplation of this lowly scene, because it is there in this stable sanctuary that we are face to face with the love of God. Later it is to be more fully revealed to us in the strong and compelling power of His Son's dedication, but here in the angelic visitations and the quietly developing events which reached their fulfilment in the inn yard at Bethlehem we have the full impact of the great fact that "God so loved the world that he gave his only begotten son that whosoever believeth on him should not perish but have everlasting life". In our struggles towards full stature in His Son we are sometimes all but discouraged by the very strength of Christ's dedication and the completeness of his active submission to his Father's will. It is at such times that we can come quietly into the moonlit courtyard and, looking upon the sleeping babe, receive into our inmost being the deep comfort of our Heavenly Father's abiding love.

2

FAITH AND FEAR

ON the fortieth day after the birth of Jesus, Mary, now growing stronger, went with Joseph to Jerusalem and there in the Temple presented herself to the priest for purification, making the humbler offering allowed for those who could not afford a yearling lamb. Following the intercession of the priest for her purification, Mary offered the babe Jesus to the Lord, and redeemed him from Temple service by the payment of five shekels. It was in this solemn and beautiful setting that Jesus was recognized and brought an ecstasy of joy to the hearts and lips of two who were waiting for redemption in Israel. It is a picture of rewarded devotion which we find repeated in Scriptural records of the experiences of the servants of God. Years of barrenness are forgotten in the wonder of consummation. Simeon was an upright and godly man who studied the law and the prophets. He realized the significance of the days in which he lived, and had been rewarded by the knowledge, given to him through the Holy Spirit, that before his eyes closed in the sleep of death, he would see the Messiah. With what trembling anticipation he would make his way through the crowded streets towards the Temple impelled by the urge of the Spirit of God. There would be no doubt in his mind that God's promise was about to be fulfilled. With a deep exultation of spirit he lifted the helpless babe to his breast, and holding the Lord of Life against his heart, he uttered memorable words. Simeon was content now to pass quietly from the scene, "For mine eyes have seen thy salvation which thou hast prepared before the face of all people, a light to lighten the Gentiles, and the glory of thy people Israel". Even Mary, who had been so well prepared for the destiny of her son by revelation and constant prayer, was filled with amazement. Simeon turned his eyes reluctantly from the child in his arms, and blessed Mary and Joseph.

His prophecy ended on a note of foreboding. Here were the first faint notes of a warning which thirty years later was to be uttered by the Saviour himself in stark reality, "I came not to send peace, but a sword". Mary was not to escape the probings of that sword, indeed she had already felt its sharpness, and Simeon's eyes would grow dim with tears as he looked into her face: "Yea, a sword shall pierce through thine own soul also".

Simeon was not alone in his recognition of the Messiah. An aged prophetess, now over a hundred years old, had lived in prayer and fasting for the eighty-four years of her widowhood. It was no coincidence that she should witness the unforgettable scene and hear the announcement from the lips of Simeon. Her recognition was instantaneous, it made no demands on a faith as devoted as hers, it found expression in a prayer of deep gratitude, and then a desire to acquaint all those who looked for redemption in Jerusalem.

We learn with a thrill of joy of that little band of waiting saints. However dark the national picture we can always find a faithful remnant who fear the Lord, and wait for the tokens of His Hand. We read of them as the Old Dispensation closes amid the darkness and sorrow in which the just retribution of God had left them: "Then they that feared the Lord spake often one to another, and the Lord hearkened and heard it, and a book of remembrance was written before him for them that feared the Lord, and that thought upon his Name; and they shall be mine, saith the Lord of hosts, in that day when I make up my jewels". Four hundred years pass, years of conflict, heroism, and intrigue, and when the light of divine revelation shines once more on the Jewish scene, we find the remnant still there: Mary and Joseph, Zacharias and Elisabeth, Simeon and Anna, and others whose names are recorded in the Book of Life.

In these darkening Gentile days we can find strength and comfort in this evidence. It also conveys a subtle warning on the distinction between watching and waiting. All Israel was watching for the coming of the promised Messiah, but only a remnant was waiting for him. It is not difficult to watch the signs of the times, but only a life of devotion, a quiet submission of heart, a complete desire to sacrifice worldly ambitions and privileges, will prepare us for that true spirit of waiting where watching is only the visible sign of the intense expectancy of the whole being.

With the birth of Jesus many ancient prophecies began to glow with life. He was probably over twelve months old when the wise Gentile philosophers sought him from distant eastern lands, acknowledged his kingship and laid treasures at his feet. We know nothing of the origin of their long journey, or the circumstances which brought them together. It is possible that the influence and message of Daniel in Babylon had not been lost with the passing years, and the thoughtful mystics of the east were waiting for the Star that should come out of Jacob. It may be that these men were shown the significance of the sudden appearance of a celestial orb by divine revelation. But we do know that they had an experience which sent each, probably from widely separated points, upon his hard and perilous road to Jerusalem. It seems from the short narrative which Matthew gives that after the appearance of the star in the east with its message which set the caravans in motion towards the king of the Jews in Jerusalem it disappeared, and their journey westwards was a journey of faith.* As they emerged from Herod's palace the star shone forth over Bethlehem a few miles to the south, and when they saw it again, probably after a lapse of many weeks, Matthew records, "They rejoiced with exceeding great joy".

Little did these travellers suspect the evil they had roused in the dark soul of the Idumean King who ruled the nation. Herod was one of those sinister characters who expose all that is worst in the human heart. By craft he had obtained a dispensation from Rome to rule Israel. His anxiety to retain that rule had become an obsession which was only satisfied by the blood of every rival. Even his wife and sons were sacrificed to his lust and jealousy. Old age found him a victim of his own vice. Living in the luxury of his new palace, this descendant of the hated Esau surrounded himself with spies, and lived in perpetual fear of retribution from an outraged people, starting at every shadow, and imagining enmity in every political move.

The arrival of so distinguished a cavalcade at the gates would occasion no little stir even in so populous and cosmopolitan a city as Jerusalem, and Herod's spies would acquaint the King of their coming. If having heard their mission these spies were reckless enough to give the king any indication of it, they would have seen his face distorted with anger and fear. The royal palace was the obvious destination of these illustrious visitors. They would have little idea of the sensi-

---

*There is a strong indication that the wise men had not seen the star between the time they had left their distant countries and the moment they emerged from Herod's presence. See Matthew 2:2, but particularly verse 9.

tive atmosphere of the court created by Herod's fearful obsession, and they could not have conceived the terrible effect of their bold inquiry, "Where is he that is born King of the Jews?" Years of deceit and hypocrisy enabled Herod to conceal the passion in his heart, and under the guise of would-be worshipper he called the chief priests and scribes and asked them where the Messiah should be born. This was no problem to those who knew their Scripture: "And thou Bethlehem, in the land of Juda, art not the least among the princes of Juda: for out of thee shall come a Governor, that shall rule my people Israel". With a gleam of triumph Herod would feel this new menace to his throne was within reach of his powerful arm, and exacting from the wise men a promise to return with more precise details, he waited impatiently for the outcome of his cruel deception. Meanwhile the magi reached their objective and worshipped him who is destined to bring the Gentiles to his light and kings to the brightness of his rising. From early Christian times their gifts have been thought to hold a significance, the gold a symbol of the Messiah's kingship, the frankincense of his divine origin, and the myrrh of his death.

Their gifts offered and their obeisance made, the wise men began their long trek eastwards over deserts and mountains to their distant homes. A divine intervention prevented their return to the impatient king in Jerusalem. Not to be divert- ed from his purpose Herod sent his soldiers down to Bethlehem, and slaughtered all the children in the town who were two years old or under. The busy noises of the little township were silenced and in their place was a noise of bitter wailing as mothers watched in helpless grief the soldiery seek out every young child.

Like the great despot who six centuries before had ruled in Babylon, Herod had failed to learn that however powerful a man may be, whatever forces he can instantly command, he is a helpless weakling when, consciously or not, he strives against God or seeks to divert His purpose. When Herod's soldiers stormed into Bethlehem, Joseph and Mary with their precious burden were far to the south west, beyond the reach of the king. They were fleeing to Egypt on the instructions of an angel who had appeared to Joseph in a dream. The journey was long and dangerous, and during the early stages they would probably sleep by day and travel by night, making for the coast at Gaza, where they would leave the almost trackless desert with its perils and its loneliness and join the ancient trade route from Damascus. We have no direct indication of how long the sojourn in Egypt lasted; the little family would probably join the Jewish colony and Joseph would provide for the needs of Mary and her son by following his trade as a carpenter. But at last the call came, probably when Jesus was between two and three years old. Herod was dead, the life of Jesus was no longer in danger. "Arise", said the angel to Joseph, "and take the young child and his mother, and go into the land of Israel." It would seem that Joseph and Mary intended to return to Bethlehem, and forsake Nazareth altogether. It may have been that they felt that this would give Jesus an opportunity of living near Jerusalem and receiving his training for his great work among his people at the hands of the learned rabbis in the Temple; it may have been that they felt it was necessary in fulfilment of God's prophetic message through Micah that they should sacrifice a natural desire to return to Galilee and make their home in Bethlehem. But as they neared the land of Israel and heard that Archelaus, Herod's son, had succeeded him they questioned the wisdom of their decision; doubt and hesitancy were removed by an angelic visitation which directed their steps northwards to the familiar countryside of Galilee and their old village of Nazareth.

3

HOME LIFE IN NAZARETH

NAZARETH will always hold precious associations to those who have come to know and love Jesus. The memories may be saddened by the reflection that the darker tendencies of human nature prevailed in the treatment he received from those among whom he grew up, yet by far the greater part of his earthly life was spent there. It was the place chosen by his Father to be the scene of his preparation for the great work that lay ahead. And for thirty years he sanctified the little town with his presence, learning the law and the purpose of God, and growing to understand the ways of men.

Nestling in the shelter of a ring of the southernmost hills of lower Galilee, Nazareth was a beautiful little town. Its white buildings spread up the hillside interspersed with orange and fig groves. For many months of the year the rocky slopes glowed with the vivid hues of the multi-coloured anemones, and the clusters of white and mauve cyclamen growing under the lichen-covered rocks, whilst the spring and early summer brought its harvest of narcissi, and the warm months saw the full beauty of the dark blue patches of cornflowers and light blue clusters of dwarf iris.

Although Nazareth was a secluded town, the stream of life passed very near it. Little could be seen from the town itself, but climbing the hillside to the edge of the basin a wonderful prospect stretched away in three directions. Perhaps the first eager gaze would be towards the west where the wooded bluff of Carmel stretched out into the deep blue waters of the Mediterranean twenty miles away. To the south and south-west lay the vast plain of Esdraelon, the scene of a score or more of decisive battles in the past and yet to be the battle-ground of man's final rebellion against his Maker. Beyond the plain to the south rose the heights of Samaria, whilst east-wards were the hills of Galilee and the Jordan crossings. Northward the hills rolled away toward the Phoenician coast broken by jagged rents where swiftly-flowing rivers and mountain streams gushed and tumbled towards the sea.

Away to the north-east it would be possible on a clear day to discern the dominating peaks of Hermon wrapped in their almost unearthly mantle of eternal snow.

This scene was animated by the movement of many travellers. The Way of the Sea which brought merchants' caravans from Damascus, skirted the Sea of Galilee, and crossing the great sweep of Esdraelon below, turned south along the coastal plain of Sharon to Egypt. From the fords of Jordan in the east the caravans of the Midianites could be seen winding down from the hills, while directly south across the vast expanse of sand and scrub, crowded with pilgrims as the festival days drew near, lay the road through Samaria to Jerusalem. Struggling among the mountains to the north of Galilee was the road from Ptolemais to the regions of Decapolis, echoing constantly with the steady tramp of Roman soldiers. Many would be the stories that the people of Nazareth would hear from the peasants in the countryside around, and sometimes from the lips of tired travellers who climbed the narrow paths to seek shelter and rest in the secluded town. They would hear of events in Egypt and in Syria, they would listen to stories of splendour and rumours of intrigue from the great heart of the Roman Empire itself; they would hear with fast-beating hearts the news of the intentions of Augustus in Palestine, of the possible successor to the throne in Jerusalem, they would exchange dark glances as they heard of still heavier taxation, and betray mixed feelings over the possibility of direct control from Rome.

The little village itself was full of life and colour. The well was seldom deserted, it provided a happy meeting place for the women who would linger there with the stone jars, resting beside them, exchanging the gossip of the place with candour; the prospect of a wedding would bring animated chatter and happy laughter, whilst sometimes their voices would be hushed and their faces saddened by the news of sickness or death. Except in the heat of the day, the steep crooked streets would be full of noise and bustle; the laughter of happy children at play, the cries of the merchants from their shops hollowed out in the walls, the occasional plaintive call of a beggar, the bray of an ass, the raucous bleat of goats, all combined to make the animated scene which formed the background to life in this hilly Galilean retreat.

It was in this beautiful and eventful setting that Jesus grew to maturity. Only one incident is recorded of him during those years. Natural as it seems to desire a greater knowledge of his childhood, we must recognize a divine wisdom in this concealment, and appreciate the fitting summary of his early life given to us by Luke, "And Jesus increased in wisdom and stature, and in favour with God and man". Jesus grew to moral and intellectual maturity as naturally as he grew physically taller and stronger, travelling the road we all travel, struggling against the temptations which are common to youth, attaining virtue by the direct assault of evil, and the triumph of personal effort. He sought strength from his Father, and found favour by repeated endeavour and steady improvement. There is a possibility that in our reverence for Jesus we overlook the implications of this gradual development, and are deprived of the true comfort of the mediatorship of him who "suffered, being tempted", who was "in all points tempted like as we are, yet without sin".

The divine reticence in the Gospels leads our minds to the simple yet beautiful picture of a growing boy helping his mother in her homely tasks, often walking with her down the crowded and lively street to make her daily purchases and fetch the water from the well, learning from her quiet example the beauty of godliness and the strength of faith. We see him as he grows older making more frequent visits to the busy carpenter's shop where the noise of the hammer and the saw proclaim Joseph's skilful service to the people around. As he grows older he begins to use the tools himself and learns the satisfaction of creative work, until his interest and skill begin to lighten the burden of the father of a growing family. There are significant indications in his teaching that these were days of struggle against poverty. The parables of Jesus are full of homely scenes which may well have had their source in his own early experience. The patched garment, the widow's feverish search for a lost coin of little value, father and children sharing a bed, the one raised lamp which could illuminate the whole house—all these seem to reflect the struggling circumstances of his youth. The humble dwelling constantly echoed with the laughter of happy children, but there were times of childish crisis too, and instinctively the younger ones would look to Jesus to settle their difficulties and calm the angry waters.

As the months lengthened into years a gradual change would have been discernible in Jesus. He grew in favour with God. That is ever a slow and beautiful process; its beginning is always hidden in mystery. It may have been on the heights above Nazareth when the rising sun was turning the hills over the Jordan valley to gold and Jesus was becoming aware of the creative power of God. It may have been in the breathless stillness of a star-filled night when a man feels the strange loneliness of his insignificance. It may have been in the flickering light of the carpenter's shop when, the day's work done, Joseph was revealing to him some of the wonders of God's deliverance and care of His people. We do not know where that flame of consciousness was kindled, we do know it grew, and that Jesus encouraged it by so diligent a study of the law and the prophets, that when he was only twelve the most learned rabbis in the land marvelled at his acquaintance with the Scriptures.*

Joseph would recognize the responsibility of teaching his children the law of the Lord. It was a father's sacred trust in Israel, even after all those centuries of disobedience and travail. "These words which I command thee this day shall be in thine heart: and thou shalt teach them diligently unto thy children, and shall talk of them when thou sittest in thine house, and when thou walkest by the way, and when thou liest down and when thou risest up." No child ever listened more carefully to the words of the law than Jesus.

How long Joseph was able to continue his spiritual ministrations we do not know. His complete disappearance from the Gospel page suggests his early death, and the probability that at an early age the responsibilities of the Godly carpenter were accepted by Jesus. When he was about six the spiritual guidance of his home would be supplemented by the instruction of a scribe at the synagogue school at Nazareth. All the synagogues had these schools for teaching the young, but a child who did not graduate to the higher education of the House of Midrash attached to the Temple at Jerusalem was

---

*Dr. H. B. Swete has a fine paragraph on this aspect of Christ's development. He says, "The consciousness of a unique relation to God, and an over-mastering enthusiasm for the spiritual and eternal, had begun to overshadow all earthly interests. Yet, as the sequel shews, they were not suffered to interfere with the obligations of human life, and the next eighteen years are summed up in the amazing words, 'He was subject to them'. Thus the spirit of the Boy is seen at once illuminating thought and prompting to duty; opening the mind to the mysteries of God, and at the same time urging the regular discharge of the responsibilities of an obscure and monotonous life" (*The Holy Spirit in the New Testament*, page 37).

not considered learned. And this was to be remembered against him in later years when Jesus challenged the scribes upon their knowledge and their conduct.

Amid the wonder and solitude of his Father's creation, knowledge was transformed by that strange alchemy into wisdom, and prayer turned to communion. There have been many examples of children with an outstanding ability to absorb facts. The development of Jesus went far beyond that. He meditated upon God's revelation, and often Mary would find his bed empty in those sacred days of preparation when meditation moved towards communion, and with a growing sense of awe Jesus began to suspect the unique significance of his life and ponder his relationship to God. Mary too would be conscious of the new sense of awareness in her son. There is no more penetrating discernment than a mother's love, and that discernment was increased a hundredfold by the things which she had hid in her heart. Watching her son returning down the hillside, the glow of the Father's presence still reflected in the light of his eyes and in the assurance of his voice, Mary would feel again the thrill of Gabriel's approach and hear once more his vibrant words proclaiming her son the long awaited Messiah of Israel. This quiet but powerful development went on as the years passed, "and the child grew and waxed strong in spirit, filled with wisdom: and the grace of God was upon him". In despised Galilee, far from the glittering opulence of the Roman court, far from the rabbinical schools of Jewish learning, Jesus grew up like a tender plant and as a root out of a dry ground, preparing himself, and being prepared by his Father, for his manifestation, first to Israel, and then to all mankind.

4

JERUSALEM

THE only recorded incident of the early life of Jesus is the adventure in Jerusalem at the age of twelve. Several reasons may be found to explain this jewel which shines in so lovely a light against a background of thirty silent years. At the age of twelve a Jewish boy became a son of the law with privileges and responsibilities which included an attendance at the Passover in Jerusalem every year. The greatest reason which sweeps the others up in its embrace would seem to be that this experience which Luke records, and which enshrines the first recorded words of Jesus, marks the point in his life when the significance of his relationship was revealed to him, and he dedicated himself unreservedly to his Father's will.

Each year Jesus would have watched his parents' preparation for the journey to Jerusalem with thoughtful eyes. His knowledge of Scripture was growing, and with that growth would come an ever-clearer perception of the significance of God's requirements. He would know that his people were a favoured race, that God had chosen them to be a special people unto Himself: a favour which bore no relation to their size or strength, but was an evidence of His faithfulness to His covenant, and of a love which was not influenced by the unresponsiveness of those who were the objects of it. With eager eyes Jesus would follow the record of his people's history: he would burn with shame as he read of their waywardness and marvel at the forbearance of God: he would sense the warmth of God's favour for Jerusalem whose very stones were precious in His sight, and, reading the prophets he would "see the end of the Lord".

The Passover epitomized all these things. To many boys of twelve its significance would have rested upon the Lord's deliverance of His people from the hand of Pharaoh King of Egypt. But the attention of Jesus would turn to the lamb of the first year, without blemish, and to its blood upon the lintels and the doorposts. His appreciation of deliverance would reach beyond the limitations imposed by the power of men, and, meditating upon the work of the "prophet like unto Moses", he would see a twofold deliverance. He would ponder for hours over the sacrifice of the lamb, and the efficacy of the blood-sprinkled doors. He would perhaps know the scroll of Esaias by heart, and although his whole being would thrill at the majesty and power of Messiah's work, and the joy and peace he was to bring as the strong Arm of God, he would read and meditate upon every word of the 53rd chapter, and recognize as the Messiah, Jehovah's servant who "was oppressed and afflicted, yet he opened not his mouth; he is brought as a lamb to the slaughter, and as a sheep before her shearers is dumb, so he opened not his mouth". But Jesus would see too something of the triumph of that sacrifice. God had said concerning him, "By his knowledge shall my righteous servant justify many, for he shall bear their iniquities". The sacrifice being made, the justification of many being accomplished, the Messiah was to have the wonderful experience of seeing the travail of his soul and feeling the satisfaction of all that had been done to prepare men for the revealed glory of God.

The day dawned for which Jesus had waited, and the preparations for the journey were complete. Before the first light of dawn the household would be astir, Joseph feeding and grooming the ass, Mary preparing the food and bedding, Jesus quietly helpful, until all was ready, and the little company made their way down the familiar street to the well where the rest of the village families were fast assembling. Amid good wishes, farewells and some envious longings the cavalcade moved away climbing steadily towards the southwestern edge of the sheltering basin whence the rocky path led downwards towards the plain of Esdraelon, and the south. It would not be long before other companies from all over Galilee would be seen wending their way across the plain. Occasionally they would overtake pilgrims whose strange dress, travel-tired eyes and Greek tongue proclaimed them Jews of the Dispersion. From every point of the compass the people of God were converging upon His city. Jerusalem like a meteoric lodestone was drawing men and women to her heart. Ploughs stood idle in the fields, vineyards and olive groves were deserted, merchants' shops were shuttered, carpenters' tools were silent: Jerusalem had claimed her people, and even now was filling and overflowing to the hills around.

Large companies of pilgrims often followed the third route through Samaria, which took them over the rough desert scrub into the plain of Dothan, across dry river beds, along stony wadys into the Samaritan hills between the twin heights of Ebal and Gerizim, towards the featureless plateau on which Bethel stands. To Jesus the journey would be a memorable one, the servants of God would emerge from the past as Joseph pointed out the familiar places which witnessed their activities and the barren landscape would become instinct with life and movement as he thought of the struggles, hardships and faith which had earned for them the favour of God. There would be darker scenes, recalled by some historic spots, scenes made more real by the gleams of hatred and scarcely-veiled hostility the boy had seen on the faces of many of the people of Samaria as they passed through. But now as the sun passed its zenith on the third day, the thoughts of Jesus moved more quickly than his tiring feet and reached forward in eager anticipation to the city of God. The words of the Psalmist described the deep, almost unutterable emotions of a son of the law as he approached the holy city for the first time; "I was glad when they said unto me, Let us go into the house of the Lord. Our feet shall stand within thy gates, O Jerusalem. Jerusalem is builded as a city that is compact together ... Pray for the peace of Jerusalem: they shall prosper that love thee. Peace be within thy walls and prosperity within thy palaces". Those deep feelings would stir the sensitive spirit of Jesus a hundredfold, and when at last the walls and the strong towers of the city lay before him, he would drink in the visible portrayal of years of reading, thought and prayer. Joseph, that great type of Israel's Messiah, had dreamed as a boy of his great destiny when even his parents and his brethren would worship him. Such thoughts may well have mingled with Jesus' dreams as he looked down for the first time upon the city which held so much in store for him. There may have been a strange sense of foreboding too. A lamb was to be slaughtered on the morrow.

There would be little room to spare in the city that night, and the pilgrims from Galilee would probably spend the night outside the city walls, sleeping in the open on the slopes of Olivet. The first rays of the Passover dawn were heralded by trumpet peals from the Temple precincts. They would be a signal for general activity, and after a hasty meal Joseph and Mary would take Jesus down the hillside and mingling with the vast crowds from nearly fifty countries, would enter the city gate and climb as quickly as the moving mass and the narrow streets would allow. As they approached the Temple precincts they would be conscious of a confusion of sounds, the bleating of lambs, the bellowing of calves, and the cooing of doves mingled with the cries of men. Voices were raised in sharp exchanges, there were accusations of theft and treachery countered by threats and challenges. Such a spectacle was not a happy introduction to the House of God, and probably Jesus felt disturbed as he watched Joseph purchase a lamb and followed him under the great colonnades of the Court of the Gentiles, up the stone steps to the Inner court of the Temple, and on through one of the nine Temple gates into the Court of the women. But his thoughts were no longer interrupted by the vulgar cries below as he stood on the sacred spot that God had chosen that His Name might be there. It was on this rock that Abraham had shown the faith of complete dedication in offering his son of promise in obedience to God's command. It was here that Solomon had received divine instructions to build a House in which God should dwell. It was here that, the building being finished, mortal man reached his highest point of communion with his Maker. "Behold, heaven and the heaven of heavens cannot contain thee; how much less this house which I have built. Have respect therefore to the prayer of thy servant ... that thine eyes may be open upon this house day and night." It was here that God accepted the petitions of His people in a glory which filled the house, preventing the entrance of the priests. The words of the Psalmist may have found an echo in his youthful heart: "One thing have I desired of the Lord, and that will I seek after; that I may dwell in the house of the Lord all the days of my life, to behold the beauty of the Lord, and to enquire in his temple". His mind may have spanned the centuries yet to be when God's House would be a house of prayer for all nations, when the knowledge of God's glory would fill the earth and the law should go forth from Zion.

That evening when the noises of the city were stilled and the thousands of pilgrims had returned to their apartments within the city or to their tents on the hills outside, excitement gave way to solemnity. The Passover was kept. The lamb was roasted and eaten with unleavened bread and bitter herbs. The traditional question from the youngest member of the family, "What mean ye by this service?" evoked a stirring account of God's deliverance of His people, probably extending beyond the experience of their ancestors in Egypt

19

to a rehearsal of His guiding hand throughout their long eventful history, the struggles in the land of promise, the halcyon days under David and Solomon, the bitterness and strife of the divided kingdom, the final penalty for disobedience in the overwhelming, first of Israel and then of Judah, by foreign despots. The rehearsal would not end on a note of despair. God had not utterly cast away His people, they lived in hope and expectation of the coming Messiah of Israel according to God's word, and the Passover was a time of deliverance. What more natural time and place for him to be revealed? This intense national feeling was responsible for the Roman legionaries placed in strategic positions in and around the city. Jesus had seen them since reaching Jerusalem.

To assess the effect of the experience of Jesus during these momentous days is but to speculate. Was it possible that in the silent watches of the night the God of Israel spoke to the eager waiting spirit of His Son; and, like Samuel, there came the ready response, "Speak, Lord, for thy servant heareth"? We do know that on the following day Jesus went out alone to seek the elders of the city, and oblivious of his parents and the passing of the hours, he talked with the learned rabbis of the great issues of the law, and of God's purpose and promises. At the end of three days we see an anxious mother break into the quiet circle, and in her conflicting emotions of relief and distress, cry out, "Son, why hast thou thus dealt with us? Behold thy father and I have sought thee sorrowing." We hear his quiet reply, not a rebuke but rather a declaration that something wonderful has happened in his life, that from now on the old relationship has changed, a new allegiance has begun, "How is it that ye sought me? Wist ye not that I must be about my Father's business?"*

These words introduce us to Jesus. For the first time in the Gospel record we hear him speak. Before the clouds take him out of our sight many are the gracious utterances that will fall from his lips, but in these first recorded words the purpose of his life is crystallized. "I must be about my Father's business." That resolution was to make great demands of him; it was to put him to the test in the wilderness, to try him amidst seething clamouring multitudes, to strain relationships, to bewilder his dearest friends. It was to demand a loyalty in which earthly relationships were to be forgotten, his

---

*The alternative, "In (or at) my Father's House", has great possibilities in connection with the outcome of the glowing moment.

brethren being those who did his Father's will. It was finally to make the supreme demand on life itself. The life of Jesus is the record of how Jesus did all these things with quiet confidence and unflinching faith, and with a clear perspective of the work he was doing in relation to the purpose of his Father.

The first demand this resolution made was by no means the lightest to the eager spirit of Jesus. His Father's business led him away from the rabbis, back over the Samaritan hills to the carpenter's shop, and kept him there for no less than eighteen years. It was a severe test. Nothing loosens the will more quickly than an inability to accept its challenge, nothing breeds doubt more insidiously than inactivity, there is no greater test of patience than indeterminate waiting. It is a lesson which all the disciples of Jesus must learn. So often, especially in the eager devotion of youth, obedience to the call of God is thought to imply an entire redirection of the whole life; there are new worlds to conquer, deep wrongs to right, great deeds to be done. Slowly we realize that the Father's business takes us back to the carpenter's shop to the things we thought we might have left behind, to the slow discipline of patience and steadfast devotion, to a long period of waiting upon God.

But we can be sure that as Jesus went about his duties at the carpenter's bench, subject to his parents, there was a new light in his eyes. He recognized his Father's will, and submitted to it gladly. Although in his new relationship he was to learn the desolation of loneliness, he was also to learn that he was never really alone, for he lived in the abiding consciousness of the nearness and the love of His Father. And that too, in humbler measure, can be the experience of every one who comes to the Father through him.

5

YOUTH AND MANHOOD

THE journey of Jesus to the Passover in Jerusalem at the age of twelve forms a natural division between his boyhood and manhood. His simple questions to his worried parents in the temple revealed his consciousness of his identity, and his willingness to respond to the demands of his Father in heaven. He recognized that the first phase of his obedience led him back to his mother's home and Joseph's bench; thither he returned with a new sense of vocation.

Those eighteen silent years were not lost. They were the source of much of the wisdom and strength that were concentrated in the arduous years to follow. The roots of knowledge, of devotion and of sacrifice grew strong and deep in the rich soil of Nazareth. There he extended and quickened his understanding of God's law, he learned with steady concentration the mission and the destiny of the Messiah, and the price that would be demanded of him: he grew in his appraisal of men, until he could penetrate their hearts and read their motives. As year succeeded year, so his life grew richer, his communion with his Father deeper, and his preparation more complete.

Looking back from the strains and tensions of his active ministry, we feel the contrast of those unruffled years in Nazareth, where in the quiet harmony of his Godly home Jesus grew strong in mind and body. With Mary's gentle spirit and Joseph's sense of justice and rectitude he would live in an atmosphere of peace and joy. The fruitfulness of those silent years can be felt rather than seen as we turn the Gospel page. The deep and wide knowledge of the Scriptures Jesus possessed leads us back to the years of diligent study which preceded his ministry. Whether he was protecting himself against the insidious attacks of the tempter, comforting those in need, exhorting his disciples or rebuking his enemies, Jesus had constant recourse to the word of God. Time and again he quoted from memory, and many of his allusions show that he knew not only the Greek translation of the

22

Scriptures but that he had studied them in the original Hebrew.* His constant reading and meditation showed him the nature of his work and prepared him for the full authority which he had to manifest and the claims he was to make when, anointed with the Holy Spirit and with power, he went forth among men with the cry, "I am the light of the world: he that followeth me shall not walk in darkness, but shall have the light of life". The Psalms which so often reveal the beauty of Christ's inmost spirit and the intense fervour of his love for God and devotion to men, surely reflect truly the work of these years of reading and contemplation. Reading the 119th Psalm we feel the full effect upon his maturing spirit reaching its highest note of exultation in the memorable words, "O how love I thy law! It is my meditation all the day ... Thy word is a lamp unto my feet and a light unto my path. I have sworn and I will perform it, that I will keep thy righteous judgments ... I have inclined my heart to perform thy statutes alway, even unto the end". In the light of his perfect dedication it seems almost presumption to hear in these words anything but the consecrated aspirations of the Son of man.

But the preparation of Jesus was not completed by his knowledge and love of God's law. It was necessary that he should experience that personal communion with Him which kindled the covenants of the written word into a living fire. As the first Adam walked with God in the garden in the cool of the day, so the last Adam found understanding and strength in the midst of his Father's creative handiwork. There on the hilltops of Nazareth he would learn that the great Creator who "telleth the number of the stars and calleth them all by their names" was also the loving Heavenly Father who "healeth the broken in heart and bindeth up their wounds". Day by day in the silence of God's presence he would strengthen those cords of love that were to give him that unique sense of union with his Father which flowed from his every word and action. His Father was opening his ear to "hear as the learned", and his whole attitude was that of one intent on listening for some sound which as yet he could scarcely hear, but which when he heard he was determined to

*Matthew 5:18; Luke 16:17. These words imply that Jesus read the Scriptures in the square characters of the original Hebrew. It should also be noted that the scribes always quoted Scripture in the original Hebrew, and it was only on that common ground that Jesus was able to meet their constant challenge. This fact gives added weight to his frequent question to them, "Have ye never read?"

receive, and receiving, to transform human destiny and bring an unearthly and eternal beauty into the lives of men. The Lord God was giving him the tongue of the learned to speak a word in season to him that was weary. He was preparing his mind and body for a living sacrifice.

These long and sacred periods of communion are reflected back into the quiet years from the pages of the Gospel where each great crisis in his life finds or leaves him praying, and we have the silent eloquence of the picture of a tired figure making his way up into the mountain at the close of a busy day to renew his strength and courage in the sacred presence of his Father. In this too David's lips express the deep emotion of his Greater Son when he cries, "O taste and see that the Lord is good: blessed is the man that trusteth in him".

These spiritual vistas expanding before him did not take Jesus from the carpenter's bench. There was waiting for him there a preparation which if it was less satisfying, was scarcely less important. From the absence of any reference to Joseph after Jesus was twelve, it seems probable that he died some time during these eighteen years, and Jesus would have upon his young shoulders the responsibilities of the home. It would be an invaluable experience to him in his ministry, bringing with it understanding of the domestic and practical difficulties that he was constantly called upon to solve. The carpenter's bench kept him in touch with men. Only those who have lived in a village can realize what an ideal place it is from which to study human nature. There is little evidence of the polished veneer of urban life: truth is not masked in conventional insincerity, there is a directness and intensity in human relationships which exposes men's hearts and scorns to hide their motives. Love and hate, good and evil, sorrow and joy stand revealed to all who pass by. Subtlety plays little part in village life, relations are plain and direct. Goodness is simple and pure, evil is often stark and elemental. It would be hard to find a greater contrast between the suave learned aristocratic Sadducee in Jerusalem, and the homely peasant of that small town of evil repute in Galilee. Jesus mingled with these men and women, he knew their difficulties, he shared their joys and sorrows, he encouraged their victories and checked their failures. With his inspiring personality visitors to the carpenter's shop would forget his youth and discuss their problems, seeking his advice and intervention. His parables show us that his knowledge extended beyond his own craft. He knew all about farming, he saw the ploughing of the land, the sowing of the seed and the gathering of the harvest. He knew the rugged sincerity of the shepherds and their ways with the sheep. We can imagine him leaving his own work to help some heavily pressed farmer to gather his crops, or to stride out over the hills with a shepherd to help him to find some straying sheep.

Deeper than all their external struggles, emphasized by their grief, but not hidden by their laughter, Jesus would discern the deep need of men. It was a need older than Nazareth, extending back through the ages to Eden itself. It was the need for God; his life's work was to satisfy that need. And with that satisfaction came a peace and a joy that no man could give or take away. Early in his record of Christ's ministry John said of him, "He knew all men, and needed not that any should testify of man: for he knew what was in man". The years at Nazareth were an early contribution to that knowledge.

Faced with the heroic obedience of Jesus, his increasing devotion and holy aspiration, we often feel dismayed at the feebleness of our discipleship. His very purity appals. In the homely life at Nazareth we can discern the true principles of preparation for our Heavenly Father's service. We can follow him in those years of diligent study and meditation upon God's word, until we experience with him those ecstatic feelings of delight in its precepts and promises. Most of us are denied the beautiful vistas from the hills of Nazareth, but we are not denied the gracious privileges of prayer and communion. And Jesus has sanctified manual labour with his own toil-hardened hands, showing how the everyday intercourse of a busy shop may be a necessary part of the training of a child of God. If we follow him in Nazareth we shall be ready, if the call comes, to follow him out into the wider spheres of service. If that call to larger service is not for us, we can remain with him at Nazareth in the assurance that his life there was rewarded by the commendation of his Father as he passed beneath the waters of Jordan. "This is my beloved Son in whom I am well pleased."

Jesus was waiting for that call to larger service. His mind had been prepared by meditation and prayer. His experience of men had revealed their strength, their weakness and their need. His body had grown strong and vigorous in readiness for the privations and rigours of the years to come. When that preparation was complete the call came. Over the Galilean hills from the Jordan fords came the news of John's preaching, and Jesus knew. We picture him striding resolutely away into the hills leaving behind a mother whose tear-dimmed eyes betrayed the anguish of the sword-thrust that had begun to pierce her heart, but whose brave smile and waving hand proclaimed her still the handmaid of the Lord.

Book Two

THE BACKGROUND OF THE MINISTRY

1

A RESTLESS PEOPLE

WHILE Jesus is striding out towards the Jordan valley, we shall pause to examine the men and women among whom he was about to work, and the atmosphere prevailing in Israel during these momentous days.

We do not need to leave the pages of the Gospels to realize that the general temper of the people was one of discontent and vague expectancy. The fact that enthusiastic crowds tried to take Jesus in Galilee, and later led him triumphantly into Jerusalem, betrays a discontent with the political powers that were shaping their lives. The fact that crowds went out first to John and later to Jesus from every city and village of Judea and Galilee is startling evidence of the dissatisfaction with which those who were responsible for the religious life of the people were viewed. Luke's comment that "the people were in expectation, and all men mused in their hearts of John whether he were the Christ or not", suggests the air of expectancy that prevailed in the land.

But we must look more carefully into this matter. Our understanding of many of the words and actions of Jesus is increased enormously by a knowledge of the conditions of the men and women among whom he worked, the motives of those who had authority over them, and the influence for good or evil which they exercised in their lives. The greatest single factor responsible for the growing discontent in the land was the economic strain under which the people lived.

When Herod the Great was given the throne as a reward for the assistance he had offered the Romans in the conquest of the land, he undertook an enormous building programme. Cities grew rapidly under his energetic hand, breakwaters stretched out into the sea at strategic points along the harbourless coasts. Public works were not neglected, while the erection and restoration of temples and monuments proclaimed his patronage of Greek culture. To placate the indignant Jews for this violation of their most sensitive loyalty, he began the rebuilding of their own temple on a most lavish scale. This last work was the most ambitious of all. It was commenced before Jesus was born, and was not completed until long after his ascension; so that each time he visited the temple he would see the labourers at work in some part of the huge building.

Whilst this great undertaking in Jerusalem did much to divert attention from the more profane activities of the Idumean ruler, another factor was introduced when heavy taxes had to be levied to meet the expenditure. These taxes were increased by the sumptuous luxury of Herod's court, and the liberal bribes he paid to Rome in an effort to retain his popularity there.

When Herod died he left the nation impoverished. The Jews unsuccessfully asked Rome to be allowed self-government. Palestine was divided among Herod's sons. Archelaus was made Tetrarch of Judea, Samaria and Idumea; Antipas, Tetrarch of Galilee; and Philip Tetrarch of Trachonitis and Iturea.* Archelaus was a failure and his tyrannies became unbearable. After ten years' rule the Jews sent an urgent petition to Rome asking to have him removed, and demanding either self-government or direct Roman control through a procurator. This latter was granted. Archelaus was deposed and in AD 6 Quirinus (translated by the AV in Luke 2 as Cyrenius) was appointed first Roman Governor.

However great the advantages of direct Roman rule may have been, the arrangement carried with it financial responsibilities unwelcome to a people with a legacy of heavy commitments. Roman taxes were not crushing in themselves (the conquerors were too wise for that) but to a nation which contributed so generously towards its religious organizations they were a heavy addition which made the burden all but intolerable. Unlike Rome's other subject nations Israel was, in spite of centuries of disobedience and punishment, still God's people. Her policies and her laws, her sanctions and her punishments, all emanated from the Temple at Jerusalem. The people's money went towards the upkeep of

---

*A Tetrarchy in the Roman Empire was a fourth part of a province. As only three Tetrarchs were appointed at this time in Palestine, it would seem that the term was used somewhat loosely.

the Temple and to the increasing affluence of the high priestly families. They made heavy demands covering almost every
activity of life, from the half-shekel Temple payment to the
tithe on cattle and crops, and even such negligible things as
anise and cummin were not excluded. Every firstborn child
was a financial liability to its parents and an asset to the
priests, while the frequent feasts and offerings all levied
their toll, in addition to taxes for the maintenance of the local
synagogue and the support of the poor.

The Roman authorities had little sympathy with Jewish
appeals for a reduction in their imperial taxes; in any case
the system was too impersonal for that. In practice Rome
simply sold the potential taxation assets of Palestine to *publicani* in the city, who in turn hired agents in the land itself,
often Jews, to collect them. Both *publicani* and local collectors
were only interested in making as much money as possible
for themselves out of the arrangement, and the Roman
authorities were not interested in the extortions made or the
methods used to enforce them. True, the embittered taxpayer
could appeal to the Roman procurator, but he, knowing the
national weakness, would in all probability point out that
they were only paying for their own protection and comfort.
They had no army to support, Rome was providing that; and
they were using the roads, the viaducts and the water supplies also maintained by Rome. Under their Idumean kings
the roads had been infested with robbers. Now with the
steady patrolling of Roman soldiers things were improving,
and eventually the dangers would be eliminated. But these
things had to be paid for. If the prospect was so difficult why
pay such heavy taxes to members of their own community?
What could the Temple authorities show for the money they
received which could remotely compare with the facilities
Rome offered? Such would be the arguments of the Roman
officials, and the Jews would have little they could reasonably say against them. They could not tell the Romans that
to withhold taxes from the Sadducees would be equivalent to
robbing God. It was equally impossible for them to seek relief
from the Sadducees whose horror would know no bounds at
the thought of the Jews suggesting any alleviation from their
sacred financial obligations. Faced with the cold decrees of
Rome, and the challenge of their conscience concerning their
loyalty to God, the Jews had no alternative but to submit to

the heavy demands made upon them. Their resources dwindled until many found it increasingly difficult to purchase any but the barest necessities of life.

Added to this economic tension was another factor with a direct bearing upon it. Many of the Jews in the rural areas of Palestine, particularly in Galilee, earned their livelihood by tilling the soil and fishing. Their prosperity depended as much upon their success in finding a good market as upon their skill. With the development of Roman culture and the introduction of Roman methods and practices, it became possible for the rich land-owners, both in Palestine and the neighbouring countries, to employ slave labour. This meant that the Jewish small-holder was faced with serious competition. Gradually all but the most prosperous were forced out of business and had to be content with a very meagre existence. Some of the less responsible characters formed parties and went off into the mountains to rob passing travellers. Sporadic rebellions broke out from time to time but they were efficiently dealt with, and the only evidence they left were homes which sheltered weeping women and hard-faced men. But all classes became bitter, until their extreme poverty and desperate anger eventually lit the flame of insurrection against the Roman authority, but the relentless power of the legions crushed their proud spirits into pathetic submission. Jesus saw this dark day ahead, but, at the time of his ministry, the situation although getting worse year by year was not desperate. The economic background could not, however, be ignored, and the temptation to make stones into bread reached beyond the alleviation of his own hunger. When, a year or so later, he fed five thousand people with a few loaves and fishes, the response was immediate. The people tried to take him by force to make him king. One of the features of his teaching in the Sermon on the Mount was an exhortation to his hearers not to be anxious about these daily hardships but to realize that they would be cared for by the loving Father who feeds the fowls and gives beauty to the lilies. It is easier for us to respond to his exhortations to take no anxious thought for the morrow than it was for many of those who heard him.

When we appreciate the strain of living and the fading hopes of the Jews among whom Jesus walked we are able to see much of his teaching in a new light. We can understand why so many of his parables had to do with money. We can see the sombre importance of men standing idle in the market place all day because no man had hired them. We are not perplexed by the woman who, finding a coin of small value that was lost, sends for her neighbours to share her joy, or by the man who had to go to his friend in the middle of the night to borrow bread for an unexpected guest. The urgency of the petition in the prayer Jesus taught his disciples becomes poignant, "Give us this day our daily bread".

These conditions were a hindrance to Jesus in his ministry. When anxiety and despair reign in people's hearts they are not usually disposed to give much heed to moral and spiritual teaching. When, however, that teaching is accompanied by gifts which even temporarily banish the anxiety, there is a human tendency to clamour for it, and Jesus was under no delusion. After the miraculous feeding at Bethsaida he said, "Ye seek me, not because ye saw the miracles, but because ye did eat of the loaves and were filled. Labour not for the meat which perisheth". When Jesus turned from the material blessings and insisted upon the fundamental truths of his identity and mission, many were offended and walked no more with him. That was an experience which was to be perpetuated down the centuries. The history of the Christian Church was to show, sometimes in most perplexing and disturbing ways, that without the abiding influence of Jesus the fleshly mind will always be stronger than the spiritual mind. Though many will follow him into the deserts for the loaves and the fishes, only a comparatively small company will respond to his deeper call to fellowship. But to those few come their Lord's assurance, "As the living Father hath sent me, and I live by the Father, so he that eateth me, even he shall live by me ... he that eateth of this bread shall live for ever".

2

THE RELIGIOUS RULERS

NONE of the classes of people who exercised authority over the Jews emerged with much credit from their contacts with Jesus. In varying degree they were all the objects of his censure; and on one occasion Jesus specifically warned his disciples to beware of the leaven of the Pharisees, the Sadducees, and of Herod. It is important that we understand something of the influence which these parties had, and how that influence permeated like leaven through the whole nation, moulding its thought and shaping its action.

The picture which is revealed is not a pretty one. There is much in it to emphasize the words of Jeremiah that "the heart is deceitful above all things and desperately wicked". The people of God grievously failed to rise to their privileges, and without the grace of God in sending His Son into the world to accomplish salvation, all men would have been eternally lost.

Superficially the Jewish nation seemed religious to the point of fanaticism, but a closer scrutiny discloses those elemental passions which have characterized nations with no pretensions to high ideals. It is true that a few wealthy families advocated the study of the Scripture, but their motive was not to turn the people to God so much as to confound the growing power of the rivals they hated; so far from submitting to the influence of the Scriptures themselves, they were pagan worldlings patronizing Greek culture and ingratiating themselves with Rome, enforcing the religious obligations which so bountifully produced their wealth. The scribes on the other hand used their high office of instructing the people in the understanding of God's law to glorify their own learning, giving their expositions a higher place than the law and the prophets, and introducing a system of casuistry which obscured the direct teaching of Scripture; while the Pharisees proved an ideal foil for the subtleties of the scribes, ostentatiously following the traditions of the elders at street corner and in market place.

Such were the powers ruling the lives of the people in the days of Jesus. With his intimate knowledge of Scripture, each visit to Jerusalem after that memorable journey at the age of twelve would show the perversity and corruption into which the people were drawn from God under the guise of serving Him. To his sensitive spirit it must have been a test of patient discipline to refrain from exposing it. But the time came when the flood-gates of his indignation burst. The cumulative effect of his anger descended upon these blind leaders, and they felt the withering power of his indictments.

Let us look more closely at these men, their systems and their motives.

The scribes had degenerated from the high office they had held for centuries when, hidden from public gaze and secure from the temptations of popularity, they had spent their lives reverently copying the books of Scripture, using special ink upon the skin of a clean animal, counting every letter, and pronouncing each word aloud before writing it. In those days the Scriptures were held in such awe that if on examining a completed sheet, one letter was found to be wrong, the whole sheet was destroyed: so conscious were they of the sacredness of their task that they would wipe their pen before writing the name of God, and wash their bodies before writing the four letters of the covenant name.

The deterioration was a slow process, and as is so often the case, began in apparently the most innocent ways. It became a practice for the decisions of the rabbis on difficult interpretations of the law of Moses to be recorded. As these reports grew in volume, classification became necessary. In course of time the further commentaries and discussions aroused were compiled and formed the Mishnah. Ultimately the scope widened, and anecdotes of school and courtroom, mingled with Jewish experiences and superstitions, found their way into another compilation of writings known as the Gemara. Mishnah and Gemara together were later to become known as the Talmud, and a knowledge of this composite work was considered "the necessary doctrine and erudition" of the learned Jew. These writings came to be honoured above the Law itself, and it was a greater crime to offend against them than to break the commands of God. But at the time of Jesus these developments had not assumed their final shape. The great distinction was that between the written law of Moses and the oral law of tradition.

Meanwhile the scribe himself had changed. He had emerged from his quiet seclusion and become the religious authority in Israel, ruling in the synagogue, teaching in the schools and the Temple courts, arbitrating in civil and family disputes, and instructing in matters of secular and ceremonial difficulty. In the Gospels we find constant references to the scribes, who are also alluded to as "rabbis", "lawyers", and "doctors of the law". The greatest of the scribes had schools of their own at which they taught the young. Several of them toured the countryside with their disciples, and were invited to minister in the synagogues of the towns through which they passed; but the majority took up their residence in the towns and villages of Judea, and particularly Galilee, where they supervised the people in the synagogues and their children in the adjoining schools.

As might be expected where the deliberations of men had so largely superseded the wisdom of God, there were several significant and fundamental differences within the ranks of the scribes. Two rival schools were most prominent during the ministry of Christ, those of Shammai and Hillel. Both schools had emerged during the century before Christ came, although as Hillel lived to be well over a hundred it is possible that he was one of the doctors of the law who interviewed Jesus in the Temple on his visit at the age of twelve. The school of Shammai, whose founder was as rich as he was careless of the stringency of his own code, was rigidly orthodox and was responsible for the unlovely extremes of ceremonial which Jesus condemned.

The rival school of Hillel was led by a man of gentle and genial poverty, tolerant to the point of looseness in some of his rulings. One of the most noticeable disagreements was on the question of divorce. The school of Shammai insisted upon adultery being the only legal ground, while Hillel taught that a man may put away his wife on the flimsiest of pretexts, even for not adequately catering for his material necessities. When the people accepted Jesus as a rabbi, the Pharisees' question on divorce, "Is it lawful for a man to put away his wife for every cause?" was not to elicit information so much as to find out whether his sympathies lay with the school of Shammai or of Hillel. In this instance Jesus showed that the school of Shammai was nearer the true attitude by virtue of its reflection of the teaching of Scripture, but generally it was this school which received the greater censure at his hands.

Most of the scribes were also Pharisees, although a small number in Judea belonged to the Sadducees. The Pharisees were by far the largest religious party among the Jews at the time of Christ, numbering according to Josephus, six thousand. Though the great majority of them were ordinary middle class Jews, they were closely associated with the scribes, most of whom were prominent members. To no small extent the scribes owed their power and authority to the Pharisees whose chief interest was to give their findings strict and ostentatious observance. Yet they maintained a certain independence by their insistence that God had given Moses an oral as well as a written law, and that the oral law had been passed to the men of the Great Synagogue successively through Joshua, the elders of Israel and the prophets. Although this belief was destitute of historical evidence it had won general acceptance, and in their efforts to keep it with all its subsequent ramifications the Pharisees had imposed upon themselves and those under their influence a burden too heavy to bear. In their meticulous observance of frivolous decisions (which at lowest level had degenerated to the refusal to eat an egg laid on the Sabbath) the simple beauty of true worship and communion was utterly lost, while their constant efforts to maintain the tradition in all its weak and beggarly elements diverted their attention from God and turned them into self-satisfied and complacent hypocrites. Unlike the Sadducees the majority of the Pharisees were neither wealthy nor opulent. They lived temperate, sometimes frugal lives, and won widespread respect among the people who felt that they were witnessing religion practised at its highest level.

However sincere many of the Pharisees may have been they were always fighting a losing battle against the system to which they were devoted. That system bred hypocrisy, and in warning his disciples against the leaven of the Pharisees it was this inevitable hypocrisy to which Jesus alluded. It produced men who, shrouded in their own conscious sense of goodness, stood aloof from the vulgar crowd and, praying with themselves, thanked God they were not as other men. The tragedy of their condition was exposed by Jesus when, answering their indignant question, "Are we blind also?", he replied "If ye were blind, ye should have no sin: but now ye say, We see; therefore your sin remaineth". A physician cannot cure a sick man who insistently protests he is in perfect health, and has not the slightest intention of submitting to an examination or listening to a diagnosis of his condition.

Thus the very sincerity of the Pharisee was an impediment to him, such was the system to which he was in bondage. And there were sincere Pharisees in Israel at the time of Christ, particularly in Galilee, where before interference came from Jerusalem, Jesus was accepted as a rabbi and invited to preach in their synagogues. But there were the unadulterated hypocrites too, men who "for a pretence made long prayers", parading their religion in public places, and shedding it like a cloak in the seclusion of their private lives. Human nature being what it is, it was inevitable that the system should breed such men, and it was the system Jesus attacked with all the power of his vital nature. We have good reason to believe that the denunciations which are recorded in the Gospels were addressed to the leaders of the Pharisees who were primarily responsible for the low spiritual condition of the people—the scribes who were also Pharisees, and who in the deepest sense were the real hypocrites.

The Sadducees were a much smaller party and were confined to Jerusalem and its neighbourhood. Unlike the Pharisees they made no effort to increase their membership, which was probably only a few hundreds. They comprised the chief priests and their families, and amassed their great wealth from the Temple system. For this reason they did all they could to encourage religious worship, but their hearts were far from God. They were worldly men with political interests rather than godly men with religious convictions. There was a very real antagonism between them and the scribes and Pharisees, but their religious differences were made the excuse for more sinister ambitions. The chief theological issue between the two parties concerned the tradition; the Sadducees refusing to accept the teaching of the scribes that Moses was given an oral law. This was fundamental and meant that they set aside as almost worthless the teaching which the scribes held to be more important than the Law of Moses. The Sadducees contended that the Pentateuch was more important and more authoritative than the remainder of the Old Testament. They rejected the belief in the resurrection and a future life because they thought it was not taught in the first five books of Scripture. It is interesting to notice that when Jesus refuted their hypothetical case of the woman who had seven husbands, he referred them to Exodus, neglecting more impressive evidence from later books, because he knew they would refuse to accept such authority.

More subtle and far-reaching was the difference in outlook between the two parties. The scribes and Pharisees, with all their faults, were intensely nationalistic and loyal to the Jewish faith they had so unhappily complicated and diluted; but the Sadducees, while fostering the national features upon which they depended for their affluence and power, looked further afield. They sought to introduce Greek culture, and played the dangerous game of expediency with the Roman court. As economic distress grew in Palestine so the Sadducees became more unpopular, until they began to lose seats to the Pharisees in the Great Sanhedrin itself, where before they had undisputed monopoly. After the terrible disaster of AD 70 the Sadducees disappeared completely from Jewish life.

The Great Sanhedrin was the supreme council of the Jews. It consisted of seventy-one members and the Mishnah traced its origin to the seventy men whom God instructed Moses to appoint to help him bear the burden of governing the Children of Israel. Although this incident may have inspired the creation of the Sanhedrin in later times, it seems certain that the divine arrangement with Moses was of a temporary nature, and subsequent references to the elders of Israel are intermittent and vague.* The Great Sanhedrin met in a hall in the Temple courts, and there it exercised its judicial power in all important ecclesiastical, civil and criminal cases. It is important to remember that in practice there were no such divisions. The Jews were a theocratic people and hence all cases were fundamentally religious. If therefore a man stole, he would be indicted both for a criminal offence and a religious one in breaking the law. Similarly in the event of a claim for damages or any other matter which we should regard as a civil case, it resolved itself into the ruling of the Mosaic Law, and was thus truly a religious matter. The Sanhedrin had extremely wide powers. Only in cases where the death penalty was prescribed was it necessary to have their sentence confirmed by the Roman procurator.

In addition to the Great Sanhedrin in Jerusalem there were similar councils in all the towns and larger villages of Palestine. These seem to have originated beyond the boundaries of the Holy Land among the Jews of the Dispersion who felt the need for the authority of a council and the worship of a synagogue. The councils of Palestine were more under the

*See page 48 of *The First Century Ecclesia*, by J. B. Norris.

control of the Jerusalem Sanhedrin which appointed their members and heard the more difficult cases that were brought before them, acting as a Supreme Court of Appeal. The members of the local Sanhedrins were usually the rulers of the synagogue. Exercising a firm and intimate control over the people, they were able to introduce a system of sanctions against any who incurred their displeasure and had been cast out of the synagogue. The parents of the man born blind were in danger of losing their livelihood by making any statement which supported the claims of Jesus and invalidated official criticism of him.

The synagogues were distributed widely throughout the towns and villages of Palestine, affording the Jews the opportunity of simple weekly worship which consisted of prayers, and a reading and exposition of the Law and the Prophets. The ruler of the synagogue was usually a Pharisee scribe who also taught in the adjoining school and presided over the local Sanhedrin.

Behind this system of worship and jurisprudence stood the great Temple on Mount Moriah, exercising its powerful unifying influence over the whole Jewish world, rising far above the puny ambitions and strifes of men. Every boy was brought up to believe that here was the point of contact between him and the God of Israel; here the High Priest went each year into the presence of God to confess the people's sins and to make reconciliation. Hither the Jews flocked for the three principal feasts of the year, filling the town and the surrounding hills. Here the Messianic hopes found their focus. Yet the thoughtful Jew saw little prospect of national deliverance through the Temple system maintained by men who sought only its own ends and strove in bitter enmity with rivals who in turn had transformed the Law of God into a complex system of ceremonial observance. Disheartened by the growing economic distress, dissatisfied with religious leaders who took everything and offered little in return, his Messianic hope was strong but vague. It was necessary for the long silent voice of the prophets to be heard again to give life and substance to the longing which lay dormant in the hearts of God's people.

3

THE WILDERNESS PROPHET

THE voice of John the Baptist ringing on the desert air
came like a clarion call to a nation whose ears had been
dulled by the monotonous chant of tradition-ridden priests.
The prediction that God would redeem His promise and send
the long-expected Messiah of Israel was, however, too deep-
rooted to be more than temporarily obscured by the ever-
growing traditions of the elders or the many perplexities of a
subject nation. National feeling was intense. The Roman
Guard had to be increased during the feasts in Jerusalem;
and clusters of rough wooden crosses with their horrible
burdens, particularly by the roadsides in Galilee, were a not
infrequent symbol of the seething unrest.

The lifeless casuistry of Temple and Synagogue, and the
relentless suppression by Rome, had given little encouragement to the Jewish people. Never had they been more in need
of that inspiring feature of their national life which had been
taken from them—the prophet of God. The divine sentence
had gone forth: "... night shall be unto you, that ye shall not
have a vision ... and the sun shall go down over the prophets,
and the night shall be dark over them". The prophet had been
an unpopular figure in Israel, not because of his revelations
of things to come, but because he represented the voice of God
indicting the people for their iniquity. Smitten by their evil
conscience the people had rejected and persecuted the messengers of God. Now, in the confusion of the dark days which
followed their withdrawal, the nation was able truly to
repent and assess their loss. It was to the prophets that they
owed their hope of a Messiah and of the restoration of their
nation to its former prosperity. Prophets had been the
authorities to whom they could turn in times of national danger
and perplexity. They alone in Israel had given them that
sense of personal approach to God which maintained their
conviction of responsibility and privilege. But though the
prophets had left the national scene their influence was still
abroad in the land, maintaining in many hearts the message

of the coming deliverer who was to redeem his people and restore their lost glory. The Scriptures clearly predicted that the Messiah's advent would be proclaimed by a prophet in the wilderness, who would herald his approach.

John the Baptist fulfilled this great role; and in so doing earned from his Lord the signal tribute that no greater man had been born of woman. He came in the true tradition of Israel's prophets, gaunt, ascetic, lonely. As foretold by the angel he brought joy and gladness to many in Israel, but at the cost of personal sacrifice and persecution. Like many of his predecessors he languished in the darkness of a prison cell until his light was finally obscured by the insatiable hatred of a woman and the voluptuous pride of a man.

From his birth John was dedicated to his task by the Holy Spirit. At an early age he renounced his priestly vocation, and went into the desert, preparing himself for his work by a life of lonely asceticism, meditating upon the message of those who had gone before him, and communing with God. Nor did the years pass without giving him an insight into the condition of Israel, the deeper motives of those who ruled, and the depravity and need of the human spirit.

At last the moment arrived when the Word of the Lord came to him. His vocation had begun. He went through the Jordan region preaching the baptism of repentance and proclaiming the coming of the Messiah. The response was immediate. The whole country caught fire. Men and women came in their thousands into the desert from all quarters. Poor peasants from Galilee jostled rich traders from Jerusalem and soldiers from Jericho. Godly souls who had waited for redemption in Israel came joyfully to join the curious sceptics and the haughty scribes. They saw a rugged, sun-tanned prophet, with tongue of fire and eyes of judgment. Impressed by the conviction and authority of his message, their hearts were stirred. On every side the cry went up, "Master, what shall we do?" John had only one answer, "Repent and prepare". The thousands who responded to his message submitted to the ordinance of baptism in the waters of Jordan, a symbol of the washing away of their sins and their recognition of the coming of Messiah. In marked contrast to the teaching of the scribes, John laid emphasis, not on what men did, but upon the spirit behind their actions. He condemned the smugness of the rulers in the delusion that they were the children of the patriarchs, and declared that God was able of the stones around which the waters of the ford were swirling to raise up children to Abraham. It was useless to claim to be of Abraham unless they were like him. The only true test was in the fruit which a tree brought forth, and the time had at last come when the axe was to be laid at the root of the tree.

The message of John bore principal reference to the first coming of Jesus. He spoke no word of a conqueror who was to overcome the foreign tyrant, humble the oppressors of the people, and establish the world-wide dominion of peace and glory which were the subject of so much Old Testament prophecy. His message concerned the relationship of individuals to God. It was a challenge to prepare for the coming of One who was to sift the wheat from the chaff and to bestow infinite blessings upon those who received him.

One day as John was baptizing in Jordan, Jesus moved through the multitudes and appeared before him. Although it is improbable that John knew his cousin by sight, he would not be deceived by the one who stood before him. As he looked into the strong face, and met the fearless eyes glowing with the light of heaven, the man who was satisfying the people's need felt suddenly conscious of his own; the man who searched the hearts of the penitents was filled with an overwhelming sense of contrition. "I have need to be baptized of thee, and comest thou to me?" The reply of Jesus is revealing: "Suffer it to be so now, for thus it becometh us to fulfil all righteousness". In his baptism of Jesus, John performed what was virtually the final office of his ministry. The appearance of the dove lighting upon Jesus was the promised visible sign which identified Jesus as the Messiah of Israel, the Son of God, whose way John had prepared. Thus John, whose work was almost done, was not without the satisfaction which is always the reward of devoted service to God.

John's recognition of Jesus was not the result of years of meditation in the wilderness, nor of a careful study of the prophets, nor was it the last step in a process of logical reasoning. John insists, "I knew him not". The recognition came as a direct revelation from God. "He that sent me to baptize with water, the same said unto me, Upon whom thou shalt see the spirit descending and remaining on him, the same is he which baptizeth with the Holy Spirit". John had that experience, and because of it he said "I saw, and bare record that this is the Son of God".

We cannot leave this matter without giving it some examination from the point of view of Jesus himself and the work he had come to do. His answer to John's objection, "Suffer it to be so now, for thus it becometh us to fulfil all righteousness", is the first evidence of his sinlessness. The multitudes had come to John confessing their sins, and had submitted to the baptism of repentance. Jesus also submitted, but his baptism was not an acknowledgment of his sin, but the demonstration of his righteousness. No words of Jesus are without weight and his answer to John indicates that it is in the spirit of humility that righteousness is to be achieved. This baptism among sinners was the preface to a greater baptism which had to be accomplished in the same spirit of humble submission to God's will, with the same great end in view, to fulfil God's righteousness. Unlike the first Adam who thought that equality with God was a thing to be grasped at, Jesus "made himself of no reputation, and took upon him the form of a servant ... he humbled himself, and became obedient unto death, even the death of the cross". And thus joining sinful men, preaching the gospel to the poor, washing his disciples' feet, and suffering the crowning indignities of his trial and death, he fulfilled all righteousness and brought to man the firstfruits of a peace with God far greater than the harmony which Adam lost. Thus the greater baptism began. Luke records that as Jesus was baptized he prayed. In this moment of complete surrender he was in the presence of God. This sublime example should be in the mind of all who come to God by him. It indicates no merely formal obedience, but a sacred submission in the presence of God. As Jesus rose from the waters, God confirmed his righteousness from heaven, and anointed him for his life of dedication by the gift of the Holy Spirit. From the age of twelve he had consecrated himself to his Father's business. Now his ears were opened to hear the voice that called him to embark upon the baptism of water and of blood through which he would eventually take away the sin of the world. The words of the Psalmist glowed with life in the spirit of Jesus, "Lo, I come, in the volume of the book it is written of me, to do thy will, O God". His Father accepted him and illuminated his path with words which would bring exultation to his burdened heart during the dark days that lay before him: "This is my beloved Son, in whom I am well pleased". Both by water and by the Spirit was Jesus baptized, and, henceforth, all who come to the Father through him would enter the Kingdom through baptism of water and of the Spirit.

Although John proclaimed that the coming one would sift the wheat from the chaff he did not live to hear the full confirmation of his message from the lips of Jesus, "I am come to send fire on earth". It is possible, however, that his disciples may have carried to him in prison the words spoken in Galilee, "Think not that I am come to send peace on earth: I came not to send peace, but a sword". It is a strange paradox that when Jesus came "not to be ministered unto, but to minister, and to give his life a ransom for many" his coming left fire and sword behind; but when he comes again in flaming fire, "taking vengeance on them that know not God", the final effect will be of peace and joy in an age when "God shall wipe away all tears, and there shall be no more death".

4

THE TRIAL OF FAITH

WITH his baptism the life of Jesus emerges in all its beauty. From now on he will always be with us, and we shall feel the strength of his presence, though our dim eyes may not see the fulness of his perfection, or our dull hearts perceive the depth of his communion with his Father. We shall see rough men growing into saints as they walk with him; we shall hear his words of instruction and comfort. We shall become conscious of his quiet confidence and healing power and know something of the peace of God. We shall learn the true meaning of love in ministration, in forbearance and in supreme sacrifice. And when at length we turn the last Gospel page we shall know that he is with us still. His invitation, "Come unto me ... learn of me", echoes yet in the ears of all who will hear, growing louder with our greater need. The wisdom of his teaching is emphasized by the appalling disasters wrought by the wisdom of men; and the certainty and need of the Kingdom he taught grow clearer with the passing years as the kingdoms of men crumble into ruin. His touch has yet its ancient power, and meditating upon him and the source of his strength we can still find a peace and joy which contrasts strangely with the tumult and discord of the world.

Immediately following his baptism Jesus was driven by the Spirit into the wilderness. The first period of preparation was completed at Nazareth; he had obeyed the call of his Father to begin the active phase of his great ministry. With the divine approval came the power of the Spirit, and now, in the Judean wilderness, the supreme test in the age-long struggle between good and evil had begun. There is a terrific urgency in that journey into the desert. It did not happen until Jesus was full of the Holy Spirit. Then he was driven. What a conflict! What final decision! We sense the atmosphere of strain in the Gospel narratives. Exaltation of spirit in the consciousness of his Father's acknowledgment and approval was sobered by the assessment of the magnitude of his task. Days lengthened into weeks. So absorbed was he that physical needs were forgotten. Yet they took their toll, and when resistance was at its lowest ebb, he felt the full impact of temptation.

It is difficult to visualize this scene without thinking of the earlier test of the first Adam. In the fragrant beauty of the Garden of God, after a period of harmony with his Maker, with all the animal creation subject to him, Adam had failed when his obedience was challenged. Now, in the fulness of time, the last Adam climbs the rugged slopes into the wilderness, its very desolation a symbol of the other failure, the animals no longer affectionate and patient but, in Mark's words, "wild beasts"; and there he engages in that struggle which in its final victory is destined to bring harmony between God and His creation in an age when the desert shall blossom as the rose, the cow and the bear shall feed together and a little child shall lead them.

There is no inconsistency in the fact that Jesus could be tempted with evil. The wilderness experience confirms that he was made in all points like his brethren, his victory there shows that he triumphantly withstood the assault of sin. There is no iniquity in temptation, but if temptation is parleyed with it quickly leads to sin. The more we allow fleshly instincts to occupy our thoughts, the greater the danger of compromise, and the desire to make terms is the first sign of defeat. In the wilderness temptations Jesus teaches that the nearer we live to God, the shorter and sharper will be the conflict with evil, just as, conversely, the lower our spiritual condition, the longer will be our fight and the greater our danger. The apostle John brings this principle into clear focus when he says, "Whosoever is born of God doth not commit sin ... he cannot sin, because he is born of God". John is not saying that it is a *physical* impossibility to sin, but that so responsive are our hearts to the love of God that it is a *moral* impossibility to sin. Jesus demonstrated this in the most exacting environment.

The first temptation was more subtle than it appears. "If thou be the son of God command that these stones be made bread." The hunger of Jesus was the cause rather than the object of the temptation; for nearly six weeks he had been lost to the needs of his body, now he becomes conscious of acute hunger: if the stones at his feet were loaves in his hand, how quickly could the faintness of his body be strengthened! Yet the temptation was deeper than this. It lay also in the suggestion of doubt. Down in the Jordan valley Jesus had heard the voice of his Father acknowledging him as His Son, and with the commendation had come the power of God. The uncertainty that increased with the lowering of bodily resistance could so easily be resolved by a harmless test which would at once relieve the ache in his body and the doubt in his mind. Jesus recognized the temptation as a trial of faith as well as of endurance, and did not hesitate. "It is written, Man shall not live by bread alone, but by every word that proceedeth out of the mouth of God." In direct contrast to the hungry Israelites who complained of their lack of bread, Jesus was content to leave his sustenance completely in the hands of God. His knowledge of the Word showed him the way of victory and his faith in it gave him the power to resist the evil thought. This victory was more than a momentary triumph inspired by a sudden challenge; it reflected a trust in God with which all Jesus did and said was instinct. With the authority of his own conquest he could exhort his disciples, "Take no thought for your life, what ye shall eat ... Your heavenly Father knoweth ye have need of all these things".

In resisting this temptation Jesus brushed aside the suggestion that he should fall back upon the divine gift of power to ease his suffering. He desired no exemption from the common lot of humanity. He demonstrated his faith by a committal of his bodily needs into the hands of his Father, and he showed the power of God's word in the presence of spiritual danger.

The triumph of Jesus points the way to victory in the lives of all those who follow him. We do not require the extreme rigours of the wilderness to tempt us to make stones into bread. Most men live by bread alone, and do not discover until too late that all is vanity and vexation of spirit. The true disciple learns that the flesh profiteth nothing, and the word of God, communicated by His Spirit, and living in His Son, is spirit and life. It is a supremely important lesson that the life is more than meat and the body than raiment.

The battle was being won but the conflict was not over. With extraordinary subtlety a new attack struck suddenly at the foundations of the previous victory. The doubt persisted, it had still to be successfully challenged. Jesus was tempted to a practical demonstration of the trust he claimed. Moreover the word to which Jesus had appealed was used to support the second test. In effect the temptation was, "You have acknowledged your confidence in God and in His Word, prove it by your actions. The word tells you that God will give His angels charge over you to keep you and prevent you dashing your foot against a stone. Throw yourself down from the pinnacle of the temple, and show your confidence in that word, and in your Father, *if* you are the Son of God. This spectacular demonstration will also be a dramatic opening to your mission and assure for you a national response". But Jesus answered with strength and courage. His reply, "It is written again", must always be the response to those who wrest isolated Scriptures for their own ends. "Thou shalt not tempt the Lord your God." The context of the quotation showed that the children of Israel had repeatedly tempted the Lord by disobedience and distrust. Time and again they had rebelled against God by a desire to go their own way. To have wavered before this temptation would have been to abandon at the outset the life of faith which Jesus came to live. He would have sought his own way to show himself to Israel, rather than the spirit of waiting upon God. There had been a subtle omission in the quotation from the 91st Psalm. The divine promise was, "For he shall give his angels charge over thee, to keep thee *in all thy ways*". The way Jesus trod was the way his Father appointed, any other way would be a faithless rebellion, and a temptation of God. Jesus was to appeal to the people's wonder not by a spectacular demonstration of power, but by so startling a manifestation of love that a hardened Roman officer was to cry, "Surely this was the Son of God!" He would give them a sign, but it was not to be a public salvation acclaimed by thousands of delirious countrymen; it was to be a victory witnessed by lonely weeping women in the solitude of a garden. Such was the Father's way, and in this way Jesus was kept by the angels who were even now waiting to minister to him.

In this victory too there is infinite encouragement for the disciple of every age to wait upon the Lord in patience and trust, neither beguiled by subtle sophistries nor tempted to subject his high relationship to artificial strains.

These had been insidious attempts to undermine Christ's loyalty and strength of purpose; the final trial was devoid of any veneer of righteousness. It was an undisguised challenge to forsake the way of God and accept the temporal rewards of the flesh. Surveying the plains below him with their cities and villages, the roads winding away into the distance, highways to the farthest dominions of the earth, he felt the temptation surge within him to forsake the strange path of suffering and humility, and use his power to bring all men to his

47

feet. His sensitive mind would readily appreciate the universal benefits of such an action. The children of God would be freed from the oppressor's yoke, and all men would enjoy the blessings of peace and prosperity. Jesus was looking for a moment along the wide straight way which leads to death. For an instant he contemplated its smoothness and its easy victories. Resolutely he turned towards the narrow tortuous path that rose steeply up among the thorns and rocks to the only true destiny. The years of communion in Nazareth had again proved sufficient. Of no other man could the Spirit through the Psalmist say, "How sweet are thy words unto my taste! Yea, sweeter than honey to my mouth! Through thy precepts I get understanding: therefore I hate every false way". Idolatry may be disguised in rich robes, but it will not deceive those whose minds are stayed upon God. To attempt to achieve even the most laudable ends in conscious defiance of the way of God is a victory for the flesh. Jesus was not deceived. With a supreme and relentless discipline of spirit he banished idolatry in all its forms, "Get thee hence, Satan: for it is written, Thou shalt worship the Lord thy God, and him only shalt thou serve".

Of the recorded temptations of Jesus, this last is the most prevalent and the most dangerous. We are confronted throughout our lives with the alternative of serving God or man. Although the apostle John does not record the temptation of Jesus, it seems almost certain that it was in his mind as he closed his epistle with the moving appeal, "We know that whosoever is born of God sinneth not; but he that is begotten of God keepeth himself, and that wicked one toucheth him not. And we know that we are of God, and the whole world lieth in wickedness ... Little children, keep yourselves from idols. Amen".

With this final rebuke to fleshly desires, the temptations were over for a season. It could not be otherwise. So complete a victory could only end in the summary departure of the vanquished. And in the place of challenge and strife came the ministering angels of God, bringing with them the fruits of victory. The battle was over and peace reigned. The victor emerged from the wilderness stronger than when he entered it. His resolution had taken the strain, and now he was ready for the work his Father had committed to his trust.

5

"BEHOLD THE LAMB OF GOD!"

A change had come over John's preaching after the baptism of Jesus. It is reflected in his abrupt negatives to a deputation of scribes and Pharisees which was sent to enquire concerning his identity. "Who art thou?" "I am not the Christ." "What then? Art thou Elias?" "I am not." "Art thou that prophet?" "No." His great anxiety now is to stand back in the shadows allowing none to see his features, that nothing of his message shall be lost. "I am the voice of one crying in the wilderness, Make straight the way of the Lord." Now that Jesus has been made manifest to him, he even minimizes the importance of his baptism, which does not purify but simply prepares men's hearts for the reception of the Christ. " I baptize with water, but in the midst of you there standeth one whom ye know not."

The deputation departed. The destiny of Israel depended upon the nation's recognition of the Messiah when he came. The gulf between the Baptist and the leaders of the people was a tragic indication of the coming conflict which was to lead to the death of the prophet, the rejection and crucifixion of the Messiah, and centuries of suffering for the Jewish race.

The following day Jesus emerged from the path along which he had disappeared six weeks before. The forty days of physical endurance and mental struggle had left their mark upon him. He came fully prepared for the world and its sin. His armour had been tested and approved. Now, waiting upon his Father for the next step in his manifestation to Israel, he had been drawn back to this gaunt prophet whose heavenly mission had yet to be completed.

John, looking up, beheld Jesus. *Now* he knew him. He had been unable to announce him before, because it was not until his baptism that John had received the divinely appointed sign, and at the moment of recognition Jesus had departed into the wilderness. Confronted by the Messiah, John knew that his work of preparation was over. All that remained for him to do was to direct men from himself to their Saviour.

"Behold the Lamb of God, which taketh away the sin of the world." Behind those words the blood of countless sacrifices had flowed. The whole structure of the Mosaic law, the meticulous details of Levitical ritual, the message of the prophets, were brought to a focus in the person of the One who now stood beside the Baptist. John could not realize the full significance of his own words, but by revelation he recognized the Messiah and knew something of the sacrifice that was to be required of him.

The following day John the Baptist was talking to two sturdy young fishermen from Galilee. John, who was later to record these events, was one, and Andrew the other. The prophet looking up saw Jesus walking some distance away. This time there was nothing impersonal in his words to his two disciples, as he looked intently into their eyes and said, "Behold the Lamb of God". His words were a command and a farewell that could not be mistaken.

So the ministry of Jesus began, quietly and unobtrusively. Such are the ways of God. In the two bronzed fishermen following the Son of man with hesitant steps and fast-beating hearts, we see the beginnings of a great impulse to follow him. We have in the simple narrative at once the birth of the church of Christ and the record of the bride's introduction to the Bridegroom.

The two men followed the silent figure; they walked on too fearful to speak to one another, almost afraid of being seen. But there was no escape for them. These men were being guided by God, they were the Father's first gift to His Son. "Thine they were", Jesus was later to plead, "and thou gavest them me." We can feel the aged John's heart glow anew, and see his dim eyes fill with tears as he lives again that breathless moment when the suspense was broken. "Then", he records, "Jesus turned and beheld them following." Those who would follow Jesus will always be subject to the moment when he makes the challenge, "What seek ye?" These men had nothing to fear. Sincere seekers after God, their search had led them to the Baptist, and their earnestness was shown by their neglected homes and livelihood. In obedience to one they believed to be a man of God they had followed the Messiah. They had sought the Lord with all their heart, and the divine promise was fulfilled, "Ye shall surely find Him".

But neither their sincerity nor the understanding that shone in the eyes of Jesus were enough to banish the emotion which stirred them and confused their tongue. "Master", they stammered, "where dwellest thou?" The one word "Master" would have sufficed, but the question that framed itself on their faltering lips speaks eloquently for them, revealing their desire to know more about him, to share his company, to prolong these vital moments. It *shows* the effect upon sincere men when Jesus turns and beholds them. "Come and see", will always be the answer. Jesus took them to some haunt in the mountainous wilderness, teaching them more powerfully than any words could convey the price of discipleship. But the privations and solitude of the desert were forgotten, because "they abode with him that day". To follow Jesus, and to abide with him will always be the essence of true discipleship.

A great experience often brings an almost painful longing to share it with those we love. So Andrew's first thought is of Simon his brother. In bringing him to Jesus he did the greatest service that one man can do for another. "We have found the Messiah", was the result of a few hours in the company of Jesus.

Jesus looked at Peter, and saw both the manner of man he was, and also the manner of man he could become by the grace of God. "Thou art Simon", was a warning of the man he was—Simon, humble, impetuous, turbulent; Simon, rash and lovable, headstrong and loyal. "Thou shalt be called Peter", was a promise. You shall yet be strong in faith and steady as a rock, an example to the Church that shall be founded upon your divinely given revelation. For many years Peter was only to have the faintest glimmerings of all that his Lord meant in those words of welcome. But later he sees and reveals, showing his brethren how they too can share this change of name; "Ye also as lively stones are built up a spiritual house, an holy priesthood, to offer up spiritual sacrifices, acceptable to God by Jesus Christ". And, looking back upon his life and inviting his brethren to consider their own transforming experience he says, "Unto you therefore which believe he is precious".

But he wrote these words nearly thirty years later. Now he was still Simon, and his conversion was not yet. There were tears and agonizing struggles before Peter should feed the flock of God, but through those years Jesus was giving him strength even at the point of his great weakness.

The day after the two had become three Jesus decided to go northwards to Galilee. Before he left he saw Philip, a fellow townsman of Andrew and Peter, and probably also a disciple of John. It may be that Philip had seen the conviction of his friends as they walked with Jesus, and sharing it, was only restrained from approaching the Messiah by his natural reticence. But looking upon him Jesus recognized him as a potential disciple; "Follow me".

The little party started for Galilee, leaving the gaunt wilderness prophet to his fading days and his lonely nights, deprived of the companionship of his four most ardent disciples whom he was probably never to see again, yet rejoicing in his loss which proclaimed work faithfully done. After three days' steady travelling, to Philip's great happiness they arrived at Cana where his friend Nathanael lived. He lost no time in finding him and giving him news which he knew would bring him joy, "We have found him of whom Moses in the law and the prophets did write, Jesus of Nazareth, the son of Joseph". This message only brought a perplexed frown to Nathanael's brow. The prophet spoke of Bethlehem Ephratah as the town from which the Messiah would come forth. Moreover Galilee was scorned by the religious leaders of the people, and Nazareth was notoriously evil even in Galilee. But Philip *knew*. There could only be one answer to Nathanael's doubts, "Come and see". Looking upon him, Jesus saw a man of prayer and simple sincerity. "Behold, an Israelite indeed in whom there is no guile" was the assessment of him who knew what was in man. Startled, Nathanael replied, wondering, "Whence knowest thou me!" Jesus had shared his communion and entered into his meditation; "Before that Philip called thee, when thou wast under the fig tree, I saw thee". In a moment of time Nathanael was led beyond Nazareth and beyond Joseph. His human observation which had only succeeded in setting limits to the power of God, was swept aside in "Thou art the Son of God, thou art the King of Israel".

We can almost see the heartening smile on the lips of Jesus as he tells him he has only seen the beginnings of the revelation of the Son of man; but his recognition and faith will be the introduction to far greater things. He was telling Nathanael what he was to tell Martha on the eve of her brother's resurrection. "Said I not unto thee, that if thou wouldest believe, thou shouldest see the glory of God?" To Nathanael he promised, "Hereafter ye shall see heaven open, and the angels of God ascending and descending upon the son of Man". These experiences had already happened to Jesus. The heavens had opened at his baptism, and the angels of God had ministered to him in the wilderness. Nicodemus will

"Now learn a parable of the fig tree; When his branch is yet tender, and putteth forth leaves, ye know that summer is nigh." (Matthew 24:32)

"Then cometh Jesus from Galilee to Jordan unto John, to be baptized of him." (Matthew 3:13)

"… he saw other two brethren, James the son of Zebedee, and John his brother, in a ship …" (Matthew 4:21)

not witness these things, but the words of Jesus will be fulfilled. Jacob had discovered that the place that had been known as Luz was in truth the House of God. Nathanael would yet see and that very shortly and in his own town, that the Heaven had been opened. He would learn that Jesus was the Way, the Truth and the Life, and that a new and living way had been opened to God through the veil of his flesh. He would come to realize that the works of Jesus, even the words he spake, were of God, and no man could come to the Father but by him.

So the Church of Christ began: five sincere men, in humble circumstances, with no religious standing, but an earnest longing for the Messiah. Two came because of the words of a man of God, one came because of a human relationship, one was invited by Jesus himself while Nathanael, who was in all probability the apostle Bartholomew, was won in spite of Jewish prejudice by the power the Father had given the Son. They all thought they had chosen Christ, but in fact Christ had chosen them, and behind that choice was the grace of God. They were not entirely dedicated to Jesus but were given the opportunity of his companionship and the time to consider the full implications of discipleship before their Master was to ask them for their final, irrevocable decision.

6

CANA

WHILST Jesus was staying in Cana, probably in Nathanael's house, a wedding was in progress in the town, and he was invited with the disciples to the feast. It may have been a courteous invitation to a visiting rabbi, but more probably the request was for the more intimate reason that a relative of Jesus was being married. Mary was there, and her subsequent concern and instructions to the servants argue a near relationship. That no mention is made of Joseph may suggest that Mary was now a widow.

The marriage ceremony in Palestine at that time was a much more solemn occasion than we are accustomed to in our modern western civilization. It lasted for several days, and was preceded by a fast. The pious Jew considered it essentially a religious occasion and looked upon it as the symbol of the union of God with Israel. He believed that his past sins were forgiven, and after a feast which, though joyful, was almost sacramental in character, he began a new life.

It was in such an atmosphere, heightened by the presence of Jesus, that the feast began. The formal blessing was bestowed, the bridal cup was emptied and the meal proceeded. Quite suddenly a difficult emergency arose; the wine had failed. This was a humiliation for the Bridegroom almost amounting to disgrace. The wine was his gift to his guests. The servants were the first to realize what had happened, but Mary, characteristically sensitive, was quick to feel something was wrong, and, ascertaining the reason, she whispered urgently to Jesus, "They have no wine".

Mary's appeal was natural enough. During the years at Nazareth Jesus had been more than adequate to deal with any situation that arose in the home or in the workshop. Mary had learned to appeal to him in moments of perplexity. She had absolute confidence in him. So now she expected him to intervene successfully. What she had heard from the enthusiastic disciples of the events in the Jordan valley had increased her confidence and possibly heightened her expectation. Moreover it is probable that the last minute invitation of Jesus with his disciples was partly responsible for the crisis.

The reply of Jesus must have startled and perplexed his mother. "Woman, what have I to do with thee? mine hour is not yet come." There was no harshness in the appellation "woman". It was often used in expressions of courtesy and reverence, and, indeed Jesus was to utter it again when he looked down upon his mother in tender solicitude from the cross. But there can be no escape from the fact that Jesus was firmly refusing to allow her relationship to direct his actions, in spite of the deep mutual love behind it. It was very natural that with the passing years and the human intimacies of home life, Mary had to learn again a lesson she had only partially learnt eighteen years before. The man of thirty had to repeat in these words the lesson the boy of twelve had taught in the Temple: "Wist ye not that I must be about my Father's business?"

With a gentle relentlessness which was to characterize all his teaching concerning human relationships, Jesus was telling his mother that the days of Nazareth were over for ever. He was saying farewell to all his earthly ties. Mary had lost her son: Jesus had lost his mother. No longer could it be "My mother and I"; henceforth it must always be "My Father and I".

Jesus does not fail Mary but he makes it clear that his actions will always be independent of the slightest human attempt to influence them; they will be the holy submission of a Son to his Father. The crisis will be averted, the feast will proceed joyfully, not because of the pleading of a woman, or the honour of a bridegroom, but to manifest the glory of the Son. What did Jesus mean by those words, "Mine hour is not yet come"? Possibly Mary, stirred by the glowing account of John's declaration from the lips of the disciples, was preoccupied by the angelic promise concerning the Messiah's destiny. Like the apostles she expected the establishment of the kingdom in all its glory at the hands of her son. Perhaps she too overlooked the humiliation and suffering to which John the Baptist with deeper understanding had alluded. She may have felt that his hour had come. Truly that hour would come when Jerusalem would be holy, and the mountains would drop down new wine, and the hills flow with milk. But before that could be possible there was another hour, the hour of death and glorification when the Son of God would by his blood cleanse those who believe on him, and make possible eternal life to those who eat his flesh and drink his blood. To this hour Jesus referred throughout his ministry until, in the upper room at Jerusalem he announced its arrival to those whom his Father had given him: "Father, the hour is come; glorify Thy son."

Mary, conscious of the sword that pierced her heart, yet without the slightest bitterness, expressed her undiminished confidence in Jesus. "Whatsoever he saith unto you, do it." Six large jars used for the ceremonial ablutions were ranged along the wall. Jesus gave instructions, "Fill the water pots with water". When each jar was filled to the brim the servants looked expectantly at Jesus. "Draw out now and bear unto the steward of the feast." The steward, knowing nothing of the crisis or the miracle, expressed his gratification at the quality of the wine, and marvelled that the best had been thus held in reserve.

"This beginning of miracles", said the Evangelist, "did Jesus in Cana of Galilee, and manifested forth his glory; and his disciples believed on him." It was the first of eight miracles that John recorded, but unlike the other Gospel writers, he always called them "signs", thus using a word specially designed to call the attention of readers to the deeper significance that lay beyond the physical event.

This distinction compels our more careful scrutiny. We recognize the importance of the first occasion on which Jesus used the power his Father had bestowed upon him to give authority to his words. We rejoice in the picture of the Son of God mingling with the children of men, walking with them in their shadowed human paths, and teaching them that joy is the fruit of the Spirit as well as of the vine. But we are led further than this. We see Jesus changing the water of ceremonial cleansing into the wine of the new covenant. The steward of the feast was the servant of the father of the bridegroom who was responsible for the purification and the sustenance of the guests. In him we are able to distinguish the features of the high priest of Israel who, presented with the new wine, did not know whence it came, or who presented it, yet unconsciously acknowledged it as better than the old. "It is expedient for us", he says, "that one man should die for the people, and that the whole nation perish not."

It was not the earthly bridegroom who had held back the good wine until now. It was the God of Israel who in the fulness of time sent forth the heavenly Bridegroom with the true wine which had in it the essence of eternal life, before which the old wine "is ready to vanish away".

Although the steward did not know, the servants knew because they listened to his words, and knowing, they wondered. But it was to the disciples that Christ's glory was manifested. His power was a vital confirmation to them of the truth of his words, and removed the last tendency to withhold their allegiance. Previously they had believed his claims, now he had vindicated them and their mental assent became a personal trust and prepared them for that moment when without hesitation they were to leave all and follow him.

BOOK TWO: THE BACKGROUND OF THE MINISTRY

Book Three

MANIFESTATION TO ISRAEL

1

THE PASSOVER AND THE TEMPLE

THE time had now fully come for Jesus to manifest himself to Israel. Pausing only a few days in the homes of his small band of followers at Capernaum he left Galilee so that he might be in the city and sanctuary of God in time for the Passover. The only appropriate place for him to reveal himself was in Jerusalem, and there could be no more fitting occasion than the feast of the Passover. The rulers must be given the first opportunity of accepting their Messiah.

But the advent of Christ meant a purge. It could not have been otherwise. Wherever self-interest and fleshly ambitions order men's lives the coming of Christ will mean a sweeping away of everything which does despite to the spirit of grace. Year by year Jesus had gone up to the temple. Each visit would reveal more of the greed and injustice of those responsible for the ordered worship of God. It was necessary for the people to bring offerings, and it was convenient that they should be readily available. It was important that the temple levies should be required in the form of a standard half-shekel coin in view of the thousands of foreign Jews who came from all parts of the empire. Arrangements were therefore made for the sale of animals and the exchange of foreign money from which the Levites and High Priestly families found a source of immense profit; and establishing a monopoly, had imposed more and more abuses upon the people who came to worship. Those who did not purchase their sacrifices in the Temple courts were not immune from the avarice of the priests because they had to submit them to the inspection of qualified examiners who were authorized to charge for each animal. These examiners were subject to human frailties and increased their revenue by receiving bribes when they found real or imaginary faults in the animals submitted to them.

The activities of the money changers were not confined to changing enough foreign money for the Temple levy and the animal offerings, but they negotiated all sorts of financial transactions. Many of their dealings led to violent dispute and not infrequently to blows and riots which needed the attention of the Temple police. These desecrations, mingling with the noise of literally thousands of animals driven through the seething masses of worshippers, made up a scene of pandemonium which must have brought smiles of contempt from the watchful Roman sentries on the walls above. They evoked a burning indignation in the heart of Jesus which frequent visits only served to intensify. Now the time had come to open his ministry and he did not spare. Twisting some cords into a whip, he drove the animals from the owners towards the great gates; he flung tables aside, scattering the piles of money. Men cringed in fear before him. "Take these things hence; make not my Father's House a house of merchandise." Slowly the storm subsided. But no man opposed him. Those responsible for the desecration came forward, but their attack was frustrated before it could begin by the silent figure standing before them, his eyes blazing with anger and challenge. Looking upon him they recognized their guilt and were powerless to charge him. There was a heavenly bearing about him that took their minds back to the wilderness and the Baptist. They remembered his proclamation of the coming of the Messiah. It was with no conscious deliberation that this man had spoken of the Temple as "My Father's House". Was it possible ...? Finally one became the spokesman of them all, but his arrogance evaporated in the presence of this scourging anger, "What sign shewest thou us, seeing thou doest these things?" If these words were in any way a renewal of the wilderness temptation, "Cast thyself down", Jesus gave no indication of it. He corrected the subtle mistake of his questioner who was only entitled to ask Jesus to "give" a sign, not to "show" one, to establish his authority as a prophet.* "Destroy this temple, and in three days I will raise it up." This was no empty challenge, it was a prophecy. The men who were responsible for these crushing abuses were the men who were to be ultimately responsible for the calamities of AD 70 when the Temple, the city, and the land were lost amid indescribable horrors. Yet the Temple then had done its work, it had been replaced by an eternal sanc-

---

*Deuteronomy 13:1–2

tuary the chief cornerstone of which was the Son of God. In the act of condemning the Temple rulers Jesus takes the first step along the road which will lead to his crucifixion, but in that act his body will fulfil the function which was only typified by the Temple and its services. And his resurrection will be the final vindication of his authority.

The Jews did not forget those words of Jesus. Nor did they ever forgive him for them. They misquoted them in their effort to condemn him and thus established their truth. But there were others who remembered them to better purpose. When despair had given place to joy at the sight of their risen Lord, the disciples "remembered that he had said this unto them; and they believed the Scriptures and the word which Jesus had said".

We cannot leave this first great incident in the public ministry of Jesus without considering the anger of Christ. There are those who find this scene difficult to reconcile with the character and mission of a Son who came to reveal the love of his Father. That may be because there is a tendency to see in the indignation of Jesus a reflection of our own angry moments. Much of our anger is a revelation of weakness, not of strength. He was silent when most men would be stirred into uncontrollable fury; he was consumed with zealous indignation when most men's lips would be sealed by cowardice, and their minds drugged by worldly excuses. Jesus listened in silence to the jibes of his tormentors, he allowed his enemies to tear his flesh and pierce his head with thorns; but when his Father's glory was questioned, or his brethren's welfare endangered, men quailed before the majesty of his wrath. We see in the anger of Christ an ingredient of his perfect character which was a manifestation of the attributes of a God of goodness and severity.

The purging of the Temple was followed by works of power. Jesus gave abundant evidence of his authority to those who had eyes to see, and while the great majority of people living in and around the city were too greatly dominated by the priests to acknowledge him, a few precious friendships were probably formed in these early days. Many believed because they saw his works, but it was a superficial acknowledgment of his power, and that is never the best reason for following Christ. Jesus who knew all men, "did not trust himself unto them". He knew their allegiance had its source in wonder, not in belief; and he acted towards them accordingly.

2

NICODEMUS

A figure moved furtively among the shadows of the city buildings. He walked quickly yet carefully, obviously intent upon avoiding recognition. Halting at last, he knocked on the door of a house and after a few whispered words was admitted.

Nicodemus was probably the spokesman of a small number of thoughtful rulers who shared the expectation of the Messiah, had pondered over the message of John the Baptist, witnessed the power with which Jesus had purged the Temple, and seen the miracles he had done in the city. He was anxious to talk with Jesus but he was also anxious not to compromise himself. He had more to lose than the Galilean fishermen. Yet he was sincere, and if he had not the courage to come boldly to Jesus in the daytime, he had at least the courage to come, and was humble enough to address this unlettered Galilean carpenter as "Rabbi".

The opening words betray the courtesy of the council chamber. "Master, we know thou art a teacher come from God: for no man can do these miracles that thou doest except God be with him." So Nicodemus, although a ruler in Israel, had little more to commend him than the people of the city who were impressed by the works of power. Jesus immediately sweeps the courtesies aside and gets down to fundamentals. "Except a man be born again he cannot see the Kingdom of God." Nicodemus had come to discourse on theological issues with one he had reason to respect. He very quickly found that he had nothing to say. In spite of his cultured approach he betrays himself as a materialist, the conventional product of a centuries-old system which had lost touch with reality. Yet in his materialism Nicodemus was nearer the truth than he knew. The new birth which brings men into relationship with God, and eventually into his Kingdom, demands childlike qualities of simplicity and trust. Patiently, Jesus elaborates his first revelation. "Verily, verily, I say unto thee, except a man be born of water and of the spirit he cannot enter into the Kingdom of God. That which is born of flesh is flesh; and that which is born of the spirit is spirit." Despite his efforts man cannot rise above his mortality. Entrance into the Kingdom demands something which is impossible of accomplishment by human endeavour, nothing less than a re-birth from above. "Marvel not that I said unto thee, Ye must be born again. The wind bloweth where it listeth and thou hearest the sound thereof, but canst not tell whence it cometh or whither it goeth: so is every one that is born of the spirit." No man can understand the divine method of election by which the power of God through His word and through His Son touches individual hearts. Such knowledge is too wonderful for us. We can only respond and worship.

But Nicodemus was looking in the wrong direction. For him the law was an end rather than a means, and righteousness was legal rather than spiritual. Jesus was speaking a language he did not comprehend, and he remained dull of hearing, his perception clouded by his religious background. For all his sincerity he did not have the spirit-quickening experience of Andrew and John when they had said, "Master, where dwellest thou?", or the sudden revelation of Nathanael when he cried, "Thou art the Son of God!" Where a Mary and a Peter, looking into the eyes of their Master apprehend truths they would have found it difficult to express, the learned theologian was ignorant; "How can these things be?"

In effect Jesus said to him, "Are you one of Israel's teachers and yet have you failed to have communion with God? Does not even the experience of prayer bring you into God's presence? I am speaking of things that are an everyday experience to me: if you do not understand these common blessings how can you soar with me into the heavenlies?" But he did take Nicodemus to the threshold and reveal to him the mystery of God's salvation. He showed him how the Son of man—a title Jesus loved to use and one which embodies both the grace of God and the highest aspiration of man—is destined to be lifted up that men, believing on him, might be redeemed from their deathly heritage in Adam and have eternal life. Such is the love of God, and such His gift to men.

But there are those who will never believe: the Son will not judge them, they are condemned already. The world judges itself in rejecting him and clinging to the flesh, thus confirming its unworthiness of eternal life.

The ruler of the Jews went out into the night. What he had expected to be a conversation had become a discourse, and one ending on a note of tension which was a challenge to him. He was destined to witness the consummation of the gift of the Father who "so loved the world". His conduct then would be beyond reproach: the movement of the spirit gradually broke down the obstacles of his training and although we hear little of him afterwards we may be confident that the lifting up of the Son of man drew Nicodemus finally to him.

From Jerusalem, Jesus went out into Judea preaching, his disciples baptizing those who responded to his call. John was still active but the presence of Jesus resulted in a further diminishing of his support as more and more people obeyed him by resorting to Jesus. The Jews either deliberately or inadvertently stirred up trouble among John's more intimate disciples over the respective baptisms, but their greatest problem was the growing popularity of Jesus and the waning influence of their austere but beloved prophet. What was a strain to the immature faith of John's disciples was a source of deep joy to John. He explains that joy to them in words which reveal his greatness. He likens his position to that of the friend of the Bridegroom, who makes all arrangements for the marriage. But when the marriage is over the friend's work is done. It would be no mark of friendship to intrude further into the relationship which he has done so much to consummate. All that remains for him is to stand aside, rejoice in the union and be thankful that he has been allowed to do so much. "This", says the great-hearted prophet, "this my joy therefore is fulfilled. He must increase, but I must decrease."

The Jewish rulers had rejected their Messiah. His ministry had begun in the Temple, then we find him in the city, now he has left Jerusalem for the country districts outside. Finally he leaves Judea altogether and moves through Samaria to Galilee. The rejection is not described in words but it is only too eloquently portrayed in these successive movements of the Messiah from the true centre of his ministry. Until he at last set his face to go to Jerusalem because "his hour" was approaching, his visits to the city were brief and disturbing. He always asserted his Messiahship there, and his claims and the works of authority which supported them gave the Jews less and less excuse for not knowing the day of their visitation.

3

SYCHAR

ACCEPTING the hostile verdict of Jerusalem, Jesus turned northwards to Galilee. John tells us that "he must needs go through Samaria". The need was a spiritual rather than a geographical one. Small parties of Jewish travellers almost invariably took the alternative route up the Jordan valley, which avoided unfriendly contacts with the Samaritans. But a work was waiting for Jesus and the events recorded in the fourth chapter of John's Gospel are both important and full of meaning.

Toiling northward along the dusty road under the midday sun, Jesus with his little band of followers reached the ancient well on the outskirts of the town of Sychar. The disciples went on to get provisions while their Master sank wearily down to rest. There is something at once saddening and satisfying about this picture. Saddening because of the knowledge it brings that in all the things that Jesus was to suffer there was no alleviation of physical weakness. Satisfying because of the sense of fellowship it brings; the recognition that he knows the long and weary way, he has trodden the path along which he beckons us: his feet have been dusty and travel sore, he has sunk exhausted at the well.

But the demands made upon him by his dedication to his Father's will were obeyed and maintained in spite of physical distress and tiredness of mind. His eager spirit soared above the limitations which nature continued to impose upon him.

His restful contemplation was broken by the footfall of a Samaritan woman who came to draw water. There are good reasons why this interruption need not have disturbed his rest. In the first place she was a woman and as such she could be ignored. Then she was a Samaritan. A long and bitter feud existed between Jews and Samaritans. Finally Jesus, who knew men's hearts so perfectly, would recognize at once in this woman one whose mode of life excluded her from decent society. None of these considerations weighed for one moment with him. His tiredness and hunger were at once

forgotten as he looked upon this woman to whom his Father
had sent him. "Give me to drink." Startled and perplexed, the
woman repeated two of the reasons why such a question
should not have been made. But as he had dealt with
Nathanael and Nicodemus so now he dealt with this woman.
It was his custom to break through traditions which were
merely stupid and meaningless, especially when they had
their source in passion and hatred. "If thou knewest the gift
of God, and who it is that saith to thee, Give me to drink;
thou wouldst have asked of him, and he would have given
thee living water." Not unnaturally this unexpected reply
brought a perplexed enquiry from the woman. She looked
down at the spring water below her, then slowly back to the
man who stood watching her. "Sir, thou hast nothing to draw
with and the well is deep; from whence hast thou that living
water?" Still Jesus refrained from answering her question
and gently continued the conquest of her soul. He persisted
in the contrast between the water he has asked of her, and
the water he can give. This water will satisfy for a moment,
and the need for it will return, but the water which can be his
gift to her will satisfy for ever. Indeed, it will be an inward
spring which will continue to quench her thirst until it finally
wells up into everlasting life. The woman's reply seems to
show that she was still bewildered, but she was impressed.
She asked for Christ's gift but her reason was that she would
be saved the trouble of future visits to the well. Her response
was limited by her ignorance, but it was a response, and
there was no mockery in it. She was ready for the next lesson
from her divine teacher. That lesson came in one short
request which altered the whole situation. The gifts of God
are not for selfish enjoyment. They have to be shared.
Andrew has to find his brother. Philip has to find Nathanael,
and later the disciples will have to go into all the world. "Go,
call thy husband and come hither." The beam of light which
had rested upon Jesus was now turned full upon her. The
question probed her life, quickening her conscience.
Unknown to her it was a challenge to confess her sin, a challenge which was evaded. "I have no husband." But Jesus was
looking into her heart. He needed neither the confirmation
nor the betrayal of her lips. He who saw the potential
strength of Peter, who was with Nathanael under the fig tree,
now told the woman that in her quick defence she had spoken
the truth. She was not far removed from a woman of the
streets making a trade of love. The glare of the light was too

strong, hastily she tried to move its penetrating rays away from herself. Perceiving that the man speaking to her was a prophet, she sought refuge in an important but impersonal question. "Our fathers worshipped in this mountain; and ye say, that in Jerusalem is the place where men ought to worship." Gently Jesus led her back: back to herself with her disordered moral life, back to the living water which brings immortality, back to his Father the source of all life. He paused only to concede one important fact in direct answer to her question. "Salvation is of the Jews." Then he pointed beyond her question to a truth which when truly perceived made the question and the bitter consequences of its insistence, quite unnecessary. It also restored the personal issue to the conversation. And however distasteful this may be to our conscience it is the only possible ground from which it can be conducted. "The hour cometh, and now is, when the true worshippers shall worship the Father in spirit and in truth, for the Father seeketh such to worship him." The woman was troubled at his answer. She had been unable to evade him, she realized that her inmost secrets lay exposed before him, she felt his love for her, but she could not understand his words. Perhaps it was a sudden premonition; perhaps in her perplexity she turned to the hope that was not far from all her people, "I know that Messias cometh ... when he is come he will tell us all things".

And then, to this Samaritan woman who had had five husbands and was living with a man not her husband, Jesus for the first time proclaimed his Messiahship. "I that speak unto thee am he."

Leaving her waterpot, the woman hurried back to the city to tell her neighbours. There is no longer any need to tell her to fetch her husband, she is anxious for all the city to come to Christ.

This strange conversation is more than a passing incident in Christ's journey through Samaria. It discloses the nature of the intercourse which takes place between God and every true seeker after Him. Our relationship begins with a demand from our Father to do something for Him. Our natural feeling is that there is nothing that we can possibly do. He is the Creator and sustainer of all things, we are puny creatures of His handiwork utterly dependent and unworthy. Yet the demand persists, and with it comes the understanding that our service conceals a far greater gift from Him. As the nature of that gift is unfolded in His word, so our desire for it grows, and although we can never appreciate it in its fulness, we plead for it. But it has its own demands. It requires us to expose all those things that are unworthy and demands that we share the gift with those around us. We cannot effectively accomplish the second without deliberately facing anything in our life which will impede our communion with God. There may easily be a strong temptation to evade this issue with specious reasoning and hypothetical problems; but we are brought back to the true issue of our personal relationship with God, and taught that in true worship, lies the conquest of sinful flesh and the way of holiness. This is all brought to a focus in the person of Jesus Christ, and our surrender is complete when we truly believe his saying: "I that speak unto thee am he".

The disciples returning from the city with provisions had seen their Master talking earnestly with the woman. They wondered but said nothing. Quietly they prepared the meal for him. Jesus was no longer exhausted and hungry; he was hardly conscious of the movement of the men around him; he was looking over the fields of waving corn towards the town which the woman was even now approaching. Finally the disciples begged him to eat. In their anxious concern for him they drew him back to temporal needs. But these things had lost all significance for him; "I have meat to eat that ye know not of". The disciples had much to learn; their understanding was as dim as the woman's had been. They thought someone had offered him food while they were away. "My meat is to do the will of Him that sent me, and to finish His work." He has eaten of that meat. The will of God has been done. Jesus compelled his disciples to look across the fields of ripening corn at the harvest that was already waiting to be gathered in. They looked at the corn and thought the harvest was four months away, but the Sower watched the men of Sychar approaching and invited his disciples to share with him the joy of reaping.

After the cold reception at Jerusalem, truly this was a joyous harvest, a prophetic one too, symbolizing the movement of the Gentiles towards him when his own people had rejected him. The Samaritans begged Jesus to stay with them. Many believed on him because of the words of the woman. Before he left belief was confirmed by their own experience. "Now", they told the woman, "we believe not because of thy saying, for we have heard him ourselves and know that this is indeed the Christ, the Saviour of the world." It is a blessed day when the disciple of Jesus can echo those words.

4

GALILEE

LEAVING Sychar, Jesus went northward into Galilee with his little band. The desolate expanses of rock and shrub they had left behind in Judea were forgotten as they reached their own fragrant countryside and heard once more the pleasant accents of their countrymen. The disciples' thoughts began to turn towards their lakeside homes, the families waiting for them, the gleaming lake and the nets. Jesus had made no demands of them yet, and they did not know that soon this dear familiar background must fade almost completely from their lives. But he had been quietly preparing them and now the last stage of that preparation was at hand as he parted from them, probably for several months, leaving them alone with their families, their nets and their thoughts. They would have plenty of time during the coming months to make their decision. In their homes and at their work their thoughts would continually go back to the Jordan valley, to Jerusalem, to Samaria. They would hear their countrymen earnestly discussing this Nazareth carpenter who had caused such consternation in the Temple and had shown miraculous powers of healing in the city. Their minds would inevitably return to Jesus, and they would feel his compelling power in his very absence. There would be a feeling of futility in the daily tasks that in the past had always been so satisfying. They would long with an ever-growing yearning to see his face again, to hear his voice, to be with him. They would wonder what he was doing at that moment, whether he was near the lake, or away in the northern hills. They were slowly coming to realize that they could not live without him. When he came back to them, a word would be all that was necessary to call them to follow him whithersoever he would lead.

Meanwhile Jesus made his way back to his own country. He came to Nazareth, the town that had become strangely remote, its traders still noisily busy in the narrow streets, the neighbours working and talking, grumbling and suffering, as they had done for the past hundred years or more. From

Nazareth he turned north-east to Cana where he probably
stayed with Nathanael instructing him further in the deep
things of the Kingdom. A warm welcome would be waiting for
him at the house of the young married couple whose wedding
he had attended nearly twelve months before. The attitude of
the people was quite different now. News of his authority and
power had been brought back from Jerusalem by those from
the towns and villages of Galilee who had attended the feast.
They received him with reverence and watched him in expectation. Nor were they disappointed, because it was whilst he
was at Cana that he received a visit from a high official of
Herod's court who was in great personal distress. His son lay
at the point of death. Hearing that Jesus had returned from
Judea, he travelled the twenty-five miles which separated
Capernaum from Cana and finding Jesus, besought him to
return with him to heal his son. In view of the man's obvious
faith shown by his making the arduous journey, the reply of
Jesus must have sounded strange, "Except ye see signs and
wonders, ye will not believe". But Jesus was going to use the
occasion to bring greater blessings than the restoration of a
dying boy. He was about to show the nobleman that the
power of God vested in him did not need his actual presence
at the scene of its ministry. There was no necessity to see the
signs and wonders. Jesus may have been speaking to the
nobleman near the fig tree in the garden where Nathanael
had learned this lesson. The other apostles had yet to learn
it. The countless company of disciples that have followed
have had to understand that the power of Christ does not
depend upon his physical presence. Herod's officer had shown
a strong yet an imperfect faith in coming to Cana; Jesus
sought to perfect it. For the moment the man's distress
clouded his perception. "Sir", he cried, "come down ere my
child die." Then Jesus made his meaning clearer by relating
it to the man's personal trouble, "Go thy way, thy son liveth".
There could be no doubt now. And looking steadily at Jesus,
the man believed his word. Yet his faith was to be tried still
further. It was impossible to start back for Capernaum in the
growing dusk; he had to find an inn to spend a night filled
with visions of the fever-ridden child he had left flushed and
restless on his pallet in Capernaum, and the quiet, confident
rabbi here in Cana. At the first glimmer of dawn he would be
on the road again, his new found faith still keeping his fears
at bay. A company of men were coming towards him; sudden-

ly he recognized one, and then another; they were household servants. He was not kept in suspense much longer. First their movements and then their faces revealed the good news that brought them to meet their master. "Thy son liveth." So his faith was vindicated. One thing remained: but the nobleman had little doubt what the answer would be when he asked his servants the hour when the change took place. It was the hour at which Jesus had spoken. The divine purpose was accomplished, the man believed, and his whole house. With a word Jesus had saved more than the single life that was ebbing away in the quiet house at Capernaum. It is quite possible that the nobleman was Chuza, Herod's steward, and his wife Joanna, who showed her gratitude by joining the company of women who ministered unto Jesus of their substance.

During the weeks that followed Jesus remained in Galilee. From the absence of any record of his actions it would appear that he spent the time in retirement. John was still preaching in Judea preparing the people to receive their Messiah. The disciples, now returned to their daily tasks were, all unknown to them, being prepared for the moment when their Lord would demand their complete surrender. Jesus could accept the last opportunity which would be afforded him to rest in the quiet seclusion of the Galilean hills until the next feast at Jerusalem called him forth to unceasing labour.

We may perhaps pause for a few moments to look at this pleasant Galilean countryside where Jesus spent these quiet months—the scene of the greater part of his ministry.

It is difficult to imagine a greater contrast than that between Judea and Galilee. The former was for the most part bare and forbidding, mountainous without the grandeur which can so often be associated with mountains. Apart from cultivated terraces around its towns and villages, it was almost devoid of trees and vegetation, a land of hot, dry rock and scrub stretching from the mountains of Samaria in the north to the wilderness of Zin in the south, and from the coastal plain in the west to the Jordan valley in the east. Galilee was a beautiful country of hills and wide valleys, green fields and golden cornlands.

The reason for this startling difference in a country no larger than Wales was the great mountain range of Lebanon which dominated Galilee in the north. From the snow-covered peaks of Lebanon and Hermon there was a steady drop to the Sea of Galilee which lay seven hundred feet below sea level. The effect of this was that the water flowed constantly down from the mountains, making Galilee a land of rushing streams, springs and wells. Its valleys were green and fruitful and its plains rich and well watered. The hard-working people accepted these natural blessings; they cultivated the plains and planted vine and olive groves on the lower slopes of the valleys, they grew corn and kept oxen and sheep, they cut the timber from the wooded hills, and they took the fish from the lake. It was a land open to the sun and the air, a land in which it was not difficult for any man to climb a height and rejoice in the creative power of God and praise His Name.

The great contrast between Judea and Galilee extended to the people. The Galileans were the true products of their countryside, vigorous, warmhearted, not easily intimidated, headstrong to the point of rashness. It was in Galilee that the Romans had most of their disturbances. Many times the hot blood would surge, Roman soldiers would march, and Galilean patriots would pay the penalty of their impetuousness unflinchingly.

It is interesting to notice that although there was such a mixed population in Galilee the Galilean Jews kept largely to their own cities. Jesus did not often go to the cities of the Gentiles in Galilee. There is no evidence in the Gospels that he ever visited Tiberias although he was constantly in its vicinity; nor do we read that he went to Sepphoris which was only five miles from Nazareth and lay on the road to Cana. Tiberias and Sepphoris were the two most important towns in Galilee. But they were Gentile strongholds.

No reference to Galilee would be complete without mention of its roads. Every valley was a natural highway worn by the dusty feet of merchants, travellers and pilgrims. Some roads even struggled down from the Lebanon mountain passes trodden by those who preferred the perils of the land to the perils of the sea. Most famous of all these roads was the one which Isaiah called "the way of the sea", connecting Damascus with ports of the Mediterranean Sea. It carried not only the merchandise of Syria, but connected the countries of the east with Europe. Recognizing its importance the Romans paved it, and exacted a tax on its traffic. One of the taxing points was Capernaum, and one of the tax gatherers there was Matthew, waiting even now for the call of Jesus.

It was in this beautiful part of the Holy Land, among these busy warm-hearted people, that Jesus spent the longest and happiest part of his ministry. With the sad exception of the people of his own town, he largely won their affection and loyalty, and although serious attempts were made from Judea to loose the hold he had on the Galileans, attempts which closed the doors of the synagogues against him, they did not really succeed, and many of the people remained faithful to the end. Thoughtful readings of the Gospels will convince us that as the hostility of the Jews intensified at the end of Christ's mortal life, Galilean hands strewed palm trees along the road to Jerusalem, and Galilean voices cried "Hosanna to the Son of David: Blessed is he that cometh in the name of the Lord". Earlier they had unsuccessfully tried to take him by force and make him king; now, they felt their hopes were to be realized. And though by his subsequent actions Jesus frustrated them, they remained faithful throughout the last dark week. The people whom the Temple authorities feared when they attempted to arrest him on at least three of the days, were not the reserved, law-ridden Jews of the city, but the people who had come down from Galilee to the Passover. It was their presence which caused Caiaphas to take Jesus in the middle of the night, rush through the Jewish trial in the early hours of the morning, and get him condemned by Pilate before they realized what had happened.

We do not know how long Jesus enjoyed the quietness of the Galilean hills because we can only assume by vague indications which feast it was which Jesus attended in Jerusalem. It could not have been less than three months nor more than nine. But with the disciples now ready for the supreme surrender of apostleship, with the net closing relentlessly round John in the desert, Jesus turned southwards once more and began the active phase of his ministry from which there was to be no respite and no turning back.

5

THE POOL OF BETHESDA

IT is not difficult for us to imagine the mixed feelings with which Jesus would attend the successive feasts at the Temple. The desire to go to his Father's House would be tempered by sadness at the things he saw and the men who ministered there.

On his previous visit Jesus had risen in indignation against the greed and profanity in the Temple Courts. He had actively protested against the money changers, and the bartering merchants whose hoarse cries rang out over the city. The Temple glittered in the sunshine, its rabbis taught endless sophistries in its cloisters, its priests impersonally accepted the sacrifices, its Sadducees received one another with formal dignity. But God was not in their thoughts and His glory had departed from their midst.

In the shadow of the north wall of the Temple, behind the stalls of the merchants near the Sheep Gate, there was a scene which was strangely remote from the activity of the Temple—a scene which revealed human suffering at its saddest level. On the steps of a great five-arched portico overlooking the pool of Bethesda crowded a multitude of people in every stage of disease and impotence. Those who were not blind watched the water below them with pathetic intensity. The pool was the subject of a well-known but uncommon physical phenomenon which caused it to bubble up at intervals. It had received and maintained the reputation of being able to cure the first infirm body which made contact with it after its disturbance. It is not hard to see how the superstition had gained credence. The power of faith over the body, particularly in cases of nervous disorders, is too well known to need emphasis. There were enough apparent cures to draw sufferers to its edge in the hope that they might be the subjects of what they believed to be angelic ministration.

The two scenes within the city bore no relation to one another. High on the hill of Zion the immaculately robed priests observed the Temple ritual, aloof and impersonal. In the shadows of its walls the halt, the blind and the withered waited for the movement of the water. Jesus, attending the feast at Jerusalem, left the Temple and making his way through the thronged streets in the north east corner of the city, stood in the midst of the suffering, expectant multitude. The water had not yet stirred and the atmosphere was tense and silent as the impotent and their friends and relatives concentrated with a selfishness born out of the greatness of their pain and need for the first shimmer of movement. Jesus watched the pitiful sight until at last he found the saddest case of all: a man was lying on the steps with no one to assist him. For thirty-eight years he had endured his infirmity. Despair was written on his face. Jesus stood over the man, but his presence awakened no response. The man did not know him, had no faith in him, and made no demands of him. Suddenly he heard a voice addressing him: "Wilt thou be made whole?" He looked up at Jesus. Had his case not been so hopeless he would have resented an interruption that might have robbed him of his chance of healing. The despair in his eyes was emphasized in his voice; what faith he had still lingered in the black waters below him. "Sir, I have no man, when the water is troubled, to put me into the pool: but while I am coming another steppeth down before me." Had the man at last found a friend who would lead him down to the water's brim and find a place for him among those that crowded the lowest step? But Jesus directed his thoughts from such lowly expectation, his clear, strong command rang out, "Rise, take up thy bed and walk". Instinctively the man obeyed; he bent down, rolled up his pallet and stood up. He found a freedom of movement he had not known for nearly forty years. He turned to face the one he had obeyed, but Jesus had gone. We can imagine the consternation that ensued. All eyes were turned towards this chronic invalid, the unhappiest of them all, now moving amongst them with tears of joy rolling down his cheeks. The waters below bubbled and subsided unnoticed. There was a greater source of power and healing in Israel.

The healed man walked through the streets towards the Temple. Perhaps he was obeying the unrecorded instructions of Jesus, perhaps he was anxious to express his gratitude to God in worship and sacrifice. It was typical of the rulers that when they saw this familiar figure no longer dragging himself painfully along, but walking with quick, eager steps, they should overlook the transformation and remember only that it was the Sabbath day. In carrying his bed he was guilty of bearing a burden. Had they had greater insight they would have been quick to discern that his bed truly had been a burden for thirty-eight years, but it was not so on this glorious Sabbath. In answer to their angry questions the man could only say that he was obeying the instructions of One who had made him whole. He could give them no information concerning the identity of his benefactor. But the healed and the healer came face to face in the Temple, and there, appropriately, Jesus completed the cure he had begun on the steps of Bethesda. Characteristically the spiritual remedy followed the natural one: "Behold, thou art made whole: sin no more lest a worse thing come unto thee".

Thus the healed man learned that it was Jesus who had cured him. He could show his gratitude by doing his part towards the complete healing which Jesus desired. But the immediate result was that he could now proclaim to those who asked him who it was who had made him whole. The result of this revelation was an issue between the healer and the rulers of the Temple. It led to the first complete statement of Jesus concerning his Messiahship and his relationship with God, set forth with clearness and decision, and the first occasion upon which his death was sought by his enemies. The conflict was to be long and bitter; finally it was to be expedient that Christ should die for the people, but that hour was not yet.

It is in the verbal conflict which ensued that we see the true meaning of the miracle and understand why John, moved by the Spirit, selected it as one of the eight signs of his Gospel. The first issue was briefly dismissed. It was the subject of the sabbath, and in answer to that challenge Jesus said quite simply, "My Father worketh hitherto, and I work". As he so often did, Jesus in a brief sentence widened and deepened the whole conception of the problem, and exposed the futility of the endless arguments and meticulous pronouncements of the scribes. He showed them by implication that God rested on the Sabbath day for the blessing of mankind. He blessed it and sanctified it. To sanctify is to set apart for His service. Had not he thus truly kept the Sabbath? Had he not blessed this impotent man with physical and spiritual health?

But in justifying his action he had exposed himself to a much more serious charge. "Therefore the Jews sought the more to kill him, because he not only had broken the sabbath, but said also that God was his Father, making himself equal with God." In answering that charge Jesus both fully revealed himself and his mission and indicted his accusers. He also plainly showed the connection between his case against the religious leaders and his healing of the impotent man. We see why he left the Temple and went down among the suffering people. His words are not so much an angry denunciation as a sad recognition of a fact. He began at a point which immediately laid bare their fundamental mistake. You, he said in effect, have only seen a man carrying a bed on the Sabbath; you knew but ignored the fact that the man had been the subject of divine restoration. I have given that man his new life, but of myself I can do nothing; I have done it because I am the Son of God, and I have been sent to identify myself with my Father's will. This restored man is the earnest of far greater works because the whole purpose of God is concealed in my obedience. The time will come when they that are in the grave shall hear my voice and come forth. You sent a deputation into the wilderness to find out the burden of John's message. John bore witness of me. But I have a greater witness than John's. At this moment the evidence stands before you in my Father's work. In spite of all your efforts to study and teach the Scriptures you have not heard the voice of God. If you had you would receive me. You search the Scriptures because in them you know you have eternal life, but that is only true because they testify of me, and you do not come to me that you might have life. You put your trust in Moses, but Moses condemns you because he leads you to me, and you reject me.

The action of Jesus in turning from the Temple to Bethesda assumes a new significance in the light of his words. The true scene of his ministry was not among the subtle analysts of the law but in the midst of suffering humanity, which knew only the greatness of its need and sought salvation with a faith which had degenerated into superstition. Into the midst he came, seeking one for whom there was no eye to pity and no arm to save. Without a plea for help, he came in his grace to bring salvation. It was altogether right that the next meeting should be in his Father's house. It was right that the healed man should give the answer to those who asked him, that Christ had made him whole. It was inevitable that persecution should follow.

This visit to Jerusalem was a microcosm of the history of the coming of the Son of God into the world. It identified those who received him not, and was an earnest of the new relationship which was promised to those who welcomed him.

BOOK THREE: MANIFESTATION TO ISRAEL

Book Four

THE GALILEAN MINISTRY

1

REJECTION AT NAZARETH

THE desert was silent again. John the Baptist had been interrupted in the midst of his work and hurried away to the grim fortress of Machaerus on the eastern side of the Dead Sea. This sudden move was made by Herod Antipas. John had condemned the method by which Herod had taken his brother Philip's wife, and in doing so he had brought upon him the implacable hatred of this woman. She was responsible for Herod's order to arrest him, and even his incarceration in the darkness and filth of the dungeon did not satisfy her savage craving to injure him. While there is no evidence that the religious leaders in Jerusalem had anything to do with this silencing of a voice which had been very disturbing to them, there can be little doubt that they viewed the course of events with satisfaction. A dangerous enemy had been removed and the manner of his going freed them from any necessity to defend themselves. They could point out to the people the dangers of listening too carefully to itinerant preachers who denounced the nation's divinely given shepherds and set at nought traditions venerated for centuries by true Israelites.

Jesus heard of the arrest of John while he was in Jerusalem. He immediately left for Galilee. From this time forward he worked without intermission, preaching, healing and instructing his disciples. It was as though this was a signal for which Jesus was waiting, and with the silencing of John's voice the people of Israel were to hear the voice of the one whom John had proclaimed.

Arriving at last in Nazareth, Jesus was once more in the environment of his childhood, surrounded by scenes he knew so well, recognized by men and women with whom he had grown up. It was but a few months ago that with his leather apron wrapped round him he had been busy with hammer and saw, fashioning yokes and ploughs and furniture, listening to the troubles of the villagers, caring for his mother and his younger brothers and sisters. How much had happened in those short months! To all outward appearances Nazareth was still the same, but to him it was already remote. The need of humanity was upon him. The strong, earnest face of Peter, the exalted cry of Nathanael, the cool breeze on the roof top, the teeming thousands searching his face with new hope and longing, these things separated him now from the carpenter's bench. He was about his Father's business. The people looked upon him with new eyes too. The news of his exploits in Jerusalem and of his miracle at Capernaum were too well authenticated to be untrue or even exaggerated. But they could not forget the wood shavings on the floor of the shop, or the noise of the hammer. They looked at Jesus and remembered Mary and her family. And when he approached those in need of healing, neighbourliness prevailed, faith failed and suffering lingered on. Only a few sick folk forgot the carpenter and believed.

Nevertheless the Sabbath brought expectation and excitement. It was the custom for the ruler of the synagogue to invite visiting rabbis to speak, and the building would rapidly fill. Some of the worshippers had seen his divine indignation displayed in the great Temple itself. How would he act now? What would he say? They would be conscious of him the moment he took his place among them. It was an occasion of the greatest importance to the people of Nazareth. The future of each individual worshipper depended upon his attitude during the next hour. It is always a momentous occasion when Jesus speaks for the first time to a man's soul.

For our Lord, too, it was a situation of no little delicacy. For many years he had attended that synagogue. Because the Spirit had not then anointed him to speak, he had kept silent through innumerable services. He could have corrected many imperfect expositions, he could have unfolded many difficult passages, but he had held his peace.

Now he was anointed to preach the Gospel to the poor. He was to be silent no longer. There can be no doubt that he had prayed and meditated upon the work that waited for him on that Sabbath morning. As in all his ways he would seek the guidance of his Father and wait for Him to prepare the way before him. There had never been a Sabbath like this in

Nazareth. The service began, the prayers were uttered, the benedictions pronounced and answered, the law had been read by several members of the congregation. At last the time came for the reading of the prophets and the sermon. The officer approached the ark, the cabinet which contained the scrolls of the law and the prophets; he took out the roll for Isaiah which was the appointed reading for the day. He removed the linen cover which protected it, and handed the scroll to Jesus. Conscious only of the guidance of his Father, Jesus opened the scroll. He began to read. "The Spirit of the Lord is upon me, because he hath anointed me to preach the gospel to the poor; he hath sent me to heal the brokenhearted, to preach deliverance to the captives, and recovering of sight to the blind, to set at liberty them that are bruised, to preach the acceptable year of the Lord." Jesus turned the scroll and handed it back to the minister. He had been standing to read, now he sat down to teach. The air was tense with expectancy, the eyes of all in the synagogue watched every movement, waiting breathlessly for him to speak to them. It could almost seem that these words were prepared by God seven hundred years before just for this moment. To his own neighbours who had watched him grow into manhood in their midst, there was no claim of divine origin, of conquest or of kinship. The context of the words he had read is an extensive one, stretching back from the forty-ninth chapter to the end of the book. It reveals the whole work of the Messiah through the days of his suffering, rejection and death, disclosing the blindness of Israel, and the significance of the sacrifice of their Messiah. The vision widens until the calling of the Gentiles is revealed, and it does not fade until Israel is restored and all mankind rests in the glory of God, ruled by a returned Messiah when Jerusalem is a rejoicing and her people a joy.

The people of Nazareth were loath to associate their carpenter with these great prophecies. But the words Jesus read to them would identify him to those who were willing to be taught. Few among them had not heard of the baptism of Jesus by John the Baptist at the fords of Jordan, and the subsequent declaration of the prophet. Few of them had not heard of his healing touch and his words of authority in Jerusalem, and even in Galilee. To sincere, thoughtful minds these things were a direct fulfilment of the words Jesus had read. "This day is this Scripture fulfilled in your ears." So Jesus began. We have no record of the way in which he devel-

81

oped his discourse. We only read of its effect upon those who listened. "And they all bare witness, and wondered at the gracious words which proceeded out of his mouth." The day of vengeance had to come, it was a day to be pondered over indeed, with a certain fearful looking for of judgment; but that was not yet, and it had no place in his immediate message. It is interesting to notice that this is the first occasion when Jesus was careful to distinguish between his first and his second coming. The discourse drew to a close. We can well imagine the spellbound silence that prevailed for a few moments until one by one his audience began to forget the words and concentrate upon the speaker. The speaker became once more the carpenter, his mother and his brethren came to life, the past thirty years began to unfold, and Jesus, knowing their hearts, realized he had failed to convince them. Already there were those who were jealous of his work of healing at Capernaum, and had noticed he had not been able to do very much among them. He anticipated their mood, and reminded them of episodes in their history. When prophets of God were in their midst, the Israelites had been passed by and aliens had been the subjects of divine ministrations. This was too much for the people of Nazareth. Forgetting the synagogue and the Sabbath, the people who a few moments before had wondered at the gracious words Jesus spoke, hounded him through the narrow streets of the town, pressed him towards the brow of the hill intent only upon hurling him to his death. When their purpose was unmistakable Jesus turned and faced them. They fell away before the awful majesty of his aspect ... He walked through their midst and made his lonely way over the mountains towards Capernaum. Nazareth, like Jerusalem, had not known the day of her visitation, and she was to suffer the condemnation of Christ's neglect. He had come to his own and his own had not received him. No longer was Nazareth to be called his city, that honour was reserved for the home town of his disciples James and John, Peter and Andrew, the town whose synagogue was the gift of a benevolent Roman, presided over by the believing Jairus, the town where even now the nobleman's family was rejoicing over the restoration of its son, and showing an active belief in Jesus. True, Capernaum was not worthy of him, and was yet to be the subject of his condemnation. But no city or place will be worthy of the coming of the Son of Man until the day when he comes to fill the earth with God's glory and bring in everlasting righteousness and peace.

2

THE CALL OF THE FOUR

THE first clear picture the Gospels give us of Jesus beside the lake of Galilee is an earnest of what he was to experience during the months ahead. Luke tells us that as he approached the lake the people pressed upon him to hear the Word of God. Although they would have heard of the healing of the nobleman's son, it was not the prospect of seeing any display of power which brought them to him; that was to follow; rather their national hopes were stirred by the things that they had heard concerning this rabbi who had sprung up in their midst and who had created such a storm in Jerusalem. They were anxious to hear him speak and confirm from the prophets the hope which they hardly dare entertain.

Among the many fishermen whose boats lay heeled over on the beach were four who had been waiting with eager hearts for this moment. Three of them, Peter, Andrew and John, we have met before. They had shared exciting experiences in Jerusalem, Judea and Samaria with him, they had seen his works of power and enjoyed the wonderful privilege of listening to him as he spoke of his Father's Kingdom. James was John's brother. They shared in the fishing undertaking which prospered under the management of their father Zebedee. There can be little doubt that in the long silent hours of the night, as their boat dipped in the inky waters, John had told his brother about Jesus. His glowing tribute and utter conviction had convinced James and, without the personal preparation which the other three had enjoyed, he was ready for discipleship.

Peter and Andrew were casting their net when they became aware of an increasing commotion. Looking up from their work they saw a vast concourse of people pressing round one who had already become dear to them. Jesus was back in their midst ! It was a breathless moment for them. As they watched they saw that he was making no attempt to satisfy the people's clamour, he was moving purposefully towards them. In a few minutes he stood facing them, and

83

they were looking into his eyes. This was the moment for which they had longed and prayed. It was the moment for which his absence had prepared them. They had found during the past months that his nearness was essential for their happiness; there had been little satisfaction in their daily toil, they had been living on their memories and their hopes. Now those hopes were realized. He was standing here before them reviving by his presence and his familiar features all the resolutions that their highest aspirations had conceived. But there was no time to lose in greetings. The crowd pressed hotly upon them, and they were in danger of being pushed into the water. Jesus had a purpose in seeking them out. "Follow me, and I will make you fishers of men." Without the slightest hesitation Peter and Andrew dropped their nets on the sand, and went with him.

A little further along the shore James and John were busy with their father Zebedee and some of the servants washing and mending their nets. The two brothers lifted their eyes to find Jesus regarding them intently. Again the senses of the Galilean fishermen thrilled as they heard words which were at once an invitation and a command. "Follow me." They responded immediately, leaving their father and their work to begin a life of no less hardship and more uncertainty: but because it would be a life in which they would remain in the company of Jesus, share his work and his thoughts, they were content.

Looking at these four sturdy, sincere men, each different yet having in common the desire to follow him without counting the cost, Jesus was under no illusion about the difficulty of the task he had set himself. But because he had implicit faith in his Father's guidance, and recognized in these men his Father's gift to him, he was able to say confidently, "I will make you ..." Many weary months of misunderstanding and doubt lay between them and their complete transformation, but by love and understanding, sympathy and rebuke, their education was to be developed until the day when they were to continue his work in the earth, worthily reflecting the glory which shone forth from him. Even now their calling was not complete. It was for three of them the third stage in their spiritual relationship with their Lord. Now they were called to discipleship; soon their vocation would be apostleship.

Having fulfilled the purpose which had brought him to the lakeside Jesus turned to the people who sought him, and were eager to hear him. He chose Peter's boat and having besought him to launch it and anchor a little from the shore,

"… Solomon in all his glory was not arrayed like one of these." (Matthew 6:29)

"… Jesus went on the sabbath day through the corn …" (Matthew 12:1)

"… when they had sung an hymn, they went out into the mount of Olives." (Mark 14:26)

"… Jesus departed from thence, and came nigh unto the sea of Galilee; and went up into a mountain, and sat down there." (Matthew 15:29)

"And they straightway left their nets, and followed him." (Matthew 4:20)

he sat down and taught the multitude. His discourse over, Jesus turned his attention once more to the men who had so eagerly obeyed his call. He was anxious to show them in a way which they would never forget, that he had asked them to revoke their lower calling for a higher one. They were to be fishermen still, but their work was no longer to be limited to the waters of the lake, and the darting silver forms which struggled in their nets. The whole world was to be their fishing ground, and the seething crowds now reluctantly dispersing on the shore were to be enclosed in their net. So the first great lesson of their discipleship began, "Launch out into the deep and let down your nets for a draught". Peter demurred. There was little any fisherman could teach him about these waters. He knew where the fish could be found, he knew the best season and time for a catch, he recognized its presence by the ripples and shadows on the water. His experience told him that there was no hope of a catch that morning. If any fish were to be caught the only possible chance was during the night, and their boats had just returned empty from their night's fishing.

Peter was willing to acknowledge the leadership of his new master in spiritual paths, but surely Jesus had nothing to teach him in his daily tasks. Ah, Peter, how wrong you are! How wrong is every disciple who fails to acknowledge Jesus as his master in every walk of life and every place of experience. Unless our surrender is complete we shall toil all the night and catch nothing. Happily Peter's doubts were redeemed by his obedience. "Nevertheless at thy word, I will let down the net."

In the presence of Jesus and under his direction the nets were lowered once more. It was immediately evident that a profound change had taken place which confounded all Peter's natural skill and experience. The sea was boiling with fish, and as the nets were drawn in they broke under the weight and strain. This was a lesson which Jesus intended for each of these men, and unconsciously Peter in his excitement brought the others into its influence; he called to James and John in the other ship to come and help them. Soon both ships were so laden with fish that they were in danger of sinking. Peter worked feverishly, his mind completely bewildered by the experience. He had seen Jesus perform miracles before, miracles that many would believe were far greater than this, but he had seen nothing that touched him so closely. He needed nothing more to convince him that he was in the presence of the Messiah. His first feelings were utter unworthiness and an overwhelming sense of sin. And, because it was Peter, he expressed himself in hasty words. He fell down at Jesus' knees crying, "Depart from me for I am a sinful man, O Lord". But Jesus was not critical of his words, he rejoiced to see how well he had learned this first great lesson of discipleship, and how truly he had been affected by a penitence of spirit which groaned in the depths of its unworthiness. "Fear not; from henceforth thou shalt catch men."

How imperfect an expression of his heart Peter's words were was shown as soon as the boats reached the shore. Luke tells us that as soon as they brought their ships to land, they forsook all and followed him.

3

A SABBATH IN CAPERNAUM

THE sabbath which followed the calling of the four from their lakeside tasks was a memorable one. It began in the synagogue at Capernaum, where Jesus was invited to speak to the people. The effect upon these eager, warm-hearted Galileans, removed from the disconcerting evidence of his lowly origin and human contacts, was profound. Even in Nazareth the worshippers had forgotten their prejudice when he spoke to them, they were lost in wonder as they listened to the gracious words which he spoke. So it was in Capernaum, so it was to be throughout Galilee and Judea. To listen to Jesus must have been an experience which could never be forgotten. He spoke with an authority which contrasted unmistakably with that of the scribes. There was a power in his utterance which was denied the most learned scribe, there was a conviction that made all the teaching which they had heard before pale and lifeless. There was more even than this; the strong, radiant character of Jesus shone forth in his teaching. As with his works, so with his words. Jesus gave himself; and those that heard and saw felt something that was utterly beautiful and holy. He spoke to them of the love of God, and the glory of His Kingdom, and told them of the demands it made of all those who responded to His call. As his hearers listened they must have been elevated far above the constricted limits of their narrow lives, they must have had visions of a beauty and a purpose they had never dreamed of; they must have seen something of the men and women it was possible for them to become. And the vision was given reality as they looked up at the face of one whose life was uncompromisingly dedicated to God. The evangelist conveys all this in his simple words, "He spake in their synagogue, being glorified of all".

The service was suddenly interrupted by the cry of a demented man. The words of grace had been too much for his tortured spirit. His voice rang through the building, "Let us alone, what have we to do with thee, thou Jesus of Nazareth?

Art thou come to destroy us? I know thee who thou art, the Holy One of God". A deathly silence followed, broken only by the fitful sobs of the exhausted man. Jesus alone remained calm, completely master of the situation. Then, with a deeper note of authority his voice was heard, "Hold thy peace and come out of him". The command penetrated into the confused brain. It produced a terrible conflict, the effects of which the horrified watchers beheld in the writhing, sweating form at their feet. Then with a final heartrending cry it was over. The man lay still, the wildness in his eyes was gone, the demoniac strength had evaporated. The power of Christ prevailed. If the teaching of Jesus had amazed the people, this supreme mastery over evil spirits awoke in them something that was entirely new. In common with both Greeks and Romans, the Jews accepted the existence of malignant spirits with an almost fatalistic tolerance. They believed that all disease was the result of indwelling demons, and in the case of mental disorders, epileptic fits and other similar derangements, one can sympathize with the bewilderment which occasioned such a belief. A person so afflicted was accepted philosophically, and few entertained a hope of cure, in spite of the spectacular efforts of the exorcists. Jesus had just stirred the people to their depths with words which both amazed and charmed them; that he should follow this by bringing sanity and peace to this madman brought forth indescribable emotions. Mark records, "And immediately his fame spread abroad throughout all the region round about Galilee".

Jesus left the synagogue with his four disciples and went down to Bethsaida to the house where Peter lived. Peter was a married man and his wife and mother-in-law, with his brother Andrew, shared the house by the lake.* It was a house which was often to be the abiding place of Jesus in his frequent visits to Capernaum, and we can well imagine with what joy Peter would welcome his illustrious guest. But on this occasion there was no welcome. No meal was prepared for the little company on their return from the synagogue. Peter's wife would not be able to conceal the anxiety which gripped her heart. Her mother had suddenly been stricken down with a burning fever, and lay desperately ill. But Jesus was in their midst, and they lost no time in telling him of the

---

*We are assuming that Bethsaida was the lakeside suburb of Capernaum. Much has been written on this and it has aroused a controversy which cannot be finally settled.

misfortune that had so quickly darkened their home. In a moment the whole scene was transformed. A few minutes before their master had been looking down at the red fever-ridden features, now the bed lay empty and the stricken woman was busily preparing a meal for them. What a happy repast it would be, with their loved one restored!

While the little company were rejoicing in their waterside home, things were happening throughout the town of Capernaum and in all the surrounding region. The news of the healing of the demoniac in the synagogue had spread rapidly from house to house. In many dwellings in Capernaum there was suffering and sorrow, as there is in every age and town. In those houses the door of hope, locked and barred perhaps for years, slowly opened, as the certainty of the miracle was established by the irrefutable evidence of many eager lips, and the information went round that Jesus was still in their midst, abiding in the house of Peter at Bethsaida. So as the evening shadows brought the sabbath to its close the pilgrimage began. Little companies emerged from humble homes all over the town, carrying or leading their pathetic burdens. As they converged upon the fisher-man's house the cries of pain mingled with the shouts of mad-men and the appeals of their guardians. The sick were laid on the ground until it was impossible to get near to the house. In the graphic language of Mark, "All the city was gathered together at the door". At last hundreds of straining eyes discerned Jesus. He was in their midst with words of comfort and power. Before him lay sick bodies and tortured minds, behind him was restoration, peace and new hope. The pilgrim-age to the lakeside had been painful and slow, the return was joyful and eager, broken bodies revelling in their newly found freedom, distraught minds delighting in their clear impression and rational thoughts. The superb picture Mark has painted by his phrase, "At even when the sun did set", presents a canvas which extends far beyond Capernaum and becomes almost symbolic. We are able to see God's anointed upon the earth, standing in the midst of suffering humanity, purging the effects of sin, bringing restoration and gladness.

The work done, the last footsteps faded away in the dark-ened streets. It had been a long, strenuous day for Jesus and his tired body cried out for rest. But it was more than rest that he needed. We cannot read the records carefully without realizing to some limited extent that Jesus did not take away suffering without great cost to himself. The very sight of the vast numbers of sick would be a poignant experience to his sensitive spirit. The act of healing was a responsive act of giving. To give to so many without intermission would be exhausting not only to the flesh but to the spirit. The body was satisfied with a few short hours of repose, but the spirit was not. Rising up a great while before day he sought the spiritual refreshment that could only be found in the presence of his Father. Long before even the early-rising fishermen had stirred, he left the house, and making his way through the deserted streets, found a solitary place among the hills behind the town, and there prayed. Some hours later the awakening household would notice the empty couch. Outside there was evidence that the activity of the night before was going to be repeated. In the first light of day people began to collect round Simon's house and wait for the appearance of the great healer. The disciples, led by Peter, began to look for him. And then, perhaps coming suddenly from behind a rock, or breasting a steep path, they saw something they would carry with them to their graves. They stood on holy ground. It would always be a precious and disquieting memory. They saw the Son of God at prayer. It is a scene too sacred to dwell upon. Each devoted heart will contemplate it, and draw its own inspiring thoughts. To Peter and his companions it must have been a revelation of the inner source of their Master's life; and as they watched his gracious ministry in the days that followed, they must have thought again of the prostrate form in the early morning light, and realized that his acts of love and power had their source in deep and sacred fellowship with his Father. They must have realized, too, that if this communion was so vital to him, it must be even more necessary for those who lacked his divine heritage and spiritual vision. This surely was the seed which developed in their minds until the opportunity came during one of the sweet moments of heavenly intercourse, and they made their request, "Lord, teach us to pray".

4

THE FIRST LEPER

STANDING on ground consecrated by the communion of Jesus with his Father, the disciples pointed back towards Capernaum where the crowds were once more gathering. Already some of the people had heard that he was missing, and had followed Peter and the others into the hills. "Lord", said Peter, "all men seek for thee." But Jesus did not return. He led his disciples away from the town towards the surrounding villages. "Let us go into the next towns, that I may preach there also; for therefore came I forth."

This apparently sudden decision to leave Capernaum may have been one of the results of his prayer. It may have been that when Jesus stood at the door of Simon's house the previous evening, and saw the multitudes of sick awaiting his gracious touch, he realized that a crisis had arisen. The all important mission of Israel's Messiah was not to be a wonder worker. His power, manifested at this moment in healing, was subservient to his greater work of revealing the truths of his Father's Kingdom, and rendering to Him the complete obedience which would make that Kingdom a reality. The miraculous works which accompanied his preaching were to be a witness to all men that God had sent him. That they were so largely concentrated upon the alleviation of human suffering is both a revelation of God's love in Jesus, and an earnest of the day when Christ's work shall be fully accomplished, when, as described by John in memorable words, "There shall be no more death, neither sorrow, nor crying, neither shall there be any more pain: for the former things are passed away". If the present emphasis continued the mission of Christ would fail. Men's temporal needs would be abundantly met, but their realization of a far greater salvation would be lost.

In this crisis concerning his work Jesus sought the solitudes, and it may well be that the decision to go further afield was conveyed to him by his Father. It was a development which could only have a beneficial effect upon the people of Capernaum, allowing time for their excitement to evaporate and giving them the opportunity of considering his works in the light of his words to them in the synagogue.

Thus began the first of a number of circuits from Capernaum into the populous regions of Galilee. It was the commencement of an almost unbelievable period of popularity. Jesus had captured the imagination of the people, his name and power were spoken of in every household, men flocked from all parts of Palestine and beyond to hear him. The multitudes grew to such proportions that it became a physical impossibility for him to address them in the narrow winding streets of the towns; he was forced to lead them out on to the hillsides and into the deserts. As he approached he drew the people from their villages for miles around, and they converged upon him from all directions, leaving only the oldest inhabitants to guard their possessions. Caravans travelling along the roads of Galilee during those months must have been subjected to many delays, Roman officials and men of affairs must have made many irate enquiries concerning the slowness of the progress and the reason for the great concourse of people. But in their haste to reach him there would be few detailed explanations. The impatient travellers would have time to reflect upon the name which was on everyone's lips, "Jesus of Nazareth! Jesus of Nazareth!" There were many sick people jostled in the milling crowds; they came borne on improvised beds, on asses, often on primitive carts. Parents carried their blind and infirm children. Class distinctions were temporarily suspended as rich and poor, freeman and slave, Pharisee and tax-collector mingled together and surged towards the place where Jesus had chosen to preach and to heal. Even an occasional leper could be seen hesitating a few yards beyond the outmost fringe of the crowd, the lower part of his face covered, but his eyes revealing his heart-rending desire to be seen by the healer, and cleansed.

We read so often the Gospel accounts of the healing of the sick that we may possibly forget to pause and meditate upon this great beneficent work of Jesus. Can we see this mother with her blind little daughter in her arms struggling to get near to Jesus, crying hysterically because her efforts are frustrated by the burly, selfish men who impede her? Can we see her finally reach him, breathless and crushed but full of triumphant faith? She eagerly lifts her arms to let him take her burden from her, she watches his sensitive fingers caress the sightless eyes, she sees his own eyes close in prayer, and when they open it is to smile a welcome into the bright little eyes that look for the first time upon the world that until this moment has only been heard and touched. The mother cannot speak, she can hardly see him through the mist of tears, but he understands, he smiles and blesses her before he turns away to heal once more. Day after day these simple, moving episodes were repeated in hundreds of families. Men and women came to him pale and emaciated, they went away glowing with health; pitiable maniacs were brought to him struggling and shouting, they left his presence with inward peace. There were some hideously revolting sights, but he quietly ministered and restored, never impatient, never too tired.

And throughout this gracious ministry Jesus preached the things of the Kingdom. The miracles he wrought had a direct bearing on his teaching. He had come to proclaim salvation, to invite men to turn to God and receive the adoption of sons. He prepared men's minds for the time when under his hand, the whole earth would be filled with the glory of his Father. In a very real sense the Kingdom of God was at hand. He was the King; his obedience unto death was to set the seal to God's purpose. The precepts which he taught were the principles upon which the Kingdom would be governed. Each miracle he wrought over disease and death was a symbol of the final abolition of sin and the final victory over death. Each mastery over the powers of nature was an earnest of the day when all the ends of the earth will remember and turn to the Lord, and he shall be governor among the nations. This thought is wonderfully expressed in the one hundred and third Psalm, where the words of the Psalmist can apply equally to the coming of the man of sorrows, and the coming of the Lion of the Tribe of Judah as king of the whole earth. "Bless the Lord, O my soul", cries the inspired Psalmist, "and forget not all his benefits: who forgiveth all thine iniquities, who healeth all thy diseases, who redeemeth thy life from destruction: who crowneth thee with loving kindness and tender mercies". Those who respond to the teaching of Jesus become children of the Kingdom. In obeying his commandments they practise the principles of his Kingdom. They can only look for persecution and sacrifice in their mortal life, because like their Lord, their Kingdom is not of this age. They live and die in the confidence that the day of the Lord is coming, and with it the full realization of all their hopes.

In his teaching Jesus therefore concentrated upon the spiritual qualifications which were necessary in all those who desired to be children of his Kingdom. His teaching as well as his miracles set all Galilee in motion. We have only a glimpse of the things he said, but it is sufficient to make us understand why men and women flocked to hear him. His words were simple so that a child could understand them, yet they searched the inmost recesses of men's hearts. He illustrated his teaching by vivid pictures of the familiar scene around him. The sky, the birds of the air, the animals of the field, the sower and the ploughman, the vineyards and the husbandman, all made their unique contribution to his message of life. Nor was the intimate domestic scene forgotten, drawn from his own experience and his observation of how men lived. The oven and the candlestick, the leaven and the salt, the clothes and the family dishes, were woven into the rich and colourful pattern of his teaching. He revealed too an intimate knowledge of the religious, political and social background, and many were the scenes given a new meaning to shed light on some spiritual truth. Listening to him as he sat in their midst, his hearers had their eyes opened, and for the first time they would see beyond the limits of their daily life to the far horizons of God's everlasting love and purpose. No longer would Jehovah be to them as remote as He is omnipotent. His Son revealed Him as a Father, intimately concerned in the welfare of His children, knowing their needs before they ask, yet desiring them to lift their faces to Him, as a parent finds joy in the upturned face of a child. He spoke to them of the great things that His Father had determined to do in the earth; of the day when all creation would unite in a paean of praise and worship: when the discord, the suffering and the hardships of the present would melt away, peace and joy would reign, and death itself would be swallowed up in life. He showed them how they could prepare themselves for that day by humility, self-discipline, and, above all, a responsive love that found expression in their attitude to one another. He had complete understanding of the difficulties of the task he had set them, but he assured them that they were not fighting a lone battle; with his help they would win through to victory. Looking into his earnest face, and feeling the authority of his words, his hearers began to see the kind of men and women they could become. When we think of the inspiring effect of Christ's words on us, the resolutions they draw from us, the insight they give us into the resources that are at our command, reaching us as they do through the comparatively cold medium of the printed word, we can form some conception of the profoundly moving influence they would have upon those who heard them from the lips of the living Lord.

It was on this tour of Galilee from Capernaum that we have the first record of a leper coming to Jesus. The fact of his approach is an arresting commentary upon the gracious ministry of Jesus. Lepers were particularly anxious to avoid rabbis or any that had the power to enforce the rigorous code of prohibitions which kept them separated from society. A leper was an outcast, spending his living death in the ruins and caves of the desert and the countryside. His hair was dishevelled, his clothes rent, and the lower half of his face covered. Although he was not allowed within the walls of a city, special provision was made for him to worship in the smaller synagogues, but it was in a place apart, and he had to arrive before the first worshipper, and was not allowed to leave until the last had gone. No one was permitted to acknowledge a leper, or stand within six feet of him. No other disease could have more effectively symbolized sin, and those who had the terrible misfortune to be its victims were treated more like criminals than incurable patients. Many of the severe restrictions were necessary for the protection of the people, but in practice they went far beyond the wisdom of expediency. Unhappily the religious leaders were sometimes guilty of the most savage mental and physical cruelty. One case is recorded of a rabbi who refused to eat an egg which had been purchased in a street where a leper had been seen: another of a rabbi who boasted that he had protected his fellow men by keeping a leper away from them by hurling stones at the unfortunate outcast.

It seems very probable from the confidence of this leper's approach that he had been watching Jesus for some time. Lingering far back behind the multitude the stricken man had been unable to hear the words of Jesus, but he was able to catch the importance of them by the wrapt attention with which the people listened. He had seen the sick being carried and led towards the centre of the crowd, but no sick returned, only empty couches and rejoicing people. Slowly a great hope was born in the wretched man's heart. Was it possible that he could approach this great healer? If only he could get through this endless, surging crowd he knew he would be cured. This man who gave the blind their sight, cured the maniacs, lifted the paralyzed from their beds and sent them walking away with praise on their lips—this man could restore his rotting flesh and deliver him from his living death. As the hours passed his faith strengthened into action. The people nearest to him were horrified to hear his dreaded cry, "Unclean! Unclean!" No longer the monotonous cry of despair but an urgent triumphant shout. They shrank away quickly, widening an avenue that led towards Jesus. At last he stood before him startled at his own temerity, the ravages of his affliction horribly evident. They were almost alone, the crowds had backed away. Looking into the eyes of Jesus he found his confidence once more: he fell forward on his face, his cry of faith rang out, "Lord, if thou wilt, thou canst make me clean". He waited a breathless eternity. Suddenly he felt firm, gentle hands close on his scaly flesh, the first human touch he had known for years, and then he heard the voice of Jesus. The leper's "if" had moved the Lord. His response was, "I will". And then with a word of authority, the evil flesh melted under his touch, the scarred and wasted body glowed with health.

Would that the deeper leprosy of the soul could be so easily dismissed! But that is a slower work, a work in which Christ can only minister with the steady co-operation of the sufferer. Faith has to be joined by a dedication of the heart and the will. But the victory can be won if the desire for spiritual health is as great as was the leper's longing for physical perfection. For the Lord's "I will" to the cry "thou canst" has lost none of its effectiveness.

The injunction of Jesus that the restored man should say nothing to any man concerning his restoration may sound strange in view of the multitudes that watched the miracle. But it can be understood in the light of two considerations. Matthew records a similar reticence of Jesus, and refers it to the fulfilment of the prophecy of Isaiah concerning him, "He shall not strive, nor cry; neither shall any man hear his voice in the streets". Men would flock to him in their thousands, but he would make no declaration of his power to increase his popularity. The clue to the second consideration is afforded by Mark when he recorded the healing of the blind man at Bethsaida. On that occasion Jesus sent the restored man to his house, with the command, "Neither go into the town, nor tell it to any in the town". A man who had been the subject of a spectacular healing could so easily go into the towns boasting of his cure, and become the centre of interest and speculation. Nothing could be worse for his spiritual welfare. If a cured man could be persuaded to tell no man, but go quietly home, meditate upon his restoration, and praise and worship his Heavenly Father, that man would be on the highway to a fuller restoration.

Jesus sent this man to the priest telling him to make the offerings of birds and lambs which Moses had commanded. The veil of the Temple had not yet been rent, and with his characteristic reverence for God's requirements, and the deep humility that marked all his actions, he acknowledged the office of those who even now were conspiring against him. Had the priest who received the restored leper had eyes to see, he would have seen an ambassador from the Messiah of Israel who had come with unmistakable credentials. But so far as we know, like so many of his kind he was conscious only of his exalted office, and the opportunity passed him by.

5

FORGIVENESS OF SINS

THE return of Jesus to Capernaum from the surrounding country excited the attention which would be expected after the momentous events of the last Sabbath he spent in the town. To the many accounts which were circulated from house to house and discussed at the corners of the streets was added the amazing story of the healing of the leper. It was not long before Peter's house at Bethsaida was once more the centre of attraction. Those who had waited in vain when Jesus had failed to return to the city after the early morning spent in prayer, were joined by many others who had come to hear and see this new rabbi who had set Galilee aflame.

There were scribes and Pharisees too, who were anxious to observe him more carefully. During that first sabbath at Capernaum they had been swept along in the general enthusiasm. By now they had had time to think, and to consider his teaching. Moreover it was necessary, they reminded themselves, in view of their responsible status, to assess their own position. Away from the compelling power of his presence, their ardour cooled. They recognized in his teaching a studied disregard for legal righteousness. This was confirmed by reports that multiplied from Judea. They realized that if they were generous in their support of this rabbi, they would incur the displeasure of the Temple authorities to whom they owed their religious vocation.

When Jesus therefore addressed the multitudes that filled Peter's house, and overflowed into the street outside, there was a sudden stir in the crowd, and a path was reverently opened up towards the house, as a number of scribes and Pharisees made their dignified passage to the forefront. What their attitude would have been had the discourse proceeded on its normal course we shall never know, because a sudden interruption changed the whole scene. Four friends of a poor man suffering from the dreaded disease of palsy were convinced that if they could get the sick man to Jesus he would be cured. When they approached the house they saw at

98

once how difficult their task was going to be: it was impossible even to reach the door. They might have waited for the discourse to finish and for Jesus to come out of the house, but great need does not brook delay, and great faith overcomes every difficulty. Most houses in Palestine had flat roofs which were approached from the outside by stone steps. There was no difficulty in carrying the sick man up. As the roof was usually made of rubble or hard earth and paved with bricks, it is unlikely that the men made any attempt to break it, which would have been a dangerous and senseless action. It is most likely that Jesus was speaking from the portico of the house which was covered by a lightly constructed canopy. This they removed and when the hole was large enough they gently lowered the sick man until he lay at the feet of the Lord. The interruption was dramatic. All eyes were turned upwards as the hole appeared and was gradually enlarged. The mat and its burden appeared and slowly descended, until it rested on the ground. Then the palsied man's wandering eyes found the object of their quest. They looked into the eyes of Jesus. Beholding him the man became oblivious of the hot crowded place, of his friends peering down intently from above, even of the illness that had emaciated his once strong frame. He was conscious only of Jesus, and of his own sinfulness. Probably his sickness was the direct result of a sinful life. His friends had brought him in faith but he had come in penitence, and looking now into the strength and holiness of the eyes that held his, his sense of despairing unworthiness, and with it, his fears, increased a hundredfold. But Jesus was lifting him up to something higher than he had ever known. He began to understand how much his need was of the spirit and how little of the body. When he made his request it was not, "Lord make me whole!" it was, "Lord, forgive". But this was a silent colloquy; the tense watchers heard nothing of it until Christ's final answer, "Son, be of good cheer, thy sins are forgiven thee".

The tension broke, the sick man felt the comfort of the peace which flowed through his whole being. But in that company many strange emotions stirred: the faith of the bearers, the relief of the stricken man, the astonishment and wonder of the people, the prejudice and opposition of the scribes. Many who watched the scene had witnessed Christ's healing power and had no doubt that the man would be healed in view of this spectacular demonstration of faith. But they were totally unprepared for these words by which Jesus showed them the true significance of this and every other miracle he performed. In offering men forgiveness Jesus occupied a province which had been the prerogative of God, but he was about to justify his assumption of this office. The people may have accepted this, but to the scribes it was a challenge which could not be ignored. The sick man may be satisfied but they were not. Yet they did not speak. They kept their thoughts to themselves, veiled behind expressionless faces. Jesus turned his attention upon them. His gaze searched their hearts. Now grace turned to judgment. "Wherefore think ye evil in your hearts?" The scribes were not wrong in questioning whether it could be possible that God had delegated His power to forgive sins to this man. They were wrong in defying the evidence that he was continually offering to prove it.

Jesus had not forgotten the cripple at his feet. He would have healed him in any case. Now, however, he accommodated his healing to their folly, not so much for their benefit as for the people who stood by. Once more he showed them his authority. It would have been equally ineffective for them to say to the diseased man, "Thy sins be forgiven thee" or to say "Take up thy bed". Although in the first case their ineffectiveness would not be seen, in the second it would be manifest by the invalid's inability to respond. But for the Son of Man it was no more difficult to forgive sins than it was to heal. True, they could not, in the nature of things, see the effect of the first but they could see the result of the second, and that proved the validity of the first. Turning to the man at his feet the word of command rang out, "Arise, take up thy bed and go into thine house". Immediately the man rose and walking through the wondering throng that made way for him, returned home peaceful in mind and whole in body. All who had witnessed the scene wondered greatly and glorified God.

The opposition of the scribes and Pharisees was stillborn; it was attacked and defeated at its source. But Jesus knew that the conflict had only begun. Very shortly, supported by men specially sent from Jerusalem, it would flare up into unremitting warfare, and doors now hospitably open would close at his approach. He had come to do his Father's will, and it should be accomplished at whatever cost. Purposefully he travelled the lonely road of self-sacrifice and hardship, deterred neither by the hatred of his enemies nor the solicitude of his friends.

The connection between sin and suffering was often misunderstood by the people of Christ's day. If a man suffered it was the direct result of a specific sin. This was one of the few current errors which Jesus stepped aside to correct. But in a general sense suffering and death are the result of sin, and one of the mysteries of suffering is that so many Godly characters are its victims. The association between forgiveness of sins and freedom from suffering is in this general sense a very real one.

In the case of this palsied man the interval between forgiveness and restoration was short. It was in Christ's purpose that it should be so. In many, many cases it is extended, sometimes for years. There are those who endure a life of suffering, and death overtakes them as a merciful release. But whether the interval be long or short, whether indeed it never come at all in mortal life, the words of the Psalmist remain true, "Blessed is he whose transgression is forgiven, whose sin is covered". For that man, whatever his physical state, there is peace and harmony in this life, and the glorious expectation of ineffable joy in the day of restoration, when the reconciliation which Christ achieved by his death finds its complete fulfilment in the Kingdom of which he preached on the hills of Galilee.

6

THE CALL OF MATTHEW

DURING his stay in Capernaum, Jesus spent most of his time by the lakeside healing and teaching the multitudes who resorted to him from every quarter. One day he approached the Custom House set at a strategic point outside the town where the famous "way of the sea" joined the Lake of Galilee. The official in charge of this post was an unpopular Jew named Matthew. All who furthered Rome's interest in Palestine were hated by the great majority of their country-men, but particularly the class of publican to which Matthew belonged. For there were two types actively engaged in collecting money for the occupying power at that time. The tax-gatherers were responsible for the normal taxes, but the Custom House officials were directly responsible to the Roman Government for the duty on the exports and imports of the country. They also received tolls from users of the roads and the bridges, from the boats which used the harbour facili-ties, and from the merchants who traded in the markets. Travellers entering or leaving Capernaum would have to stop at the Custom House, unload their mules or camels and subject their merchandise to the keen eyes of the Customs official who would require duty which ranged from 2½ to 12½ per cent according to its nature. It will be readily seen that these officials had numerous opportunities for bribery and extortion, and there can be little doubt that most of them used these means to amass quick fortunes, enjoy their power, and the patronage of those wealthy families to whom they granted immunities which were denied to the poor. As we should expect the scribes and Pharisees were particularly opposed to all publicans; whilst perforce they had to admit them into their synagogues they lost no occasion of showing their distaste and contempt. Should any synagogue official ever succumb to the temptation of getting a more lucrative living by joining the publicani, he was forthwith expelled from his duties.

Sitting day by day outside his Custom House Matthew would undoubtedly see and hear much of Jesus. He would see the steady procession constantly moving down the wide paved road towards Capernaum, from the poor homeless wanderers to the impressive caravans of the rich with their attendants. He would see the sick and the halt and the blind carried and led towards the place where Jesus was preaching. Ships would come across the lake bringing their burden of people eager to join the throng. He would answer the countless questions that would be breathlessly put to him concerning the present whereabouts of the prophet. He would without doubt have been personally acquainted with Peter and Andrew, James and John, and would have heard, perhaps with amazement, possibly with understanding, that they had left their homes and their trade to be the disciples of the prophet Jesus.

There were probably times when moving along the shore, Jesus would stop to heal and preach within sight and sound of Matthew's roadside Custom House, and amid repeated interruptions he would hear many of the gracious words that Jesus spoke, and see a pale face change to a healthy glow under his touch, and a raving madman become calm and joyful at a word of command. He would be strangely impressed by the contrast between the teaching he listened to, and the law-bound repetitions of the scribes; by the way in which he ministered to the lowest and meanest suppliant, people from whom the scribes would have shrunk in horror. He would be encouraged to hope that with this man there would be sympathy and encouragement, where everywhere else there was bitterness and scorn.

Then because of his unique position he would be one of the first to learn that all was not well between Jesus and the religious rulers in Capernaum. They were his enemies too, and he would feel a bond of fellowship with this gracious teacher.

And so it seems very probable that gradually, all unknown to himself, Matthew became in spirit a disciple of Jesus, but a disciple who could never acknowledge his allegiance or hope for the favour of the Master he watched with growing eagerness. But on this morning Jesus paused when he reached the Custom House, his shadow fell athwart Matthew's desk. Looking up, Matthew met eyes of ineffable love which conveyed to him the message even before the lips could utter the words "Follow me". And the man who during long years had become hardened to angry words and bitter looks left the parchments and the money chest in the road-side cabin to become first a disciple and then an apostle. The official who for so long had added to men's burdens was about to enter into the intimate service of him whose life's work was to remove them. Instead of his pen being inspired by selfish gain to record transactions in his ledger, it was to be his gracious privilege, inspired by the spirit of God, to open a new account in the record of the eternal purpose of the Father as now revealed in the life and the words of His beloved Son.

The call of Matthew is a striking example of the complete disregard of Jesus for the opinions of men. It also illustrates how he quietly pursued a course which, from a logical point of view, could only do his cause a great deal of harm. There can be no doubt that the dramatic choice of Matthew led to a deterioration of the people's opinion of him as well as a hardening of the opposition of the scribes and Pharisees. From the point of view of his ability to keep the support of the people and alleviate the disapproval of the religious rulers it would have seemed much wiser to have ignored Matthew and accepted the scribe who was prepared to follow him whithersoever he went. But Jesus had the perspective of the ages. He knew that his work was only beginning with the completion of his earthly mission. His choices and decisions were based upon the future as much as the present. This is one of the less easily recognized and more difficult paths along which his disciples are called. It is only after long association that we can make mature judgments which are based upon the true recognition that the things that are seen are temporal and the things that are not seen are eternal.

That Matthew was a comparatively wealthy man can be gathered from the great feast which he arranged at his house following his call. It was a gesture which affords us a glimpse of his character because the guests he invited to meet Jesus were his fellow publicans. The occasion was both a farewell and an invitation. It marked the end of his life of affluence and the beginning of a life of poverty. But he was quick to recognize that in reality it was exactly the opposite, and we can believe that he was anxious that his former associates would be similarly persuaded when they met his Master, and make a renunciation like his.

Jesus came to the feast, accepting this expression of gratitude gladly, knowing its source and its object. As in all things he judged the heart, but others were not so charitable. The event did not escape the notice of the local scribes and

Pharisees, and with a cunning which reflects little credit upon them they approached the disciples, realizing no doubt the harm they could do Jesus by sowing disquiet in their minds. "How is it that he eateth with publicans and sinners?" The Master did not allow his immature disciples to be exposed to the subtlety of these men. As was his custom then, so it is his promise now, that he will intervene in these crises of challenge and persecution, and we are thankful to his enemies, not because of their opposition, but because they evoked this gracious reply of Jesus on behalf of his disciples. His defence for loving the unloved is among the most beautiful of all the things which Jesus uttered, full of heavenly pleading and exquisite pathos. None can bring out the character of a man better than his enemies, and here as so often in the Gospels the sheer beauty of Christ's shines forth as he answers these scowling, unfriendly men who seek only his humiliation. In their blindness and perversion they question the company he keeps. With simple dignity he assures them that this is his rightful place. He was a doctor, and no doctor worthy of the name would spend his time among the healthy. His true place was with his patients, and the more serious the illness the longer he would be with them and the more frequent his visits. A complete answer to their challenge, it was also an indictment of those who made it. It exposed as bad physicians those who had been given the responsibility of healing. Instead of strengthening the weak they avoided contact with those who needed their help and were in obvious fear of infection. But there was far more in his answer than this for those who would thoughtfully consider its implications. It provided the true interpretation of his healing work among the bodily sick. All men were guilty in God's sight and worthy of death. In His grace the Eternal Father was pleased to give that guilt another name, and call it sickness. But it was still a sickness unto death, and it could only be cured by the Physician of God's provision. Thus when Matthew records the healing of Peter's wife's mother, he adds, "That it might be fulfilled which was spoken by Esaias the prophet saying, Himself took our infirmities, and bare our sicknesses". Yet deliverance was not complete until God sealed it in the wounds of His beloved Son.

Jesus was careful not to accept the postulate of their question. The obvious inference they made was that they were righteous. "Go ye and learn what that meaneth, I will have mercy and not sacrifice: for I am come not to call the righteous but sinners to repentance." The object of Jesus in making this quotation from Hosea will be seen when we too go and learn what it meaneth. The message of this prophet, as indeed of all the prophets of Israel, was the sickness of Israel, an indication of their punishment, and a glimpse of the restoration which would finally be granted in the mercy of God. None but the God of Israel could accomplish this, and then only in the greatness of His loving kindness. Thus, the spirit through Hosea says the Assyrian could not heal them. But the healing would come, and the word comes to the prophet, "I will heal their backsliding, I will love them freely: for mine anger is turned away from him". In the sixth chapter where we are given a prophetic insight into the New Covenant when the mercy of God will be manifest to Israel, words which point with wonderful significance to the death and resurrection of the Messiah are prefaced by Israel's acknowledgment of her sin and God's ability to heal, "Come and let us return to the Lord; for he hath torn and he will heal us: he hath smitten and he will bind us up".

If only those scribes and Pharisees had obeyed the Lord's injunction and meditated upon the words to which he directed them they would have learned that they were in dire need of the Physician. They needed him more. Their sickness was greater than the publican's because of their faithlessness to their trust.

This exchange between Jesus and the local synagogue officials was followed by an interruption from the disciples of John the Baptist. It is possible that their question was inspired by the Pharisees. A certain affinity seems implied by their challenge.* "Why do we and the Pharisees fast oft, but thy disciples fast not?" With beautiful appropriateness Jesus led them back to their own Master's words, words which each of them would remember because they were so often repeated by the prophet who now languished in prison. "Ye your-selves", John had said, "bear me witness that I said, I am not the Christ, but I am sent before him." Jesus identified him-self with John's words. He was the Bridegroom. His disciples had recognized and acclaimed him, and because he was still with them it was an hour for rejoicing and not for fasting. But the bridal feast was not yet: the Bridegroom must leave his disciples alone, that would be their time of sorrow and fasting.

*We cannot rule out the possibility that when John was imprisoned many of his disciples turned to the Pharisees.

Jesus sealed his argument by the two metaphorical parables of the garment and the wine, both associated with the Bridegroom. "No man", he said, "putteth a piece of new cloth into an old garment." The ceremonial fasting of the Pharisees and of John's disciples was part of an old system that was ready to vanish away. It had been superseded by the arrival of the Bridegroom who had come to consecrate a new and living way. The garment which is worn out to the point of uselessness cannot be made serviceable again. The new material will only emphasize its poverty.

And then, as his manner was, Jesus changed the figure and deepened the truth he was expressing. "No man putteth new wine into old bottles." The garment had only to do with the outward aspect. Now Jesus turns to something which affects the inward condition. His mission from God as the Physician and the Bridegroom was to turn a deathly heritage into an eternal one. But this great gift could not be received in the unregenerate, darkened life. A transformation had to take place, gradual, painful and unmistakable. Jesus conceded that men do not straightway desire the new; they say the old is better. It is the cry of the flesh clinging desperately to its natural inclinations. But when Christ truly enters, it becomes a despairing cry in the light of the recognition that the flesh profiteth nothing, but that his words are spirit and life. Thus graphically Jesus anticipated in this parable the words of his great apostle to the Gentiles, "If any man be in Christ he is a new creature: old things are passed away; behold, all things are become new."

7

LORD OF THE SABBATH

DURING this period of activity in and around Capernaum Jesus came into open conflict with the Pharisees on the question of the Sabbath day. It was inevitable that it should come sooner or later, and the amazing popularity of Jesus together with his complete answer to their charges and criticisms before the multitudes, led them to watch him with the utmost care. If they could find something in which they could irrevocably condemn him they would restore their damaged prestige and also do his cause a great deal of harm. The Sabbath offered them the best opportunity to do this, because although he always attended the synagogue to worship, he was also prepared to continue with his ministry of healing.

Walking through the cornfield with their Lord one sabbath day, the disciples paused to eat some ears of ripening corn. Several times during these active days when Jesus moved unweariedly among the people teaching and healing, neither he nor his disciples had the opportunity to pause long enough for a meal. The Pharisees were carefully watching for such an opportunity. There was no Sabbath calm and reverence in their hearts. Scarcely had the disciples begun to eat than their Lord was challenged, "Behold! thy disciples do that which is not lawful to do on the Sabbath day".

Jesus could so easily have turned upon them with withering scorn, and exposed their littleness. He could have pointed out to them that his disciples were perfectly justified by the law of God, but had only broken their puny tradition. But if these men in their hatred had disclosed their ignorance of the significance of the Sabbath, Jesus had not: his shining example emphasized the meanness of their quibbles. Mercy still prevailed over judgment, giving his enemies a further span to see the error of their ways. With all the persuasion of sweet reasonableness Jesus dealt with their accusation. He called upon the law and the prophets to justify the actions of his disciples. What would be your attitude towards King David and his followers who, like my disciples, hungered on the Sabbath? He went into the House of God and took the shewbread which it was only lawful for the priests to eat. He did not ignore a tradition, he broke the law of God. And would you find fault with the priests who in the execution of their duties profane the sabbath? But as he so often did on such occasions he widened and deepened the context, and gave a new meaning to the whole conception of the Sabbath. "The Sabbath was made for man, and not man for the Sabbath ... the Son of Man is Lord even of the Sabbath day."

In sublimely simple words Jesus did far more than defend his disciples. He went back beyond the law to the divine purpose in instituting the Sabbath. It was not a burden imposed upon man, but a blessing bestowed upon him. Like sacrifice, it was not ordained to give man the opportunity of doing something to show his goodness, but rather to give him the consciousness both of his need and of the divine provision to meet it. Its immediate significance was in rest for the body and solace for the spirit. The Pharisees had failed to understand even that proximate end. They had brought low this beneficent law of God by introducing innumerable restrictions which showed how much they had lost the spirit of God's dealings, and indeed of His character. Under their heavy hand the Sabbath had become an intolerable burden.

When a life is dedicated to God, its purpose steadfast and its motive pure, the man-made restrictions to attain legal righteousness become not only irksome and unnecessary but positively harmful. The whole teaching of Jesus created the incentive to seek and to love God: in doing so he freed men from impositions which at their best could be but a poor substitute for true piety and morality, and at their worst could encourage the grossest self-esteem and hypocrisy. The denial of these ordinances did not prevent adequate expression of spiritual life; rather it cleared the way for it. Jesus gave incentive and power to a holiness and consecration undreamed of in the law. He demonstrated it by his own radiant example. He showed that response to God's love lay not in the bondage of the letter but in the liberty of the spirit.

This fundamental conception was the great gulf that was fixed between Jesus and the religious rulers of his day. The things that the scribes and Pharisees taught had become the acknowledged standard of religious life. Jesus exposed them as the great evil of his time, forming a barrier between man and the true knowledge and worship of God. The conflict was as inevitable as it was bitter. It had of necessity to be unto death.

If only these men had forgotten their littleness for a moment! If, in the light of his words, they had dispassionately viewed their charge against the disciples, they could hardly have failed to perceive that it was almost laughable. They were not accusing them of taking the corn—that was permissible—but according to the mature judgment they were enforcing, the action of rolling the ears between their hands constituted the process of threshing! It was because their minds were full of this pettiness that they were unprepared for the revelation which followed, "But I say unto you, that in this place is one greater than the Temple". The priests ministered in the Temple on the Sabbath. Both Sabbath and Temple must give way to one who is greater than either, and he is standing in their midst. The Sabbath is not an end in itself; it is typical of a rest that remaineth for the people of God. The Temple was but an evidence of the condescension of the Almighty to the limitations of men; its chief significance lay in its essentially prophetic character, pointing forward to the time when the tabernacle of God shall be with men and He will dwell with them. Both these features were dependent upon God's purpose of redemption in Christ. He was thus higher than both, Lord of the Sabbath and greater than the Temple.

One of the great tragedies of that and every age is that men and women are so preoccupied with their real or imagined rights and privileges that the great revelations of God which have power to transform their whole lives are unheeded. It is an evil which can have its victims in the Household. At times when the rights and wrongs of an issue are the subject of heated discussion it is always wise to pause and listen to the voice of Christ. He can restore the true perspective.

However complete a truth and however sublime a teacher, men's understanding is blunted when their hearts are darkened by malice and evil. The following Sabbath found the scribes and Pharisees watching with unabated intensity. All eyes were upon Jesus as he entered the synagogue and approached a man whose hand was withered. Would he dare to break the Sabbath law before them all in the House of God? Jesus knew their thoughts and deliberately chose to make the issue clear beyond the slightest doubt. Turning to the afflicted man, he commanded him to rise and stand forth in their midst. Then he challenged them, "I will ask you one thing, Is it lawful on the sabbath days to do good, or to do evil? To save life, or to destroy it? What man shall there be among you, that shall have one sheep, and if it fall into a pit on the sabbath day, will he not lay hold on it and lift it out? How much then is a man better than a sheep?" His questions went unanswered. No man spoke. Impervious alike to his pleading and to the need of the man whose arm hung helplessly at his side, they waited for him to act so that they might accuse him. Jesus looked upon them with anger in his heart at their unrelenting hardness. This was the spirit which would dog his footsteps through Galilee and Judea, endeavouring to thwart every gesture of love. It would not bend to the warmth of Christ's pleading, but eventually it would break under the heavy blows of Rome.

But his anger turned to love as he turned from them to the suppliant who waited eagerly for his healing power. "Stretch forth thine hand." Obedience brought restoration to the sufferer and frustration to the enemies of Jesus. They went away, anger crystallizing into settled hatred and envy. They held a council and even consorted with the Herodians. Their one preoccupation was how they might destroy him. Their persistence which was at last to win its terrible reward is a bitter commentary upon the depravity of the human spirit. It is also a wonderful revelation of the grace of God shining through His beloved Son that when Jesus heard of the evil councils he withdrew himself; and when great multitudes followed him, he healed them all.

8

THE TWELVE

THE deliberate and concerted opposition of the religious leaders in Galilee and the council they convened to discuss the best method to destroy him led Jesus to a decision which was a landmark in the Gospel history. There were undoubtedly other good reasons why Jesus selected twelve men from among his many disciples to become apostles. The very term suggests one of them. An apostle is 'one sent': on at least two occasions the Master sent forth these men to undertake a work which was growing out of all proportion to the power of one to fulfil. The longer journeys which he contemplated as the sphere of his activity extended, made it imperative that some selection should be made. It is very probable that at this time there were literally hundreds of disciples of Jesus of varying degrees of loyalty, who followed him from place to place. To have taken them to the coasts of Tyre and Sidon would have been to impede rather than help his work. But as the life of Jesus proceeds we see that there was a greater purpose in his action which these other considerations only serve to throw into higher relief. The twelve were destined to be far more than companions; they were to be his witnesses, taking over the responsibility of propagating the Gospel in the utter conviction of the identity and divine mission of the Messiah. There was much for them to learn in the few months that lay before them. They had to be educated in personal dedication, learning the lessons of prayer, of humility, of discipline and of self-sacrifice. From now their Master was to divide his time between the multitudes and the Twelve, spending more and more time with them as the first great wave of popularity spent itself and the forces of opposition gathered to accomplish his destruction.

So it was that when Christ's earthly mission had been completed the work went on, still with the authority and power of God, in the lives of these men, who had discovered and tapped the sources of their Master's strength, and who had learned, at times with almost painful slowness, the great purpose of his Father. In the dangers and difficulties of their work they overcame because they had been with their Lord in all the crises of his eventful life, they had seen him in those exposed hours of loneliness and strife, of weariness and disappointment when the true nature of man is revealed. In the intimacy of daily fellowship he was to teach them by precept and example. They were to learn that following him was a mental and spiritual process as well as a physical one. That is probably an easier lesson for us to learn than it was for them. Later disciples without the privilege of walking with him through the crowded streets and over the verdant hills of Galilee find much of their inspiration in a prayerful contemplation of his words, the demands they make, and the light they throw upon the holy and devoted mind that uttered them. But for the twelve the example would be even more powerful than the precept: they would never lose the tender picture of their Master kneeling before them with basin and towel: they would always feel the gentle touch of his hand upon their feet. Here lay their incentive for loving one another. They would watch him return from a sleepless night in the hills, peace, radiance and renewed strength exuding from his whole being. Thus they would be instructed in prayer. From his life they would learn the lesson of sacrifice that we learn chiefly from his death. Examples of his love, his devotion and his discipline would remain fresh long after many of his words were only half remembered.

Before Jesus made his deliberate choice of twelve men he spent the night with his Father. All the great events in his life find him or leave him in prayer. It is the natural expression of the dedication of one whose meat and drink was to do the will of Him who sent him, whose words and actions belonged to his Father, who of himself could do nothing. There is here a personal lesson for every disciple, a lesson too clearly portrayed for any to miss, too vital to the sincere heart to need any further stress.

The number of the disciples is of great significance. It linked the work of the Messiah with the divine Kingdom of Israel when the twelve tribes had prospered under the powerful hand of David, and it pointed forward to the restoration of that Kingdom under David's greater Son, when the twelve tribes would be ruled by the twelve men Jesus had appointed under the hand of God. It was thus a number which had design as well as convenience behind it. It was based upon the framework of the whole purpose of God.

Of the twelve whom Jesus chose (assuming the identity of Nathanael and Bartholomew) seven are already known to us. Of the other five only two emerge again in the Gospels; Thomas whose scepticism has earned for him a notoriety that has overshadowed his equally evident qualities of courage and loyalty, and Judas whose treachery even at this early stage is branded with the words, "Which also betrayed him". We know very little of the remaining three beyond the certainty that they were made of the right material for the moulding purpose of their Master. Judas Thaddeus (also incorrectly called Lebbaeus in the Authorized Version of Matthew) has earned our lasting gratitude by asking a thoughtful question during those last precious hours in the upper room. It evoked what to most of us must be at once the most disturbing and the most comforting truth that Jesus spoke. Simon Zelotes as his name implies was a former member of a secret fanatical Jewish nationalist organization sworn to exterminate Roman rule in Palestine. His choice is a further example of the complete indifference to public opinion. The enemies of Jesus would not fail to pounce upon this as evidence of his political aspirations. They would use it to make others see a sinister design in the man who was drawing the whole country under his banner. But looking at this choice from the true point of view we see the vigorous loyalty of a courageous man turned from devotion to a false cause into devotion to a noble one. The reflection brings an inevitable comparison with the call of the apostle Paul. James, the son or brother of Alphaeus, remains obscure in spite of many attempts to identify him. It is possible that he was James the less, so called to distinguish him from the son of Zebedee. If this is true he would be the cousin of Jesus.

Such were the men Jesus chose to be with him. Unlettered, uncultured, unknown: men of widely different interests, fishermen, taxgatherer, dangerous revolutionary. It is illuminating to see Simon the fanatical hater of Rome, and Matthew the Roman hireling, finding fellowship in common devotion to Jesus. Doubtless there would be occasions in the absence of their master during their early association when natural animosities would be aroused in their worldly discussions, but that would be inevitable in the formative process to which they were being subjected. Gradually their former loyalties and ambitions would die away before their common hope, and side by side they went forward bringing to men the good news of a Kingdom which would usher in blessings infinitely greater than could ever be achieved by the might of Rome, and would surpass in glory and extent the palmiest days of Israel's history.

It is difficult to see how Jesus could have chosen from any other than the poor and insignificant class in Galilee. Those whom he called were representative of those to whom he had come. It was the poor who heard him gladly and followed him whithersoever he went. The priestly and aristocratic classes had rejected him and proclaimed their unbelief. Their wisdom reared up as a barrier between them and discipleship. It was altogether fitting that the great Physician should choose as his students men who had recognized their need of him and had complete confidence in his healing touch, men who had in effect echoed the words of their spokesman, "Depart from me, for I am a sinful man, O Lord". They were simple truly, but it was the humble simplicity which is the beginning of true wisdom and Jesus rejoiced in them because they were able to receive the message of heaven which was hidden from the wise and prudent. The simple, rugged faith of these men made the cultured approaches of some of the leaders seem like unworthy patronage. Their minds may have been uninformed in many things, but their hearts were warm and so their love deepened their knowledge, and wisdom grew apace; not indeed the knowledge of the Temple courts, but the understanding of the things of the kingdom and the qualities which the eternal Father desires in each of his children. They were not taught in the cloistered edifice of man's construction, but in the amphitheatre of God's creative work. They did not draw their lessons from the laboriously prepared casuistry of men, but from the One who, coming to reveal the mind of the Almighty, extracted from His handiwork truths of eternal significance.

There is great comfort for us in our contemplation of this choice which Jesus made. It clearly illustrates the divine revelation that the wisdom of this world is foolishness with God, that He has chosen the weak things of the world to bring to nought the things that are strong. The qualifications for discipleship remain even in this age of universal knowledge. Indeed it is probably true that there has never been a time when concentrated learning for its own sake can do so much to impede the childlike faith and the receptive heart which is the threshold every disciple must cross. It is still the poor of this world, rich in faith, whom God has chosen to be the heirs of the Kingdom.

Jesus continued his ministry from this point with a new and vital object added to his work. He had the constant companionship of those twelve who through much weakness and many falterings were to abide with him on the arduous path to Jerusalem and beyond. Each experience provided another lesson in their education and prepared them for their momentous calling, so that when the time came they were ready to go forth with the authority of their Lord, suffering the inevitable impact of unbelief and persecution, but willing to follow him even unto death.

"Then the devil taketh him up into the holy city ..." (Matthew 4:5)

"... after six days Jesus taketh Peter, James, and John his brother, and bringeth them up into an high mountain apart ..." (Matthew 17:1)

"Salt is good: but if the salt have lost his savour, wherewith shall it be seasoned? It is neither fit for the land, nor yet for the dunghill ..." (Luke 14:34,35)

9

THE BEATITUDES

HAVING made his prayerful choice of the men who were destined to be rulers in the kingdom which he had come to manifest, Jesus took an early opportunity of instructing them in the principles of that kingdom. He led the Twelve to the foothills which look back over the gleaming lake of Galilee and upon the villages which fringed its western shore. Reaching a large plateau among the heights, he sat down in their midst and taught them. It was not long before they were joined by the multitudes which had become such a familiar sight wherever he went.

The discourse which followed, familiar to us as the Sermon on the Mount, is recorded most fully by Matthew. The greatest intellects of each generation have contributed their meditations upon its teaching. But no man has ever plumbed its depths or ascended its heights. They are words which form the basis of all righteousness. They constitute the rock upon which all Christian endeavour is built. Jesus had come to demonstrate in his life the attributes of his Father. He had come to lift the faces of the sons of men towards the Fountain of light and life; to call upon them to abandon their selfish grovelling in the darkness of human ambition and willingly follow him into the cool clear air of the spirit, ever progressing towards the perfection embodied in the exhortation which is the climax of the discourse, "Be ye therefore perfect, even as your Father which is in heaven is perfect".

The teaching and precepts of Jesus expressed in the clear symmetry of the Sermon on the Mount are not abstract ideals, as beautiful as mountain peaks and as remote, to be preserved and worshipped in devotional hours and ignored in the hurlyburly of daily living. They form a working philosophy of life which is the only road a disciple can tread. A steep and difficult road truly, but one which Jesus himself was treading. Nor did he demand that his disciples should tread it alone. He reached out his hand and led them towards its summit.

117

Jesus was teaching the twelve and the multitude of disciples who should follow them how to live on his high level. The whole discourse forms a portrait of the Teacher himself. In it he reveals the secret of his life. Showing his disciples the way, he describes the fountain from which all his own actions sprang, disclosing a heart dedicated to his Father's will.

It is as important as it is interesting to consider the general structure of this discourse. Broadly it falls into three divisions. The first, which takes us to the twentieth verse of the fifth chapter, illustrates with the words "Ye are" and "ye have" the basic character of the child of God. By far the largest section, continuing to the 14th verse of the seventh chapter, deals with the outward manifestation of that basic character in the vicissitudes of life: actions which are the inevitable outcome of the spiritual condition and do not have their motives "as the Pharisees", to be seen of men. It is here that the twelve are repeatedly reminded of the distinction between the justice of the Mosaic Law which required obedience to the letter, and the love of the law Christ was giving them which demanded a responsive obedience to the spirit of grace. Finally there follows a warning against the stumbling-blocks and by-paths on the road to perfection, and a graphic parable which conveys far too vividly for complacency the fundamental importance of man's attitude to his precepts.

From this broad analysis it can readily be seen that the Beatitudes are the seed from which all the other aspects burst into radiant expression. The secret of the law of Christ does not lie in the disciple loving his enemies or in turning the other cheek—that is the natural expression of the blessed condition to which he calls them in his opening words. The man who is poor in spirit will not seek the mote in his brother's eye. He that truly mourns will not be guilty of the disfiguring deceptions of the fasting Pharisee. One who is pure in heart will have made those painful sacrifices which have deprived him of offending hands and feet and eyes. He who hungers and thirsts after righteousness will not be over-anxious to get his share of the lesser blessings of this life.

As the general sermon submits to analysis, so it is possible to appreciate the symmetry of the Beatitudes themselves. The first great need of the spiritual man is poverty of spirit. From that we are able to advance along clearly defined paths towards perfection. We see the death and then the burial of self-righteousness. The blessing of meekness takes its place.

Meekness prepares the heart for the flowing in of
spiritual life by a hunger and thirst after righteousness.
Consciousness of divine gifts gives birth to a profound sense
of gratitude for mercies received, a gratitude which can only
be satisfied by a responsive mercy to our fellows. Purity
increases with the exclusion of all that is foreign to a true
reception of spiritual experience. With the singleness of
desire and purpose, conflicts of loyalty cease, struggles of the
flesh diminish, and the blessedness of peace fills the disciple's
heart. Righteousness has ever been at enmity with evil. The
more advanced our spiritual life, the more bitter will be the
assaults of "the powers of darkness", and the more comfort
will be found in the final Beatitude, "Blessed are they which
are persecuted for righteousness sake".

But these fundamental truths which sum up all that Jesus
has to say about discipleship demand more than a cursory
reference. To understand them and attempt to apply them is
to be numbered among those who forsook all and followed
him.

The word "blessed" which runs through the Beatitudes
stands not for a passing joy but for a continuing condition of
the heart. "Blessed *are*", indicates an inner experience, something not controlled by circumstance or regulated by environment: a state of heart not of life. If the listening Twelve, or
the multitudes of listeners that have followed them, can
attain this blessedness which, by God's grace, is the reward
of a diligent endeavour to keep these commandments, then
all the circumstances, difficulties and temptations of life will
be met and controlled by this condition of a heart which beats
in harmony with the heart of Jesus.

The first stage in discipline is poverty of spirit: a deliberate
renunciation of many things which the flesh finds attractive.
Immediately the way of Jesus struck away from the way of
men. He taught that self-sacrifice, not self-culture is the true
vocation of those who would follow him. The disciples were
shown at the outset that they had to make a choice even more
important than the decision to leave all and follow him. It
was impossible for them to travel upon two roads leading in
opposite directions. Jesus showed them that they could not
begin to accept the gifts of God until they were prepared to
give up the prizes the world had to offer. The spirit that fights
for its rights, that demands adequate rewards for natural
endowments, may indicate wordly wisdom, but that wisdom

119

is foolishness with God. He also showed them that the end of poverty of spirit is not poverty; it is riches. They would commence a journey which leads them high above the thoughts and ways of men to the mind of the Creator. "Theirs is the kingdom of Heaven." When the work of their Master rises to its consummation at his return to the earth it will be those who have willingly broken their lives and renounced their spirit to serve him who will be the children of the Kingdom. In that day those who have sacrificed the dubious pleasures of a godless world, manifesting a longing, never-satisfied desire to enjoy the fellowship and accept the responsibilities that Jesus offers, will receive the unspeakable gift of immortality and will shine like stars in the Kingdom of his Father.

Spiritual mourning is the natural outcome of the renounced spirit. When his own temporal ambitions and wants are resolved, the thoughts and activities of the disciple can turn to the needs of others. He is able to share their burdens and enter into their sorrows. Losing concern for himself, not so much deliberately as inevitably, he begins to manifest love for others. Jesus himself had done just that. In the wilderness of Judea he had resolved his own problem; he returned to give his whole attention to the needs of men, loving them even to the uttermost. Now, in that same spirit of love, he teaches them that the trials, disappointments and sorrows of many hearts are concentrated on the heart of the true disciple. Answering his call to a life of love and service, they are entering into the fellowship of his sufferings. The vale of tears lies before them. But by bearing the burdens of others they would fulfil his law, and with the mourning came the promise of the blessing of comfort. The literal meaning of this word comfort is "strengthened by being with". This godly sorrow was to bring to his disciples a companionship more precious than his physical presence, a deep spiritual union from which they would draw strength from his strength. Thus they would receive a measure of peace and joy far exceeding the measure of their grief.

Meekness is not weakness when it is the quality born of the two previous Beatitudes. The spirit of renunciation and the spirit of loving service combine to produce the man who is meek. It is a state which emerges from a breaking and softening process. To the world it sounds effeminate and tasteless, but upon the lips of Jesus the eager disciples realized that it was a quality to be found only in the bravest and strongest characters. It is not the natural meekness suggestive of tameness which belongs to the placid easy-going amiable man. It is the hard-earned reward of a purging spiritual experience which has demanded a high degree of courage and self control. The blessing of meekness is inheritance. "Blessed are the meek, for they shall inherit the earth." It could not be claimed in the light of the apostles' subsequent experience that this blessing was offered to them as a present possession. The earth was under the temporary domination of the proud and the arrogant. Already they had had evidence of the temper of those who occupied the highest places in the earth, evidence that would accumulate until their Master hung on the cross. But that would not always be. Although for a season they would suffer under the injustice and cruelty of men, their inheritance remained. An heir is one who is not of age but who is coming into his possession at some future time. Thus Jesus was sowing to his disciples' mind the seed of a truth which he was later to develop in many wonderful ways. By a strange paradox, by forsaking the world they were to inherit the earth. This Beatitude is a paraphrase of the thirty-seventh Psalm which gives the picture of evil now prospering and the wicked flourishing as a green bay tree. The godly man is exhorted not to fret over their power nor be envious of their prosperity. Though he suffer adversity at their hands he must continually delight in the Lord and commit his ways unto Him. The day will come when evil doers shall be cut off and the meek shall inherit the earth, and shall delight themselves in the abundance of peace.

Although the final reward of the meek will wait upon the return to the earth of their Lord, the disciples would have lost the spirit of their Master's words had they ignored the present spiritual compensations that they would enjoy as they strove to follow him. In the very process of their struggles they would experience a peace passing understanding, a fellowship and a deep sense of communion which would be for them, and can be for us, an earnest of the eternal inheritance which awaits those who are true sons of God.

10

THE BEATITUDES *(Continued)*

FINDING life by letting it go is an emptying process. It empties the disciple of the ingredients that produce the satisfactions of the carnal mind. But a life cannot remain empty. Something is needed to take the place of those things that have been sacrificed. "Blessed", said Jesus to the men who were determined to follow him, "blessed are they which do hunger and thirst after righteousness." A man who is satisfied with the world is not a hungry man. Being full, he has no interest in spiritual food. He cannot enjoy the rich fruits of the spirit because his capacity for enjoyment is limited by his chosen environment. Spiritual hunger no less than natural hunger is a craving which must be satisfied or we perish. It should not be necessary to be led into the darkened stillness of a death chamber to realize that all hearts are empty unless God fills them, nor should we wait for the disillusioned confession of a broken heart to bring home to us the truth that all desires fail except they crave after God. Appetite is quickened by the attractiveness of food. To the listening disciples on the Mount the righteousness to which Jesus called them was not the legal righteousness of tradition. They could see that every day on the street corners, it was not even the abstract righteousness of the law. It was embodied in the one who sat in their midst. The hunger and thirst of their renounced spirit was to find its satisfaction in Christ. As their life with him grew into an abiding fellowship so the pangs of hunger died and their thirst was quenched. They experienced a partial fulfilment of his promise that they should be filled. It was impossible for them to tap such sources without powerful results. They had not all the same capacity, but, with one exception, they were all filled. Truly there were fleshly interruptions from time to time, but these only emphasized the distance they had travelled, and threw into clearer relief the goal towards which they moved.

Appetite for righteousness cries out to be softened by mercy. The twelve were in little danger of losing sight of this while Jesus was with them, his hand constantly raised in blessing and restoration. But this many-sided picture of the mature disciple was not for that time alone nor for those ears alone. The days were coming when he would be taken from them and they would continue the greatest task ever committed to frail men. In turn they would be followed by generations of disciples each striving after the perfection which their Lord was describing in simple trenchant words among the hills of Galilee. Without the constant lesson of Christ's example there is a very real possibility of the heart hardening under a passion for righteousness. Rigorous self-discipline can lead to a disturbingly harsh attitude towards the failings of others. There are few things more unlovely than the righteousness of the Pharisees of each generation. There is nothing more inspiring than righteousness matured by mercy and sympathy. Understanding of the love of God is the birthplace of a responsive love in the disciple's heart. It is responsive because it must find expression. It can no more be confined to its birthplace than the delicate loveliness of the rose can be confined within its bud. It has to burst out into fragrance and beauty bringing charm to all those who come within its influence. Such was the life of Jesus. Such was the character he desired of those he had chosen to be with him. The first indication of the presence of this responding love is an intense desire to serve—to do something in the service of him who has done so much for us. Love for God can only find adequate expression in love for our brethren. Mercy is one of the precious fruits of love. Saddened and depressed by the burden of some sin or weakness we sink to our knees in confession and plead for forgiveness. What words can describe the sense of relief, the subdued exaltation, the peace which fills our being as we leave our burden with the Lord and experience the grace of forgiveness? The fulness and beauty of that forgiveness is the measure of God's love for us. We cannot give like God, but we can try to forgive like Him. We can only begin to achieve it by loving our fellows and having a sincere zeal for their spiritual welfare. As long as we love we shall be able to forgive.

Compelling and exacting as is the picture Jesus has so far drawn, it is not yet complete. He turned his disciples' attention now from the circumference to the centre. "Blessed are the pure in heart, for they shall see God." Unless their heart was pure their life could not be, however much their action seemed to suggest that it was. The natural heart untouched by God's grace is "deceitful above all things and desperately wicked". That is a truth of which every one has had personal experience. How is it possible to transform naturally wicked and deceitful hearts to the purity demanded by Christ and blessed with the vision of God? A large part of the answer lies in the steps of renunciation, of penitence and intercession, of meekness, of spiritual longing, and of mercy, that have already been taken. To have proceeded so far makes this goal nearer, and the desire for it greater. We may hope for success as we concentrate all our powers and affections on Him who is absolutely and eternally pure. Purity of heart is more than the spiritual counterpart of the seventh commandment. It is not the exclusion of one form of grossness but of all. The origin of the word is "unmixed". Gold is only pure when there are no alloys left. The heart cannot be pure if its own private interests are mixed with its loyalty to God. The full beauty of the reward of purity in the vision of God is reserved for the day of glory, but blessed is he who even in the day of weakness so surrenders his heart to His refining discipline that for one or two moments in a lifetime he has felt something near to it: moments of highest aspiration when all thoughts of self have gone and he is conscious only of the presence and power of the Father. To Jesus this must have been an abiding possession. To his disciples it can only be a rare and passing moment of sublime devotion, but it holds within it the promise of eternity.

Jesus showed his disciples that the effectiveness of their work for him would be based upon the effectiveness of his work in them. As peacemakers they would be disciples who had travelled some distance along the road that led to the fulness of the stature of their Lord. A true peacemaker is far more than a composer of quarrels. The mediation between two individuals or factions striving against each other is a small part of a work of deeper significance. There is nothing negative about it. It is a glorious creative work. It is peace "making". We cannot make peace by avoiding action or adopting a "peace at any price" policy. Like every virtue, peace has its counterfeits, and an attitude which will allow vice to go unchecked and unattended wounds to fester is a shameful disguise. The peacemaker is not the man who betrays the selfish geniality of a comfortable Christian. Before the disciple can go forth as a peacemaker into the striving world his own restless spirit must be quietened in the presence of God, and his own inward strifes must be stilled by the peace which is the precious gift of his Master. When that is attained he will carry with him the blessings of peace. His presence will shed a fragrance and impart strength into the lives of all those with whom he comes in contact. Such men and women shall be called the children of God.

124

The twelve living with him amid the sunlit hills and shining lake realized what he meant as he unfolded his precept in gracious words and deeds. They saw one who will one day speak peace to the nations, bringing peace into the hearts of simple people as he revealed to them a Father of infinite love and compassion. He makes peacemakers of his disciples by giving them his peace.

The disciple's character is now complete. It has emerged strong and compelling. But the world will not find it attractive. Jesus took an early opportunity of emphasizing what most of the men surrounding him had already seen. It is a mistake to think that one who exhibits the qualities called forth by Jesus will spontaneously draw men to him. They will live to see how grave an error that can be as they watch the net closing around their Lord, and later when, taking up his work, they feel the full impact of men's hatred and cruelty. The measure of faithfulness will often be the measure of persecution. But Jesus showed them their true attitude in the face of persecution. "Rejoice and be exceeding glad." The reason for their joy would be that they were enduring for his sake. How much easier it would be for that reason! What a difference it would make and what an incentive it would give! In the days to come many of them were to go to prison and to death. The brave light that shone in their eyes, the courageous smile that hid their agony, would reflect the vision of the one who was now in their midst, but who would then be but a precious memory. They would die in the triumphant knowledge that they were suffering for his sake. And knowing this they would be content. Persecution strengthens character, saves from selfishness, develops trust in God. Remembering their Master it was not so difficult for them to forget the injustice in the privilege.

So the true disciple of every age sits at the feet of his Lord and learns the manner of man he would have him become. His progress becomes a triumph not of words but of works. The world sweeps by him largely unconcerned, but when it does take heed it is disturbed and it persecutes. But there are always hearts waiting to be touched by the appeal of a Christ-like spirit. So the great work goes on. More powerful than the perplexities of life and the subtleties of the flesh the disciple hears the voice of his Saviour, "Lo, I am with you alway, even unto the end of the world".

11

THE LAW OF LOVE

HAVING delineated the salient features of the true disciple, Jesus used three striking metaphors to show the Twelve the great responsibility that they had incurred in following him. "Ye are the salt of the earth ... ye are the light of the world ... a city that is set upon a hill cannot be hid." Salt gives savour to food and, far more important, it saves it from corruption. Such is the vocation of the disciple; but only of the disciple whose character has been set forth in the Beatitudes. It will be the example of the preacher which will give authority to his message. A call to regeneration without the transformation of the prophet is worse than valueless. Disciples whose words have lost the support of their conduct will never save men from corruption. They will only bring shame upon him who appointed them. Their power for harm is as great as their power for good.

But mingling with the world and saving it from corruption, they must also live above it. They are as lights shining on high, spreading radiance far and wide. As a lamp illuminates the blackness, so they must seek out the dark environment where the Gospel of love can be preached and the works of compassion undertaken. In the midst of evil, men must feel the contrast of their goodness.

The emphasis in these metaphors remains where it has been in the Beatitudes, not on what the disciples do, but on what they are. Salt that is good inevitably exerts a wholesome and saving influence. Light which is not obscured cannot do anything but illumine the darkness. So disciples who show the qualities Jesus has described cannot fail to be worthy of him that sent them. A city that is set on a hill cannot be hid. It may be welcomed as a haven of rest by the weary traveller, it may be avoided as a den of vice. But it cannot be hid. A man who claims discipleship cannot be ignored. His profession has elevated him and he stands exposed to the public gaze for good or ill. In all ages men will assess Christ not so much by his precepts as by the lives of men and women they see and know, who profess to be his disciples. This is as it should be. Jesus told the Twelve that this many-sided character which would develop under his care was not to be a cloistered virtue. They were men with a work to do. That work was the salvation of men and the glory of God. It would only be accomplished when they let their light shine that men, seeing their good works, would glorify their Father.

With these metaphors the course of the great discourse turned into the practical issue of how the disciples could translate the qualities Jesus demanded of them into terms of everyday living. The moral and spiritual standard of life was set out in the Law. The Twelve and perhaps even more particularly the multitudes who surrounded him, thought, not without some excuse, that Jesus spoke with an authority which set aside the law. His attitude to the observance of the Sabbath and the rituals of fasting and purifying gave them some ground for doubt. But Jesus now reassured them in the clearest terms. "Think not that I am come to destroy the law and the prophets. I am not come to destroy but to fulfil." He went on to establish for all time the necessity for obedience, even to the smallest detail, of the law of God. Failure to realize this will be reflected not in the expulsion of the disciple from the Kingdom, but in his position there. Yet there was a far greater mistake than failing to keep the law, and that lay in misinterpreting the very nature of righteousness. The scribes and Pharisees were guilty of that even whilst they meticulously obeyed its injunctions. This would exclude them from the Kingdom. The righteousness of the scribes and Pharisees was the exact opposite of the character that emerged from the Beatitudes. It was a righteousness which was concerned solely with outward observance, completely disregarding the condition of the heart. The goodness Jesus portrayed was the response to the love of God which transformed heart and mind. From this condition good works flowed as an inevitable result.

With specific illustrations Jesus then showed his hearers the manner in which he came to fulfil the law. It was not in the sense that the Pharisees kept it by formal observance for their own glorification, but by discerning the spirit of the commandment and tracing it back from the circumference to the centre. The Law said, "Thou shalt not kill". But murder is the last stage of a long process which begins with anger, envy and hatred in the heart. It was there that Jesus attacked it. "But I say unto you that whosoever is angry with his brother without a cause shall be in danger of the judgment." It is easier to attack and defeat the germ of murder in the heart, than to allow it to mature there until it bursts out into violent words and at last festers into ugly intentions. Thus Jesus attacked the source while the law only protected men from the final outrage. The law condemned adultery, but adultery begins with a lascivious look. There it can be easily defeated in a short sharp battle. Any thought can be dismissed by a determined "not wanted". Jesus teaches us to win our warfare at that stage. It will be done by the one who displays the qualities of heart which he has described in the Beatitudes. No sacrifice is too great to ensure purity of heart and mind in the powerful antagonism of the lust of the flesh. Rather than approach the dangerous waters where the Law demands its penalty, it is better to pluck out the right eye or cut off the right hand. But these sacrifices will only be necessary where the first spark of passion is not immediately extinguished.

Jesus went on to speak of divorce. His words here are only a part of his teaching on a subject to be considered later. He gave as a further illustration of his fulfilment of the law, the question of oaths. The Jews held that their word was only binding when it was confirmed by an oath. Such an attitude served only to weaken men's sense of truth and stimulate irreverence. Once more Jesus did not contradict the law, but he went beyond it. As in divorce, so here, the Mosaic Law made a concession to human weakness. A man swore an oath to impress upon himself and others the solemnity of his undertaking. But to the disciple, revealing the qualities Jesus had described, it was not necessary. Yea and nay were completely binding. There are no gradations of truth, no compromises, no subtleties. Nothing that will weaken the foundations of trust and confidence and lower the estimate of truth must be tolerated. Truth and reverence are the two things which become suspect by the emphasis imposed by an oath. They are the very things upon which discipleship is based. Jesus came into the world to bear witness to the truth of His Father's word. His disciples' calling is based upon that truth, and the fear of God which is the beginning of true wisdom.

Finally Jesus comes to the most powerful, the most practical and the most difficult and exacting illustration of the deeper fulfilment of the Mosaic Law. It concerned disciples' attitude to those who wronged them. No better illustration of the contrast between the law of Christ and the law of the world can be found than in this teaching of Jesus that the responsibility for reconciliation rests upon the one who is wronged rather than upon the offender. There would be occasions when they would be confronted by men who physically assaulted them, who sought to deprive them of their goods, who abused their authority by making unjust compulsions. The Law said that retribution should be exacted, based upon the nature of the offence. Such a system of justice has found its place in greater or less degree in every civilized country. It has undoubtedly made a substantial contribution to moral and social standards wherever it has been enforced. But this was not enough for the discipline of Jesus. His Father was not moved by considerations of justice when He sent His Son into the world. "God so loved the world that he gave his only begotten Son." The sacrifice that the Son was to make in a few short months bore no relation to justice. As his hour approached he was to confide to these men, "Greater love hath no man than this, that a man lay down his life for his friends". The supreme gesture of the Father and the Son was revealed in the love that they manifested. Thus as an inevitable condition, the true vocation of the disciple of Jesus was to be revealed in the love which they manifested in their relations with men. Every day would bring them opportunities of doing this. They would be exposed to the malice of men. Because of their allegiance they would be persecuted for righteousness' sake. They were to prove their discipleship not by refraining from retaliation; not by demanding retribution, however just, but by showing the same spirit as their Heavenly Father and His Beloved Son. This did not mean that if a man struck them on the cheek they were meekly to resign themselves to their fate. Indeed they were to accept the challenge and fight back. But the fight was to be transferred to the higher battlefield of love. They were to turn the other cheek, to give the cloak also, to walk the second mile. That is action, but it is the action of love, in which the disciple wrests the initiative from the offender and fights him with weapons he cannot understand or resist. Jesus had already shown the Twelve, and he was to show them most clearly of all in his death, that it is only in this way that right triumphs over evil. Wrong has no answer to the assault of love. Justice may check it by fear, but love conquers it. A wrongdoer understands retaliation. He is prepared to accept the penalties which justice demands. But confronted by the offensive of love he is either baffled and beaten, or he responds and is transformed.

The redemption of the world has its foundation laid upon this divine principle. It was only by learning it as they heard it unfolded by their Master in his revelation of the Father, and as they watched it unfolded in his own daily relations with man, that they could begin to respond to the exhortation which was the climax of his whole discourse, "Be ye therefore perfect, even as your Father who is in Heaven is perfect".

12

THE LAW OF LOVE *(Continued)*

THE disciples were continually surrounded by those who regarded themselves or were regarded as the true patterns of religious life. Jesus had told them that unless their righteousness exceeded that of these Pharisees there could be no place for them in the Kingdom of Heaven. Now he proceeds to enlarge on that. He contrasts true and false worship in its three phases; in relation to man, God, and self. He begins by removing the veneer from the religious exercises of the Pharisees and exposing their real motive. "Take heed that ye do not your righteousness before men to be seen of them." Theirs was a religious life born and sustained in self-interest. It gives alms, prays and fasts, not as spontaneous expressions of devotion to God, but because they are the price it is necessary to pay for the good opinion of men. They pay the price. They receive the reward. The transaction is over. How different are the spiritual devotions of the true child of God. Jesus was revealing to them the great love of God towards them, a love that could only be satisfied by a responsive love, expressed in worship and adoration to Him, in good works to men, and in careful discipline of self. Such was God's claim upon them, and such was the only true motive for the performance of religious duties. Sincerity could therefore be the only test by which these devotions could be judged. There was a great need for the giving of alms. The act may be expanded to represent all the material benefits which they could offer to their fellows. But because of the source from which the action springs the left hand will not know what the right hand gives. The gift will not be made openly to be seen of men, nor will it be done self-consciously to be seen of himself. The admiration of men and the satisfaction of self are twin dangers which will only be avoided if service is a humble response to the Father's love.

There could have been no display of hypocrisy more revolting to Jesus than the sight of the Pharisees standing in the prominent places of the city in ostentatious piety at the times of prayer. They loved to be seen of men. They had their reward. The true place of prayer was in secret when the door was shut and the soul was alone with God. Already Jesus had taught his disciples this by example rather than by precept. It would be impossible for them to remain unaware for long of his relationship with his Father. They saw an awareness of God and a dependence upon Him which had not been seen since the days of David. They saw an even fuller interpreter of the heart-cry of the Psalmist, "As the hart panteth after the water brooks, so panteth my soul after thee, O God. My soul thirsteth for God, for the living God". They had seen Jesus return to them from his sleepless night on the distant hills, his step firm, his face aglow, a new glad light in his eyes, eager to face the arduous tasks of another day. No precept could impress them more than an example like that. But he told them that such lonely communion was to be the nature of their prayer. He gave them a pattern which disciples ever since have treasured as "The Lord's Prayer". It obeyed the injunctions of its author in its simplicity. It focussed attention first upon God and His purpose, and then turned to the suppliants' needs, limiting its request for temporal things to immediate necessities; concentrating more upon the needs of the heart—forgiveness and the breadth of spirit to forgive, an appeal for deliverance from temptation, and a final ascription of eternal power and glory to God.

The prayer has been called "The Alphabet of Prayer". According to our needs and circumstances each of its sentences can be enlarged and developed. What vivid pictures are stirred into life by the brief petition "Thy Kingdom come"! What heart searchings! What earnest longings! What a challenge may be evoked by those simple words, "As we forgive"! This prayer can be translated and enlarged into the terms of every disciple's life. It can lose its formality and become intensely personal. Yet if our spirit is right and our desire great, by repetition of its simple words we can keep close to God in those barren days when we "wist not what to say".

The course of the great discourse turned at this point, and Jesus went on to discuss with his disciples something that was implicit in all that he had already said. He spoke of the difference in motive and outlook, and therefore in values, between the disciples as children of the Kingdom, and the children of the world. They had already seen from his opening words that their blessedness bore no relation to the earthly possessions upon which the natural man places such store. Their continued state of blessedness depended upon keeping unwaveringly to the standard of values which had prompted them to forsake all and follow Christ. In doing that they had shown where their treasure was, and therefore where their heart was. The ungodly piety of the hypocrites had its reward. It was immediate and final because it was of the earth, and like all earthly treasures, subject to moth, rust and extinction. As long as the disciples kept their perspective their whole being would be pervaded with light. If it was forsaken the whole spiritual vision would not merely be clouded, it would be lost. It was not only unwise but impossible to serve two masters. There could not be two controlling influences in the heart. To set the affections on the world was to give up the Kingdom. "Ye *cannot* serve God and mammon."

But in turning away from the world and avoiding the lust for its riches and rewards the disciples were exposed to a lesser danger, the danger of anxiety. Of this Jesus now spoke; not in the severe terms in which he spoke of divided loyalty, but in appealing words of exhortation. He reminded them that they will not be destitute because they are not spending their lives seeking means of sustenance and comfort. The loving Father who had already provided them with a body with all its wonderful faculties, a life instinct with great possibilities, was both able and willing to maintain it. They had only to look about them to see not only God's creative power but also His protective care. The birds banking and wheeling in the bright sunlight above their heads, the unconscious beauty of the anemones nestling among the grasses at their feet, were joyous witnesses of the provident care of their Creator. How much greater would be the love and provision He would extend to the highest work of His hands, especially those whose lives were dedicated to Him, and whose one great object was to give Him pleasure. There was every incentive for trust and none for doubt. The great object of the disciples' vocation remained. Unmoved by the false glitter of the world's rewards, unhampered by anxieties concerning their daily needs, they were to lay up treasure in Heaven, to serve God alone, and to seek first His Kingdom and His righteousness.

"Sufficient unto the day is the evil thereof." But there is evil in every day which no disciple can avoid and each must fight. How is he to fight it? In language of great severity Jesus told his disciples that it is a battle that begins with themselves. It is tragically easy for us to see the evils around us. We find little difficulty in discovering the faults of others. Jesus warns the disciples that the faculties that are so acute in perceiving another's weakness must first be used unsparingly upon themselves. There can be no more powerful discouragement to the tendency to pass judgment than the realization that "with what judgment ye judge, ye shall be judged; and with what measure ye mete, it shall be measured to you again". Even deep devotion and dedication to God has its own subtle temptations. Jesus warned his disciples against censoriousness by drawing the vivid picture of a man all but blinded by an obstruction in his eye absorbed in the task of removing the veriest splinter from his brother's eye. It was an illustration which would probably provoke a smile, but one which they would never forget. It is a timely reminder to disciples of each successive generation of one of the most insidious and prevalent dangers. It is also an exhortation to reserve their condemnation for themselves and their love for their brethren.

But whilst Jesus gave his disciples this graphic warning against seeking out and judging evil in others, he also showed them the error of going to the opposite extreme and ignoring the existence of evil altogether. "Give not that which is holy unto the dogs, neither cast ye your pearls before swine, lest they trample them under their feet, and turn again and rend you." The disciple has to pursue the true course which lies between the evil of judging and the evil of squandering his blessings. It is possible to expose the holy things of God to desecration. Whilst his great work, like that of his Master, is to preach the Gospel by word and example, it is possible to do this work not only unprofitably but injuriously. The secrets of God's grace and the confession of deep spiritual experiences can be recklessly divulged bringing shame upon the Word and needless persecution upon the unwise disciple. "A wise man's heart discerneth both time and judgment", and to decide when to speak and when to forbear must be one of many responsibilities which are the accompaniment of divine privilege.

The immature disciples may well have felt despondent about such exacting requirements and subtle pitfalls. Their Lord brings them fresh courage with his renewed assurance of divine help and guidance. "Ask and it shall be given you, seek and ye shall find; knock and it shall be opened unto you." There is a sense of progressive intimacy in this threefold encouragement and promise. Jesus reintroduces the subject of prayer, but not now as a religious duty exercised with a sincerity which contrasts with the hypocrisy of the Pharisees, but as a power in the life of the disciple which will enable him to make true decisions, avoid the many evils which beset him, and keep his feet on the path of love and service, which will lead him at last to the Kingdom of God. Accepting this privilege which will keep their hearts right with their Maker, Jesus showed that it would enable them to keep their hearts right with their neighbour also. "Therefore all things whatsoever ye would that men should do to you, do ye even so to them: for this is the law and the prophets." It was the complete vindication of his teaching that he had come not to destroy but to fulfil. His words are the positive attitude of love which he demanded of himself and required of his disciples.

On this high note the Master completed his description of the principles of the Kingdom he had come to proclaim. He had shown the Twelve the blessings which were associated with it both in this life and also in that which is to come. He had not hesitated to set forth the price it demanded of them in self-control, self-humbling and self-sacrifice. For this very reason the great mass of humanity would find it unattractive and prefer selfish pleasures and temporary rewards. Only the few would tread the narrow path of life. But they were among those few and to them his invitation went forth, an invitation as stirring and challenging as the "Follow me" which had preceded it. "Enter ye in at the strait gate." In drawing the comparison between the two ways the emphasis remained where it had been right through the discourse, not upon the destruction of the one and the life of the other, but upon the price it demanded of them. He appealed thus to all that was noble and good in them.

Jesus warned the Twelve against the false prophets who would arise in their midst, disguising their deceit in specious pretentions. Their efforts will fail and their identity be discovered if they are recognized by their fruits. Truth in the heart brings forth good fruit in the life. But the test by which the credentials of the prophet are proved is also the test which will be applied to the disciple in the day of account. There will be many professions of allegiance at the Judgment Seat, many eager recitals of works accomplished. But he will know by their fruit those who have responded to his precepts of love and thus done the Father's will. They alone shall enter the Kingdom of Heaven.

Finally the great discourse draws to its close on an awe-inspiring note. There will be a junction even on the narrow road. It is one thing to hear, understand and assent to the will of God as set forth in the revelation of His Son: it is another to translate that assent into terms of everyday living. The man who hears and obeys has hard work before him. He digs deep into solid rock. With painful slowness and many setbacks the building is erected on the foundation. But it stands firm against assaults from without and strains from within. The man who hears but obeys not, ignores the first essential of building, he does not bother about the foundations. He builds upon loose sand. However beautiful and imposing the structure may look, it shudders and falls under the impact of the first storm.

This impressive parable with which Jesus brings to a close his charter of the Kingdom of God is a solemn challenge to every disciple of every age. We are so familiar with this great sermon on the Mount. We have known and loved its passages from childhood. Our very intimacy with it demands an answer which will determine our position in the day when the Law Giver and the Mediator assumes the role of Judge. Are we doers of the Word?

13

THE LORD OF LIFE

JESUS returned from the mountain and entered Capernaum surrounded by apostles whose minds must have been much occupied by the things they had heard. The multitudes that had listened to him, accepting him as a scribe, marvelled that he spoke with authority. Immediately it was known that he was back in the city he was once more the centre of importunate crowds pressing their needs upon him.

Quartered at Capernaum at that time was a remarkable Roman officer. He was a Centurion in charge of foreign troops in the town, but unlike the great majority of Romans he had come to respect the Jews, their God and their laws. Although it is evident that he had not gone so far as to become a proselyte he had built the Jewish synagogue. But the Centurion had a greater commendation. He possessed unbounded faith in Jesus. He showed a care for his slave which was almost unique in a man of his standing. There was a humility about him which came strangely from a responsible Roman.

There can be no doubt that he knew a great deal about Jesus. His behaviour suggests acquaintance with the nobleman of Herod's court who had hurried to Cana a few weeks before when his son was at the point of death. He had probably heard how Jesus had spoken the word which had restored his son twenty-five miles away. Thus it was that when he heard that Jesus was back in the city the Centurion sought aid on behalf of his sick servant. In his humility he would not go to Jesus himself but asked the rulers of the Jews to make the appeal on his behalf. It may be that some members of the deputation acceded to the request reluctantly, but their indebtedness to their benefactor prevented refusal. Their approach did not reflect the humility which the Centurion would have desired. Instead of laying stress upon the Roman's need and faith they emphasized his worthiness and his generosity. They "besought him instantly that he was worthy for whom he should do this: for he loveth our nation and hath built us a synagogue". But Jesus recognized the faith and the humility behind the request, as he recognized the quality of a Centurion who would concern himself so deeply over the health of a slave. He went with them towards the Roman's residence. Before the company could arrive the Centurion once more intervened. He sent out his friends to Jesus with the message that it was not fit that Jesus should defile himself by entering his home, nor did he consider himself worthy to come out and speak with him. He expressed his belief that all that would be necessary for the healing of his servant could be accomplished by a word. He went on to give the grounds for his faith, interpreting the power of Jesus in terms of his authority as a soldier. He believed Jesus under the authority of God could command sickness by a word just as he himself could command his servants in the name of Caesar.

There are only two instances in the Gospels where it is recorded that Jesus marvelled. He marvelled at the unbelief of his fellow townspeople at Nazareth. He marvelled at the belief of this Roman soldier.

Jesus faced the deputation of the Jews. Consciousness of their divine favour contrasted strangely with the humility of this Gentile. Their unbelief presented an even more forceful enigma in the light of his profound and reasoned faith. They were of all people the children of faith. They were the natural offspring of faithful Abraham. God had sent His Son into their midst seeking a faithful response to his words of life, words which had been given the testimony of miraculous works. But that response was not to be found in Israel. It was found at this moment in the heart of a Roman Centurion. Jesus turned to the men who, in introducing the needs of the heathen, had so smugly referred to "our nation". He assumed the role of a prophet. "I say unto you that many shall come from the east and west and shall sit down with Abraham, Isaac and Jacob in the kingdom of heaven. But the children of the kingdom shall be cast out into outer darkness: there shall be weeping and gnashing of teeth." These words were the confirmation of the promise of God to Abraham and of the testimony of the prophets. Yet there can be no doubt that the rulers of the synagogue could have received no ruder shock to their cherished beliefs than they did outside the Centurion's house that day. They had unwittingly set the scene for a demonstration which was a complete inversion of a hitherto unquestioned picture. They had a very clear conception of their favoured position not only now, but in the end of the world. That they should forfeit their ancient and natural prerogative was unthinkable. That they should be cast into outer darkness in anger and sorrow whilst heathens from all over the earth enjoyed the privileges they had lost, was altogether beyond their comprehension. But that Jesus had present and undeniable evidence of a faith that put their unbelief to shame they could not deny. His pronouncement would do nothing to heal the breach that had already appeared in his relations with them. Although they had no answer now, it would not be long before they showed their hand. Meanwhile the word of power had gone forth. The Centurion's servant had been restored according to his faith. In spite of superficial appearances in Matthew's account it is conclusive that the soldier had no personal contact with Jesus. With that wonderful reverence for human personality which shines forth in so many of his contacts, the Lord respected the man's sincere humility; showing him by his absence how truly he had understood his heavenly mission, he paid silent tribute to his robust faith.

These were busy days in Capernaum. Jesus had little time to do anything but attend to the ceaseless needs of the multitudes. So great was his concentration upon this ministry and so much did he neglect himself, that several of his friends sought forcibly to restrain him, fearing he would become completely exhausted. When Mark says, "For they said, He is beside himself", his words did not mean as much as they imply: they suggest an acute apprehension that his mind and body would be unable to stand much more strain. Their concern was a tribute to their regard for him, but it also showed a lack of understanding of the dynamic and all pervading purpose of their Lord, and of the unfailing source from which his strength was renewed.

Shortly after the healing of the Centurion's servant Jesus left Capernaum to begin another circuit of the surrounding towns and villages. Accompanied by the Twelve and followed by many people he went south-westwards over the Galilean hills towards the Plain of Esdraelon. It was springtime. The fresh green of the awakening countryside would bring happiness and a sense of well-being to many of the people as they followed. The disciples too would probably feel a new sense of eagerness as they left the familiar streets of their own city to begin their first campaign as the Twelve whom the Master had chosen to be his apostles.

It would be evening before they had covered the twentyfive miles which brought them within sight of the town of Nain.

It soon became apparent that there was no little stir in the place. A crowd was streaming out of the city gate, and the echoes that came faintly up to them lingering among the hills, proclaimed a time of mourning. A funeral procession was making its way towards the burial ground on the road to Endor. It was not long before the two multitudes met and mingled, the crowds who followed the Prince of Life and those that accompanied the victim of Death. It was a great and solemn moment when Jesus reached the bier and looked down at the dead face of the young man; an inevitable moment. He turned to behold the agonized features of the widowed mother, who heedless of the interruption, continued her bitter wailing. Jesus would see far more than her present anguish. He would see the sad change from wife to widow in the humble home: her love for a son who took his father's place: her increasing dependence upon his industry and strength. He would know that nothing now remained but sorrow, and poverty and loneliness. Such insight would stir to emotion the most callous man. Looked upon by one who knew the human heart so well it could not fail to move his spirit and evoke his compassion.

"Weep not!" Words! Empty words! What comfort could they give? Could they restore to her the life of the son she had brought to birth only to mourn at his grave? Could they sweep away the load of grief that bowed her body? Could they remove the years that stretched away before her? Ah! dear, lonely stricken soul, they can do all these things. The Lord of Life is standing at your side. There is authority mingled with the love in his words. Reluctantly she lifted her tear-stained face. Her eyes sought and found the face of Jesus. In a moment she realized the words were no longer words. Before he stepped forward and touched the wickerwork that held her son she knew. "Young man, I say unto thee, Arise."

And in the evening light before the hushed multitudes, the young man sat up and spoke. And Luke records with simple significance, "He gave him to his mother".

So it was that among the hills of Galilee overlooking the plain that has been and is yet to be so typical of man's conflict and death, the apostles learned the highest ministry of their Lord. Multitudes would continue to stream forth from the city gate bearing their dead. But the Redeemer had come to say to those that mourned, "Weep not", and to follow his words of love with power so great that death itself could not prevail against it.

A wave of awe swept the people. God was glorified: His prophet was acknowledged and his fame spread abroad. The great tragedy is that the beneficent effect faded with the passing years, and the Lord of Life was to take a lonely road to his garden grave. The tragedy continues despite the final triumph of the empty tomb. The multitudes pass by unheeding, or pause to watch and wonder and forget. Only the disciples remain. But to them he gives power to become the sons of God. Though death may step in to rob them of their promise now, he who is alive for evermore and has the keys of the grave and of death, will one day stand at the graveside to crown their mortal strivings with eternal blessings.

14

A MESSAGE FROM PRISON

IT was whilst he was preaching in the vicinity of Nain that
John the Baptist, languishing in the fortress prison above
the Dead Sea, sent two of his disciples to Jesus to ask the
unexpected question, "Art thou he who should come, or look
we for another?"

Much has been said and written concerning what many
consider to be an evidence of the Baptist's faltering faith.
Allowances are made; mitigating circumstances are urged;
the privations of prison life have been emphasized. It has
been suggested that the reports that Jesus had been feasting
with publicans and sinners and refusing to allow his disciples
to fast, had created a germ of doubt which developed rapidly
in the loneliness of the prison cell. It has been said that
John's question did not betray more than a need for assurance
in view of the failure of the Messiah to manifest his power in
establishing the Kingdom.

But is there any evidence that John doubted at all?
Certainly it would have been a reversal of all that we know
of his character. The privations of prison can hardly be urged
against a man who from his earliest days had known nothing
but the hardships of the wilderness. The effects of loneliness
cannot be deplored when they refer to one who had spent
years of lonely meditation far from the haunts of men, waiting
for the day when his active work would begin. Moreover the
reluctance of Herod Antipas to have him beheaded and the
facilities he was allowed for converse with his disciples,
suggest that John may have had some relief from the solitary
confinement to which he was committed.

Whilst we may say that, knowing human nature, this was
yet possible, we also have to face the fact that John's doubt
would have been a betrayal of his divine calling. He had been
given the Holy Spirit from his birth; his whole mission was
guided by God's power. It was thus that he had departed into
the deserts. It was thus that he knew when the time had
come for him to lift up his voice and call the multitudes to

him. Above all, it was in this way, by his own acknowledgment, that he recognized the Christ. By the power of the Holy Spirit he knew that his work would only be successfully accomplished when his influence waned before the greater light of the Messiah whose path he prepared.

And does not this last consideration give us the clue to the real meaning of that journey which two of John's disciples undertook? John no longer needed or desired disciples. His work was finished. Any who clung to him in spite of his protestations were an embarrassment to him. Yet there were those who did cling. They remained faithful to him even after he had been carried away to the confinement of Machaerus. They had no intention of leaving him to join the disciples of Jesus. There is evidence that the Pharisees had seized the opportunity of antagonizing some of them against Jesus. Doubtless John had finally persuaded most of his followers to leave him and go to Jesus. But some were stubborn to the end and would not be persuaded that Jesus was the Christ. Is it not possible that John, realizing the temper of these two men, decided to allow Jesus to convince them himself by his works? Alone they would never have gone to him, but armed with a commission they went obediently enough. John, obeying the Lord's precept to be "as wise as serpents and as harmless as doves", had probably sent them to examine the claims of Jesus and come within his influence, knowing that Jesus would understand his motive and convince them.

That Jesus responded is evident from Luke's account. "And in that same hour he cured many of their infirmities and plagues, and of evil spirits; and unto many that were blind he gave sight." Then Jesus sent the two back to John with a parting message meant, not for the prisoner, but for them! "And blessed is he, whosoever shall not be offended in me". We can imagine two very thoughtful disciples making their long journey south-eastwards. And when finally they arrived and recounted to John all that Jesus had done, can we not hear the voice of the austere prophet, still strong and resolute. "Now will ye not believe him?" If indeed he ever saw them again, for the end was at hand. But we may hope that they were among the many blind whom Jesus healed. Thus we may believe that the greatest prophet went to his death not saddened by doubts which could only detract from his greatness, but with a last faithful effort to fulfil his vocation of directing men to the Messiah.

143

When the messengers had left, Jesus turned to the multitudes and spoke about John. It is immediately evident that his words were not about one who was offended in him but one who believed through persecution, imprisonment and death. "What went ye out into the wilderness for to see? A reed shaken with the wind?" No! John had not been shaken by the wind of persecution. Did you expect to see a man clothed in soft raiment? He had every right to it. He could have lived delicately. No! They went out to see a prophet. But he was much more than a prophet. The function of the prophet was to announce God's purpose. John had been raised up to introduce God's Son. No greater work could have been assigned to mortal man. No greater man had been born of woman. But the work of the Son was to prepare the world for the Kingdom of God, and great as John was, the humblest place in the Kingdom would represent something greater than anything John could see or know in his mortal life. With wonderful humility Jesus beckons John to his side as one like him, who through the ages that had passed was destined to come, and like him was to suffer rejection. The Kingdom of Heaven, symbolized alike in the precursor and the Messiah, was to suffer violence. Both were to be taken by force. The publicans had responded to God's counsel by believing John's message and submitting to his baptism. The Pharisees and the lawyers by refusing to accept the teaching and the baptism of the prophet had rejected God. But in that very act they had condemned themselves. Jesus turned upon them now. How shall I describe you? 'You are like wilful, peevish children who have come out into the market place to play. When your friends prepare to dance you refuse, and when they try to accommodate you by playing at funerals you are just as sulky and stubborn. Your whole life professes to be a dedication to God. But when He sends His ascetic wilderness prophet you say, "He hath a devil"; and when the Son himself appears in humble fellowship with men your verdict is, "Behold a man gluttonous and a winebibber, a friend of publicans and sinners"'.

The religious leaders had brought condemnation not only upon themselves but also upon those they led. Out of sympathy with the prophets of God, satisfied only with themselves, they had tainted their generation with their conceits. But the sombreness of the picture is not unrelieved. A study of God's ways teaches us always to look keenly upon the little point of light which glimmers in the darkness. At last God's light will flood the world. Around him were the Twelve, men who knew the temper of the sea and the changing moods of the sky, but who lacked careful tuition in the gentle art of intrigue and the polemics of domination. To them the Saviour had not come in vain. Their comprehension of his words was delayed, like the gradual summer dawn creeping over the slopes of the lakeside hills, but he spoke a language they understood, and they responded.

They had recognized the wisdom of God in the austerity of John, and they were growing to learn it in all its wonders in the companionship of the one who condescended to the table of publicans and sinners. The impressive sophistries, the rapier thrusts, the sparkling wit of the wise of that generation has long since passed into the limbo of forgotten things. The staunch loyalty of the fishermen, swept on under the impulse of the swiftly moving drama to unshakable conviction, glows today drawing men through severe strains, and heart-searching, from darkness into its eternal light.

15

SIMON THE PHARISEE

STILL journeying through Galilee in the company of his disciples and followed by thronging multitudes, Jesus received an invitation to dine at a Pharisee's house. Simon (not to be confused with the leper at Bethany many miles to the south) had his reasons for inviting Jesus. His cool reception of his guest suggests curiosity rather than homage. But although he knew both the motive and the heart which inspired it, the one who ate with publicans and sinners was equally willing to accept the hospitality of those whom men esteemed greater. His message of salvation was offered to all. It was man's individual response, not his social state, that determined whether he should enter the Kingdom. Only the complete inability of the majority of the rich and the self-righteous to realize their poverty and pride had finally driven Christ into the company of those who recognized their need.

The meal was interrupted by what must have been an unprecedented outrage to the astounded Simon. A shadow flitted across the threshold as a woman came swiftly into the room, approached the reclining Jesus from behind, and fell at his feet in an abandonment of grief. Pitifully she wept. The hot tears coursed down her pale, suffering face and dropped on his unburdened feet. She wiped them away with her abundant hair, covering his feet with kisses.

We have no record of the events which led this harlot into the Pharisee's house. It would have been no surprise to see her prostrate herself before him in the streets of the city, or even in the houses of the publicans. But that she should thus invade the privacy of the austere Pharisee whom she had so much reason to fear seems to demand our attention. It is obvious that she was moved by an overpowering sense of urgency. She must see Jesus now, wherever he was. That her enquiries led her to the Pharisee's house mattered not at all. What lay behind that urgency, those hot tears, those passionate kisses? Had not the Lamb of Cod entered into the Kingdom of sin and won an overwhelming victory? It may have been that for idle or evil reasons she had mingled with the crowd that pressed about Jesus. She had probably watched as one poor victim of disease after another was transformed into radiant health under the loving touch. He had spoken of the beautiful things of life and God's way of holiness, until she had burned with shame. Perhaps he had raised his head and looked into her eyes. She would defy him for a time, all the barriers up to protect her sin from his penetrating gaze. But not for long. Soon, like her mother Eve, she would be conscious only of her nakedness and her desire to hide. Jesus had gone his way. The multitudes had dispersed. The woman had tried to forget. But she knew she never would. His love had begun a fire in her soul that no rebellious tears could quench. It went on, burning away her sin. But when the fire had consumed all the sin, the degradation and the shame, something sparkled in the blackened ruin: something too small for her heart to recognize. But it grew apace. It demanded recognition. It roused her from her prostration and drove her to Jesus. It was only when she kissed the feet that were damp with her tears that she knew it was love, love too great to define. With her tears and her hair and her hands she was able to give it expression and ease her heart of something too big to carry far.

But what could Simon know of all this? He could only see the external and translate it in terms of the convention. O, Simon, blind pathetic Simon, Simon of every age: can you not see that you must do more than invite the Saviour into your house? He must be welcomed into your heart. It will only be when you have felt the pain of the blows and the scorchings of the fires which his coming brings that you will understand the grief of that woman lying at his feet. Then, and only then, you will see the wonder of the love which has elevated her. Then you will see why, whilst you were conspiring the death of the Saviour of the world, a woman stood in the garden at the dawn of day, filled with a love stronger than death.

Recovering from his shocked surprise Simon suddenly saw in the situation an answer to his doubts concerning Christ. If he were indeed the Messiah he would recognize at once the identity of this woman and would drive her away. That he failed to do so was convincing evidence of the falsity of his claims. How wrong Simon was! Little did he suspect that Jesus not only knew all about the woman, but knew also the intimate thoughts which were even now passing through his mind. Simon had a lesson to learn. If he received it his pride would be badly shaken, he would have rents torn in his cloak of righteousness, yet he would be able to begin a new life which would put to shame the arrogant smugness of his false piety.

"Simon, I have something to say to thee."

"Master", he said, "speak."

"There was a certain creditor which had two debtors: the one owed five hundred pence the other fifty. When they had nothing to pay he frankly forgave them both. Which of them will love him most?" Simon replied, "He, I suppose, to whom he forgave most." "Thou hast rightly judged." Then turning for the first time to the woman, he brought home the lesson to Simon, "Simon, seest thou this woman? I entered into thine house, thou gavest me no water for my feet: but she hath washed my feet with tears, and wiped them with the hairs of her head. Thou gavest me no kiss, but this woman since the time I came in hath not ceased to kiss my feet. My head with oil thou didst not anoint, but this woman hath anointed my feet with ointment. Wherefore I say unto thee, her sins, which are many, are forgiven: for she loved much: but to whom little is forgiven, the same loveth little". Then, addressing the woman he said, "Thy sins are forgiven. Thy faith hath saved thee: go in peace".

In using his illustration Jesus had also used Simon's estimate of the relative need of forgiveness between himself and the woman. He did not necessarily endorse it. Indeed some of his subsequent parables show that it was at least possible that in his sight it was the woman who owed the fifty pence and Simon who owed the five hundred. Because the woman knew the depravity of her sin and had felt the grace of forgiveness she had loved deeply. It was because Simon thought he had so little to forgive that he loved little. It is only when we take off the outer garments of hypocrisy and contemplate the majesty of God, and His attributes shining forth in the character of Jesus, that we begin to form a true estimate of our indebtedness. It is only then that the fifty pence will change to five hundred, and the lip service will be transformed into a deep devotion which leads us with tear-filled hearts to the shadow of the Cross.

Thus we have this moving account of the first sin-burdened penitent laying her load at the feet of Jesus, and going away with peace in her heart and love surging through her whole being. She was the first of a multitude whose con-

"… some (seed) fell on stony ground, where it had not much earth …"
(Mark 4:5)

"Jesus therefore walked no more openly among the Jews; but went
thence unto a country near to the wilderness …" (John 11:54)

"… he withdrew himself into the wilderness, and prayed." (Luke 5:16)

science has been stirred and whose eyes have been opened by the purity and love of the noble figure who trod the hills of Galilee as the Messenger of the Covenant. In remorse and gratitude they have sought him out, and, oblivious of the supercilious glances of their fellows, they have demonstrated their affection. By some strange alchemy their load of sin and care has mingled with the tears and with the ointment, and they have gone on their way in peace and joy, desiring only fresh opportunities to manifest their new-found love.

16

THE WOMEN WHO FOLLOWED

IT is possible but by no means certain that the penitent woman with flowing hair was none other than Mary Magdalene. We do know that when Jesus continued his journey after this incident in Simon's house we read that Mary Magdalene was with him ministering to his needs. It is also not without significance that she is described as the woman from whom Jesus cast seven devils. It is not profitable to linger too long on this identity, but if Mary of Magdala was indeed the woman who prostrated herself in the Pharisee's house, we can understand the sublime devotion with which she followed her Lord. Love possessed her more completely than the seven demons had ever done. Who can watch her without deep emotion as she clings to him by night and day, following with weary but persistent steps as he strides out over tough mountain and rocky valley. When the inevitable storm breaks over him and the thunder rolls across the sky we see her horrified face illuminated for an instant in the lightning flash. And she is clinging more closely still. At last she can follow him no further. She stands near the foot of the Cross, her haggard eyes still seeking her dying Lord. Even his death could not separate her from him. With unfailing loyalty she followed behind those who carried him to his tomb. While bewildered disciples mourned their weakness she watched where he was laid. On the first day of the week she faced an empty grave. Her cry of despair tugs at every heart string. "They have taken away my Lord, and I know not where they have laid him." But when she thought he was furthest away he was nearest to her, and at last she learned the greatest lesson of her life. He taught her that although her physical eyes may not behold him, although her clasping fingers could not touch him, although she might not hear the rich accents she loved so well, he was with her always, to the end of the world—and beyond.

Great as was the work of Jesus in easing men's physical load, healing their sickness, restoring their sight, the life of Mary Magdalene shows that it was not so great as his unseen work in the heart of man. No miracle can be more wonderful to the discerning mind than the picture of the woman lost in the lowest degradation of sin transformed into a saint glowing with a love too deep to express. It is both a comfort and an incentive to realize that while the hand of the Redeemer is no longer lifted in gentle ministration to take away our physical infirmities, his greater work goes on. No abyss of sin and despair is too deep or too dark for him to reach; no heart too cold to warm into devoted love and service.

There were many other women who followed him in Galilee, ministering to him of their substance. Susanna is mentioned by name. There was also Joanna, the wife of Chuza, Herod's steward. This woman may have been the wife of the Capernaum court official whose son Jesus had healed by a word spoken at Cana. If that is so it was a beautiful way of showing her gratitude, and one which must commend itself to her sisters for all time. Although their Lord is no longer in their midst it is still possible for them to follow him, and minister to him of their substance in conscious response to his blessings. He is yet to show the lovely significance of a cup of cold water and the precious secret of his identity hidden in the lonely, the suffering and the needy. It is a blessed truth that the Master still makes it possible for devoted women to follow him beside the gleaming lake and on the solitary road which leads to Jerusalem, inspiring all men by their loyalty and their love and leading many to his feet.

When Jesus reached Capernaum from his long journey through the cities and villages of Galilee, the people brought to him one possessed who was also blind and dumb. The afflicted man was restored, and those who witnessed the miracle were amazed and said, "Is not this the Son of David?" Such incidents happened daily at this period of Christ's ministry, but Mark adds a fact which is probably the reason for its prominence. He tells us that scribes who had come down from Jerusalem intervened to challenge Christ. It would seem that the popularity of Jesus was becoming so disturbing, particularly after the resurrection at Nain, that a deputation was sent quickly from Jerusalem to use its considerable power in an effort to check it.

These scribes lost no time in launching their campaign against him. Their attack was more subtle than may be at first apparent. They could not deny that Christ was performing miracles, but they could question the source of his power.

Miraculous powers and the ability to expel unclean spirits were commonly claimed among the Jews at that time, and such activities were countenanced by the scribes and Pharisees. Their point of attack was not therefore on whether Christ performed miracles but by what power he worked. "This fellow", said they, "doth not cast out devils but by Beelzebub the prince of the devils." How quickly and decisively Jesus confounded them! What paltry figures they made confronted by his truth and purity! If their allegation was true then the Kingdom of Beelzebub must be in considerable confusion. It was obviously doomed to fall in its state of civil war. How can it be otherwise if, in the name of Beelzebub, he is freeing men from the domination of Beelzebub? To add to their perplexity Jesus went further. Your disciples cast out devils too. In whose name do they cast them out? Obviously their power could not be from the same source or they would be bound in honour to believe in him. "Let them be your judges."

Having reduced their challenge to absurdity, with irresistible logic Jesus brought home to them the only alternative "But if I cast out devils by the Spirit of God, then the Kingdom of God is come unto you". He went even further. In coming to bring the Kingdom of God, Jesus had come to engage in mortal combat with the devil and his works. Sin in all its ramifications had to be stamped out. He would achieve it finally when his hour had come. His work with those who were afflicted with the terrible effects of sin was an earnest of that coming victory. He was entering into the strong man's house and spoiling his goods. To do that he needed the power of God to bind the strong man. He required also the faith of those he released. Otherwise his work for them could only fail. "He that is not with me is against me, and he that gathereth not with me scattereth abroad."

But Jesus had not yet finished with these men. He had shattered their attack. Now he turned from his own defence to denounce them. It was brief but it was terrible; every one of them must have gone cold with fear as he convicted them. Without answering him a word they went their way.

There is something far worse than a lack of faith which is, after all, only passive opposition to the working of the Spirit of God. Jesus was faced with an active, organized opposition which for selfish reasons sought to work on the side of the enemy Christ had come to destroy. It not only denied him the

Spirit of God but attributed his power to Satan. That was something which could never be forgiven. Blasphemy against the Son, evil as that was, could be repented of; but to speak against God by denouncing His Spirit as evil was to be guilty of eternal sin and to be for ever unpardoned. This dreadful indictment the scribes brought upon themselves, "because", says Mark, "they said, He hath an unclean spirit."

It was on this occasion that Christ's mother and brethren came to Capernaum and asked for him. His attitude to them suggests that their mission sought in some way to impede his ministry. Whether it was that Mary had heard of the concerted efforts which were being made against him and, moved by fear and affection, was anxious to persuade him against continuing his work, we do not know. But it seems certain from his apparent refusal to see her, that the maternal instinct was pressing strongly still, in spite of two rebukes which had already wounded her sensitive spirit. We find it hard to criticize a mother's protective and possessive instinct. The sword must pierce her soul once more. Jesus does not condemn his mother, but he is still about his Father's business. His whole life is dedicated to founding a spiritual relationship far exceeding the bounds of earthly ties. He can no longer acknowledge their authority; it is for them to acknowledge his. It is unhappily significant that they waited outside desiring him to come to them. It could never be so. They could go to him; he could never come to them. "Behold my mother and my brethren! For whosoever shall do the will of God, the same is my brother and my sister and mother."

17

TEACHING IN PARABLES

LEAVING the city with its scheming scribes, its crowds and its delicate demands of loyalty, Jesus moved away towards the seashore. Reading the thirteenth chapter of Matthew we can almost sense the freedom of spirit which liberated him as he reached the water's edge and met the fresh breezes fragrant with the scent of the summer and the tang of the sea. Stepping into a boat he would ask the disciples to push out a little from the shore so that he could command the vast audience which was assembling in the natural rising amphitheatre of the bay.

We like to picture the scene as Jesus began to teach. It was probably nearing mid-summer, the warm sun was bathing everything in its golden light; the blue sky, made deeper by the silvery spinnakers of cloud, threw its deepness on the breeze-stirred water. The waves collapsed on the shingle in short, flat crashes. Beyond the stirring multitudes the hills curved upwards to meet the overhanging sky, their slopes a radiant tapestry of flower and herb and rich brown earth. And when the crowds had settled and become expectantly silent Jesus opened his mouth to teach. His mind caught and held the spirit of the moment and he lent eternity to the distant wheatfield shining a premature gold in the sun, and to the humble activities which were visible from his gently swaying pulpit.

It is interesting to notice that from this time Jesus used parables with a new emphasis. The method was quite familiar to the Jews who were instructed by the rabbis in this way. But even cursory comparison shows that in this as in his direct approach, "he spoke with authority and not as the scribes". Apart from the fundamental difference of motive, what had the rabbis to offer which could compare with the pictures drawn by such a loving student of sea and sky, who watched successive seasons bring to birth changing colour, growth and song: who knew the ways of men in all the shadowed and sunlit paths of their human life: who wove into these things he knew and loved so well the heavenly truths

154

he had received from his Father? The parables which Jesus spoke have been well described as "the outlined shadows — large, perhaps, and dim — as the light of heavenly things falls on well-known scenes, which correspond to and have their counterpart, in spiritual realities".*

Difficulty may be experienced concerning the explanation which Jesus gave to his disciples regarding his use of parables. It is Mark who records Christ's answer in the most unequivocal words, "Unto you it is given to know the mystery of the Kingdom of God: but unto them that are without, all these things are done in parables; that seeing they may see, and not perceive; and hearing they may hear, and not understand: lest at any time they should be converted, and their sins should be forgiven them". These words have caused many to wonder whether Jesus used parables deliberately to conceal truth which could have saved his hearers. It is important to notice that this inability to see and understand is confined by the Lord to "them that are without". Nor must it be forgotten that but a brief hour ago Jesus had been in conflict with scribes from Jerusalem, whom he had condemned as being guilty of an unforgivable sin. Those scribes had growing numbers of their supporters in Galilee. The crowd which had assembled round the shore that day was sharply divided between those who were his disciples or were sympathetic hearers, and those who were his implacable enemies. His parables would have a very different effect on these two classes. Those who desired to be "scribes instructed in the Kingdom of Heaven" would receive them thoughtfully, and if they found anything too difficult they would seek him out with the request, "Declare unto us this parable". Thus they would gradually learn, in a way they could never forget, the mysteries of the Kingdom. But in the heart of his enemies there would be no such desire. Their careful attention was due to an anxiety to take hold of some word upon which they could condemn him. They saw and they heard, but their failure to perceive and understand was the result of their deliberate blindness and hardness of heart. Jesus seems to confirm this in his further word of explanation, "For whosoever hath, to him shall be given, and he shall have more abundance: but whosoever hath not, from him shall be taken away even that he hath".

It is outside our purpose to deal in detail with the parables which Jesus spoke on this occasion. But we cannot pass them

*EDERSHEIM, *Life and Times of Jesus, The Messiah* (Vol.1, page 582).

without noticing both their general import and the wonderful harmony which exists between them. Four of them were spoken from the boat, three were given to the disciples when Jesus had sent the people away and returned to his house.

All seven of the parables recorded in the thirteenth chapter of Matthew are parables of the Kingdom. They were a vindication of the words uttered to the scribes earlier that day, "If I cast out devils by the Spirit of God, then the kingdom of God is come unto you". They were also a justification of his welcome into intimate relationship of those who believed on him, in answer to the human claims of his mother and his brethren.

This series of parables has to do with the beginnings of the Kingdom of God under the limitations imposed by the present era of sin and mortality. Later on, as his ministry drew to its climax, his parables dealt with the full and final aspect of the Kingdom when the King shall return from his Father's side, demand the retribution of evil-doers, and bring blessings of faithfulness to those who have served him well.

It was impossible to convey clearly all the aspects even of the first stages of the Kingdom in one parable. In his wisdom Jesus told the story in a succession of pictures each supplementing the other. The first two long parables—the Sower, and the Wheat and the Tares, describe successively the birth and the progress of the preparation for the Kingdom of God. The two shorter ones—the Mustard Seed and the Leaven—show how the individual seed develops until the harvest.

In the parable of the Sower we see the husbandman throwing the seed over the whole field irrespective of its condition. That seed only grows strongly in places. It is not the fault of the Husbandman nor of the seed, but of the land that receives it. No seeds flourished on the hardened paths, the stony places, or amid the thorns. But in the deep, well ploughed ground it grew abundantly. The parable of the Wheat and the Tares takes up the story of the Kingdom. Jesus takes away from us the picture of the whole field and brings into focus the good soil where the seed is established. The seed is no longer the word, it has become the children of the kingdom. The world outside is ignored. We see only the Kingdom of God in its embryo form. Among the growing wheat all is not well. There are seeds growing strongly that have their origin not from the Sower but from the earth. They have sprung up threatening to check the vigour of the corn.

But the wise Husbandman allows this persecution and suffering. To remove the opposition would be to weaken the roots of the corn. The harvest is coming and then the purging will take place and the fully developed wheat will be gathered into barns.

These two parables do little to indicate the full extent and glory of the kingdom of God: indeed they rather emphasize the limited nature of the Sower's effort, and the struggle for the survival of the seed, even in the rich responsive soil. But in the Parable of the Mustard Seed which follows, Jesus shows that this small and difficult beginning will end in something which is infinitely greater. In the Parable of the Leaven he teaches that the little leaven, all but unnoticed in the three measures of meal, will eventually permeate the whole matter into which it was introduced. These two parables do not describe the gradual growth of the Kingdom either in the hearts of men or in the Church, but they form a perfect complement to the parables of the Sower and the Tares, for they show the end of the Lord. A Galilean carpenter surrounded by a few unlettered countrymen, first discredited and then ignominiously crucified by the leaders of his country, it is hard to imagine a smaller or less significant beginning, yet the final result will be seen in the day when every tongue shall confess that Jesus Christ is Lord, to the glory of God, the Father.

The three parables which Jesus spoke later in the house were intended only for those who symbolized the corn which was already beginning to sprout up in the good ground, the hearts which were even now changing under the beneficent influence of the Son of God. To them Jesus showed the transcendent value of the find they had made. It was like treasure found in a field, like a pearl of fabulous price, something which men would gladly surrender all they had to acquire. In the Parable of the Drag Net he warned them not to esteem their treasure lightly. When the Gospel net was full there would be a separation among the children of the Kingdom and only the righteous would survive the divine judgment.

So, within the scope of a few short parables, Jesus gave a complete picture of the impact of his coming and his Gospel both upon the world and upon the believer. The rejection of the former would lead to destruction, but the faithfulness of the latter would bring indescribable blessing in the day when the righteous shall "shine forth as the sun in the Kingdom of their Father".

18

THE STORM ON THE LAKE

THE long day was at last drawing to its close. Jesus must have been near the end of his physical resources. He had returned from the strain of an exacting tour through the cities and villages of Galilee to meet the impact of Capernaum with its crowds, its needs, its hostilities. The whole history of his ministry had been enacted in those few hours since the dawn. He had healed the blind and dumb demoniac, engaged in bitter controversy with the scribes from Jerusalem, taught the multitudes and privately instructed the disciples. Now, looking out across the Lake in the stillness that pervaded the air as the familiar beauty of day quickly darkened in the mantle of the night, Jesus must have felt an overwhelming desire for rest and seclusion. Matthew tells us that "seeing the great multitudes about him, he gave commandment to depart unto the other side". And Mark adds that the disciples "took him even as he was, in the ship". As is so often the case in the Gospels these short comments are full of meaning. They showed both the need of Jesus to leave the crowds and rest, and the suddenness of his decision to get away immediately.

The departure was delayed by a scribe who came to him full of enthusiasm, "Master, I will follow thee whithersoever thou goest". These were strange words on the lips of a scribe, but we have no reason to doubt their sincerity. He had probably listened with the multitudes on the seashore earlier in the day, and had not unnaturally been emotionally affected by both the words and the person of the Lord. In a moment of sudden resolution he had decided to throw everything overboard and join the band of disciples. Scribes were unusual converts to the cause of Christ. Emotion is a dangerous condition in which to make life-long decisions. Jesus put him to the test. Did he know the path the Master was treading? "The foxes have holes, the birds of the air have nests, but the Son of Man hath not where to lay his head." The urgent need for rest which Jesus felt as he said those poignant words would probably be hidden from the scribe by the self-control which

completely mastered his physical condition. But we can see
it, and feel the pathos the more. That was the road he trod.
The fox pursued by relentless enemies can find its secluded
hole deep in the ground where it can safely rest. The bird of
the air, dropping from the strain of its winged pilgrimage, can
come to rest on some leafy branch, but the Son of Man,
because he is the Son of Man, has not where to lay his head,
no place to call his home, no retreat from the urgent demands
of his mission. Within the hour that tired head will rest on
the steersman's cushion in the fishing boat, only to be disturbed again by the disciples' need and the surging tumult. It
will not find true rest until it bows slowly to his breast outside the city wall. Will you follow him now, O scribe? Now
that you know the road he takes? Or growing pale before the
price he asks, and seeing the truth of it in his eyes rather
than on his lips, will you return to the security of your
sheltered life?

It was at this time too, that one of the disciples had apparently received news that his father had died and asked Jesus
for permission to attend to his burial. The uncompromising
answer from the one who ministered so tenderly to sorrow
seems hard, perhaps even cruel. "Follow me and let the dead
bury their dead", and Luke adds, "But go thou and preach the
Kingdom of God". It is only after careful thought that we see
in it the characteristic love of the Saviour of the world.

First of all this man was already a follower of Jesus, not
committed to the complete service of apostleship but certainly to the obligations of discipleship. Then we notice that by
the very nature of his answer Jesus has justified his refusal
by changing the present circumstances into a spiritual
metaphor. The world is a world of perishing mortality—of
dead men. Jesus had come to bring life. By associating himself with Jesus the disciple had left the congregation of the
dead. But if he withdrew from Jesus he would enter it once
more and would be in danger of attending his own burial as
well as his father's. A great surgeon, spending all his time at
the hospital saving men from death, does not pause in his
labours to bury the dead. Nor does the medical student leave
the master's side for that or any other purpose. So it was with
the disciple of the great Physician. By learning from his Lord,
and then in his turn going out to preach the Kingdom of God,
he was performing a work of love and service which made his
present request paltry and insignificant.

In the growing darkness Jesus stepped into the boat followed by his disciples, whom he instructed to steer to the farther shore. At last exhaustion, defied for so long, exacted its price. He lay down and slept.

The sudden storms which develop on the Sea of Galilee when the wind whistles down the narrow gorges from the northern mountains were well known to the fishermen disciples. Such a tempest swept down upon them now. It quickly developed into a fury they had never experienced before. The wind lashed the sea into a seething caldron. It roared through the rigging. It swept up the boat in its rage. The mountainous waves lashed the helpless craft and the seas poured in unchecked. Soon it began to founder. All the experience of the hardened fishermen was unavailing. Their frenzied shouts were torn from their throats and lost in the surging darkness. Their faces grew pale with fear.

And still, completely spent, their Master slept.

All their efforts useless, they suddenly realized their Lord was in the boat. "Master, Master, we perish." Jesus awoke. In a moment he understood. But before he turned to the wind and the waves, he brought peace to their frenzied hearts. "Why are you fearful, O ye of little faith?" Then to the wind, he cried, "Peace", and to the waves "Be still". And there was a great calm. The disciples, shaken and ashamed, marvelled saying, "What manner of man is this?"

How many are the lessons borne to us on the winds of that storm! The passage over the sea to the distant shore is the disciples' journey through life. The frail boat that undertakes the crossing is the human heart. But Christ is there. His protecting influence will remain however sudden the storms, however dark the night. But he will not be awakened by the fury of the gale nor the shudder of the boat. Only the voice of the disciples will rouse him. Then he will bring peace into the heart and save the life from disaster.

The memory of the disciples working feverishly to save themselves, with fear in their eyes and despair in their hearts, should be a warning of our own insufficiency: and the sublime picture of the Master sleeping peacefully amid the raging storm should be an abiding incentive to a living faith in him who "stilleth the roaring of the seas, the roaring of the waves, and the tumult of the peoples".

19

AMONG THE GERGESENES

GERGESA was a town of some importance on the eastern shore of the Sea of Galilee. One of the ten cities of the Decapolis, a region of Greek culture, it was ruled over by Herod Philip. To-day its ruins and its tombs can still be seen by the side of the solitary cliffs that rise precipitously out of the water.

It was here that Jesus stepped ashore in the early dawn that followed a momentous night. The disciples would still feel shaken and full of wonder. Could they ever forget the transformation they had seen? One moment they had looked upon the intensely human picture of their Lord asleep, the next they had gazed at a figure they did not recognize, who commanded the elements with majestic authority. Now they were about to witness a fresh unveiling of his power.

Among the tombs of Gergesa there lurked a raging madman more terrifying in aspect than they had ever encountered. Matthew speaks of two demoniacs, Mark and Luke only of one. It would appear that the man who described himself as "Legion" was by far the most formidable, and therefore the one upon whom Jesus concentrated his attention whilst, of course, healing both. For the purpose of narrative we follow Mark and Luke and speak only of one. The composite picture presented by the Evangelists is a fearful one. We see an unclothed maniac roaming the mountains and the tombs: a grotesque monster who could not be bound, even with chains. Bleeding from the gashes of self-imposed wounds, exceedingly fierce, he prevented anyone from venturing near him. Seeing the boat pulled up to the shore and its occupants making their way towards the tombs the demented man dashed down upon them. But suddenly, while he was still some distance away, he stopped. Something in his disordered mind felt a power greater than his madness. He ran forward, only to fall at Christ's feet. Jesus immediately began the heavy task of mastering his will and overcoming his hallucinations. He commanded the evil spirit to come out of the man. But it brought a frenzied outburst, "What have I to do with thee,

Jesus thou Son of God Most High?" How was it possible that this poor madman could have any knowledge of the Christ? We cannot tell. But we do know that Jesus always demanded a responsive faith in those he cured. Unbelief had prevented his beneficent work in Nazareth. Is it not possible that Jesus impressed his identity upon the tortured mind and thus gave the man the opportunity of making that contribution of faith necessary to his own healing? The knowledge that he was the Son of God was only the first stage in the cure. It evoked a greater tumult in him. "I beseech thee, torment me not!" Steadily Jesus persevered. Still preparing him for the moment of response, he asked, "What is thy name?" The simple question broke through his defences. He had believed with all those of his day that if a man became demented it was because evil demons had taken possession of him. "My name is Legion", he cried pathetically, "for we are many". He pleaded that Jesus would not send them away into the country. Then looking across at the cliff top the man saw a great herd of swine feeding. "Send us into the swine that we may enter into them." Here was the opportunity which would give the man ground for faith. If he had visible evidence that the demons had departed from him he would believe. Watching with pitiful intensity he saw a sudden movement among the animals. It spread rapidly. Several rushed headlong down the slope; they were followed by the others in a mad stampede. Unable to check the gathering impetus they plunged into the sea. The man looked at Jesus for the first time with faith in his eyes, and Jesus healed him.

There was a sad sequel to this moving incident. The keepers of the swine hurried to the city to tell their story. The whole population came out towards the tombs they had deserted so long. There the people found the man who so recently had been a raging maniac, sitting quietly at the feet of Jesus, clothed and in his right mind. And Mark says, "They were afraid". That reaction was altogether natural. Fear can be a low form of faith. But the tragedy came when they learned what had become of their swine. They began to plead with Jesus to depart from their coasts. They did not seek his identity, they brought him no sick, they offered him no hospitality. They besought him to leave them. And Luke says quite simply, "He went up into the ship, and returned back again".

But for a brief moment the sun broke through. The collective prayer of the inhabitants was followed by a single prayer.

The man who had called himself Legion prayed for discipleship. He besought Jesus that he would allow him to come back with him. Granting the prayer of the multitude Jesus left them to their fate. Refusing the desire of the man he had healed to stay with him, he conferred upon him the obligations of discipleship, and Luke tells us, "He went his way, and published throughout the whole city how great things Jesus had done for him".

Some controversy has surrounded this miracle that stands so uniquely in the midst of the Galilean ministry. This can, however, be dismissed. We can turn to the simple record and learn with gratitude that the miracle itself is its own justification. He who commands the wind and the sea has the same wonderful power over the minds and hearts of men. No obstacle of mind or spirit is too great for him to transform when faith is born.

The great question is not—why did the Lord permit the destruction of two thousand swine? That question supplies its own answer. The life of the man was of more value than many swine, more than ever so because that man was destined to be, not only a disciple, but in measure an apostle also. For was he not a forerunner of the great Apostle to the Gentiles, telling the men of Decapolis the great tidings of what Jesus had done, evoking their wonder?

No! The important question is—why did the Gergesenes beseech him to depart? It is important because these lakeside inhabitants have a large posterity, descending to our day, and capable of infiltrating even into the houses of those who profess allegiance to him. The keeping of swine is no sinful occupation. The cares and responsibilities of this busy life, the sustenance of our families, the modest target our ambition sets, are all legitimate. But when Christ makes a demand endangering them—there lies the challenge! It is then that each has to answer for himself. Do I want to see the little boat sailing back across the lake? Do I want to be left with my swine?

20

THE HEM OF HIS GARMENT

THE sun would be high in the heavens when the little boat made its way back over the placid waters of a sea that had hardly recovered from the rebuke of its Master. Jesus appears to have said no word to the people he was leaving. He had quietly gone away. Looking back now at the crowd on the receding shore, he must have felt the sadness of their rejection. It was an inoffensive refusal but it was an ominous foretaste of the brutal one that lay before him. Jerusalem must have seemed far away during these busy days in Galilee, but it was always there, away to the south, hostile, implacable—waiting. The bitter attack of the scribes yesterday and the rejection of the Gergesenes to-day brought it nearer. We imagine him watching his disciples as they went unconcernedly about their work in the boat, the sun shining on their bronzed faces and rippling muscles. How little they knew of the road that lay before them! How could they understand that their beloved Master who moved everywhere on his mission of love and healing was going forward to meet a surging wave of hatred and brutality that would not be sated until he hung bleeding on a cross? How could these carefree men dream that they would tread the bitter road of remorse and black despair? Gently he will have to prepare them for these shocks. He will have to show them that discipleship means more than this lovely companionship in the Galilean hills.

Recording the arrival at the opposite shore, Luke seems to have caught the spirit of contrast between the resentful crowd who had silently watched Jesus leave them, and the eager multitudes who waited to receive him. In an indefinable way he conveys the warm glow their sincere homage brought to the heart of Jesus. He tells us, "When Jesus was returned the people gladly received him, for they were all waiting for him". They were probably waiting with some anxiety. No ship could have ridden out the raging tempest of the night before. Many of the little ships which Mark had mentioned must have broken from their moorings, the shore would be strewn with wreckage. What had happened to the fishing boat that had carried the Lord into the darkness and the storm?

News of his safe arrival spread rapidly. It brought to him an eminent man in deep distress. The only daughter of Jairus, a little girl of twelve, lay dying. Matthew's expression, "My daughter is even now dead" must be attributed to the extreme brevity of his description. It is inconceivable that Jairus knew his daughter was dead when he first came to Jesus. In their longer accounts Mark says, "lieth at the point of death", and Luke, "she lay dying". Casting aside all his dignity he fell down at Jesus' feet in the midst of the people who had respectfully made way for him; for Jairus was the ruler of the synagogue at Capernaum. He seems to have remained aloof from the disturbances that had occurred over the Sabbath observance. He had had abundant evidence of the power of Jesus, yet he had not come before. His daughter must have been desperately ill yesterday when Jesus was in the city, but he had waited until it was almost too late. What had held him back? Was it a fear that his colleagues in the synagogue would disapprove? Did his faith need perfecting? Certainly it was going to be sorely tried before he returned to the stricken bedside. The precious minutes were passing and Jesus could hardly move a step forward for the thronging crowds.

And then someone else stood between Jairus and his daughter. There was a woman in the crowd who was in great need of help. For twelve years she had had an issue of blood, and no physician had been able to help her. There were twelve prescribed cures for this complaint, some of them particularly revolting. Mark says, she "had suffered many things ... and was nothing bettered but rather grew worse". We see a pale, emaciated woman, made timid by the consciousness of her affliction. But she knew of Jesus and had perfect faith in him. If only she could reach him she knew that she would be cured. Her great problem was her courage. Even if she could get to him she could not stand before the crowds and tell him of her need. Then her faith devised the answer: "If I may touch but his clothes I shall be whole". Thus she embarked upon her great adventure.

When Jesus landed he had been immediately encompassed by the multitudes, but spurred on by boundless confidence in him, she edged nearer. Roughly she was pushed back, she was crushed and bruised, she felt weak with exhaustion, but she kept her despair at bay and struggled on until at last she stood behind him. Surely her heart stood still as in one breathless moment she stooped forward and grasped the hem of his garment! Immediately the current of his power surged through her frail body. She knew she was healed. In a confusion of joy she sought to steal quietly away. Suddenly the voice of Jesus arrested her. "Who touched me?" He turned about and quietly searched the faces round him. Peter, surprised at what must have seemed to him a frivolous question, answered, "Master, the multitude throng thee, and sayest thou, Who touched me?" But Jesus knew; "Somebody hath touched me". Knowing that she could no longer be hid, the woman came tremblingly forward and fell at Jesus' feet. Jesus listened while she confessed the reason for her action and witnessed to her cure. Then, commending her faith, he sent her away.

We may wonder why Jesus did not let this poor woman escape with her precious secret untold. Matthew suggests the answer. She had said within herself, "If I may but touch his garment, I shall be whole". That was an error which Jesus found it imperative to correct and so her secret had to be revealed. The power was not in his garment but in her faith. "Daughter, be of good comfort, thy faith hath made thee whole." Her faith was great, but her knowledge was imperfect. Without her confession, and the blessing of Jesus, she would have known of his power, but not of his love.

There is a notable significance in Peter's puzzled question. There is a lesson in it too. It was true that many people thronged and pressed upon Jesus, yet they felt no surge of power, and he felt no virtue leave him. The crowds are with him still, acclaiming him, pressing him on every side. Yet for many there is no contact and therefore no cure. But from time to time one with deep faith in his power comes infinitely wondering, and stooping, touches the hem of his garment, and knows. And in that same instant his Master knows also. That man or woman goes forward with the blessing of peace and joy which only the Lord can give.

This delay must have been a sore trial to Jairus whose daughter's life was hanging by a thread. But it was the lesson his faith needed. Jesus could have cured the child with a word at any moment as he had done with two other prominent men in that very city. But he did not. Even as he was speaking to the woman, a messenger from the house pushed his way through the crowd and told Jairus it was too late; his daughter was dead. Looking into the tragic eyes, dulled with sudden grief, Jesus gently urged him back to faith with the gracious words he had so recently addressed to his frightened disciples, "Be not afraid: only believe". With the crowds pressing hard around him he came at last to the gate of the courtyard. Here he left them, and taking only Peter, James and John he went with the stricken father into the house. For the first time these three disciples were separated from the others. They were to be present at this greatest miracle, they were to witness the highest glory of their Lord's earthly life, and they were to enter into his deepest sorrow.

The scene in the house was one of bitter wailing, that melancholy tumult which always preceded an eastern funeral. With an imperious gesture Jesus cried out, "Give place". The mourners were no longer needed. This had ceased to be a place of death; the Lord of Life was here! "The maid is not dead but sleepeth." The wailing changed to laughter. Surely the mourners were hired!

In the inner chamber when the father and mother were ready to receive their child into their midst, and the three disciples were waiting to behold the glory of God in His Son, Jesus went over to the bed, and with tender affection he took the slender hand as though rousing her from her nightly rest. "Little Maiden, arise!" Obediently the child rose up and walked over to her speechless parents; whilst Jesus, manifesting his greatest power, yet thoughtful also of the humblest need, bade them give her something to eat.

21

BLIND MEN AND SIGHT GIVERS

NOT without instruction do we notice that the woman who had come secretly and hoped to depart unobserved, was asked by Jesus to reveal her experience before all the people; while he who came publicly was led away from the multitudes to the seclusion of his house and exhorted to silence. The common need of all who sought the healing power of Jesus was their infirmity. There the likeness stopped. Their character, their background, their deeper spiritual wants were all diverse. When they came in faith the Lord gave physical healing to them all. At that point his ministration to their spiritual needs began, differing with each according to his character. The nobleman has to spend a restless night far from home; the paralytic must receive the consciousness that his sins are forgiven; the disciples have to watch their boat filling with water; the man that was called Legion must remain on the farther shore; the woman has to confess her secret; Jairus must reveal nothing to the questioning crowds that are even now waiting at his gate.

Nor is it greatly different with us. The general ministration of Jesus ends when we rise from the waters of his mystic grave; general only because it is the experience of grace to all those who come to him in faith. It is a supreme and solitary occasion to the individual: a crisis in which he feels the cumulative power of all Christ's miracles. The leprosy of sin, the blindness of ignorance, the paralysis of fear have all been washed away. He starts a new life which begins with that touch of power. But there the peculiar need commences. By living upon every word that proceedeth out of the mouth of God, by exercising the wondrous privileges of prayer, communion and fellowship, we shall continue to receive the ministrations of Jesus, revealing and correcting our weaknesses, supplying our own particular needs and preparing us for the glory of his return.

The silence which Jesus imposed upon Jairus would seem to have been for his own spiritual benefit. Certainly the secret could not be long withheld. Where the hand of Jesus rests there is no occasion for convalescence, and the maiden was immediately ready to enter again into the joyful companionship of her friends. Thus it is no surprise to learn from Matthew that "the fame hereof went abroad into all that land". It was impossible for Jesus to stay in Capernaum, so he left the Lake, crossing the richly cultivated and beautiful Plain of Gennesaret, climbing upwards into the hills where the corn and the fruit gave place to the steeply sloping vineyards, and then turning towards the south-west he approached the familiar landscape surrounding Nazareth.

During this journey towards his former home two blind men followed Jesus crying after him, "Thou Son of David, have mercy upon us!" They recognized him as the promised Messiah and knew he could cure them. As his ministry went on and all men saw his power, we find Jesus making increasingly heavy demands upon their faith. So it was here. Jesus did not pause to heal them, he walked on, apparently unheeding. It was probably a long time before he reached a house for rest and refreshment. By dint of great effort and much pleading with their fellows the blind men were still behind him, and finally they groped their way into the house and found him. "Believe ye that I am able to do this?" Fervently they made answer, "Yea, Lord". Once more faith became the link between the poverty of man and the abounding goodness of God. Jesus touched their sightless eyes. They opened to look upon the most precious vision human or spiritual eyes can behold. They looked up into the face of Jesus.

Jesus had sad memories of the last visit he had paid to the town of his childhood and youth. With murder in their hearts his townsmen had taken him up the surrounding heights intending to fling him to his death. Although during the intervening months his fame had spread to every quarter, he found things little better on this occasion. Where there is no response to the love of God there can be no hope of change in a man, a town or a nation. On this occasion the people of Nazareth made no attempt on his life, but they were unable to surmount the obstacle of that little house on the hillside with its adjoining workshop: nor could they forget his mother and his brethren. When he would heal their sick the responsive faith was missing and he could do few works of power. At last he left them never to return. He went to the surrounding towns and villages where greater faith brought richer rewards.

During his ministry in the neighbourhood of Nazareth, Jesus sent out the Twelve on their first great commission as apostles. One object in doing this was undoubtedly to spread both the Gospel and the power of the Gospel far and wide. An even more imperative reason was to prepare them for their ultimate high vocation. They had learned by a hundred tokens the authority which lay behind the words of their Lord. They had sheltered behind him when critics had taxed them with their conduct. They had grown dependent upon him in times of physical danger. But already he saw the first signs of a storm which would not abate until it took him from them. With that love which marked all his dealings he bestowed power on them and sent them forth. They would go conscious that he was not far from them; whilst the power they had received would give them growing confidence in the true work for which they had been chosen.

It is no surprise that before he sent them forth on their great adventure, Jesus gave them both instruction and counsel. His words to them are most fully recorded by Matthew. It seems that as he spoke the whole vista of discipleship opened before him, and he saw their work continuing long after their own labours were over. But the warnings and the promises which both met and passed beyond their own day were true in principle for all who follow, just as the instructions given specifically for them represent the spirit of true ministry to every age.

The direct instructions the Twelve received were to go to the lost sheep of the House of Israel and preach the advent of the Kingdom, confirming their words by works of healing. They were not to make careful preparations for their journey; but upon entering a city they were to search out who in it was worthy, and there stay and receive the hospitality that was due to them. They were given power to bring peace into a household, and to utter judgment upon family or city.

Jesus then seems to have lifted his eyes to watch these men going forth a few years later on the same great mission, to be met by hatred, imprisonment and death. He will no longer be with them, save in spirit, so he speaks to them now: words of wisdom and love which they may treasure in their hearts, and must never forget. He tells them that when they are witnessing for the truth in those future days they must realize that they are not alone. There will be no need to prepare their own defence; "It shall be given you in that hour what ye shall speak". He sees the time when allegiance to him will bring a sharper sword than a weapon of war, a sword that shall cleave through a family, dividing son from father, and daughter from mother. He reminds them they will be treading His road. It is the privilege and price of discipleship that the disciple shall be as the master. Following him, they will be harmless as doves: they must also be as wise as serpents, not going forward stubbornly to meet unnecessary persecution, but fleeing from city to city, that the things they have learned in secret may be proclaimed from the housetop ... Nor must they lose their perspective. "Fear not them which kill the body, but are not able to kill the soul: but fear him which is able to destroy both soul and body in hell."

Jesus gave them his assurance that in doing his work amid all this hostility and danger, they were in his Father's special care. The very hairs of their head were numbered. He put the incentive before them as something which would give meaning to their sacrifices and sweeten all their sufferings. "Whosoever shall confess me before men, him will I confess also before my Father which is in Heaven."

Finally their Lord reaches the climax of his discourse in words treasured and feared by disciples down the ages; "He that taketh not his cross and followeth after me is not worthy of me. He that findeth his life shall lose it, but he that loseth his life for my sake, shall find it". So might he have beautifully summed up his Sermon on the Mount, but he brings it into the context of this remorseless conflict which is inevitable for those who follow the man who moved steadily to the cross. The disciples did not then, of course, understand the fateful connection between the cross they must take and the Master they must follow. They did understand in the fulness of time; and then they spoke, not of their cross, but his. For the moment they understood the cross to mean the deepest disgrace and ignominy which it would be necessary for them to suffer for his sake, and they saw dimly what they would perceive with greater clearness soon, that, following Christ, they could only find life by letting it go.

So Jesus sent forth these men with counsel and guidance which, taking them far beyond the needs of the present expedition, would help them to join the great company of those of whom the world was not worthy, but who having obtained a good report through faith, will at last receive the promise.

BOOK FOUR: THE GALILEAN MINISTRY

Book Five

LESSONS IN DISCIPLESHIP

1

THE DEATH OF JOHN THE BAPTIST

FOR many weeks the cities of Israel heard the Gospel of the Kingdom and witnessed the power of God. Journeying in pairs through the land, the lowly men of Galilee spread abroad the fame of Jesus. Nor did their Master cease from his constant activity. He too, probably with other disciples who were later to take part in an even larger campaign, moved from place to place teaching and healing.

Away to the south in the great fortress of Machaerus four thousand feet above the eastern shores of the Dead Sea an event occurred which altered the whole course of the Lord's ministry. The nobles and the high military and civil officials of Galilee would have no suspicion of the significance of the occasion as they gathered from all parts of the province to the birthday feast which Herod Antipas had arranged. John, worn out with the privations and sufferings inevitable to his confinement, could not know that even his untimely death would play its part in the divine purpose that was slowly unfolding.

Herod Antipas, like his father, Herod the Great, and his brother, Archelaus, had little to commend him. Cruel, suspicious and sensual, he stopped at nothing to satisfy his desires. During a visit to Rome he had fallen into an intrigue with Herodias. Neither the fact that she was the wife of his half-brother Philip, nor the inconvenience of his having already married the daughter of Aretas, King of Arabia, were allowed to stand in his way. He robbed his half brother, repudiated his own wife, and brought Herodias to his throne. The new queen had never forgiven John for his condemnation of this incestuous union. His imprisonment might have satisfied her but for one disturbing thing. There was something about this gaunt, fearless prophet which fascinated Antipas.

Mark tells us unexpectedly, "Herod feared John, knowing that he was a righteous man, and a holy, and kept him safe. And when he heard him, he was much perplexed, and he heard him gladly". Herodias could never be sure that John would not be pardoned and released. She watched carefully for the opportunity finally to silence him.

The great banquet is at its height in the brilliantly lit hall of the fortress; wine has flowed freely; immoderate shouts of laughter echo through the building: coarse jests are bandied; debauchery is in the air. The dissolute king seeks fresh excitement for his guests. With depraved familiarity he calls for his step-daughter, Salome, to quicken their drunken senses. They watch her sensual movements with delight. The exhibition over, intemperate voices roar acclamation. Antipas, his vanity flattered, rouses himself from his stupor. She shall be rewarded for this, he shouts loudly, "to the half of my kingdom". He utters an oath. This is too much for the girl to decide; she must find her mother. A slow smile of triumph lights the evil, beautiful features of the queen. Her opportunity has come. "The head of John the Baptist." Salome stands once more before the king. He suddenly sobers as he hears her words. A half-shocked, half-guilty hush falls on the scene. He searches the faces of his guests, the grandeur of their attire contrasting with their bemused and stupid faces. He thinks of the strange, silent man in the darkness of the dungeon and he feels a great remorse. But the oath! ... It must be done! Mark records, "Immediately the king sent an executioner and commanded his head to be brought".

John's few remaining disciples went sadly to the castle and bore the headless body away. Reverently they buried it, and went northwards to tell Jesus the tragic news.

Thus died this rugged man of God, as he had lived, with a grandeur of purpose and a moral dignity unequalled among the children of men.

The widespread propagation of the Gospel extended the whole scope of Christ's ministry. It would cause no little anxiety to the scribes and Pharisees who saw it bursting out into a national ferment with far-reaching political consequence. Reports would reach Jerusalem, and even the lordly Sadducees would be stirred, whilst the Zealots, that intensely patriotic minority, would wait hopefully for some sign of open revolt. The Passover was near at hand; could it be that with a million fervent Jews around the city the Messiah would march southwards and strike for freedom against the Roman oppressor?

Herod Antipas, in the remoteness of his castle, heard and feared for both personal and national reasons. It may appear strange that the King had not heard of Jesus before this: that he had not received reports of the multitudes that had been drawn by his teaching from every corner of the land, and of the miracles that he was continually performing. There are two probable reasons. Herod was a man who cared little for the people; he was out of touch with their needs and activities; his whole time was devoted to keeping his relations right with Rome, and giving his pleasures and ambitions as much satisfaction as his ample means and power would allow. It is also possible that Antipas had not been in Galilee since Jesus had begun his active ministry there. It is true that he had a palace at Tiberias, but he spent much of his time at his two strongholds in Perea, at Julias and Machaerus.

The murder of John the Baptist seems to have had a profound effect upon Herod. A melancholy descended upon him which left him restless and superstitious. When he heard of this preacher in Galilee surrounded by vast crowds, and doing unbelievable miracles, his conscience smote hard. "It is John whom I beheaded. He is risen from the dead." But Herod did nothing about it. Later on during his ministry some Pharisees were to tell Jesus that Herod sought his life, but it seems to have been their own effort to alarm him and drive him away, rather than any active hostility on the part of Herod. The time was coming when, with Jesus standing before him, he would have a wonderful opportunity of atoning for his miserable betrayal of John, but he only descended further into the abyss. He mocked the Bridegroom as he had mocked his friend, and allowed his soldiers to besport themselves. We can find no pity in our hearts for Herod when we learn that his future held nothing but disgrace. He was deprived of his kingdom, spent his last days in exile, and at last he went unto his own place.

The tragic tidings from the Dead Sea seem to have coincided with the return of the Twelve to Capernaum. They came back full of glowing reports of all that they had achieved in his name. The city itself was full of activity as the news spread that Jesus was in their midst, and the apostles had returned from their long mission.

But with the death of John, Jesus must have felt more than ever the grim reality of the Cross. The resentment of the priests in Jerusalem, and the mounting opposition of the scribes in Galilee had cast its shadow across his path. But now, words had changed to deeds. The forces of evil had struck. Righteous blood had flowed. The staunch prophet of the desert whose life's work had been to prepare the people to receive him, lay murdered.

From this time the tenor of Christ's ministry changed. Capernaum hardly saw his gracious figure in her streets again. The multitudes found him demanding an allegiance they were loath to give, and many drifted away. On every possible occasion he showed a desire to get his disciples alone privately so that he could reveal to them progressively, as they were able to bear it, the true course of his life and the nature of his death.

So it was now. He led them away from the busy city down to the lakeside where their long neglected fishing-boats lay tugging quietly at their moorings. "Come ye yourselves apart unto a desert place and rest awhile."

2

THE FEEDING OF THE FIVE THOUSAND

THE deliberate withdrawal of Jesus from public observation had its effect upon his enemies. Mistaking it for weakness, they pressed home their attacks against him with greater vindictiveness. Their assaults exposed their own wickedness and called forth from Jesus indictments more severe and penetrating than anything they had yet heard. But in the absence of the constant impetus of his miracles, the charges of the scribes and Pharisees bore increasing weight with the curious and selfish elements in the multitudes, and they began to drift away. Even the wider circle of his disciples were repelled when his teaching assumed a more mysterious and deeper tone.

All this did not happen suddenly; it gradually becomes apparent as we read the records of the second part of the Galilean ministry which began with the news of the Baptist's death. Now Jesus is at the height of his popularity, that period when "whithersoever he entered, into villages, or cities, or country, they laid the sick in the streets, and besought him if they might touch if it were but the border of his garment, and as many as touched it were made whole". Thus it was that when Jesus took his disciples away privately, crossing the Lake to the desert beyond Bethsaida, the multitude watched the course of the boat and, divining its destination, thousands set out on foot round the northern shore, undertaking a journey of some eight or nine miles, so that they might be with him. The purpose of Jesus was thwarted; his great need for quietness and meditation was left unsatisfied. But as he watched the crowds, tired from their long walk, leading their blind, carrying their sick, moving slowly, their faces and their steps turned towards him, he had compassion on them. They were to him like sheep in need of their shepherd. What a characteristic picture of Jesus this is! How comforting for each of us to know that, in spite of our waywardness, if we seek him earnestly, tired from our travelling, weakened by our load, he will turn to us in compassion and minister to us in his abounding love!

Putting aside the purpose of his journey, Jesus taught the people and healed their sick. As the day wore on a problem arose. There were well over five thousand people out here in the desert; they had arrived weary early in the day and were now tired, hungry and miles from home. Jesus anticipated their need, and leading Philip to one side he made it the occasion of a test for him. John is careful to tell us that Jesus himself knew what he was going to do. Why was Philip thus singled out? He was a native of Bethsaida, but the true reason seems to have been that he was in particular need of this challenge to his faith. He was the disciple who had said to Nathanael, "We have found him whom Moses in the law, and the prophets, did write". Had he learned since those early days that looking upon Christ he was looking upon the Father? That the power of the God of Moses was manifest in His Son? "Philip, whence shall we buy bread that these may eat?" But the disciple's faith wavered before the magnitude of the problem. He related it to the limitations of the common purse. "Two hundred pennyworth of bread is not sufficient." It is well to pause before we criticize this failure, and perceive the danger in which every disciple stands of making a similar mistake, and showing the same lack of confidence in Christ.

Evening came, and the other disciples saw the problem that Jesus had previously raised with Philip. "This is a desert place and the time is now past: send the multitude away that they may go into the villages and buy themselves victuals." Their Master had a different plan; "Give ye them to eat". Though they had just returned from doing marvellous works in His name, these men, like Philip, could not take the suggestion seriously. They too had still to learn. Taking the five barley loaves and two small fishes from the youth who stood near, Jesus told the disciples to make the people sit down on the grass in orderly companies of hundreds and fifties, and, offering his Father thanks and blessing the bread, he gave the morsels to them to distribute. Five thousand men beside women and children were satisfied with food, and twelve baskets of broken pieces were collected.

Discussion upon the manner in which the bread was multiplied will yield little profit. All God's creative work is an appeal to faith to the thoughtful man. It is an adventure in faith to believe that "the worlds were framed by the Word of God, so that things which are seen are not made of things which do appear". Those who live and toil in constant touch with the creative power of the Almighty, watching the seasonal transformations of each successive year, the golden miracle of the harvest, and the continual wonder of newborn life, have less difficulty in understanding this sign which Jesus gave and was soon to unfold in its deeper meaning. And will not that deeper meaning reveal a greater miracle still? The broken body of the Son of God was destined to distribute the bread of life among a multitude which no man can number from every kindred and tongue and people and nation.

Walking for miles along the muddy, uneven shores of the lake, these people had sought for Jesus: forgetful of their physical needs, they had listened to his words. How beautifully he fulfilled his promise that, seeking first the Kingdom of God, temporal needs will be added. And although the fuller significance of this ministration was to wait for the morrow, can we not see in the twelve baskets remaining a symbol of the love that fulfils the desperate need of man and gains in the giving?

The effect of this miracle was immediate and spontaneous. The sheep needing a shepherd became a people wanting a king. They were staggered by the greatness of the power which this man wielded. They accepted with awe his healing qualities directed to the needs of a single sufferer, but this was stupendous power directed to the needs of a hungry nation; power on a national scale. Here, surely, was the One who should come, the Messiah who should destroy all opposition and bring in the Kingdom of God, restoring Israel to her proud place as head of the nations in an age of righteousness and peace. The Passover was at hand—that time when national hopes were high, when the oppression of Rome was most bitterly resented. The murmuring grew in volume until it became an ominous roar. The people surged around their Messiah intent on marching with him upon Jerusalem and declaring him their king. Jesus looked at his disciples. They were obviously affected by this mass hysteria. Action must begin with them. Matthew records, "And straightway Jesus constrained his disciples to get into a ship, and go before him unto the other side, while he sent the multitudes away".

With the disciples gone, Jesus turned to the people, quietened their clamour and sent them on their long journey homewards. When the last straggler had disappeared round the bend of the distant shore, Jesus turned upwards into the hills in the gathering darkness, to commune with his Father.

He needed his Father's strength and guidance especially now in these difficult days when the course of his ministry was changing. He must have felt keenly the death of that stalwart wilderness cousin, the increasing pressure of his enemies, the uncertainty of his disciples, the misconceptions of the multitude. When the heart is overwhelmed its only refuge is in the shadow of the Rock that is higher than itself. It must have been so for the Saviour with his greater burdens and his greater strength. If we dare to lift for a moment the veil that conceals this sacred communion we feel that his prayer was not for himself alone. His thoughts would also be with the men toiling in the darkening waters of the Lake. There he stayed on in the lonely heights until in new found strength and peace he was able to return to his loving ministrations below.

Meanwhile the disciples struggled in the darkness against a turbulent sea and a contrary wind. The sails were useless, so they rowed into the gale. The long hours of the night dragged on but they made little progress. And this time they were alone. There was no Saviour asleep in the stern sheets. Their Master had begun that special instruction which the Baptist's death had made urgent and imperative; this was their first great lesson. With characteristic significance John says, "And it was now dark, and Jesus was not come to them". It was necessary for them to learn that not only were they safe with him in the vessel, there was nothing to fear with him on the heights above in prayer with his Father. His physical presence was not essential for them to overcome their conflicts. Indeed the time was approaching when they would be alone in the midst of perils; when the prophet would have become the priest, interceding on high; when the blessing for them and for all that followed them would be because they would believe though they would not see him.

In that darkest hour which precedes the dawn, he came, walking upon the water. The fitful moon lit up his raiment as he made as though he would pass them. But their cries of fear brought him towards them. "Be of good cheer, it is I; be not afraid." The single voice of Peter came back to him across the water, "Lord, if it be thou, bid me come unto thee on the water". This was characteristic of Peter; that impetuous anxiety to show his love and confidence: that spirit which in spite of this imminent lesson is yet to cry, "Though all men, Lord ... yet not I". Peter had asked for this lesson. Jesus would not quench his earnest spirit by refusing it; "Come". Confidently

"... rivers of living water." (John 7:38)

"… a certain householder, … planted a vineyard, and hedged it round about, and digged a winepress in it, and built a tower …" (Matthew 21:33)

"… what woman having ten pieces of silver, if she lose one piece, doth not light a candle, and sweep the house, and seek diligently till she find it?" (Luke 15:8)

"… he cried with a loud voice, Lazarus, come forth." (John 11:43)

he clambered over the side and walked towards his Lord. But he did not keep the beginning of his confidence firm unto the end. His eyes left his Master's face and looked fearfully out into the boisterous night and at the swirling waters below him. In that moment his faith had gone. He began to sink. "Immediately Jesus stretched forth his hand and caught him, and said unto him, O thou of little faith, wherefore didst thou doubt?" His failure lay not in his decision to come, but in his loss of confidence in his Lord when his adventure of faith had begun. The disciples gladly received him into the boat, and once more a calm descended on the lake and they were able to get to Capernaum immediately.*

Many lessons emerge from this night on the sea: nor are they all for the benefit of the immediate disciples alone. Life can present a picture of a dark and turbulent sea with Jesus afar off. It is the slow triumph of faith to see him on the heights above in communion and intercession with his Father. Sometimes he comes to us in the midst of the storm and darkness, in unfamiliar form which we must learn to recognize. We are quick to appreciate, if we are slow to learn, that when we walk over the waters to meet him, we must not be dismayed by the darkness, the winds or the waves; we must believe that his power is greater far; that he can save even unto the uttermost: that faith can only be sustained by keeping our eyes fixed lovingly and obediently upon him.

Finally, few will miss the significance of this miracle for these last troubled years. The sea and the waves are roaring, men's hearts failing, their resources almost spent. But in the last watch of the night the Son will leave his Father's presence and come with his word of peace to those who yearn for him. And with him will come the dawn and the desired haven.

---

*The words "Immediately the ship was at the land whither they went", John 6:21, are, I think, in contrast with the fact that they had been toiling in rowing for the wind was contrary (Mark 6:48). Thus the meaning would be that they had no further difficulties and proceeded straightway to land.

3

THE BREAD OF LIFE

THE excitement which followed the miracle of the bread in the desert did not quickly subside. The people had allowed Jesus to dismiss them, but they were loath to go. Many must have spent that wild night in the vicinity of Bethsaida; others had probably gone back only to return early the following morning. They had noticed that the disciples' boat had been the only one on the shore, and as Jesus had not re-crossed the lake in it, and the wind had been blowing across all night from the Capernaum side, they had every reason to believe that he was still in the vicinity. But, unable to find him, they at last decided that somehow he must have rejoined his disciples at Capernaum. They found a number of boats which had come from Tiberias (probably fishing boats driven before the wind during the night and beached on that desert shore), and in them they made their way back to Capernaum and found Jesus with his disciples. Hence their surprised question, "Rabbi, whence camest thou hither?"*

Jesus looked at these people who had taken such pains to find him. His answer was a challenge to their clamourings of yesterday and their excitement to-day, "Verily, verily, I say unto you, ye seek me not because ye saw the miracles, but because ye did eat of the loaves and were filled. Labour not for the meat which perisheth, but for that meat which endureth unto everlasting life, which the Son of man shall give unto you". They had tried to make him king because they wanted assurance of the bread which perishes. In a single gesture Jesus swept into oblivion the mighty work of yesterday; he all but repudiated it because it had dazzled their eyes, and diverted their attention from the true bread. The bread was nothing: those who were temporarily sustained by it would be nothing in a brief span of time. Their only hope

---

*This order of events is dictated by a comparison of Matthew 14 and John 6, where one record independently supplies the reason for the events related in the other. It is these little things, perhaps as much as the greater issues, which impress the seal of inspiration upon the record.

lay in labouring for that food which his Father had sent him into the world to give; the food which is not subject to change and decay, but endures as a transforming power, issuing finally into everlasting life. The difference was not one of degree; it was absolute. It had been so with Nicodemus. It had been so with the woman of Samaria. The Son of God had not come into the world to offer something better. He had come to offer life in direct contrast with death. There was no alternative: there could be no compromise.

The people were impressed: they asked a natural question, "What shall we do that we might work the works of God?" "This", Jesus answered, "is the work of God, that ye believe in him whom He hath sent." The answer startled them and made them suspicious: they may have anticipated some code of precept or doctrine. But it was an answer which summarized the whole conception of faith and works. Effective works of love can only spring from belief in Christ. The Sermon on the Mount embodied a dedicated life which could only be built upon the rock of belief in its author as the one sent by the Father to give life unto the world.

The attitude of the listeners changed: they wanted a sign: not that they might believe *in* him, but that they might believe him—a different thing. Truly he had fed them yesterday in the desert, but Moses had given bread—literally "out of the blue"—to thousands in the wilderness for years, and he made no such claim. Jesus pointed out their mistake. It was not Moses but God who had given bread to their fathers, and that bread was not the true bread. "The true bread is he which cometh down from heaven and giveth life to all the world."

Visibly impressed, the people uttered the inarticulate cry of all mankind, "Lord, evermore give us this bread". "I am the bread of life: he that cometh unto me shall never hunger; and he that believeth on me shall never thirst." Here was the sign they had asked for that they might see and believe. But though they had seen they had not believed. They had come to him eagerly, but they had not truly come; they had eaten of the bread he gave, but not of the true bread that he was.

The unbelief of the people was not an indication that God's purpose had failed. It is as the Father wills. The Father makes the choice. The Son has come to fulfil his Father's will. That will is that whosoever believes on the Son may have everlasting life and be raised at the last day.

Bewildered murmurings broke out among the people. On what possible grounds could this man claim to have come from heaven? They knew all about him, his father and his mother. Was he not the son of Joseph? But Jesus reiterated the truth they had interrupted. He insisted that those who would come to him for living bread would only be those whom his Father had drawn. The initiative was and would always be with the Father; the children of Zion would be taught of God: the response would always be the influence of that divine teaching upon the heart, and the work of completion would always be with the Son, "I will raise him up at the last day".

Jesus then goes further in that revelation of himself as the bread from heaven. "I am the bread of life; your fathers did eat manna in the wilderness and are dead. This is that bread which cometh down from heaven, that a man may eat thereof and not die. I am the living bread which came down from heaven: if any man eat of this bread he shall live for ever: and the bread which I will give is my flesh, which I will give for the life of the world."

The true meaning of the bread broken on the opposite shore, and the proximity of the Passover, emerges here. The bread is not only the bread of life from heaven that man must eat to have everlasting life; it is also the living bread which the Son identifies as his flesh which must be given for the life of the world.

Once more the Jews broke into the discourse, striving between themselves, but Jesus repeated his words with a clarity which could not be misunderstood although the meaning eluded them, "Verily, verily, I say unto you, Except ye eat the flesh of the Son of man, and drink his blood, ye have no life in you". The Son prophesied not only of his death but of the everlasting life which would come forth from it. As the living Father had sent him, and he lived by the Father, so, by partaking of his flesh and his blood, those who had been taught of God should live by him. The deep meaning that lay behind those words was not revealed until he spoke to the Twelve alone in the upper room: it could not be understood in its fullness until he rose again from the dead.

Most of those who then heard, placed a crude construction upon these words and alienated themselves from Jesus. It was a great apostasy.

There was unbelief among many of his disciples too. "Does this offend you?" There will be a greater strain upon their faith in days to come. It was not the actual eating of his flesh that would give life; it was the conscious assimilation of his life conveyed through belief in his words. Jesus knew from the beginning those who had been drawn by the Father and committed to his care; he knew, too, the terrible role to be played by one of the Twelve. The crowds had left him, the disciples were divided, the apostles had a cell of wickedness in their midst. "From that time many of his disciples went back, and walked no more with him." There is a compelling significance in the words, "went back". They returned to the company of those who ate manna in the wilderness and were dead. There could be no compromise between life and death. A few hours ago Jesus had had to compel the multitudes to go away from him; no compulsion was necessary now. Puzzled and antagonized, they left him.

It was a moment of crisis for the Twelve also. The physical storm on the waters the previous night was followed by a spiritual upheaval as violent and dangerous. Their Master constrained them to take this voyage of faith as certainly as he had compelled them into the boat. As the crowds left him, the moment of decision came. Had they understood their Master's words the general desertion would have troubled them not at all, but the night was dark, and their Lord seemed far away. He turned to them now. Can we not discern an understanding smile? "Will ye also go away?" No! The crisis was past. Little as they understood the deep things he had said, they believed on him with all their hearts. Peter again became their spokesman. Once more his voice carried across the dark waters of doubt which had for a while separated them from their Lord. "Lord, to whom shall we go? Thou hast the words of eternal life; and we believe and are sure that thou art that Christ, the Son of the living God."

There was one abstention from that expression of confidence. One of the Twelve should have gone back with the unbelievers. He did something far worse. He stayed in their midst, a false accuser in disciples' guise. And Jesus knew. "Have I not chosen you twelve, and one of you is a devil? He spake of Judas Iscariot the son of Simon, for he it was who should betray him, being one of the Twelve."

4

CRUMBS FROM THE MASTER'S TABLE

IT may have been news of the attempt to make Jesus king, carried by Passover pilgrims to Jerusalem, which was responsible for a further deputation of scribes and Pharisees to Galilee. It is obvious that they had come with the intention of joining issue with Jesus immediately. The feeding of the multitudes had given them the clue to their approach. It would have been impossible for all the people to have observed the important rite of washing the hands before eating.[1]

The scribes had little difficulty in discovering the disciples at fault in this. They approached Jesus, "Why walk not thy disciples according to the tradition of the elders, but eat bread with unwashen hands?" They could not have been prepared for the withering attack that met them. The battle was joined. No quarter would be asked or given until the end. Jesus, neither justifying nor apologizing for his disciples, exposed the fatal gulf between the law of God and their tradition. We can hardly appreciate the full significance of the crude blasphemy which the rabbinic writings contained, and which were included in a tradition made more binding than Scripture itself.[2] For the first time he flung at them the charge of hypocrisy.

"Well hath Esaias prophesied of you hypocrites, as it is written, This people honoureth me with their lips, but their heart is far from me. Howbeit in vain do they worship me, teaching for doctrine the commandments of men."

---

[1]The traditions of the elders demanded careful obedience to this ordinance, giving instructions concerning the manner in which it was to be done. The hands were to be held upwards after washing, so that the whole hand might be covered to the wrist, and the water contaminated by the washing not run down the fingers again and pollute them. Failure to observe this ritual resulted in the defilement of any food that was touched. One rabbi who failed to enforce it was actually buried in excommunication. (See EDERSHEIM, *Life and Times of Jesus*, Vol. II, page 10).

[2]*Ibid.*, Vol. II, page 15.

They must have been startled by this sudden attack, with its accusation made more devastating by his holy wrath. But he had not finished with them yet. The crowds stood a little way off, watching in amazement this wandering Rabbi from Nazareth who had become a symbol of fiery judgment. He returned to the attack, dealing a death blow to their traditions, exposing them as self-condemned to all who had ears to hear. Not only did they set aside the law of God, they positively rejected it in order to replace it with commandments ingeniously compiled to serve their selfish ends. He quoted the case of "Corban" by which a man might be released from God's command to honour his father and mother by dedicating his wealth to the altar. But the sin was more terrible than that. It freed him by deceit from obedience to God. His gift was a pretence. He was under no obligation, in spite of his promised "Corban", to lose his money. "And", said Jesus "many such like things do ye."

Turning to the wondering multitude he commanded them to come near and hear his answer to the charge. He spoke with great earnestness, compelling their attention. "Hearken unto me every one of you, and understand", he said; and a moment later, "If any man have ears to hear, let him hear". He was about to tell them something of the greatest importance which showed the striking contrast between his teaching and that of the scribes. They had found fault because the disciples had eaten with unwashed hands, thereby defiling the food they ate. That, he maintained, was impossible. Defilement does not go into a man from without: it comes out from within. Here lay the essential difference between the commandments of men, and the law of God. The scribes supported the teaching that said that because the hands were not washed, the bread was polluted, and the eater defiled. Jesus said it was what was in the heart of man, which issued out of him in evil thoughts, murders, pride, and wickedness which defiled him. He showed that the scribes were fundamentally wrong because by a tradition of externalism they sought by outward observances to influence the inner man. That could never be. The law of God, presented by Christ, addressed itself to the inward man, transforming the heart, and therefore the qualities which issued from the heart, the character and conduct. The whole of the teaching of Christ, crystallized in the Sermon on the Mount, was dedicated to this task.

The disciples, on reaching the house, asked him for a clearer understanding of this. He gave them the appalling catalogue of depravity hidden in the natural heart. He was also giving them hour by hour, and day by day, the perfect example of the qualities which shone forth from a heart which was entirely dedicated to God.

The scribes do not appear to have had any desire to renew their attack, nor were they now to have a further opportunity. It was still the obvious desire of Jesus to move away from the crowds and find a secluded place where, free from interruption, he could continue to instruct his disciples and unfold to them a picture of the days that lay ahead. They must not be irretrievably lost when they see the nature of the crown that is destined for his head. They must remember these words in the Galilean hills. The desert on the eastern shore of the Lake had proved to be too near the centre of his popularity. This time he decided to withdraw far beyond the range of the importunate crowds. He travelled north-westwards for about thirty miles into the mountains of Upper Galilee, reaching at last the borders of Tyre and Sidon. There is no reason to believe that Jesus went over those borders into the land of the Gentiles, the evidence suggests that he did not. He entered into a house on the Galilean side of the boundary, and, in Mark's words, "would have no man know it".

But "he could not be hid". A Syrophenician woman was in deepest distress because her daughter had an unclean spirit. She had heard of the fame of Jesus and, crossing the border, sought for him. After anxious enquiry she found him. How her heart would leap with joy when she saw him! She threw herself at his feet. "Have mercy on me, O Lord, thou Son of David, my daughter is grievously vexed with a devil." She had found him. Her faith would suffice. She lay there at his feet. Her ears waited for the word which would turn the anguish in her soul into joy. There was no response from the quiet figure. No gracious hand lifted her up. No power flowed forth to meet her cry of faith. No word of comfort broke the stillness. In silence he watched her piteous appeal for help. Quietly he left her with her burden and her grief.

Still she clung to her belief in him. She followed crying, imploring, beseeching, until her persistence disclosed a hardness in the hearts of disciples which must yet be softened. "Send her away", they besought the Lord, "for she crieth after us."

Where lies the secret of his silence? Why are the fountains of his mercy sealed? Surely the answer lies in the manner of the woman's approach. Jesus was too great to be patronized. In her need she had addressed him as "Thou Son of David". What could she know of the meaning of this title she had so glibly used? David had not been king of Syria; his greater Son had not crossed the borders of Galilee. Like the woman who had touched the hem of his garment, she too has something to learn. Spiritual discernment of her relationship with Israel must take the blindness from her faith. Jesus makes answer to the disciples, not to her: "I am not sent but unto the lost sheep of the house of Israel". Quickly she discerns her mistake. Worshipping him she implores once more, appealing to him no longer as the Son of David who belonged only to Israel, but as the Lord, the universal helper of all mankind. She accepts his rebuke, but she will not leave him. Her need is desperate. "Lord, help me."

At last he speaks. His words press the teaching home. She will never forget now that salvation is of the Jews. It is a hard saying, but he has spoken, and in his words there is a gleam of hope. "It is not meet to take the children's bread and cast it to dogs." With that sudden inspiration which so often comes in the presence of Christ she accepts his answer. There is yet hope. There are crumbs! "True, Lord, yet the dogs eat the crumbs that fall from their Master's table!" Surely it was given her in that moment what to speak! How could she have known that the children had so recently refused the bread? How had she learned that they had driven him at that moment to the very border of the table? And was not he the master of the dogs also? Was not she here in faith at his feet?

How beautifully Jesus responded to this woman who had wrestled with the Son and had prevailed! Her sorrow had endured for a night, but joy had come in the morning. "O woman, great is thy faith: be it unto thee even as thou wilt." Enlightened faith had at last called forth the responsive power of Jesus, and away over the border in a heathen land, a little girl stirred upon her bed and then lay back with a smile of peace.

5

FEEDING OTHER SHEEP

FROM the borders of Tyre and Sidon, Jesus and his small band of disciples turned eastwards into the mountains of northern Galilee, travelling probably across the foothills of Lebanon and Hermon with their high gorges and swirling torrents. It was a long and lonely journey which would give Jesus abundant opportunity for instructing the Twelve. He would be able to discuss with them the adventures they had had on their mission without him, the problems that had presented themselves, the difficult decisions they had been forced to make. And listening to them Jesus would help each one according to his temperament, giving advice which would guide them in the years ahead. He would tell them something of what discipleship meant as both a privilege and a responsibility. There can be little doubt that during the arduous days that followed their Lord's ascension they would often call to mind the things he told them on some vividly remembered occasion, when perhaps the evening sun was striking the topmost peaks of Hermon, turning the powdered snow into a rosy pink, when the foaming waters were splashing and eddying through the rocky chasm, and the mountain pines were leaning against the steeply rising cliffs until they were lost on the snowline. Precious moments these. Moments not denied even now to those who leave the crowded shore and seek to be alone with Christ.

How long this joyful sojourn in the mountains lasted we cannot tell. But at last it ended, and they took the road southwards through Ituraea, reaching the eastern shores of the Sea of Galilee from the province of Decapolis.

Long before they had their first glimpse of the rich blue of the sea, Jesus had been recognized. They had travelled through the country of the Gergesenes where Legion, now a peaceful evangelist, was spreading abroad his fame. It may well be that the seed he had sown had brought forth fruit. When Jesus reached the top of a mountain he was besieged by a multitude of people bringing with them their blind, dumb and maimed. This was the first time such a scene had occurred outside the confines of Israel, and it had a profound effect upon these semi-Gentile people who "glorified the God of Israel". The scene must have surprised the disciples who themselves had been carefully instructed to go only to the lost sheep of the house of Israel. But it was a scene which foreshadowed the time, not far distant, when the blessings which had been confined to the Jews since the days of Abraham would be extended to embrace all mankind.

Mark singles out one particular miracle at this time. The people brought to him a man who was deaf and, probably because of his deafness, suffered also from an impediment in his speech. It is an inspiration to watch Jesus deal with this man who cannot hear the word of life nor cry for release from his infirmity. Jesus led him away from the multitude and, entering into his limitations so that he might draw forth the man's faith, he healed him by signs. First he plunged his fingers into the deaf ears, moistening his own finger with saliva he touched the tongue that was tied, then looking up to heaven to direct the afflicted man's attention to the true source of his healing, he sighed. None of these actions had produced any result. But they had given the man an understanding which was the seed-bed of faith and the preparation for blessing. At last he spoke; "Ephphatha—Be opened", and, Mark tells us, "straightway his ears were opened and the string of his tongue was loosed, and he spake plain". Jesus charged him, and those of his friends who had left the multitude to witness the miracle, to tell no man. But as on previous occasions, they published it the more.

As with so many of the works of Christ, this miracle has features which give cause for reflection. We notice that Jesus drew the man away from the crowds that he might heal him. The reason was probably to take him from influences which would distract his attention during this supreme preparation of faith. Alone with Jesus he could concentrate upon him, and understand the meaning of every gesture he made. There are times when such a process is necessary for the spiritual healing of those who follow. The Lord God has given His Son the tongue of the learned that he might speak a word in season to him that is weary. Sometimes our ears are dull of hearing, and when they are we usually find that we have also an impediment in our speech. To take us away from the multitude to the isolation of a sick bed, or into that mental detachment which comes from solitude, is perhaps the only way towards the healing which will give us ears to hear the joyful sound of his Gospel, and voice to speak forth all his praise.

For three days the people stayed with Jesus as he healed their sick. Whether he taught these Gentiles the things of the Kingdom we do not know, but there can be no doubt that he had words of comfort and guidance for them which would be a preparation for the evangelizing work of the apostles in a few years' time. Now the hour of his departure had come. His work at Decapolis had been short. He was leaving them and they would not see his face again. But his love was with them to the end. As he was about to go he saw their need. They had been with him for three days. To send them away would mean that many of them would faint before they reached their homes. Once more he was moved with that tender compassion which needed so little encouragement to flow out in loving service. Once more the disciples failed to believe that his power was as great as his love "Whence should we have so much bread in the wilderness as to fill so great a multitude?" As if to remind them of the occasion a few weeks ago only a few miles along the same shore, Jesus repeated his question, "How many loaves have ye?" Whether the question was a rebuke to their faith we do not know. They answered simply, "Seven, and a few little fishes". Having commanded the people to sit down, Jesus once again blessed the bread and gave it to the disciples to distribute. All were filled, and seven baskets were taken up. Four thousand men beside women and children had been fed.*

---

*Two interesting points of contrast between the feeding of the 5,000 and the 4,000 emerge. (a) The first miracle occurred earlier in the year when the grass was lush and green; Mark mentions "the green grass" (6:39). John says, "Now there was much grass in the place" (6:10). The second miracle happened when the early grass had been burned up. In both records the writers simply say that the people sat on the ground. (b) Different containers were used to collect the fragments in the two miracles, but both words are translated "baskets". Those used for the second miracle seem to have been larger, for Paul was let down from the Damascus wall in one. The distinction is invariably made in all the Gospel references. Thus when Jesus warned the disciples against the leaven of the Pharisees, he says, "Do ye not ... remember the five loaves of the five thousand, and how many 'baskets' took ye up? Neither the seven loaves of the four thousand and how many 'panniers' took ye up?" (Matthew 16: 9–10). There are indications that the twelve baskets of the first miracle were in fact the twelve disciples' dinner baskets. This suggestion will bring many fruitful thoughts, particularly the connection between John 6:12 and John 17:12.

It may be difficult to understand the attitude of the disciples on this occasion. There is abundant evidence in Scripture to show that they do not stand alone. Israel and even Moses himself failed in the midst of evidence of God's power. It is easy to take an optimistic view of the faith we expect in others; the real test must always be with ourselves. There is just the possibility that the disciples had not forgotten the previous occasion, nor doubted their Master's power, but did not expect it to be manifested towards the Gentiles as it had been to his own people. Such an attitude would make their question tentative rather than doubting.

The two miracles of feeding taken together can be found to have spiritual significance. Jesus came to his own to feed them first, but when they refused him he departed and offered bread to the Gentiles. The hesitancy of the disciples to understand the first ministration, and their reluctance on the occasion of the second lend strength to this typical interpretation.

So Jesus departed across the lake to the coasts of Magdala. The long Galilean ministry had virtually closed, the short one at Decapolis was at an end. Both had concluded with a feast provided by Jesus. Our thoughts go forward to the close of the Judaean ministry. We find Jesus eating the last Supper with his disciples, not indeed on a mountain, but in an upper room. The five thousand who followed him become twelve, then eleven. He will not ask them now, "Will ye also go away?" Following the traitor out into the night they will presently leave him. But the feast will not be interrupted by their departure. The bread will be broken, and in its breaking the apostles will be united to their Lord, and to them down the centuries will be joined disciples from both the Galilean and the Decapolis shore, all awaiting the final feast when their Lord and Master, returned from his Father's side, will eat bread and drink wine in his Kingdom.

6

LEAVEN

JESUS had hardly reached the familiar western shore of the Lake after his long absence when he was challenged by Pharisees and Sadducees who "came forth" to meet him, and tempting him, demanded a sign from heaven. The presence of Sadducees so far from the limited confines around Jerusalem is some indication of the alarm which was intensifying there as the popularity of Jesus spread through Galilee.

The demand for a sign would not have been an insult had not the actions and words of Christ been constantly supported by the authority of his miracles. It was the responsibility of the leaders of Israel to test a prophet by asking a sign.* And their Rabbinical writings show a number of cases where it was asked and given. Here was a prophet who set at nought the tradition of the elders, who broke their precepts and whose teaching differed gravely from theirs in several important particulars. Moreover he had openly counter-charged them with hypocrisy when they had opposed him. They acknowledged his power but not its source.

How easily Jesus could have satisfied their request! He could have left them pale and trembling by the might at his command. But that was not the way of Jesus. He allowed them to be their own judges; because of the hardness of their hearts that was the worst punishment they could have for their contempt of the Son of God. There would be weeping and gnashing of teeth. He who comes to Christ whether in challenge or inquiry cannot demand a spectacular display of power: enduring trust will come from a gradual appreciation and an assimilation of love—a love that glows in humble glory. Such trust finds its birth in the dimly-lit stable of a crowded inn, and leads on to a lonely Son of Man carrying the burden of all humanity to a rough wooden cross outside a city wall. These Pharisees and Sadducees had not learned this. Countless of their countrymen had learned it, and so had a Roman centurion and a Syrophenician woman. The great

---

*Deuteronomy 13:1-5

LEAVEN

army of Galileans glowing with restored health had no
message for these supercilious leaders from Jerusalem. They
needed a sign from heaven. They tempted him.

Did Jesus know that at this very place less than forty years
hence the sea would be dyed with Jewish blood when the
armies of Vespasian marched upon Galilee from the north? He
sighed deeply in his spirit. He understood their motive, he
knew their hardness, he foresaw the ruin they were bringing
upon themselves and their country. Only a wicked and an
adulterous generation would seek a sign in Israel at this time.
He refused the demonstration they asked for, but he gave
them a warning. They looked into the heavens in the morning
and the evening, and from the colour of the sky they could
discern the signs of the approaching weather. Could they not
lift up their heads in Israel and see the signs of a coming
storm? Their present mission was an omen. Yes, he would give
them a sign!—the sign that the Ninevites received when their
judgment appeared imminent, the sign of the prophet Jonah.
The people of Nineveh accepted the preaching of Jonah. The
three days was a sad and terrible symbol. If it was ignored,
that threatening storm would break over their heads with a
relentless fury Nineveh had not known.

Having given them a sign which could have proved greater
than any display of power had they the desire to have
received it, Jesus left them and went with his disciples into
the boat. They now embarked upon a further journey away
from the crowds towards the northern mountains. They
beached their boat on the desert shore of Bethsaida, the place
which had been the scene of the first great miracle of the
bread. It would appear that Jesus had been silent during the
crossing, reflecting on the encounter he had just had with the
Pharisees and Sadducees. Immediately upon landing he
spoke to his disciples, "Take heed and beware of the leaven of
the Pharisees and of the Sadducees". The disciples were perplexed by his warning and reasoned among themselves. They
finally decided that it must have something to do with the
fact that they had forgotten to bring bread.* Jesus sternly

*It has been suggested that the disciples thought Jesus meant that
they had deliberately forgotten the bread so that they might receive
a sign such as the Pharisees had demanded. Another suggestion is
that they thought Jesus was telling them not to take bread from the
Pharisees. Neither of these rather forced ideas seems necessary. It
appears more likely that the disciples were confused by their
Master's words, and vaguely felt that they must have something to
do with their failure to bring bread.

195

reprimanded them for their lack of faith, and reminded them of his ability to supply bread. Then they perceived that he spoke of the doctrine of the Pharisees and the Sadducees.*

In warning his disciples against the Pharisees and Sadducees, Jesus did not speak of the leaven of each, but of the leaven that was common to the two. We have seen that superficially the two parties were widely different: the one was strict, intensely nationalistic, and preoccupied with ritual, the other was lax, sympathetic to outside culture and philosophy, and sceptical. The leaven of the Pharisees was hypocrisy: the leaven of the Sadducees was materialism. Each had to be avoided. Yet they had joined on the opposite shore in common cause, and therefore the leaven to be particularly careful of was the result of their attitude to Christ. The key to the danger takes us back to the charges Jesus had already laid against them. His accusation was that as sign-seekers they were wicked, adulterous and blind. It was an accusation levelled against them for their common attitude to the things of God. They were all of this world. The Pharisees in their hypocrisy used their devotions "to be seen of men", and, patronizing this world, they had their reward. The Sadducees in their scepticism and licence made little pretence of seeking anything other than temporal rewards. Both parties joined in hostility against Jesus because he represented the things of God. Both were ungodly, alive to self and dead to God.

If our study of the life of Jesus is to bear fruit truly in our own lives we must be continually learning the lessons in which it abounds. The leaven against which Jesus warned his disciples has not been destroyed. Hypocrisy is not extinct, nor materialism. They unite in that baser leaven of ungodliness which can by its very nature permeate our lives and estrange us from Christ and his kingdom.

Before Jesus and his disciples left the village of Bethsaida to begin their journey northwards, the people brought a blind man and besought Jesus to touch him. He did not comply with their request. Instead we have the moving and significant picture of Jesus leading the blind man by the hand, and taking him out of the town into the country, where he would

---

*Mark substitutes "the leaven of Herod" for Matthew's "leaven of the Sadducees". Some Sadducees, emphasized their political interests and became partisans of Herod These Sadducees were also known as Herodians.

be free from the embarrassments of the crowds and where his first vision would be of the creative works of God, and of the Saviour who was the beginning of God's new creation. This healing differs from similar miracles because it was performed gradually. First Jesus put his own saliva on the man's eyes, touched them, and asked him if he saw. The man looked up and with blurred vision saw in the distance the crowds from the town coming out towards him. "I see", he said, "men as trees, walking." Once more Jesus touched him, and this time, looking up, he saw every man clearly.

We may wonder why Jesus thus delayed the perfect cure. Without the instruction afforded by the record we do not know; even then we can only reverently surmise, being careful to avoid presumption. Thus it would seem, as it has often been shown in the Gospels, that the answer lies in the imperfect faith of the sufferer. This man did not come to Jesus himself, he was brought to him by the townsfolk. Even when he stood before him, he had no word of supplication: the people appealed on his behalf. In this we see a further object in Jesus leading him out of the town. As we have noticed before in cases of immature faith, Jesus sought to perfect it in the process of healing. Thus, when the blind man looked up to see, even dimly, for the first time, his faith would soar, and he would believe that Jesus could complete the cure. Thus prepared, the second touch perfected his sight. The restored man was told to avoid the town and go straight to his home.

The lesson and the warning of this miracle can be clearly seen. According to our faith will our spiritual vision be. So often, perfect faith comes only slowly in a development which begins with the blurred vision of men as trees walking. We need the courage and honesty of the blind man in confessing his immaturity. Finally, our first service when we have received sight must be undertaken in the seclusion of our own hearts. There in worship and gratitude we may prepare for a dedication which will later find expression in witnessing to his name in the city.

7

"THOU ART THE CHRIST"

THE journey from the shores of Galilee to Caesarea
Philippi took Jesus and his disciples through some of the
most striking scenery in Palestine. To reach this capital town
of Herod Philip they would travel twenty-five miles due north
through the upper Jordan valley. For the first ten miles the
mountains rose steeply on both sides of the river, but gradually the narrow rocky way ascended until the little band
reached the uppermost lake, known to us as Lake Huleh.
There it opened out into a marshy plateau into which poured
and mingled the mountain streams from Lebanon and
Hermon. Well watered and with a southern aspect this was a
region of rich wheatland and olive groves. Climbing higher
towards the still distant triple heads of Hermon, the cultiva-
tion became more ragged, the olives gave way to terraced
vineyards, and they in turn were left behind as the country
became wilder. Now they were among the valleys of great
basalt rocks and rushing torrents. Wild roses, honeysuckle
and clematis clung in tangled luxury to hillsides crowned
with the mighty oaks of Bashan. Pausing from time to time
they could look back at the panorama of the Jordan, cleaving
its turbulent path through the mountains until it emptied
itself into the distant expanse of the Sea of Galilee. All
around mountains rose to over four thousand feet, and now
to the north-east Hermon towered over them, its features
more discernible, yet its proud peaks rising nine thousand
feet, as remote as ever. Far to the north-west the heights of
the Lebanon range would just be visible.

Caesarea Philippi lay delightfully situated at the head of
the steeply rising valley of the upper Jordan. From an
immense cavern above the town sprang the mountain torrents
known as "the upper sources of the Jordan". From the
ancient times this had been a place of pagan worship. The
Greeks had made it a sanctuary to the god Pan, and only a
few years previously Herod Philip had built a great white
temple there dedicated to Caesar. He had also enlarged and
transformed the town, calling it after Caesar, but adding his
own name to distinguish it from the coastal port.

We have described this environment at some length because it was the appropriate setting for the momentous happenings which were now to take place. Even the most superficial reading of the Gospels will give the sense of an impending crisis. The turning point in the ministry of Jesus had come with the discourse on the bread of life which had ended his active work among the Galileans. We dare not presume to enter too closely into the thoughts and emotions of Jesus, but we must feel something of a restlessness, a desire to get away from the crowds and the highways into the remoteness of the mountains. We see him in prayer so intense that he is oblivious of the presence of his disciples. With feelings of deep reverence we sense rather than see the struggle and the need of the Redeemer as he waited to take the road that led to Jerusalem. Almost instinctively we know that it was the Lord himself who yearned for a sign from heaven, not to point the way, but to give him strength to tread it. It is only after prayerful meditation that we write of this. It is for each humble disciple to feel for himself something of the sacred and lonely conflict of his Lord before he went forward with unflinching purpose to his ultimate sacrifice. To enter into that as a deep inner experience is to love him more intensely and serve him with greater zeal.

It has been well said that whilst the Gospels only record the events of his life, Jesus himself becomes articulate in the Psalms. Pouring out the emotions of his own exiled spirit, the Psalmist could not know that in his words the infinite sadness and the sublime courage of the Son of God would find expression.

"O my God, my soul is cast down within me;
Therefore do I remember thee from the land of Jordan,
And the Hermons, from the hill Mizar.
Deep calleth unto deep at the noise of thy waterspouts:
All thy waves and thy billows are gone over me."
. . . .

"Why go I mourning because of the oppression of the enemy?
As with a sword in my bones, mine adversaries reproach me,
While they continually say to me, Where is thy God?
Why art thou cast down, O my soul?
And why art thou disquieted within me?
Hope thou in God, for I shall yet praise him
Who is the health of my countenance and my God."

199

The manner in which the crisis affected the Twelve is more evident. Things had changed since those happy days in Galilee when all men sought for Jesus. True, when the multitudes had gone and most of the disciples had drifted away, they had risen to a loyal assertion of confidence which must have gladdened their Lord's heart. But such spontaneous assurances are apt to be tried by remorseless events. His continued desertion by the people must have been a severe shock to them. This was quickly followed by further opposition from Jerusalem which had led to open and unsuccessful conflict. While this had been somewhat neutralized by the tour of the borders of Tyre and Sidon and the spontaneous enthusiasm of the people of Decapolis, an ominous event had succeeded these experiences. The Pharisees, supported by the Sadducees, had asked him for a sign from heaven; Jesus had refused, and had immediately left them to enjoy their triumph. The Twelve had probably seen some complacent smiles among those eminent men as the boat pulled away from the shore. Deserted by the people, successfully challenged by their enemies, resorting to the farthest extremity of the country, here was a sadly changed state of affairs!

Nor was this all. It was not without cause that following the general desertion in the synagogue at Capernaum, Jesus had turned to his loyal disciples and said, "Have I not chosen you twelve, and one of you is a devil?" One of the disciples had expected great material blessings from his discipleship, and for him things were going badly. A wonderful opportunity had been inexplicably lost when the people had tried to make his master king. Baffled, he had heard the discourse in the synagogue, and he began to feel a bitter disillusionment. Resentment welled up within him against the Lord who had called him to a vocation so different from the one his ambition had proposed. The recent sharp exchange on the western shore of Galilee served only to confirm his fears. Jesus knew of all this. He had given Judas his first warning at Capernaum. He had repeated it at the beginning of this journey into the mountains. Not for nothing did their Master warn the Twelve of the leaven which was in their very midst. The powerful personality of Judas and his subtle murmurings could do much to offset the influence of Jesus on disciples bewildered by the sudden change that had overtaken them.

In his own time Jesus faced the issue which had brought him into this land of mountains and waterspouts. Luke introduces the crisis in words which must be a precious paradox to all those who love the Lord and seek to follow him in the path of prayer. In a manner which seems to convey the sense of strain and the urgent need of waiting upon God, Luke records his sublime detachment, "And it came to pass as he was alone praying, his disciples were with him, and he asked them saying Whom say the people that I am?" It was an enquiry which was only important because it led forward to the supreme question. They told him that some said he was John the Baptist, others Elijah, and others one of the old prophets. The people among whom he worked had had a great regard for him. There was no doubt that at one time most of them had regarded him as the promised Messiah. But the disciples' answer showed that this failure to fit the people's conception of what action the Messiah should take, added to the steady opposition of the scribes and Pharisees, had changed their opinion of him. He had been relegated to the status of a prophet.

"But", said Jesus, reaching the supreme crisis, "whom do *ye* say that I am?"

Without hesitation Peter cried out, "Thou art the Christ, the Son of the living God". It was a moment of great exaltation for Jesus. In spite of all that had happened to discredit the claim of his Lord, Peter knew. "Blessed art thou, Simon, son of Jonas for flesh and blood hath not revealed it unto thee, but my Father which is in heaven."

Jesus knew in that moment that his church was founded. At the furthest possible point from the Temple and ritual of Jerusalem, among the mountain torrents where pagan culture had made its shrine, and the Roman fortress proclaimed the might of temporal power, this rejected leader with his little group of exiles established his church.

Peter had justified his Lord's choice of his new name. His confession was the rock upon which the whole assembly of the called out ones would be built. Although it would be subjected to many assaults the forces of wickedness and unbelief would not prevail against it.* Jesus promised Peter the keys of the Kingdom of heaven and told him that what he will bind on earth will be bound in heaven, and what he shall loose on

---

*This point is carefully discussed on page 10*ff.* of *The First Century Ecclesia*, by J. B. NORRIS.

earth shall be loosed in heaven.* This was a promise which Peter was later to share with the other apostles, but his inspired pronouncement gave him the right to be first. Thus we find that Peter made the first great revelation of Christianity on the day of Pentecost to Jews, "devout men out of every nation under heaven". And although Paul was the apostle to the Gentiles, it was Peter who was sent to open the Kingdom of heaven to the first group of Gentiles.

---

*The binding and loosing was an idiom taken from current Jewish practice. It implied the prohibition and sanction by the Scribes of actions as unlawful and lawful under the tradition of the elders. First Peter, and then the other apostles, were to have that prerogative. But they would not be arbitrators of the traditions of men but of the law of God.

8

"IT IS GOOD FOR US TO BE HERE"

THE true revelation of Jesus as the Messiah was for the Apostles alone. The time had not yet come for them to reveal what they had themselves not fully understood. So he charged them to tell no man that Jesus was the Christ. But upon the basis of their confession he was able to begin immediately to show them the true nature of his Messiahship, where it was destined to lead him, and what it was to mean to them. "From this time forth began Jesus to show unto his disciples how he must go unto Jerusalem, and suffer many things of the elders, and chief priests, and scribes, and be killed, and be raised again the third day."

This revelation of a suffering and rejected Messiah was too much for Peter. His love for his Lord was too great to accept the terrible picture of imminent persecution and cruel death. "Be it far from thee, Lord", he burst out, "this shall not be unto thee." Ah! Peter, your very love can be a stumblingblock to yourself and an offence to your Lord. Its stimulus is human and not spiritual! The temptation which Peter suddenly brought to Jesus at this critical moment was greater because of the horror and despair in the disciple's eyes. He could bear the enmity of his enemies better than the love of his friends. Every disciple has to learn that the love of our nearest and dearest may be a greater danger to our spiritual welfare than the opposition of many foes. The test must always lie in the source and the nature of their love, whether it is human or spiritual. "Get thee behind me, Satan, thou art an offence unto me." It was not that Peter loved too much, nor that Jesus loved Peter less, but, "Thou savourest not the things that be of God, but those that be of men."

In a moment, the sudden temptation had gone; the sword-thrust from his impetuous disciple was healed; the road to Jerusalem shone clearly down the valley to the south. With characteristic beauty, Jesus used Peter's lapse to show the disciples their part in the purpose of God which lay before him. The cross which had forced a cry of horror from Peter's lips was the lot of the disciple too. Whether it became a real one, was not important; their life as men who followed him must be a life of sacrifice, denying the desires of the flesh, and savouring only the things that be of God. He had come to give life. Accepting this gift meant losing many of the glittering prizes the world held out, but from the ruins of the temporal loss there would emerge a life that was of far greater value than the present conquest of all the world.

Finally Jesus put their Messianic expectation in its true perspective. They had been right to expect a King who would come in majesty and power to exalt the nation and establish a world-wide kingdom of righteousness and peace. But this cross which had so horrified Peter must come before the crown. Then, in the fulness of time, "the Son of Man shall come in the glory of his Father, with his angels; and then he shall reward every man according to his works".

From now on Jesus was to maintain that perspective and make it clearer for them in teaching and parable. Meanwhile, to give them an earnest of its fulfilment, and courage to bear their cross and follow him, Jesus promised, "Verily, I say unto you, There be some standing here which shall not taste of death, till they see the Son of Man coming in his kingdom".

About six days later Jesus fulfilled that promise and three had the unspeakable honour of beholding his glory. We have no record of the events of those days but we may be certain they were occupied in preparation and prayer. Then the day came for which Jesus seemed to be waiting.[1] He took with him Peter, James and John and climbed with them towards the top of one of the lower heights of Mount Hermon.[2] The choice of the three most intimate disciples was undoubtedly of supreme importance. They had already been drawn apart to witness the raising of the little girl in the death chamber at Capernaum; they were yet to be nearest him in his hour of deepest sorrow. Now they were about to witness the moments of his final dedication to the cross, and to see the glory and the victory that lay beyond the desolation of suffering.

---

[1]The Greek words translated "bringeth them up into a high mountain apart" (Matthew 17), are unusual. They imply that Jesus deliberately took the three up to share an experience he was expecting.

[2]They would not ascend the 9,000 feet peaks of Mount Hermon itself: that is still a task for experienced mountaineers. Mount Tabor is sometimes mentioned as the traditional Mount of Transfiguration. Tabor is 50 miles to the south and its summit was dominated by fortified buildings. It is also out of keeping with the context of the Gospel records.

We can picture the little group starting on their way when the mid-day sun was past; climbing steadily up into the higher passes of the giant massif that towers into the sky until its peaks dominate the whole land of Israel. Reaching the snow-filled crevices they would be able to pause and trace the course of the Jordan as it cut through its mountain walls and tumbled into the broad expanse of the Sea of Galilee.

As the evening approached the peaks above them would blush in the dying rays of the sun. The fissures and chasms would become sharply defined, while the great bulk of the mountain itself would cast its own shadow out across the eastern plains towards Damascus. Gradually the shadows would lengthen, the sun, now a ball of fire, would slip down to be extinguished in the deep waters of the Mediterranean. Darkness would creep up the Jordan valley until its vapours stole towards them from the ravines below.* Presently the rising moon would turn the heavens into a luminous depth of light. One by one the stars would begin their night vigil over the slumbering earth.

Jesus had brought his three most loved disciples into a high mountain apart to pray. Here, remote from the haunts of men, they communed with God.

How long they prayed we do not know. The disciples, probably a little apart from their Lord, grew heavy with sleep. They had climbed steadily for hours, and, as often happens, the intensity of their prayer brought a physical reaction. Exhaustion proved too strong for sustained devotion.

For Jesus it was far otherwise. It seems as though he had come in obedience to a call from his Father. As he prayed "the fashion of his countenance was altered and his raiment became white and glistening". The disciples opened their wondering eyes to behold a scene of unearthly radiance. Their Lord was bathed in the light of heaven. Talking with him were two men whom, with the heightened sensitivity of spiritual perception, they immediately recognized as Moses and Elijah. The Son of God, who had come to fulfil the law and the prophets, was in earnest discourse with their greatest representatives. They were talking of the death which Jesus should accomplish at Jerusalem.

*The evidence seems to indicate that the Transfiguration occurred at night. The disciples were heavy with sleep. Also, Luke says, "On the next day, when they were come down ..." (Luke 9:37)

205

The vision faded. The two figures had gone. Peter, now thoroughly roused from the stupor of sleep, cried out, because his impetuous nature demanded expression. But he wist not what to say. All that he knew was that he wanted this wondrous glory perpetuated. "Master, it is good for us to be here: let us make three tabernacles, one for thee, one for Moses, and one for Elias." Peter had yet to learn that only the road to Jerusalem leads to the time when the tabernacle of God will be with men.

The peaks of Hermon had glowed but palely in the excess of light. Slowly they were obscured altogether as a cloud descended upon them. But it was no ordinary cloud—it must have been luminous with an aura of glory. The disciples trembled with unspeakable dread as it enveloped them. The stillness was broken by a voice from the mists, "This is my beloved Son: hear him".

How long the disciples lay prostrate we do not know. But a gentle hand touched them, and they heard a dear, familiar voice, "Arise, and be not afraid". They looked up to see Jesus standing over them—Jesus in his rough home-spun robe. The cloud had gone. The moon shone coldly on the distant peaks.

We cannot read the account of this sacred experience without a sense of gratitude that we have been allowed a glimpse of that night of destiny. Our reverence and awe should be too deep to allow us to discuss its nature. We have seen what the disciples saw. We dare not seek to know what Jesus saw and heard. With Peter we "wist not what to say", for the brightness of the glory fills our hearts. But we can understand the effect of this night of wonder. For Jesus surely it was an experience of the joy that was set before him. It was a renewed anointing for his death, to the glory of his Father and the redemption of all mankind. The disciples would feel that nothing could ever be the same again. John would later write, "That which was from the beginning, which we have heard we have seen with our eyes, which we have looked upon, and our hands have handled, of the Word of life; that which we have seen and heard declare we unto you, that ye also may have fellowship with us". Peter would write, "For we have not followed cunningly devised fables when we made known unto you the power and coming of our Lord Jesus Christ, but were eye-witnesses of his majesty. For he received from God the Father honour and glory, when there came such a voice to him from the excellent glory, This is my beloved Son, in whom

I am well pleased. And this voice which came from heaven we heard, when we were with him in the holy mount.”

But meanwhile, John would remember that moment as he looked up at the bowed head covered with blood and sweat. Peter would remember it after he had cried, “I never knew him”, and would go out into the night and sob as though his heart must break.

9

"HELP THOU MINE UNBELIEF"

WHEN the morning rays of the sun turned to gold the tops of Hermon, it was in truth the dawning of another day for Jesus and his three disciples. As they made their way down to the plains where men lived and toiled there can be little doubt that, like Moses before them, they wist not that their faces shone. The three apostles had been shown something which even their Master could not have taught them. Now in the cool, sunlit air they would be conscious of the peace which always follows communion with God. As soon as they reached the foot of the mount they would reveal to their fellow disciples something of the wonder they had seen. They would tell them that there was no longer need for concern, whatever may befall; Jesus was the Son of God, and they had seen his glory. Yet this was not to be! "Tell the vision to no man until the Son of Man be risen again from the dead." This revelation was for them alone.

An experience like that cannot be shared. No words could begin to convey what God's glory had revealed. This remains true to-day. If in God's grace there come moments when Christ enters into our hearts, and we feel the strength of his presence and the power of his love, we are conscious that we have had one experience which we cannot share. There may be times when "deep calls unto deep", and on some moorland tor, or in the flickering light of a winter fire, we unexpectedly find ourselves confiding in a kindred soul. These are rare and joyous hours. But such experiences can never be related with the intention of demonstrating the power and beauty of Christ in the human heart. Each one yearns for the hour of visitation and waits in hope and prayer. And one day, he comes, and like Peter, James and John we find ourselves reluctant to leave the mountain heights and descend to the plains below.

It was not surprising that the thoughts of the three disciples should be occupied by the things they had witnessed. The scribes had taught that Elijah would be revealed before the coming of the day of the Lord. They wondered how this might be, and what part the vision had in the course of

208

events. "Master", they said, "why say the scribes that Elijah must first come?" Jesus did not hesitate to confirm the accuracy of the scribes' interpretation of the message of Malachi. He told them that it was true that before the final manifestation of the Messiah, Elijah would be sent to restore all things and prepare for the establishment of the Kingdom. Yet (as is so often seen in God's dealings with man) there was also a sense in which Elijah had appeared already in the person of John the Baptist, and the nation had done to him whatsoever it listed. The scribes had not the complete picture of the two Elijahs and the two advents of the Messiah. Jesus brings that out in a counter-question recorded by Mark, "How is it written of the Son of Man that he must suffer many things and be set at nought?" If John's work saw the complete fulfilment of the preparation for the Messiah and his Kingdom, where is the place of Christ's suffering?

The descent of Jesus to the plain bears a striking resemblance to the coming of Moses from the mount. From the glory, harmony and peace of heaven he returns to discord, mockery and unbelief on the earth. Three factors were responsible for the scene which he witnessed. The nine remaining disciples had lost their Lord, and with him had gone their faith: an urgent case of need had come to test that faith; and the scribes, no longer content for Jesus to come into their midst, had tracked him up the Jordan valley. A man had brought his terribly afflicted son to be healed, and learning the whereabouts of Jesus probably from the people of Caesarea Philippi, he came to the foot of the mount, followed by crowds from the city. In the absence of Jesus the man had appealed to the disciples, but they had proved impotent. This presented a wonderful opportunity for the scribes, who took full advantage of their failure to bring ridicule upon their Lord.

So it was that the Son of Man returned from receiving the glory and honour of his Father to encounter the mockery and unbelief of men. His coming had a profound effect upon the people. Mark tells us, "And straightway all the people, when they beheld him, were greatly amazed, and running to him saluted him". We wonder whether the disturbance fully accounts for their amazement and greeting. Is it not possible that the light of God's glory still lingered about him? And is it not a significant contrast that when Moses came down from the Mount his shining face brought fear to the people, but the coming of Christ from his Father's presence brought warmth and joy?

With his coming the tumult ceased. The scribes were embarrassed by their accusations, the disciples by their failure. "What question ye with them?" But the scribes, so quick to condemn him in his absence, had nothing to say. The explanation was made by the man who was responsible for the disturbances. Kneeling before Jesus, he told him that he had brought his only son who was pining away in the grip of epilepsy. He was dumb, and so terribly afflicted that he writhed foaming on the earth, gnashing his teeth.* "And", he said, "I spake to thy disciples that they should cast him out, and they could not."

The cry of Jesus seems to have in it something of the contrast between the mountain heights and this vale of tears, the glory of the Father's presence, and the reproach of men. It has in it too, the yearning for the completion of his work, that all this suffering and discord may cease. It was a cry of protestation which included them all—the mocking scribes, the unbelieving disciples, the anxious father. "O faithless generation, how long shall I be with you? How long shall I suffer you?" But his rebuke was no refusal; his impatience of the wilful need of man was not impatience of his ministry of love. That is inexhaustible. Until death itself is swallowed up in victory the gracious invitation will remain, "Bring him unto me".

Coming to Jesus the poor youth was seized with a paroxysm such as the father had described. Jesus watched him as he writhed at his feet. The commotion that had followed the disciples' failure, the challenge of the scribes, the shouting of the people, had made the atmosphere a tense and difficult background for the calm confidence of faith. Jesus sought to bring peace into the disturbed heart of the father which would inspire in him that belief which alone would save his son. Seeking, as he always did, those adequate grounds of faith, Jesus turned to the man, and asked him how long he had been like this. "Of a child", he answered, and took the opportunity of telling him more of the effect of the malady on his son. So great was his distress that the boy lost all control of his faculties, often falling into the fire and water. "But", he cried in sudden entreaty, "if thou canst do anything have compassion on us, and help us." Ah, foolish man! Let the greatness of thy need excuse thy faithless heart! As well may

---

*Luke describes the youth as suddenly crying out. This in no way contradicts the statement in Mark that the boy was dumb. It is not difficult to imagine inarticulate cries being forced from him in his terrible paroxysms.

he take a bucket to the brink of the fathomless ocean and cry, "If thou canst!" With infinite love Jesus turned the question round, and doing so, gave him an impetus for faith. He was looking pleadingly at Jesus, yearning to see his son restored. Jesus led him back to the inmost recesses of his own heart. Do not demand it of me, I am willing; demand it of yourself. "If *thou* canst believe." His son was in his hands. His faith alone could release the power that Jesus was willing to give.

In a moment the man saw it. A spark of grace had been kindled in his heart, and by its light he saw for the first time the depths of his faithlessness. It will always be so. Jesus alone can reveal to us the exceeding sinfulness of sin; he alone can show us the fetters of unbelief chaining us to our prison wall. The father realized he could be his son's worst enemy. Implicit in that knowledge was belief in Jesus. He cried out pathetically yet triumphantly, "Lord, I believe; help thou mine unbelief".

Clinging desperately to Jesus, conscious only of his insufficiency, but praying for help, he was, all unknowingly, a wonderful example of true faith. For what can we add to that? Tears of penitence, acknowledgment of weakness, words of profound conviction—those are the ingredients of faith. We hardly need to hear the sequel. "And Jesus rebuked the unclean spirit and healed the child, and delivered him again to his father."

When they were alone the nine disciples asked Jesus why they had so dismally failed. "Because of your unbelief", he answered, "for verily I say unto you, If ye have faith as a grain of mustard seed, ye shall say unto this mountain, Remove hence to yonder place; and it shall remove; and nothing shall be impossible unto you. Howbeit this kind goeth not out but by prayer."

They had thought that they had faith in him, but it was a profession grown languid in the ebb and flow of daily life. It was not a faith which could win for them a place with their companions on the heights of Hermon, nor save the name of their Lord from shame on the plains below. The faith that Jesus required of them was an intense vitalizing force which sought only the Kingdom of God, and His righteousness; that was sustained by prayer. Faith of *that* kind, though only as small as the proverbial mustard seed, could remove mountains. The smallest faith if it is true faith, can overcome the greatest obstacles, because it is the channel which links the believer to the infinite power of God. Without it we can do nothing; with it we can do all things.

10

"FOR ME AND THEE"

THE distant parts of the land of Israel were no longer
secluded resting places for Jesus and his apostles. The
scribes had come, and the multitudes were once more
gathering around. Moreover, the purpose of the northward
journey had been accomplished. The glory of the mount was
more than a memory; it was for Jesus a glorious incentive,
and for the three disciples a precious and unforgettable
secret. The little company therefore made its way southwards to Galilee, but not this time to the crowds who again
would have eagerly responded to the teaching and the power.
Mark says that they "passed through Galilee, and he would
not that any man should know it. For he taught his disciples
..." Nor do the evangelists leave us in doubt concerning the
nature of his teaching: "The Son of man is delivered into the
hands of men, and they shall kill him; and after that he is
killed he shall rise the third day". A few hours before Jesus
had cast an unclean spirit out of a lunatic. He takes no step
to cast the devil out of his own treacherous disciple, nor does
he seek to move the mountain that rears its skull-shaped
form outside the city wall. His great desire is that his disciples
shall see the full picture of their Lord's destiny. They must realize that before the world can be for the Messiah, the Messiah
must be for the world. "Let these sayings sink down into your
ears he said. They were exceedingly sorrowful: but they could
not understand. Peter their spokesman was silent. The sting
of his Lord's rebuke was fresh and painful. So, though they
were bewildered and depressed, they were afraid to ask him.

It would seem that Jesus remained in Galilee for some
little time, avoiding public notice and instructing the disciples.
When at last they returned to the familiar streets of
Capernaum, the collectors of the temple dues approached
Peter privately and asked whether his Master offered the
half shekel which under the law was payable by every Jew
over twenty.* It is not certainly known whether or not the

---

*Exodus 30:11–16.

"… it shall be more tolerable for the land of Sodom in the day of judgment …" (Matthew 11:24)

"… the foolish said unto the wise, Give us of your oil;
for our lamps are gone out." (Matthew 25:8)

rabbis were exempt from this yearly payment, but it appears that the collectors approached Peter in a spirit of deference and enquiry, rather than criticism. Either from his knowledge of the past, or in his confidence that Jesus would willingly render what God required in His law, Peter answered for his Master without hesitation. When he reached the house he found Jesus waiting for him, fully aware of what had taken place. But there was no reproof in the Lord's words, "What thinkest thou Simon? Of whom do the kings of the earth take custom or tribute? Of their own children or of strangers?" "Of strangers", he answered readily. "Then", said Jesus, "are the children free." Peter must have realized at once how hastily he had committed his Lord. On his own recent acknowledgment, Jesus was the Son of the King of Heaven. The temple was his Father's house, and on those grounds alone there could be no question of his paying for its maintenance. But the implication was deeper than that. The Son of God was greater than the temple made with hands. He was the true sanctuary of which the building was only the type. The flowing of the blood of bulls and goats would be finally staunched when the blood flowed from his broken body. The glory of God would leave the temporary abode of Mount Moriah and be revealed in the Son. When his perfect offering was accomplished with his approaching sacrifice the present building was ready to vanish away: a new and living way into the Holiest was about to be prepared through the veil of his flesh. The half shekel "atonement money" required of the Israelites was to be fully paid within the year. The Son was free from the impositions required for the physical temple. In prospect, the apostles were free too, because they were associated with the true temple of God. They were to pay their dues to him: not the contribution of a fixed sum, but the abiding dedication of their whole life as sons of God and ministers of the true temple.

Having made the position clear to Peter and thus protected him from any misunderstanding in the future, Jesus once more manifested that humility of spirit which characterized all his actions. "Nevertheless, lest we should offend them, go thou to the sea, and cast a hook, and take up the fish that first cometh up, and when thou hast opened his mouth thou shalt find a piece of money; that take and give unto them for me and thee." It cannot be without significance that Peter must render this service for his Lord in his natural occupation as fisherman. In this act of obedience he would learn

213

that the heavenly treasury was ever open to the faithful child of God, despite the protest of reason. How much work of the Lord has been neglected because we have not the faith to go to the water's edge and throw out our hook? Peter knew the ways of the sea; he could easily have argued against the reasonableness of his commission. But natural knowledge is irrelevant and can be dangerous when we are under the instructions of Christ. Peter had arrived at that blessed state where he had more confidence in his Lord than in the familiar paths of his daily life.

Some features in the events of the last few days had disturbed the disciples, stimulating thoughts which they would be loath to admit were often in their minds. It concerned their status in the Kingdom of God. Only three of them had been selected to witness the Transfiguration, whilst nine remained below: Jesus was frequently to be seen in tender intimacy with John: in the most natural way the synagogue officials had approached Peter as the spokesman of the apostles. It is not unlikely that the favoured ones felt that their pre-eminence was a happy augury for the day when their Master revealed himself as the nation's Messiah. It is even more likely that some of the others were resentful at what they felt was favouritism, and moved by envy, they stubbornly resisted the real or imagined claims of their brethren. With Jesus out of earshot, conversation turned to dispute. The disciples returned to the estate from which they had been called, pressing their rights, forgetful of the claims of their Lord.

As they neared Peter's house and realized that they must meet their Master they would make hasty attempts to curb their tempers, but their red faces and darkly glowing eyes would reveal how imperfectly they had succeeded.

"What was it that ye disputed with yourselves by the way?" So he knew! His absence had not prevented his sharing their conversation. He could enter into their moments of nobility, and be with them in their hour of shame. His love would encourage them in the one yet would not abandon them in the other. Sensing this the disciples openly asked him, "Who is greatest in the Kingdom of Heaven ?"* Jesus answered them unexpectedly. He did not say, "He that loveth most", or "He that serveth best". His answer is at once no answer and the only possible answer, "If any man desire to be first, the same shall be last of all". Making his reply even

*Matthew 18:1

214

more eloquent he leaned forward and drew towards him one of the children who were so often to be seen near him. Taking him in his arms, he said, "Verily I say unto you, except ye be converted and become as little children, ye shall not enter into the kingdom of heaven. Whosoever shall humble himself as this little child, the same is greatest in the kingdom of · heaven".

They were to find again the childlike trust that loves unquestioningly and has utter confidence in the Father; to regain the simplicity of those years which were free from the selfish speculations of later days. This is to understand the call of Jesus and to become children of the Kingdom. We are only truly converted when, having gone forth to meet the stress and storms of life, we emerge from the conflict with a trust in God as strong as that which we had shown as children in our earthly parents. We can only win such a victory by unswerving loyalty to Christ and uncompromising obedience to his precepts. To offend one of Christ's little ones is to bring down the judgment of heaven. Offence will come against the servant as against the master, "But woe unto that man by whom the offence cometh". Because the power of their Father is commensurate with His love, the children are never beyond the scope of His care, however bitter the persecution they may suffer, and their final emergence into His presence is assured. Indeed although their enemies may persistently assault them there remains a very real sense in which they cannot be offended: "Great peace have they which love thy law, and nothing shall offend them".

The world is not the only offender of Christ's "little ones". Where his love is not fully present there is always grave danger of offence by word and example. Jesus warns his own disciples, "Take heed that ye despise not one of these little ones, for I say unto you that in heaven their angels do always behold the face of my Father which is in heaven". We may not often think of this intimate ministration of the angels. We are content to consider them as powerful messengers of God, accomplishing His great purposes, commissioned to the earth on dramatic occasions when the Eternal Father condescends to reveal His will to men, but for the most part attending the Throne of God in glory. Here Jesus shows another work that is assigned to them, and pondering his words, we become conscious that similar references to the work of angels in other parts of Scripture shine in a new light.

When a child of the world becomes a child of God, it is the Father's good pleasure to appoint one of His Holy Ones to have him in his keeping. Thus it appears that, whilst they are above and beyond us in our present estate, they serve us, because we are called to the glory of Christ. The world itself received the service and guidance of the angels in a general way under the Hand of God, but here we have a glimpse of their personal charge. So highly does God honour those who obey Him in a spirit of meekness and love! It is a wonderful inspiration and comfort to realize that when we give our lives to God in humble dedication, He appoints us a guardian angel, not to appropriate the work of Christ, but to accompany us throughout our lives, guiding us through the difficult paths and dark places, helping us in moments of spiritual danger. We probably forget the angels far too much. We neglect to tell our own "little ones" of their protecting power and guidance. To do so is to despise their loving condescension, and to be guilty of irreverence toward Him who sent them on their mission of love.

Let us meditate prayerfully upon the angels: let us lift up our hearts in grateful acknowledgment to our Heavenly Father for the mighty one whom He has sent to stand guard over our life. Let us constantly remember him whose sacrificial love made this relationship possible. Then we shall see a Bethel wherever a child of God is found.

11

"NEVER MAN SPAKE LIKE THIS MAN"

THE summer was almost over and the great feast of Tabernacles was at hand. It was a popular and joyous feast, celebrating the time when God brought out the Israelites from Egypt and caused them to sojourn in the wilderness before bringing them into the promised land. Combined with this celebration was what would be known to-day as a Harvest Festival, where thanksgiving was rendered after the fruits of the land had been safely gathered in. A happy atmosphere prevailed throughout the seven days of the feast, particularly among the younger Jews. All who were physically able to do so left the comparative comfort of their homes and constructed temporary booths where they lived in carefree "hardship" until the feast was ended. To the observer looking down over the hundreds of hastily erected tents on the Mount of Olives, Jerusalem must have presented a strange and stirring sight. Each building would have its own covering of thickly-leaved branches, whilst in every available space clusters of tents would make their mushroom growth. It was a period too of intense ceremonial activity. More sacrifices were offered than at any of the other feasts, there were daily processions round the altar, solemn marches to the pool of Siloam, the singing of the Hallel, the reading of the law, the lighting of the four great candelabra in the Court of the Women. The whole picture was one of joy and thanksgiving.

Jesus had not been to Jerusalem for many months. But now the city was to impel him towards his crowning work. His ministry in Galilee was virtually over. Although the majority of the common people there were still loyal and would remain so to the end, their grateful and welcoming voices were now mingled with shouts of opposition and blasphemy. During the past weeks he had left the multitudes, and sought the peace of remote places to find seclusion with his little band of disciples.

As the feast of Tabernacles drew near and companies of Galileans from the towns and villages began to make their arrangements to travel together to Jerusalem, Christ's brothers approached him and suggested that it would be advisable for him to come with them to the feast. They give the appearance of being puzzled rather than hostile. That Jesus was accomplishing remarkable things in Galilee they had no doubt, but they were sceptical of his claims and anxious to put them to the more conclusive test of the temple rulers. In view of what they could only believe to be weakness in his attitude to the local scribes and Pharisees, it would not be long before he was forced to confirm that weakness or reveal his strength in the more important setting in Jerusalem.

But Jesus had no desire to accompany his brothers. There are many things he must tell his disciples which cannot be shared by sceptics whatever the blood relationship might be. The world and the church cannot accomplish a journey to Jerusalem together. "My time has not yet come: but your time is always ready. The world cannot hate you: but me it hateth because I testify of it that the works thereof are evil."

So it was that his brothers went away without him, and Jesus, after abiding in Galilee for a little while longer, eventually set off with his disciples, "as it were in secret".

Meanwhile, in Jerusalem his absence caused more disturbance than his presence. The Jewish rulers searched for him: they were now determined upon his arrest. Unable to find him they asked each other, "Where is he?" There was equal speculation with less decision among the people. Many said, "He is a good man". Others, "Nay, but he deceiveth the people". Much subdued murmuring prevailed. Only true knowledge of his identity and serene confidence in him will save men.

The whole background of the incidents at this feast is pulsating with disturbance and perplexity, with unreserved scorn and timid loyalty. There was speculation among the people and divided opinions in the council chamber. Temple police sent to arrest him returned empty-handed. In ordinary circumstances their excuse would have had dire consequences for them; now it only brought forth a sarcastic protest. There was even a token rebellion in the Sanhedrin itself.

When we seek the reason for this commotion we realize that it was inevitable. Jesus had been away from Jerusalem for a long time, During the interval the whole of Galilee had acclaimed him. He had had to restrain the people from making him king and marching with him into Jerusalem: he had shown miraculous powers in dealing with individuals and multitudes. Only the disciples had received the revelation of what lay before him in Jerusalem. The great majority still clung to the hope that he would manifest himself in power at the right moment. There could therefore be nothing more significant than the appearance of Jesus in Jerusalem at one of the great feasts. The Jewish rulers awaited his coming with apprehension. The people were half hoping and half fearing. Those from Galilee would undoubtedly anticipate his advent joyfully, convinced of his intentions: the people of Jerusalem, absorbing the opinion of the priests, would answer that he was a deceiver.

The great feast was half over when Jesus came. He went quietly into the Temple courts and began to teach. The people hearing him were immediately impressed, and wondered among themselves whether the failure of the rulers to apprehend him was explained by their knowledge that he was indeed the Messiah. But they were perplexed by the lack of mystery which surrounded his origin. "Howbeit", they said, "we know this man, whence he is: but when Christ cometh, no man knows whence he is." Jesus pointed beyond the beginnings which they thought they knew to the real purpose of his coming and the identity of the One who had sent him. There lay their fatal ignorance. Such statements always provoked the rulers of Israel. There was a stir in the crowd. Several Pharisees started forward with dark scowls, intent on dragging him away. But as suddenly they hesitated and drew back. The people were quick to notice this indecision: it was a moral victory for Jesus. Many believed on him and said, "When Christ cometh will he do more miracles than these which this man bath done?" Perceiving the growing influence of Jesus over the people, and realizing their own inadequacy to deal with the situation, the Pharisees sought the co-operation of their enemies. For quite different reasons the chief priests were anxious to comply, and the temple police were sent to take him. But Jesus was not taken. His hour had not yet come. He spoke to the people of remaining but a short while with them and then going away to the One who had sent him. When he had taken that journey they would seek him but would not find him. This intrigued the Jews: did he intend to go beyond the confines of Israel and teach the people of the Dispersion? What a plea there is in these exchanges for the humility and teachableness of that little child who lay for a moment in his arms in the house at Capernaum!

On the last day of the feast Jesus stood forth in the temple area and made his great proclamation, "If any man thirst let him come unto me and drink. He that believeth on me, as the Scripture hath said, out of his belly shall flow rivers of living water". It is probable that Jesus made this announcement as the priests were carrying the golden vessel containing the waters of Siloam which they were to pour over the altar. How appropriate those words were from the lips of the one who was about to be the smitten rock destined to give the water of life to the children of God in the wilderness! Once more his words caused strife and divided opinions. Many proclaimed him the prophet, others, the Christ, whilst with strangest irony there were those who refused to believe at all because the Messiah should be the seed of David, and be born in Bethlehem!

Presently the Temple officers returned to the rulers empty-handed. The failure of their mission is most eloquent testimony to the power of Christ's teaching. Going to arrest him, probably without the slightest compunction, they had been arrested themselves by his bearing and his message. Their hands thrust out to take him had dropped to their sides: their harsh words of command were never uttered. They left him, to confess their failure, their fear of him giving them courage to face their own masters, "Never man spake like this man". How often, and in how many different ways that scene has been enacted since! The Pharisees, who at this time were the most anxious of all the rulers to apprehend him, chided with the soldiers, giving vent to their disappointment and bitterness. So this man had managed to deceive them too! Is it not enough that the rulers refuse to accept him? The people doubtless are moved, but they know nothing of the law and are cursed.

Quite unexpectedly the quiet, courteous voice of Nicodemus intervened. His knowledge of Jesus and his sense of justice overcame his natural reticence. He showed how wrong the Pharisees were, It was not true that none of the rulers believed on him. And it was the Pharisees, not the people, who appeared to be ignorant of the law, by condemning a man without hearing him or considering his claims. But his courage quickly evaporated when these baffled men turned the full venom of their scorn upon him. "Art thou also of Galilee? Search and look, for out of Galilee ariseth no prophet." Nicodemus did not accept a challenge he could have taken up successfully. He had no spirit left in him. "Every man went unto his own house. Jesus went unto the mount of Olives."

12

CASTING THE FIRST STONE

THE rulers of Israel left the temple for the comfort of their own homes, the Messiah of Israel left the temple and climbed the slopes of Olivet to pray under the starry sky. How often Jesus did that! The familiar slopes that looked out over the temple had been sanctified by many nights of communion for the supreme dedication which was to be made when the hatred that seethed within those walls had exacted its price.

Early in the morning Jesus was once more in the temple. The people crowded to him and he sat down to teach. Although the feast was now over, it is probable that many of the worshippers stayed in the city because of the presence of Jesus. The events of yesterday though not dramatic had created a situation of tension. There can be no doubt that the scribes and Pharisees were determined to apprehend him, awaiting only the smallest pretext. So far their efforts had only brought humiliation upon themselves, but who could say when they would break through his defences and effect his arrest?

The Pharisees had not learned their lesson. They were humbled but not discouraged. Determined to achieve their object they did not hesitate to use a woman's shame to achieve their ends.* The quiet scene in the courts was interrupted by a group of scribes and Pharisees dragging to him a terrified and dishevelled woman. Careless of her feelings, they sought only to make her the instrument of their enmity against him. "Master, this woman was taken in adultery, in the very act." Here was the irrefutable evidence; now they could lay their snare. "Moses in the law commanded us that such should be stoned: but what sayest thou?" It was a problem not without subtlety and danger. These men knew the attitude of Jesus towards publicans and sinners, and they were reasonably certain that he would not allow her to be stoned. This would immediately expose him to the accusation

---

*Doubts have been cast upon the genuineness of this account. The problem is carefully discussed in *The Gospel of John*, by JOHN CARTER (pages 100–1).

that he was deliberately refuting the law of Moses, an accusation which would be only partly mitigated by the fact that stoning was not now the general practice in such cases. In the remote event of his endorsing the law of Moses their victory could be greater. He would both incur the displeasure of the people for his inconsistency and the political charge that he was challenging the prerogative of Rome. Thus his enemies thought they had a strong case. At best they would arrest him, and in any event they would succeed in breaking the people's confidence in him.

They had set the scene of this unhappy drama. They watched him now, triumph and hate shining in their eyes. The crowds pressed round breathlessly. The half clothed, bareheaded woman, taut with a shame even greater than her fear, stood exposed to their hungry gaze. She dare not lift her eyes to this man whom the rulers had appointed to be her judge. She knew nothing of the plot that lay behind this last terrible hour. But her judge did not look at her. Entering into her feelings, his love spared her that. He bent forward from his sitting position and wrote in the dust. His action was a silent plea to the conscience of those men, made heartless by their hatred. With an eloquence which no words could equal he was telling them to leave the poor woman alone, to relieve him of the constraint of speaking. He gave them time to allow their own hearts to convict them. Had they gone away then they would have been humbled, but it would be as nothing compared to the abasement to which Jesus was so loath to commit them. As was so often the case they mistook his strength for weakness; they were blind to everything but his apparent indecision. They continued their demand, spurning the escape he had offered them.

The moment came when there could be no evasion of the judgment for which they asked. The Lord stood up and searched the faces of these rulers of Israel who had stooped so low. His eyes burned with anger as he looked from one to the other. Never before had they so felt the stature and holiness of the man who stood before them. They became conscious that they were mean and graceless. Their assurance shrivelled under this steady gaze which seared into their souls sparing none of the evil things now exposed there. They saw the enormity of their action. Then he spoke: "He that is without sin among you, let him first cast a stone at her". That was all he needed to say. He stooped and resumed his writing, waiting once more for their consciences to work. In the morning shadows of their temple, in full view of the expectant crowds, they looked strangely one at another until they could bear each other's glances no more. He had not accused any of them: he had left it to each one to decide. Jesus was taking no notice of them, he had no desire to be a witness of their humiliation. He was only grieved that it had become necessary. They watched his stooping form conscious that at any moment he could stand up and challenge them, and they would have nothing to say. Silently each made the inevitable confession of his guilt. The eldest of them edged into the crowd and was lost to view. One by one the others melted away until none was left. The woman could have gone too, but she stayed. Something bigger than her fear and her shame kept her near Jesus. He rose, and for the first time he looked her full in the face. "Woman, where are those thine accusers? Hath no man condemned thee?" "No man, Lord." She was not so distracted that she was blind to the reason for the slow departure of her accusers. Looking into the face of Jesus, strong, pure, heavenly, she saw the full degradation of her wilful passion. Surely there are tears of penitence in her eyes! "Neither do I condemn thee: go, and sin no more."

Jesus did not condone her sin, did not even offer her forgiveness and peace. Sinners could not condemn her; neither would the one who was without sin. Jesus left it to her to merit forgiveness by her future conduct and faith: but he had given her a glimpse of the mercy and grace that were waiting for her appeal. Although we hear nothing more of her we may hope that though she went away at his command, she would come back of her own free will, her desires sublimated, to join the little company of women who loved much because they had been forgiven much.

This incident has proved invaluable in Christian history. It is a graphic exposition of the Master's words on the mount, "Judge not, that ye be not judged". However damning the evidence may be against our brother, if we pause and look into our own hearts, we shall go quietly away and leave him with his Lord. There are times when it becomes necessary to take action, but that action must not be taken because we have condemned our brother. It will be taken in the painful consciousness of our own unworthiness, and with a love which will plead intercession before the Throne of Grace. We shall wait with eagerness for the first signs of penitence so that we can joyfully restore the erring one to the fellowship of the saints.

13

"THOU HAST SEEN HIM"

LATER the same day Jesus stood up in the temple and proclaimed himself the light of the world. The claim was immediately repudiated by the Pharisees and a verbal battle ensued which resulted in many of the people and even some of the rulers believing on him. But in most of them it was a superficial faith which failed to stand the test to which it was now exposed. The Jews resorted to the familiar claim that they were the children of Abraham: this would not do, Jesus observed, since unlike them, Abraham had rejoiced to see his day. "Thou art not yet fifty years old", they cried, "and hast thou seen Abraham?" "Verily, verily, I say unto you, Before Abraham was, I am." This dramatic assertion was altogether too much for them. Deeds, not words, could be the only answer to this apparent blasphemy. They took up stones, but Jesus moved away into a crowd that was not altogether hostile, and left the temple.

A thought of surpassing loveliness is often lost by the artificial break between the eighth and ninth chapters of John. If we link the two verses it immediately becomes apparent. Following the dispute in the temple, "the Jews took up stones to cast at Jesus; he went out of the temple, going through the midst of them, and so passed by. And as he passed by, he saw a man that was blind from his birth". Escaping from men intent upon his hurt, Jesus found the need of man a barrier he could not pass. Here is an epitome of his life. From the beginning of his ministry this persecution had gone on, intensifying with the passing months until it reached its terrible climax. But it never interrupted his gentle ministration of love, or dulled his ear to the cry of man. His enemies did not succeed in diverting him from his purpose, and, by a sublime paradox, when at last they nailed him to the cross, he achieved his greatest victory in satisfying man's deepest need.

The blind man was probably begging in the precincts of the temple. The knowledge that he was born blind indicates that he was a familiar figure there and his history well known.

The disciples, puzzled by the general belief in the close relationship between sin and suffering, asked Jesus whether this man had sinned or his parents. The Jews persisted in believing in this connection in spite of the lesson of the book of Job. They took it to illogical lengths, so that when they found a man afflicted from birth, they were driven to the point of proclaiming it to be the result of pre-natal sin.

That there is an affinity between sin and suffering, and sometimes a direct connection, Jesus did not deny. But to assume that connection in every case by a cruel scrutiny of the secret life of a sufferer was false in principle and morally wrong. "Neither hath this man sinned, nor his parents: but that the works of God should be made manifest in him." Jesus refrained from discussing the subject, confining his attention to this man's need, and his power to help. God's purpose was that His works should be manifested in this blind beggar, and that by his natural and spiritual sight he would be a witness to the Light of the World. As the shadows of this day were lengthening, so the day of his own earthly life was drawing to its close, and with it would go these opportunities of loving service. "I must work the works of Him that sent me, while it is day: the night cometh when no man can work. As long as I am in the world I am the light of the world." No more fitting work could be found for the Light of the World than the opening of the eyes of the blind, unless it were the opening also of the eyes of his understanding. And such was his purpose now.

The blind man was leaning against the wall of the temple. He had been crying out to passers-by for alms; now as the sound of footsteps stopped before him, he waited expectantly. The inconsiderate words of the disciples had little effect upon a man hardened by years of charity. But for the first time he heard the voice of Jesus. With the enhanced sensitiveness of the blind he felt instantly the strength of the one who spoke. He had heard of the man from Galilee who was creating so much stir in the temple. The words he now listened to were beyond his comprehension, but he knew that this man intended to do something for him. Suddenly he felt his eye-lids touched by strong, purposeful fingers. A damp heaviness pressed against them. Then that rich voice spoke again, but this time directly to him. "Go wash in the pool of Siloam." Without hesitation he obeyed. He began his long journey through the narrow crowded streets of the lower city.

225

Reaching the end of the temple wall his rapidly tapping stick would no longer find the familiar landmarks. He would lift his voice to cry, not for alms, but for guidance to those waters which would take away his blindness and bring him into a new world of light and beauty. Passers-by would look in astonishment at the man with a clay-spattered face, groping uncertainly but with set purpose along the tortuous streets, calling with pathetic eagerness to be led to the pool of Siloam. Perhaps a friendly hand would take his arm and shorten his journey. At last he stood beside the waters washing his eyes. In a breathless moment he looked out upon a world of movement and colour. The sounds and sensations of a lifetime took form and beauty. John says simply, "He went his way, therefore, and washed, and came, seeing".

He would no doubt make his way through his new world to seek his benefactor. Unable to find him he would joyfully hurry to behold for the first time his parents and his home. Neighbours looking upon this figure, so familiar yet so changed by his radiant smile, and his shining eyes, questioned his identity, only to be assured that he was indeed the man who had sat and begged.

The neighbours decided that their best course was to take him to the Pharisees. To them he answered simply, "He put clay upon my eyes, and I washed and do see". This stirred up that division among them that had been evident all day. There were those who dismissed the Lord's claims because he had broken the sabbath, but there were others who reflected "How can a man that is a sinner do such miracles?" But the hostility prevailed. The timidity on the side of conscience continued to the end, and only found full expression when there was left a lifeless body to wrap in grave-clothes and place reverently in a tomb.

The interview which followed is an example of the power of simple truth over perversity. The Pharisees were made to look ridiculous; their only remedy to preserve their tattered dignity was to hurt the man Jesus had healed.

The next question betrayed their confusion. What did he think of his benefactor? "He is a prophet!" Question and answer solved nothing. A moment ago they had appeared satisfied about the genuineness of the case. Now they re-opened the matter by questioning the man's parents. This was futile. They confirmed that he was their son, and that he had been born blind. With the threat of excommunication hanging over them they felt their announcements sufficiently bold: "He is of age, ask him; he shall speak for himself".

They turned to him again. "Give God the praise; we know that this man is a sinner." He replied with sincere humility but with none of his parents' fear, "Whether he be a sinner or no, I know not". But his words unconsciously turned to irony as he added this simple truth, "One thing I know, that, whereas I was blind, now I see".

The Pharisees had been driven back to their starting point. They asked him again how Jesus opened his eyes. But under this fatuous inquisition the young man grew impatient. How they hated his benefactor! Their stubbornness was stimulating his faith in Jesus. "I have told you already, and ye did not hear. Wherefore would ye hear it again? Will ye also be his disciples?" His artless reply stung them to the quick. He could have said nothing more calculated to reduce them to impotent rage than the suggestion that they should be disciples of Jesus. But he had succeeded in turning their attack into defence. "Thou art his disciple, but we are Moses' disciples. We know that God spake unto Moses: as for this fellow, we know not whence he is." Yet in appealing to Moses they were appealing to one who proclaimed the coming of the greater prophet to whom they must turn or be consumed. The restored man would know nothing of this, but their words had revealed to his quick brain a gaping hole in their reasoning. With growing confidence the man who sees begins to instruct the blind. At first he had confessed that he knew not whether Jesus was a sinner: now they had fully convinced him that he was not. "Why herein is a marvellous thing, that ye know not from whence he is, and yet he hath opened mine eyes. Now we know that God heareth not sinners: but if any man be a worshipper of God and doeth his will, him he heareth. Since the world began was it not heard that any man opened the eyes of one that was born blind. If this man were not of God, he could do nothing."

This was altogether too much for the Pharisees. The interview had assumed a grotesque form. It could only have one ending if they were to salvage the slightest vestige of dignity. They still had the power to ruin him. "Thou wast altogether born in sins, and dost thou teach us? And they cast him out." It is an age-old remedy. Not only would he no longer worship, but he was ostracized from society, and would find all the doors of employment closed to him. Even those who engaged in conversation with him would be frowned upon. In view of the timidity of his parents it is possible that he would be turned out from his own home.

But the record does not end there. Such loyalty to Christ will always have the same glorious sequel. How many days of loneliness and persecution the young man endured we do not know, but he was ready now for the complete enlightenment of spiritual vision.

Jesus heard that he had been cast out, and he went in search of him. "And when he had found him, he said unto him, Dost thou believe in the Son of God?" The estranged man would immediately recognize that voice and know who stood before him. For the first time his eyes reverently searched the face of the one who had made him whole. His reply seems to sense the impending revelation and promised obedience. "Who is he, Lord, that I might believe on him?" With what loving appropriateness Jesus finally reveals himself by reminding him of the evidence which supports his claim. "Thou hast seen him." And to remove the last shadow of doubt, "It is he that talketh with thee." And so this poignant scene ended in the only possible way. John records it: "Lord, I believe. And he worshipped him".

We cannot leave this dramatic incident without briefly suggesting its lessons. As we have seen, the "signs" of John's Gospel contained the particular purpose of illustrating the great spiritual truths of Christ's work. This miracle set forth the claim that Jesus had made in the temple a few hours before. It showed him to be the Light of the World. The blind man begging at the gate of the temple is a powerful symbol of the blindness and poverty of man, proclaiming his need at the gateway of heaven. The power to remove both (for the one is largely determined by the other) is revealed by the coming of the Son of Man. Our blind eyes are touched by the ointment prepared by the mingling of the dust of the ground with the moisture from the mouth of him who was sent from heaven. But this does not cure us. We receive the command to go and wash in the waters of Apostleship (John is careful to point out that Siloam means Sent). It is a long and difficult journey. Some do not undertake it at all; some begin only to give it up and resume their begging at the gate. Often it is made shorter and easier by the friendly guidance of one who can see. It is the responsibility of all enlightened ones to listen for the tapping of the stick and the cry to be directed to the waters of Siloam. But faith and obedience are rewarded. With the washing of the waters we enter a new world illuminated by the Sun of Righteousness. This may mean estrangement, persecution and sacrifice, but it will also be an opportunity for witness and loyalty. Jesus will know. He will seek us out and invite us into a fellowship so deep and abiding that all the former relationships are like the phantom sounds and movements of the dark world from which we have been delivered.

"For judgment I am come into this world, that they which see not might see; and they which see might be made blind."

BOOK FIVE: LESSONS IN DISCIPLESHIP

Book Six

TOWARDS JERUSALEM

1

"HE STEDFASTLY SET HIS FACE"

FOLLOWING the eventful days at the Feast of Tabernacles Jesus returned to Galilee, but not to resume his ministry there, nor indeed to stay any length of time. He gave his disciples the opportunity of bidding farewell to their homes and families, because Galilee would see them no more until the Son of Man was risen from the dead. Luke, who records the memories of this Jerusalem journey in far greater detail than the other evangelists, describes this final departure from Galilee. "And it came to pass, when the time was come that he should be received up, he stedfastly set his face to go to Jerusalem"—words which eloquently convey both the sense of dedication, and the glory that lay beyond the cross. His time was now only a few months away, his witness was almost over. His voice had been drowned by the clamorous opposition round the populous shores of Galilee; the priests of Jerusalem were watching carefully for the first opportunity to arrest him. Even the Samaritans were about to refuse him.

The aspect of Jesus must have changed during these last months of continual opposition; a tenseness begins to creep into the Gospel narrative. The joyful days on the shores of the sunlit lake when all men followed and acclaimed him, had gone. The times when he could sit on the gentle slopes of the hills, watch a great crowd settling on the grass, and speak of the wonders of his Father's Kingdom, were quickly fading memories. His words convince us that lines of care could be traced in his face; resolution, almost fearful in its intensity, shone in his eyes. This change never affected his love and thoughtfulness for those to whom he ministered, but it betrayed that suffering of his soul that becomes articulate in the Psalms. It is with relief that we watch his features relax as he takes a child into his arms, and we feel a glow of joy when we see the hospitable doors of Bethany open to receive him. His journey now takes him through Samaria, Perea and Judea, visiting many towns and villages on the way, but his goal is always Jerusalem. Nothing remained now but to go resolutely forward and finish the work his Father had given him to do. Now the tenor of his teaching changed. He openly declared himself to be the Messiah of Israel. His parables no longer portrayed the present aspect of the Kingdom, but emphasized the day of his return in power and judgment. All men should know him as the Christ, the Son of David, and if they rejected him they must reject him as the Messiah.

The last scene in Galilee is one of tender sadness. The Christ of God looked out upon the cities of the lake— Bethsaida, with its busy water front and its humble dwellings; Capernaum, commanded by its stately synagogue, its cluster of roof tops gleaming in the sunshine; away inland to the northwest the hazy outline of Chorazin. Their teeming thousands had followed him so readily. But their fear of the priests had been greater than their loyalty to him. They had left him with his handful of faithful disciples. They had made their terrible choice, and even their final support at the coming Passover would not avail them.

"Woe unto thee, Chorazin! Woe unto thee, Bethsaida! for if the mighty works which were done in you, had been done in Tyre and Sidon, they would have repented long ago in sackcloth and ashes ... And thou, Capernaum, which art exalted unto heaven, shalt be brought down to hell ... It shall be more tolerable for the land of Sodom in the day of judgment than for thee."

The disciples looked in alarm at this loving Master who had suddenly become a prophet of desolation, pronouncing a doom from which these cities would never recover. Gradually his features relaxed; he looked upon these men who stood around him, loyal through many trials. Once more the prophet became the Master. Lifting up his eyes to heaven, he prayed. "I thank thee, O Father, Lord of heaven and earth, because thou hast hid these things from the wise and prudent, and hast revealed them to babes. Even so, Father, for so it seemed good in thy sight."

The little company looked out over these gleaming waters of Galilee which Jesus would not see again on this side of the Cross, and his disciples not until they had undergone strain and suffering almost beyond endurance. The first shadow of the coming end had been cast by these words of Jesus on the cities of their birth, the scene of their childhood and later of their youthful ambitions and their daily tasks.

Once they had willingly left it all to follow Jesus. They had said their first farewell to their dear ones and their homes, they had forsaken the little boats, and the lake whose moods they knew and loved so well. They had turned away from the green fields, the waving corn, the fragrant copses of lovely Gennesaret. Now, on the eve of their final departure their Lord had turned to condemn and prophesy extinction upon this world of happy memories: upon their friends and their homes.

It was a severe test for these silent men, they felt baffled and sick at heart. Only the strong, devoted figure at their side could command such loyalty. He felt the aching of their hearts, the emotions too deep to be trusted with expression. He looked at them his eyes kindling with a warmth of love that left them breathless and showed them that no sacrifice can be too great for him who offers his care and companionship. "Come unto me, all ye that labour and are heavy laden, and I will give you rest. Take my yoke upon you, and learn of me, for I am meek and lowly in heart: and ye shall find rest unto your souls. For my yoke is easy and my burden is light."

Would they ever forget this last lingering moment before they turned away toward the south? Nor must we forget it. When we are tempted to consider the price loyalty to Christ demands of us, we must go back to this scene, watch these silent men, and listen to the voice of their Master and ours. Can any sacrifice of ours measure up to theirs? Jesus led them away from everything that man calls worthwhile. He directed them to a place of suffering, danger and death. They accepted his guidance because he was with them and his words of courage and comfort sustained them. Even when in the final bitterness they faltered, he was eager to welcome them back to his side, stronger and wiser for their experience. The centuries have passed and the times have changed, but the principle of sacrifice and service remains, and, though our mortal limitations have imposed the condition of faith, the assurance of the nearness and love of our Lord is with us still.

Their way to the south lay through Samaria, and Jesus sent messengers before them into a village to make provision for his little company. The Feast of Tabernacles was over, and the Feast of Dedication was near. These were times when the Samaritans, never well-disposed towards the Jews, turned deliberately hostile. Pilgrims to Jerusalem, as we have seen, usually avoided Samaria. So it was that Jesus found these people less friendly than the people of Sychar had once been. The messengers returned to say that they would not receive him.

For the first time James and John reveal the quality which had given them the name of "Sons of Thunder". "Lord, wilt thou that we command fire to come down from heaven and consume them, even as Elias did?" It is interesting to notice that these vengeful and even bitter words followed so quickly after their Master's judgment of their own cities. Capernaum and Bethsaida had never refused Jesus this hospitality. Indeed the people had always welcomed him back joyfully from his travels through Galilee. If they had merited divine retribution, how much more this Samaritan village which refused to receive him and to accord him the ordinary courtesies of oriental custom? With this was undoubtedly mingled a feeling of anger at this insult to their Lord. Their language possibly suggests too that the experience on Hermon was still fresh in their minds.

But Jesus rebuked them. His anger was not against the villages who had refused him, but against these two disciples who, after so many lessons of his love, had still not caught the spirit of his ministry. "Ye know not what manner of spirit ye are of. For the Son of Man has not come to destroy men's lives but to save them."

Jesus did not, of course, imply any criticism of Elijah's action. The prophet's mission was to exercise the righteous judgment of God. Wrath and punishment are as much prerogatives of God as love and mercy. But the coming into the world of the Son of God was a dispensation of love, and while that dispensation remained, love prevailed. The time would come when men's refusal to accept this ministration would again bring wrath. Meanwhile the people of the Samaritan village brought judgment upon themselves. Their sick and blind could have been healed; they remained sick and blind. The eyes of their understanding were dark but they received no light. Jesus went on to another village.

2

"WHO IS MY NEIGHBOUR?"

BEFORE Jesus continued his journey southwards he made a final and widespread appeal to the people of Israel. Calling together seventy disciples whom he had probably carefully chosen and prepared for the work, he sent them "unto every city and place whither he himself would come". As the Twelve were destined to be the true rulers of the tribes of Israel, so the seventy were perhaps set in contrast to the Sanhedrin, with a greater claim to spiritual descent from those appointed to help Moses in his ministry. Their instructions did not differ greatly from those which Jesus had given to the Twelve in Galilee earlier, but there is a greater impression of urgency. They were to go forth in the knowledge that the harvest was great, but the labourers few: they were to salute no man by the way, nor go from house to house.

How long or how far the seventy pursued their mission we do not know. Following his record of their departure, Luke immediately goes on to give the details of their return, omitting until afterwards any allusion to the events which had transpired in their absence. They reported that the power which Jesus had given them had been manifested with spectacular results. They did not say anything of the effects of their preaching, nor of the houses where they had found peace. They did not say how many had repented of their evil ways, and now joyfully awaited the coming of the Messiah.

Their delight was centred upon themselves and the works they were able to do. "Lord", they cried, "even the devils are subject to us." "In thy name" seems almost an after-thought. Without discouraging them Jesus quietly restored their perspective, "In this rejoice not that the spirits are subject unto you; but rather rejoice because your names are written in heaven".

It was about this time that a lawyer came to Jesus with a simple but profound question. "Master, what shall I do to inherit eternal life?" Luke says he was tempting him, an expression that need not mean more than trying him. Whether his motives for doing this were good or evil is deter-

235

mined by the context. Many such questions were asked with
the intention of humiliating and confounding him, and were
suitably dealt with by Jesus. The care which he took with
this lawyer indicates that his enquiry was made in the better
spirit. "What is written in the law? How readest thou?" The
man answered confidently, "Thou shalt love the Lord thy God
with all thy heart, and with all thy soul, and with all thy
strength, and with all thy mind, and thy neighbour as thyself". Like Jesus, this lawyer had selected the two commandments which were the fulfilment of the whole law. Jesus
acknowledged it. "Thou hast answered right; this do, and
thou shalt live."

At this point the lawyer betrayed the weakness of those
who concentrated upon the meticulous observance of the law.
He was anxious to know the exact limits of his obligations.
Who were those who in his particular station of life had
claims on him? Was it not possible that he was already obeying the law? Perhaps he might justify himself. "And who is
my neighbour?"

This question laid bare his need. He knew nothing of the
responsive love towards God which finds delight in every
opportunity to express itself in love to man, acknowledging as
its only limit the physical inability to proceed further.
Without hesitation Jesus ministered to that need.

He told him the story of a man who went down the
desolate road from Jerusalem to Jericho. He was set upon by
brigands who stripped him of his clothes, wounded him, and
left him bleeding by the roadside. Here lay a wonderful
opportunity of demonstrating obedience to the first commandment by keeping the second, and of finding the eternal life
which the lawyer sought. First, a priest came down that way.
He saw the man there, lying in a pool of blood. But his
important service in the House of God made it quite impossible to defile himself. Was not there a Levite travelling behind
whose time was less important and whose social status was
more suited to deal with this matter? He passed by on the
other side. The Levite approached. He stood and looked down
upon the wounded man. He saw his life ebbing away, he
watched the effect of exposure and shock on the trembling
flesh. He too, crossed to the other side, and went his way. He
had several good reasons for doing so. Had not the priest
before him ignored the man? The outrage had only just
occurred, the robbers must still be in the vicinity. He was in

danger; he must be on his way without delay. In any case the poor fellow looked beyond help now. The priest, intent on his religious purity, the Levite, satisfied with his excuses, hurried on, leaving their countryman to die on the roadside!

But a certain Samaritan came that way. This man had somewhat better reason to steel himself against pity at the plight of the detested Jew. Yet he climbed off his ass and went over to him. Ignoring the danger and the need for haste he knelt down and, tearing strips from his own garments, bound up the gaping wounds, pouring in oil and wine. Gently lifting him from the ground, he carried him to his waiting beast and brought him to an inn. Nor did he even now consider the ministration finished. He "took care of him, and on the morrow, when he departed, he took out two pence, and gave them to the host, and said unto him, Take care of him; and whatsoever thou spendest more, when I come again, I will repay thee."

"Which of these three thinkest thou", said Jesus, "was neighbour to him that fell among the thieves?" There could only be one answer, yet the lawyer could not bring himself directly to acknowledge the good work of the hated Samaritan. "He that showed mercy on him." "Go", said Jesus, "and do thou likewise."

Beautiful as this parable is, its full message escapes us if we fail to see also a portrayal of the work of Jesus. In the Jew who left the city of God and descended across the barren wilderness to Jericho, we have a picture of Adam's fall. The price he paid for his journey we see in the mortal blows that left him dying by the roadside. The law looked upon him, but could not minister life. But in the fulness of time the Good Samaritan* came along this road of suffering and blood; he was despised and rejected, but he stooped to minister to man's need, binding up his wounds. The oil and the wine invite our grateful contemplation. The instructions to the innkeeper remind us of the charge to Peter, and all Peter's true successors, "Feed my sheep", and the promise to come again and repay needs no emphasis.

Shortly after the departure of this lawyer, Jesus went away to a quiet place to pray to his Father. It must have been a wonderful thing for his disciples to see the effect of prayer upon their Lord, and it is no surprise to find one of them coming to him now and asking him to teach them to pray. Once

*John 8:48

more their Master outlined the form of prayer he had already given them at the beginning of his ministry, but this time he added invaluable thoughts on prayer by parable and precept.

Jesus described a man who had unexpected midnight visitors. He had no bread to give them, so he went to his friend who answered in vexation, "Trouble me not, the door is now shut, and my children are with me in bed. I cannot rise and give thee". With continued pestering, however, the householder rose reluctantly and attended to his need.

This is a parable which has troubled many. It is thought to be a bewildering illustration of the Father's attitude to men's needs, portraying Him as one who does not want to be disturbed, and can only be moved to help by being persistently worried. The answer to this difficulty lies in the way in which Jesus used parables. Some parables (for example, that of the Good Samaritan) were intended to be interpreted according to the sequence of the narrative: but in others, Jesus had no such intention, and to try to force a literal interpretation leads only to perplexity. In these parables Jesus is simply using a story to emphasize a great spiritual truth, and the details are of little significance.

Perhaps the principle can best be shown by changing the thought from verbal pictures to literal paintings. There are those artists who paint a country scene in all its wonderful detail. We readily recognize its features and it needs no interpretation. But other artists seek to convey some great truth or abstract subject. Rembrandt painted the head of an old woman; her bowed face was so shadowy that none of her features could be recognized. High up on her cheek bone shone a single glow of light. As the portrait of a woman's face, the picture was a failure, but Rembrandt called his picture "Grief", and it was a masterpiece.*

So now, Jesus only used the story of the parable as a background to illustrate the two truths, of the urgent need of man, and the ability of God to satisfy that need. In the words that follow there is no suggestion of reluctance on the part of God to supply man's needs. "If a son shall ask bread of any of you that is a father, will he give him a stone? ... If ye, then, being evil, know how to give good gifts unto your children, how much more shall your heavenly Father give the Holy Spirit to them that ask him?"

---

*This example was given in a Broadcast talk many years ago.

3

THE OUTSIDE OF THE CUP

AS Jesus made his way towards Jerusalem the opposition became more evident than the enthusiasm. Although he attracted multitudes wherever he went, their supplication was giving way to accusation and he had to contend more than to heal.

Thus when he paused to cure one who was dumb, although the people wondered, he became the centre of a storm of abuse. The familiar cry that had begun in Galilee had grown more confident: "He casteth out devils through Beelzebub, the chief of the devils". Words of life and power were stayed as Jesus patiently showed them their unreasonableness. They were not satisfied. Thwarted, they resorted to another challenge that had grown familiar, and simply served to show the meagreness of real evidence against him. They demanded a sign from heaven. Jesus dealt with them as he had dealt with their fellows by the lakeside at Magdala.

Suddenly the voice of a woman was heard above the tumult, "Blessed is the womb that bare thee, and the breasts which thou hast sucked". Were it not for the Lord's answer we should be thrilled with this evidence of loyalty at a time when he was sorely pressed by his enemies. But the Son of God was greater than that. He is never in need of the patronage of men. The words of Jesus are sufficient answer to those who down the centuries have echoed this eulogy of his mother. The woman's outburst was unrelated to the things Jesus had been saying. It was the word of God alone that could bring forth blessing in the fruitfulness of those who heard. Mary had been blessed in her submission to that word of God; she had heard and believed. There is a warning here to all who may be prone to shallow outbursts of affection for Christ. Our devotion will not be measured by them, but by the fruitfulness of our lives.

Jesus now received an invitation from a Pharisee to dine at his house. This man had evidently not heard of the attitude of his guest towards the venerated traditions. He marvelled that he had not washed before the meal. This was an outrage.

239

The washing of hands had become far more than a custom; it was now a religious obligation. As the guests entered a house, water was brought, and they washed one hand. When later they reclined at the table, a basin of water was once more placed before them, and they washed both hands before beginning their meal. Bitter controversy had raged between the rival schools of Hillel and Shammai over the consideration of whether the hands should be washed before or after the cup was filled with wine, and over the position in which the towel should be placed for drying the hands. Jesus coolly dispensed with this elaborate mummery.

His abstention had a devastating effect upon that large and distinguished gathering. The Pharisee would burn with shame, feeling that this Rabbi had not only insulted him, but also his guests. To have invited one who flagrantly set aside their cherished traditions would be severely condemned and even misinterpreted. But Jesus had only begun the lesson: "Now do ye Pharisees make clean the outside of the cup and of the platter; but your inward part is full of ravening and wickedness. Ye fools, did not he which made that which is without, make that which is within also?" The meticulous care they took over their outward ceremonial, combined with their disregard for inward purity, made a farce of the whole conception of the law of purification. True purity is reflected from within rather than demonstrated from without. Next Jesus with growing sternness turned to condemn their exacting of tithes from the minutest herbs. It was a practice which exhausted their religious energy, leaving nothing for the exercise of their true function of dealing justly and exhibiting the love of God. And all the time they were concealing what they really were, by a pretence of what they were not. "Ye are as graves which appear not, and the men that walk over them are not aware of them."

At this point, one of the scribes at the table intervened. He saw the Lord's indictment was more than an attack upon the Pharisees: it struck at the foundation of the tradition for which the scribes, too, were responsible. Therefore they were also insulted. Saying this, the scribe brought the Lord's denunciation upon himself and his fellows. The scribes were responsible for those binding impositions which robbed men of the last vestige of freedom, and did nothing to ease their burden. Certainly they perpetuated the work of their fathers—but their fathers killed the prophets, and they built their sepulchres.

Solemnly the Son of God pronounced judgment upon these men. The blood of all the prophets shed from the foundation of the world should be required of this generation. They had the means and the responsibility for propagating knowledge, and had hidden the key. How prophetic the words of Jesus were was shown within the next few months, just as the "woe" he had proclaimed was shortly to be sealed in their own blood.

While provocation and denunciation proceeded within, commotion was growing outside. From all parts of Perea the people gathered to see Jesus, so that when he came out there was "an innumerable multitude of people", treading upon each other in their anxiety to hear him. Fresh from the scene within the house, Jesus warned them against the leaven of the Pharisees, revealing to them the contrast between the punctiliousness of these legal custodians and the loving care of their heavenly Father.

There was a man there who was not listening to Jesus. His mind was occupied with a sense of private wrong. Financial interests blotted out thoughts of a loving Father who counted the very hairs of the head. He interrupted Jesus, "Master, speak to my brother, that he divide the inheritance with me". Jesus turned to the man whose thoughts were so far removed from the great truths he was revealing. "Man", he replied, "who made me a judge or a divider over you?"

He refused to arbitrate between two selfish claims, but he showed them the condition of heart in which no such dispute would be possible. "Take heed, and beware of covetousness." Without covetousness there would have been no claims to settle. "A man's life consisteth not in the abundance of the things which he possesseth."

To bring home the lesson Jesus told the story of the rich fool. A farmer was blessed in the fruits of the field. The earth brought forth abundantly and his barns were quickly filled. Because the man had forgotten the Giver in the enjoyment of the gifts, his problem of accommodation became a crisis in his life. The words of David should have warned him, "If riches increase, set not thy heart on them". But instead he pondered the question, "What shall I do, because I have no room where to bestow my fruits?" The solution could not have been far away. There were many barns lying empty around him, many mouths hungry for the good things which embarrassed him. But he was too busy glorying in the things of the flesh to look beyond the confines of his own estate. He made his decision:

"This will I do: I will pull down my barns and build greater, and there will I bestow all my goods and my fruits". Then Jesus tore down the veil between action and motive, and revealed the true reason for his decision. "And I will say to my soul, Soul, thou hast much goods laid up for many years; take thine ease, eat, drink and be merry." Here was a man who literally made provision for the things of the flesh, to fulfil the lusts thereof. With what insight Jesus made the man address his own soul!

But while the man was conversing with himself on his future delights, the Creator he had forgotten had determined his end. "Thou fool; this night thy soul shall be required of thee." In a moment his foresight was turned to folly; the years of comfort reduced to a few short hours; the accumulated treasure was to be enjoyed by others. Now, his poverty was manifest. He could not willingly commit himself to God in the joyous consciousness that his true riches were yet to be. He would be torn away from his earthly riches to face a spiritual bankruptcy which would be final, "So", said Jesus, "is he that layeth up treasure for himself and is not rich toward God."

Jesus did not attribute this tragedy to the fact that this man, blessed of God, was rich, but to his lack of real acknowledgment of the Giver of every good and perfect gift. That grievous error led to the next; he loved his possessions, using them for his own fleshly ambitions rather than as an instrument through which he could express his thankfulness in loving service to the need of others.

The interruption was not, after all, a break in the context of the Lord's discourse. It was rather a warning which demonstrated the unhappy effect of self-sufficiency. So he was able to continue where he had left off and tell them in words which will never lose their force that man's sufficiency is of God. The only man who is truly rich is the man who is rich toward God; nor will he be poor in the things of this life for he is in the care of the One who feeds the ravens and adorns the lilies of the field.

It was on this occasion that Jesus spoke for the first time openly of his return to the earth. To-day these words become an urgent challenge. "Let your loins be girded about, and your lights burning; and ye yourselves like unto men that wait for their Lord, when he will return from the wedding; that when he cometh and knocketh, they may open unto him immediately."

4

"EXCEPT YE REPENT"

DURING Christ's ministry in Perea a number of Jews described to him an incident which had occurred in Jerusalem when Pilate had sent his soldiery amongst the temple worshippers and mingled their blood with the sacrifices. Such tragedies were not uncommon in those turbulent days, testifying alike to the fanatical patriotism of the Galileans and the stern character of the Roman rule. But it is obvious from the answer which Jesus gave these men that their problem was merely a philosophical one. They were concerned as the disciples had been in the case of the blind beggar, with the relationship between their suffering and their sinfulness. These men, they had argued, must have been guilty of some heinous sin, that God should bring so terrible a judgment upon them, that in the very act of worship their blood should be required.

Jesus, however, emphatically denied their cruel insinuations. "Suppose ye that these Galileans were sinners above all the Galileans, because they suffered such things? I tell you, Nay: but, except ye repent ye shall all likewise perish." He turned their attention from the tragic scene to themselves. Death will come to all; the means by which it comes is relatively unimportant. What is important is to recognize the evil of human nature, and turn to God in repentance. He reminded them of another tragedy. Eighteen men had been killed when the tower of Siloam fell. Once more he emphasized the lesson, "Unless ye repent ye shall all likewise perish".

We should probably have taken this warning only in a personal sense had it not been for the Parable of the Barren Fig Tree by which Jesus related his warnings to the nation of Israel. In view of that parable, the words "likewise perish" assume a sombre aspect. Israel did not repent and the day came when, with the Romans at their gates, strife broke out among themselves in that very temple. Once more human blood flowed with the blood of the sacrifices; whilst facing the relentless enemy onslaught, thousands of Jews perished under the falling masonry of their city.

243

With prophetic insight Jesus spoke of those days. He told them of one who planted a fig tree in his vineyard. Because it bore no fruit after three years of careful tending, he determined to cut it down. But his hand was stayed for the moment by the intercession of the dresser of the vineyard, who promised to dig about the tree and dung it for another year in a final effort to save it. If his work on it failed it should be cut down.

Israel was unique among the nations of the world. It had unparalleled opportunities for bearing fruit and giving glory to God. In his wisdom and love Jesus forebore to relate the sequel he saw so closely. He did nothing to encourage a fatalistic acceptance of doom. While the fig tree would undoubtedly fall under the axe of divine judgment, the personal aspect remained, and Pella was waiting to receive those who obeyed his word. So it is to-day. The judgments of God will be executed in the earth before His glory is finally revealed. That is a call to acknowledge the righteousness and justice of God, and an incentive to recognize the evil of our nature, and turn to Him with penitent hearts.

The following Sabbath, Jesus went into the synagogue of one of the towns or villages of Perea. It was his first visit; but the way had been prepared for him by the seventy. His immediate approach would be heralded by the activity which he always excited, drawing the inhabitants from the surrounding countryside. A particularly distressing sight awaited him. A woman was crouching in the dim light of the synagogue. She was doubled up, her bones locked, her muscles dried away. For eighteen years she had suffered this prostration. Unable to lift herself, her eyes looked up into the Master's face. No appeal was made; none was necessary. Jesus called her to him, and offered her the release which her faith had justified and his love could in no wise refuse. Bending forward he put his hand upon her rigid frame. "Woman, thou art loosed from thine infirmity." The cords that had long locked her bones together fell away, and for the first time for eighteen years she stood upright. In the joy of her freedom she lifted up her voice to glorify God.

There were some who did not share in the rejoicing. Chief among them was the ruler of the synagogue. He had not the courage to accuse Jesus; he had probably heard of the rashness of such a course. Rather he made his attack through the people who came to be healed, criticizing them for thus profaning the sabbath. "There are six days in which men

"O Jerusalem, Jerusalem, ... how often would I have
gathered thy children together, ... and ye would not!"
(Matthew 23:37)

"Behold, your house is left unto you desolate." (Matthew 23:38)

"And they shall fall by the edge of the sword, and shall be led away captive into all nations: and Jerusalem shall be trodden down of the Gentiles, until the times of the Gentiles be fulfilled." (Luke 21:24)

ought to work", he said, "in them therefore come and be healed, and not on the sabbath day."

But it was not so easy to evade the issue. The ruler found himself face to face with the one he had sought indirectly to condemn. "Thou hypocrite! Doth not each one of you on the sabbath loose his ox or his ass from the stall, and lead him away to watering? And ought not this woman, being a daughter of Abraham, whom Satan hath bound, lo, these eighteen years, be loosed from this bond on the sabbath day?" And so the day ended on a note of rejoicing and righteous refutation. Those who had thought more of their oxen than of the infirmity of their fellows were ashamed, but the people rejoiced as they witnessed all the glorious things that were done by him.

Jesus continued his journey through the country east of the Jordan. Luke records that he went through the cities and villages teaching and journeying towards Jerusalem. There are quite a number who have found difficulty in understanding why many of the sayings of Jesus are repeated in the Gospels, at what is evidently a much later time in the ministry. It has not been ignored by the critics. We have to remember that on this journey, which only Luke records in any detail, Jesus was breaking new ground. His teaching was familiar in Judea and Galilee, but not in Perea. The questions which had previously been asked earlier in his ministry were asked again by people who had never heard him before. They were questions prompted in nearly every case by the impact of the teaching of Jesus upon what the people had been taught by the scribes. Jesus dealt with these questions in words similar to those he had used when answering the Galileans; frequently in his discourses he used the same figures and appeals.

As so often happens, our faith in the Gospel record is enhanced rather than weakened by more careful study. We find quite different reactions on the part of the religious rulers in the three different regions of Christ's ministry. In Judea, which means principally Jerusalem, there was little desire to hear his teaching. He faced not only bitter opposition but downright persecution. Nearly all his discourses were rudely interrupted, some with the crude arbitrament of stones. In Galilee, Jesus was given every opportunity to expound his teaching. It was the only place where the Sermon on the Mount could be preached. Except in Jesus' own town of Nazareth, the opposition confined itself to polite questions until roused by the arrival of emissaries from Jerusalem determined to poison the atmosphere. Even then the change was gradual, and was only hastened by the hard sayings of Jesus himself. In Perea the attitude was different again from either Judea or Galilee. The scribes and Pharisees there had obviously heard a great deal about Jesus, but the majority had had no contact with him. They were perhaps embarrassed by his decision to spend some time in their region on his way south to Jerusalem. They had neither the astuteness of the rulers of the temple, nor the open-mindedness of the rulers of Galilee. All they wanted was to persuade him to leave them as soon as possible. The enthusiasm of the people added to their discomfort and forced their hand. But they were clumsy in their methods and collapsed under direct attack.

Thus we notice that the ruler of the synagogue made no attempt to challenge Jesus directly for his sabbath healing, nor did he speak to the woman who was healed. He made an attempt to oppose Christ by attacking the witnesses. The same awkwardness is seen afterwards when the Pharisees tried to persuade him to leave them. They took advantage of what was possibly a rumour, but their effort may not have even that redeeming feature. They warned him that Herod sought to kill him. It was palpably false. On the only occasions we have any record of Herod's attitude to Christ, we find he was interested in him and anxious to see him.[1] It was a stupid ruse, yet one which had apparently been thought out. Had it succeeded it would have had several satisfactory results. It would have put an end to his protracted stay in their country; it would have hastened his journey to Jerusalem where they knew his arrest was imminent; and it would have betrayed in him a personal fear which would have had a profound effect upon the attitude of the people towards him.

The reply of Jesus exposed their intrigue. They had advised him to go away; he told them to depart and see Herod. "Tell that fox" contains a subtle implication to these foxes to go and concert with this bigger fox. Such threats did not affect him or his work. He had his ministrations of love to perform, casting out devils, and curing the infirm; that work will go on to-day and to-morrow.[2] It will come to an end, and then, his work accomplished, he will be perfected. But he *will*

---

[1]Luke 9:7–9; 23:8

[2]The expression "to-day and to-morrow and the third day", can only be taken figuratively. It was a current colloquialism.

depart when his work in their midst is finished; "For", he says, with deep irony, "it cannot be that a prophet perish out of Jerusalem".

So it was that the rulers of Perea joined those of Judea and Galilee in rejecting the Son of God. There was no sign of life on any of the main branches of the fig tree. All this careful tending was of no avail. Yet there were some who heard and believed. They were being prepared for that repentance and conversion to which Peter would call them when this greatest of all God's prophets had gone to Jerusalem to die, and to be perfected. One of the loveliest aspects of the ministry of Jesus was the way in which, in spite of these severe setbacks, he never despaired of men and women, nor ceased exhorting them, by precept and example, to aspire after the perfection of God.

5

MARY CHOOSES THE GOOD PART

AN expanse of limestone rocks interspersed with shrubs and a few stunted trees forms the high plateau extending east of Jerusalem. It breaks suddenly into a shallow glen. There the little village of Bethany nestles amid olive groves, clusters of figs and terraces of vine. To this sheltered spot Jesus directed his steps on his way to Jerusalem to attend the Feast of Dedication.

For the first time we learn of that delightful family which did so much to ease the load which Jesus carried during the last fateful days of his mortal life. We are given no hint whether this was the first time that Jesus saw Mary and Martha. It may be that some time previously, Lazarus, meeting Jesus in the temple, had been attracted to him and invited him to his home. It is possible that some of the seventy disciples had been well received there and had spoken to Jesus of the warm welcome they had been given by this pious little household. But whatever the circumstances, the name of Bethany will always be fragrant, and bring a sense of love and thankfulness into our hearts, as we think of those hours of restfulness and peace which contrasted so sharply with the conflicts of the temple courts.

It is not quite in harmony with this peaceful spirit that the first incident which was recorded in that home should have been the cause of so much discussion. But the responsibility for that must rest with those who, failing to catch the true significance of the words of Jesus, have tended to distinguish between practical Marthas and contemplative Marys, thus dividing the service of Christ into two distinct spheres, and in the process finding no little sympathy and justification for Martha. Let us picture the scene and try to draw from it some of the wealth which the counsel of Jesus always yields.

The coming of so distinguished a guest into her home was a wonderful experience for Martha, and she was anxious to do him the highest honour within the power of her generous nature. She busied herself with preparations worthy of such an occasion. It was evidently a household of some means, and Martha went out of her way to prepare a feast. Luke speaks of her as being "cumbered about much serving". It would appear that she had had some notice of his coming, and Mary, her younger sister, had helped her until Jesus had arrived. With his coming Mary had forgotten all else in her loving homage, and in a few moments was sitting at his feet absorbing his words of life.

For a time Martha continued her work, pre-occupied with her anxiety to give of her best. But as the time went by she grew increasingly aware of her sister's absence, and watching her sit there at the feet of Jesus she began to feel resentful. Once such thoughts are harboured they grow apace. Resentment soon turned to something remarkably like anger. Unable to restrain herself any longer, she went to Jesus, and beginning reverently by addressing him as "Lord", she soon lost control of herself and gave way to her feelings. "Dost thou not care that my sister hath left me to serve alone?" How thoughtless such resentment can be! It had distorted the lovely character of Martha, revealing features quite unlike her. When we allow resentment and anger to affect our judgment, we are brought down to a common level. For how serious are the implications of her words!

First of all, feeling disturbed herself she tries to break into the peace of Jesus, desiring that he might share her disquiet. She presumes to expect that the Master will be deeply interested in the good things she is so carefully preparing for him. Admitting that Mary had already helped her, she suggests that she is doing nothing now but sitting idly at his feet. So highly does she assess her work in comparison with his, that she would have him left alone whilst her final preparations are made. The implication here is that Jesus has come primarily for the food that she will give him, and that Mary therefore, listening to him, is wasting her time. "Bid her", she says, "that she help me." She instructs Jesus to cease his talking and send Mary to her to engage upon a more worth while task.

Martha would have no idea of all her hasty words involved. When these consequences were revealed she would be the first to repent them. They are a warning to us not to make careless statements and pass thoughtless judgments where the things of God are concerned. In the light of grace they may reveal a spirit which we would deplore.

"Martha, Martha", Jesus repeats her name, calling her out of her busy confusion, "thou art careful and troubled about many things." He was telling her it was not necessary for her to prepare these many things to welcome him into her house. We see a smile of reproach in his eyes. O, Martha dear, in spite of your generous nature and your warm hospitality, you have forgotten who I am. You have not realized what I have brought for you. It is still true that I have come not to be ministered unto but to minister. He looked down at the silent figure at his feet. "But one thing is needful: and Mary hath chosen that good part, which shall not be taken away from her."

There were two meals being prepared in that Bethany home, one by Jesus, the other by Martha. Who would dare to say that Martha's meal was the more important? The bread which perishes has little significance in the presence of the Bread of Life. Only one thing was needful, and Mary, sitting at his feet, had chosen it. The time would come when sickness or age would deprive Martha of her part, but these could not take away what Mary had chosen. If only Martha had made the same choice and had sat down with Mary at his feet, she would have risen so fortified by the food he had given her that when her turn for service came she would have ministered to him with joy and peace in her heart.

By dividing all disciples into Marys and Marthas we do neither woman justice, nor do we understand the import of the words of Jesus. There is no evidence that Mary was less practical than Martha. There is everything to suggest that Martha was deeply devout. It is just one of those human incidents which we often see in the Gospels, and experience in our lives; but it is made fruitful by divine wisdom. Martha, over-conscious for the moment of the greatness of her guest, and of her responsibilities as his hostess, overlooked the blessings which he had come to bestow. That perspective lost, the seed of resentment had nothing to stop its growth, until the gentle chiding of Jesus awakened her, and brought her to join Mary at his feet.

But a great lesson emerges; one which no disciple can afford to miss. It has a wider application than the love of two women, and takes us beyond the oven and the kitchen sink, though it by no means excludes them. It is the lesson that all service for Christ begins at his feet. There, learning of him and understanding what he requires of us, our hearts are filled with the glow of his joy and the serenity of his peace. Only then can we arise and serve him in that quiet confidence and love which will guard us from self-righteousness and pride.

This great principle shines forth in the lives of all God's servants. They come forth from the solitude of prayer and meditation to serve. Those we deem most active were men of prayer; and those we associate with contemplation were men of action. Paul's supremely active service was preceded by three years in the desert at the feet of Jesus. John the beloved, a disciple almost mystical in his spiritual apprehension, was also a man of action.

Many of us run energetically around, almost grimly determined to serve him, growing weary in our labour and perhaps a little angry with our brethren. Let us learn the lesson that Jesus taught Martha, that our service is not a self-inspired attempt to minister to him. It is for us to resort to him, allowing him to feed us, so that we can rise in quietness of spirit and deep humility of mind to minister to his needs.

6

WHERE JOHN FIRST BAPTIZED

FROM Bethany, Jesus went westwards over the barren plateau and reached Jerusalem in time for the Feast of Dedication. It was now winter. Two months had passed since he was here before. Only four months separated him from the final Passover.

The Feast of Dedication was one of the smaller feasts of the year. It could be observed by Jews without the necessity of coming to Jerusalem. It commemorated the deliverance of the Jews from Syrian oppression by the Maccabees, and had special relation to the cleansing of the temple, the re-dedication of the altar and the restoration of national worship that followed.

Jesus made his way to the temple and waited in the shelter of Solomon's Porch which stood in front of the Beautiful Gate, the main entrance to the Court of the Women. As soon as it was known that he was there, the Jews surrounded him, demanding his true identity. "How long dost thou make us to doubt?" they cried, "if thou be the Christ, tell us plainly." When John speaks of the Jews he is referring not to the people but to the temple officials. Their anxiety was not as genuine as it sounds. They merely sought an opportunity to find in his answer something which would justify an arrest. Firmly, yet with wonderful patience, Jesus dealt with them. They have had ample evidence for belief already: their refusal to accept it is a proof that they are not his sheep. His sheep hear his voice, and he gives them eternal life. No man shall take them from him, nor can any man snatch them from his Father's hand, because his Father is greater than all. What is true of the Father is true of the Son, "for", he said, "I and my Father are one".

Once more these rulers seethed with anger before the confidence and grave reasoning of the man who stood in their midst—before the enormity of his claim. They picked up great stones that the builders had left scattered about the temple courts. But they hesitated in the act of hurling them at him. Unperturbed by the extreme danger that threatened, Jesus directed their attention from his words to his works. "If I do not the works of my Father, believe me not. But if I do, though ye believe me not, believe the works: that ye may know and believe, that the Father is in me and I in him."

There was no answer to this. The people, only too conscious of his works, looked menacingly at their leaders. One by one the stones dropped at their feet. But they decided they had enough evidence to arrest him. They started forward, but he had disappeared into the crowds. He left the temple and the city for those remote regions of the Dead Sea which had been the scene of John's great witness to his coming. Could it be possible that it was less than three years since he had left the carpenter's shop at Nazareth, and stood at this spot watching the rugged prophet calling upon men to repent and prepare themselves for the Messiah? How much had happened since then! The first call upon the priests in Jerusalem; the lovely months in Galilee when the little fishing boats came swinging home against the sunset. Men seemed to need him in those happy days, until that cloud, no bigger than a man's hand, had grown into this raging storm, so intense that a visit to the temple meant stones and police. John had been dead for nearly a year. Soon Jesus would return to Jerusalem for the last time to make the supreme sacrifice for which a perishing world had long waited. The years had become months, the months were now weeks.

Yet it was here in these swirling waters that he had been acknowledged by his Father's blessing; here his great work which was soon to end in Jerusalem had received the seal of dedication by the Spirit. There could have been no better place for Jesus to come, nowhere from which he could more confidently set out to accomplish his culminating sacrifice. He did not now move far from this sacred spot. John says, "There he abode. And many resorted unto him and said, John did no miracle; but all things that John spake of this man were true. And many believed on him there".

Jesus now accepted an invitation from the chief Pharisee in the district to join him at meat one Sabbath day. In spite of their meticulous and rigid laws, in practice the Sabbath was by no means a day of rigour and austerity among the majority of the Pharisees. On the contrary the Jews were more than once accused by foreigners of making it a day of riot and drunkenness.

Before the feast began, Jesus was approached by a man suffering from dropsy. Probably it was the first time people in this part of Palestine had had an opportunity of witnessing the well known attitude of this rabbi towards the Sabbath. They watched him carefully. Jesus met their challenge. "Is it lawful to heal on the Sabbath day?" Their silence showed that they were not acquiescent. He took the man aside, healed him, and let him go. Then he turned to them, using the unanswerable argument with which he had so often confounded his contemporaries, "Which of you shall have an ass or an ox fallen into a pit, and will not straightway pull him out on the sabbath day?" They had no answer. They turned away from the courtyard towards the feast chamber.

It was evidently a large gathering of friends, kinsmen and neighbours, all affluent, all no doubt pleased to be the guests of the chief Pharisee. Jesus followed them. It was his turn to watch them. He saw their manoeuvres, some subtle, some overt, to reach the best places at the table. Some, no doubt, felt they had good claims to precedence, others were anxious to improve the occasion by insinuating themselves with their host. It was a revealing picture. It spoke eloquently of the ways of the flesh. What perversity lay in the hearts of this Pharisee and his elegant guests, so quick to oppose him in his sabbath ministration to the needy, yet now blatantly revealing their selfish interests, and smacking their lips in anticipation of the rich dishes to be set before them, and waiting for the heady wine to flow freely!

Jesus remained silent until they were settled, the wealthy and arrogant in their seats of prominence, the relatively poorer in their humbler places. Then he spoke. "When thou art bidden of any man to a wedding, sit not down in the highest room; lest a more honourable man than thou be bidden of him; and he that bade thee and him come and say unto thee, Give this man place; and thou begin with shame to take the lowest room." There could be no avoiding the frankness of his words. These pious leaders of the people who rejoiced in their descent from Abraham were no true children of the Kingdom whose only entrance was through a low door called Humility.

This host was not the first Pharisee to regret inviting this guest. He looked at the red, uncomfortable faces round the table. He realized how keenly they were feeling this insult. Jesus turned to him. No, his mistake was not in inviting the

Messiah to his table; but rather in welcoming these men of means. "When thou makest a feast", he said, "call the poor, the maimed, the lame and the blind, and thou shalt be blessed; for they cannot recompense thee." The recompense would come from a higher source, at the resurrection of the just.

One of the guests, perhaps with some sincerity, spoke of the blessedness of him who should eat bread in the Kingdom of God. This drew from Jesus the parable of the Great Supper, in which a certain man had invited many guests. When everything was ready they all excused themselves on material grounds, which indicated in the spiritual application that their earthly pre-occupation robbed them of all desire to participate in the things of God. Angry at the way in which his hospitality had been despised, the host ordered his servant to go into the streets (still within the boundaries of the city) and bring in the poor, the halt, the maimed and the blind. The servant reported that, though he had obeyed his lord, there was still room. So a further command was issued, and the servant received his last commission—to go beyond the city wall, out into the country, and bring in those from the highways and the hedges.

The last phase of the parable had changed from the historic to the prophetic, but there would be no doubt in the minds of the hearers concerning its implications. It was to remain true that those who were asked first to the feast would not taste of the supper, but as individuals admitting lameness and blindness they would still be welcomed by the servant who had come with the great invitation to the poor of the Jews, to be extended finally to those who were without.

Returning to the fords of the Jordan, Jesus found great multitudes waiting to hear him. It was like the early days of his ministry, when John's work had been diminishing, and all men were coming to hear the One of whom John testified. Once again, as he had done then, he taught them the deep truths of discipleship. He showed them that to follow him meant the sacrifice of even the natural relationships of life. It meant bearing a cross, whose shadow was becoming more clearly defined with every passing hour. He spoke to them of the need for carefully considering the responsibility of their decision. A man building a tower counts the cost before he begins to build. A king, contemplating war against a formidable opponent, weighs his strength and his weakness, and then decides whether to attack or to make terms. There is no easy way into the company of the disciples. Each one has to measure the price, and then deliberately decide upon his course of action. The cost is not something he can easily afford. "Whosoever he be of you that forsaketh not all that he hath, he cannot be my disciple."

7

"WHEN HE WAS YET A GREAT WAY OFF"

WHEREVER Jesus went he drew to him publicans and sinners—men separated from their fellows by their means of livelihood and their way of life. It was one of the Pharisees' greatest problems. They could not understand the attitude of Jesus in allowing these men even to approach him. That he should talk with them, and sink to the depravity of accepting their hospitality, was horrifying. His wonderful answer that he had come as a physician to tend the sick, and must therefore be among them, had not satisfied these Pharisees. So developed was the sense of their own righteousness, and so ingrained their contempt of these people, that the simile seemed lost on them. They could only understand the righteousness which was marked by separation from sinners. They had no difficulty in appreciating the asceticism of the Old Testament prophets, and even that of John the Baptist in the wilderness. But this man encouraged these outcasts from decent society, and whether he was in Judea, Galilee or even out here in the Jordan valley, they flocked to him. Now, whilst he was speaking of the demands of discipleship, they had surrounded him; he had even shared a meal with them.

The latest example of their aversion led Jesus to a more detailed justification of his attitude than he had yet expressed. We may be thankful for it, because it evoked the three great parables of the lost sheep, the lost coin and the lost son. In these human stories Jesus brought out the wonderful truth that while the Pharisees were murmuring on earth, and keeping their distance from these men who had come to Jesus, the Father Himself and the holy angels were rejoicing that they who had been lost were now found. Moreover the further lesson emerges, that the position of the sinner who comes to the Father is far happier than that of those who cling to their ceremonial righteousness. They may not have gone astray in any conventional sense, but they have not come to Jesus. There is more joy in heaven for a repentant sinner than for them. The three parables form a beautiful harmony. The first two show the seeking love of God in his Son and in his Church, and the third traces the progress of the responsive love of man towards God.

The first parable is a vivid and faithful picture of the true Shepherd who, discovering that one of his sheep is lost, dedicates himself to the task of finding it. He does not count the cost: he is undeterred by the weariness of the way, the rocks that bruise his feet, or the thorns which tear his flesh. At last he finds it. Artistic imagination has painted it high up on some well-nigh inaccessible rock, lonely, hungry and help-less. There is no anger in the shepherd's voice as he calls; no rebuke at the waywardness which has caused him such trouble. He is the shepherd still. He does not drive it back toward the pasture; he does not even call it to follow him. Reaching out, he gently lifts it to his tired shoulders, and brings it to the fold amid heavenly rejoicings.

In the second parable Jesus becomes prophetic. The picture is a more intimate one. The wilderness has become the house, the hundred sheep become the ten coins. The rich landowner has become the poor woman who has lost a coin, and lighting a candle, sweeps the house, and diligently searches until she finds it. Then she calls her friends and neighbours bidding them to rejoice with her because she has found what she had lost. Jesus seems to be speaking here of the time when his disciples, continuing his work, have become his Church. But the emphasis remains upon the love of God, the importance of those that were lost and the joy of restoration.

The story of the Prodigal Son is surely the most moving of all the parables of Jesus. Its three characters were the very actors in this drama by the fords of Jordan: the publicans and sinners who, ashamed of their ways, had come to Jesus to be lovingly received and protected from the scribes and Pharisees; the representatives of legal righteousness who betrayed their true character in their lovelessness, and in their unconscious admission of their hypocrisy; above all, the love of God revealed in Jesus which is the true home of both brothers. It is a love which goes out to meet the younger one, when he has come to himself and realized the folly and degra-dation of natural propensities. It is also a love which gently reasons with the uglier disposition of the elder, imploring him to come in to the feast and share the Father's blessings.

We shall be the poorer if we do not often meditate upon this beautiful parable shining in the sunlight of the Father's love in Jesus. It bears an intensely personal application for each one of us. We do not often go with the younger brother quite so far away from home, nor are many of us reduced to the degradation which was needful for him. Yet dare any of us claim that our feet have not strayed out into the selfish paths of our natural inheritance? Has not every one of us sought to use the portion of goods that falleth to us for our own pleasure?

Few of us are so surly and hypocritical as the elder brother, but a sensitive awareness will show us when we are taking upon ourselves his likeness. It is a sober thought that the fact that we never leave our Father's home does not mean that we are nearer to Him than is our brother who, though far away among the swine, is beginning to realize what he has left, and is saying in his heart, "I will arise and go unto my Father".

Dominating the whole scene is the love of God. If we are far away it seeks us out across the wilderness to call us home. If we dwell beneath its wings it penetrates into the dark corners of our hearts and searches our motives. Responding to it the elder and the younger brother can meet together, their hands clasped in fellowship, and enjoy the love-feast the Father has prepared for them.

We cannot leave this parable without seeking to extract from it a lesson in prayer. The younger brother's first approach to his father was the natural cry of a child, and is the spiritual cry of an immature Christian. It was a petition, "*Give me* the portion of goods". But when experience had taught him wisdom he began to understand the true meaning of fatherhood. Eventually, having come to himself, he approached his father once more. But it was no longer "*Give me*"; it was, "Father, *make me*". So it is with us. Only the varied experiences of our spiritual warfare which brings increasing confidence in God, will give us that maturity which leads us from simple prayers of petition to the intense habitual communion which seeks only the Father's transforming love, and desires only to be like Him.

The Pharisees heard this story with some grimness. They could not miss its meaning, nor its invitation to join the publicans and sinners in enjoying the blessings of his Father's love. But the elder brother maintained his surliness. He preferred to continue his hurt self-righteousness, and thus also to retain that approbation of men which he so dearly loved.

Jesus saw that the appeal of his word pictures was lost upon them. He turned to his disciples and described these men to them, bringing out their inconsistency and summarizing all hypocrisy in trenchant words which reached beyond the history of those men who served God to please men. "No servant can serve two masters: for either he will hate the one, and love the other; or else he will hold to the one, and despise the other. Ye *cannot* serve God and mammon."

The scribes and Pharisees, stung by his words, curled their lips in sneers. But Jesus reminded them that however much they sought to justify themselves before men, God knew their hearts. That was the final test. To bring home its force he told them the parable of the Rich Man and Lazarus. In doing so he used their own conceptions of the after life, not because they were literally true, but because they forcibly illustrated the lesson he was teaching them.

In the eyes of men the condition of Lazarus could not bear comparison with the comfort and opulence of the rich man. Yet when their relative positions in the sight of God were revealed, the situation was exactly reversed. The rich man had become the beggar in dire straits, longing for the simple gift of a drop of water from the hand of him who had once desired the crumbs from his table. The beggar had become the rich man enjoying comfort and plenty. In his wonderful way, Jesus used the occasion to bring home a further lesson which the Pharisees needed. Having drawn the picture in colours which compelled their attention, he represented the tormented man pleading that someone may be sent to warn his brethren of this completely different standard of values. Thus, repenting of their ways, they might be saved from bitter disillusionment. But the ways of God *have* been revealed. The relationship between God and man, and the standards God requires, have been fully shown. His constant warnings against hypocrisy were clear and forceful. "If they hear not Moses and the prophets, neither will they be persuaded though one rose from the dead."

Within a week their conduct would prove the accuracy of his words. Was it a strange coincidence, or was it divine foreknowledge that a Lazarus should rise from the dead? Faced with the evidence of his resurrection, the Pharisees and priests "from that day forth" took counsel to put Jesus to death.

8

"THE MASTER IS COME AND CALLETH FOR THEE"

TRAGEDY now came to the little family at Bethany. Lazarus, the beloved brother of Mary and Martha, was struck down suddenly with a fatal illness. Looking at him as he lay on his bed, they saw the pallor of death was already upon him. Their thoughts flew to Jesus. He alone could help them. They knew he was somewhere in the Jordan valley. How could they get to him? Here was a reliable man who could be trusted to find him with the minimum delay; they gave him the message: "Lord, behold, he whom thou lovest is sick". That was all; no urgent request for him to come. It was enough that he knew their need. The messenger departed. In his absence Lazarus grew rapidly worse. Probably during that night he died. The trust of the sisters was being severely tried. The burial had to take place almost immediately. Mourners came to perform their sad rites, villagers flocked to the house and followed the bier to the tomb outside the town, many friends came over from Jerusalem two miles away. Everybody seemed to be in Bethany. Everybody except Jesus. He had not come.

The messenger found him on the banks of Jordan. He received an answer to take back to the sorrowing sisters, "This sickness is not unto death, but for the glory of God, that the Son of God might be glorified thereby". But it was already a house of death to which the man returned. Surely the rabbi had made a terrible mistake! Yet faithfully he repeated the words of Jesus. Bewilderment was added to their grief. What could he mean? So even Jesus had been wrong! Even he could not help them now! Did Mary understand? No, not even Mary. If only he had spoken the word. He had not even come. Was the messenger sure the rabbi had said nothing about coming? No, he had turned away and continued preaching. Heavy footed, she went into the house in bewildered despair and grief.

But Jesus had not forsaken those weeping sisters. As if to assure us, John records, "Now Jesus loved Martha and her sister, and Lazarus". Coming where they do, the words

261

assume a lovely significance; they suggest that his love for them was a test of his resolution. For two long days, while the women wept in Bethany, Jesus "abode still in the same place where he was". An even greater love held him back, the love that desired to comfort their hearts with the assurance that he was the Resurrection and the Life.

The two days accomplished, Jesus turned to his disciples, "Let us go into Judea again". The words brought them apprehension. They had not forgotten the menacing shadows of the temple, the cries of abuse, the stones. Yes, the stones above all—they seemed too sharp a reminder of the things their Lord had told them were waiting for him there. "Master, the Jews of late sought to stone thee; goest thou thither again?" Jesus reassured them. There were still some hours of daylight left before the hour of darkness came. With him, even in Judea, they will be in the light, and will not stumble. Without him it matters not where they are, they will be groping in darkness. He told them the reason for his departure. "Our friend Lazarus sleepeth: but I go that I may awake him out of sleep." Seizing eagerly the opportunity to remain in safety they suggested that the crisis seemed to be over; if he slept he would recover. Jesus spoke plainly, "Lazarus is dead". He was glad he had not been there. Could his resolve have outlasted his love had he seen the silent suffering of those he loved at Bethany? Thomas, honest and loyal, fearful but faithful, gave voice to his fear and his love: "Let us also go that we may die with him".

At Bethany the burial was over, the tomb was sealed, but the mourners remained to console. Martha was told that Jesus had come; she climbed the hill to meet him on the outskirts of the little town. Mary stayed in the house. "Lord", cried the elder sister, "if thou hadst been here, my brother had not died." But looking upon him after these days of anxiety and grief, she felt once more the strength of his presence. A flicker of hope stirred in her heart. She dare not dwell upon the full implications of it, even to herself. But suddenly it found expression. "I know, that even now, whatsoever thou wilt ask of God, God will give it thee." Jesus knew. "Thy brother shall rise again." Yes, she believed that. He had been a dear, good man. There was the resurrection. But what of this aching void in her heart? What of the lovely home hidden now among the vines: the home that had suddenly become lonely and cheerless?

Gently Jesus lifted her thoughts higher—beyond the present grief, beyond even the joy that her brother's restoration would give her for a few years before this scene was repeated. He had come to bring life, life more abundant, life that would triumph over this mortal span of years. Fellowship with him will bring her into relationship with divine life, triumphant in its victory over death.

"I am the Resurrection and the Life: he that believeth in me, though he were dead, yet shall he live: and whosoever liveth and believeth in me shall never die." He looked into her face, "Believest thou this, Martha?" Ah, that was a challenge indeed! With true sincerity she could say she believed in *him*. "Thou art the Christ, the Son of God, who should come into the world."

With an indefinable hope she left him there. Back in the little home where she had been taught the secret of true service, she found Mary surrounded by her friends. She drew her aside. "The Master is come and calleth for thee." Breathlessly Mary rose and left the house. At last! At last! *He* had come. Half running, she climbed the hill towards him. The mourners watched her anxiously. "She has gone to the grave to weep there", they thought: "we cannot leave her." It was the Lord's purpose that they should follow to witness what was now to be done.

Mary found her Lord waiting for her. With her heart bursting with relief and anguish she threw herself at his feet. Brokenly she repeated what she had said to Martha so many, many times during the last few days: "Lord, if thou hadst been here, my brother had not died." She could say no more. She lay at his feet quietly weeping. The mourners could bear the sight no longer. Watching this sad figure prostrate, they wept. Jesus, the Son of God, looked on and was troubled in spirit. Gently he lifted her up. "Where have ye laid him?" "Lord, come and see."

They reached the tomb. The gravestone, cold and final, shut in Lazarus from the world of life and light. The silence was only broken by the weeping of the woman. But beyond the silence a prayer ascended. Jesus, now deeply moved, looked upon the scene—the stricken sisters of the family he loved, the mourning women, the rock-covered tomb, grey and silent. It was a picture in miniature of all that sin had wrought, this scene enacted down the ages and through ages yet to come. He will staunch these tears, but they will flow afresh. They will stream down the cheeks of those who have no comforter to bring restoration. Jesus wept. The mourners, watching in amazement, whispered one to another, "Behold, how he loved him." Behold, rather, how he loved all mankind! And behold not here in Bethany. Look out over that distant shoulder of rock that leans towards Jerusalem. There you shall behold how he loved.

Reaching the cave where Lazarus lay, he asked Martha to have the stone removed. But Martha, practical still, said "Lord, by this time he stinketh". Martha had forgotten the words the messenger had brought from beyond Jordan, "Said I not unto thee, Thou shalt see the glory of God?"

The stone was rolled away, the cave yawned open. The prayer that Jesus offered even whilst he wept, had been answered. "I thank thee, that thou hast heard me ... because of the people which stand by, I said it, that they may believe that thou hast sent me."

Turning to the tomb, his voice rose to a ringing command, "Lazarus, come forth". "And he that was dead came forth."

We turn to Christ in our moments of suffering and trial. Our need is enough for his love. But sometimes he remains away, and we do not understand the message he sends. The crisis comes and goes. Perhaps we are left grief-stricken and alone. But one day we shall hear the summons, "The Master is come, he calleth for thee". Before the open grave he will show us that he is the Resurrection and the Life, and he that believeth on him, though he were dead, shall live. Then we shall see the completed pattern of our lives, and we shall know that the sorrow and the suffering made up the fulness of his love.

Book Seven

TOWARDS CALVARY

1

"BUT WHERE ARE THE NINE?"

THE resurrection of Lazarus had profound repercussions. Historically it led directly to the death of Jesus. Some of the people who had witnessed the miracle told the Pharisees what they had seen. The Pharisees passed the information to the Council, and from now on it was the Sanhedrin itself which took steps for the apprehension of Jesus. The Sadducees were more concerned with the political effect of the miracle. Lazarus seems to have been a prominent man; the Passover was near. They could not ignore the possibility of an insurrection which would bring upon them the retribution of Rome, and lead to their own downfall. Caiaphas, the high priest, cast aside the querulous arguments in the council chamber, and summed up the matter in clear, cold logic: "Ye know nothing at all, nor consider that it is expedient for us that one man should die for the people, and that the whole nation perish not".

The beloved apostle John, looking back upon these days many years later, spoke of the prophetic nature of those words, but showed also their double application in the great redemption which was to be achieved in gathering together in one all the children of God.

Meanwhile the counsel of the high priest was confirmed, and action immediately followed. It was determined to arrest Jesus and put him to death. Any man knowing his whereabouts was to report to them immediately.

As the preparations began for the final Passover, Jesus left the city and went northwards into the mountainous country near the town of Ephraim, and stayed there with his disciples.

This retirement would afford him the last opportunity for solitary communion with God. It would also give him time to prepare the disciples for the events of the coming week; although in his love and understanding, he was to make care-

ful arrangements that his final exhortation and encouragement should be reserved for the few hours before his arrest.
There was little interruption in this mountainous country.
Although the Passover was approaching, the pilgrims were
keeping well to the east, avoiding the Samaritans.

The little company had reached the borders that divided
Samaria from Galilee and were approaching a village when
their attention was drawn to a group of men. As they drew
nearer it was evident that in spite of their anxiety to attract
attention, they were also anxious to keep their distance. Over
the still air came the concerted cry, "Jesus, Master, have mercy
on us". It was evident that Jesus had come across one of those
colonies of lepers that were dotted over Palestine. They hud-
dled together in a common bond of loathsomeness. Jew and
Samaritan knew no enmity here. One of the many distressing
features of leprosy is the failure of the voice. But under the
stress of their need these ten men made themselves heard.

Steadily Jesus drew near. "Go", he said, "show yourselves to
the priests." Once more we wonder at the way in which Jesus
suited his instructions to the needs of those who came to him.
His was no conventional healing. He was always more conscious of the spiritual need than the bodily infirmity. The ten
looked down at their scarred and pitted flesh. There was no
sign of a cure. Yet this man was telling them to act as though
they had been cleansed. Here was a call to faith, not in words
but in deed. They turned and began their journey towards the
village, and Luke records, "As they went they were cleansed".

Presently Jesus saw one man coming towards him; a man
who was excited. His features were not familiar. His clear
complexion gave no indication that here was one of the
pitiable wrecks who had stood before him less than half an
hour ago. When he spoke his tone was strong, full of thankfulness. With a loud voice he glorified God, and, reaching
Jesus, he fell at his feet, giving thanks.

There was no need for Jesus to look up and scan the
countryside. He knew this man was alone. "Were there not
ten cleansed? But where are the nine?" No, only the
Samaritan had returned to give thanks. Not far away the
other nine were rejoicing in their release, but they had forgotten the source of their healing. "Go thy way", Jesus said,
"thy faith hath made thee whole." The Samaritan had been
more deeply cured than his fellows. The Word of the Lord had
penetrated beneath his scaly flesh and touched his heart.

How often our plaintive cry is heard before the Throne of Grace: yet when responsive blessings flow, how many retrace their steps to Jesus, and falling at his feet, glorify his Father? Thankfulness, rendered to God, and manifested in our actions towards men, is as rare as it is seemly. Sometimes a Samaritan teaches us the lesson.

When Jesus reached the adjacent village he found the people dumbfounded at the sight of the lepers in their midst. The Pharisees, obviously impressed, came up and asked him when the Kingdom of God should come. But it was too late to ask that now. In a few days' time the Passover will be held, and the King will be crucified. It cannot now come with observation. Men will no longer be able to say, "Lo, here" or "Lo, there". For "Behold", he said, "the Kingdom of God is in your midst". The disciples were puzzled by his words, and so Jesus explained them. The time was at hand when they would desire to see the days of the Son of Man, but would not see them. He was to suffer many things and be rejected of this generation. But the day would come when the Son of Man would be unmistakably revealed in his Kingdom. "For as the lightning that lighteneth out of the one part under heaven, shineth unto the other part under heaven, so shall also the Son of Man be in his day."

He spoke to them of the dangers and the false alarms prior to his coming. He exhorted them to be loyal and courageous. Their attitude in the difficult days ahead was to be one of prayer. He told them the parable of the unjust judge who was pestered by the constant pleadings of a poor woman. After many refusals he finally righted her wrong, because her repeated visits were bothering him. "And shall not God", said Jesus, "avenge his own elect, which cry day and night unto him, though he bear long with them?"

About this time Jesus noticed, probably in the larger body of his disciples, a marked degree of self-righteousness among some; it was made more distressing by a tendency to despise their fellows. To these Jesus addressed a parable conveying a pointed lesson for all who suffer from a presumptuous imagination of their righteousness.* "Two men went into the temple to pray, the one a Pharisee, the other a publican." To the Pharisee this was always a cherished occasion. Majestically he walks towards the most prominent place, and satisfied that he is conspicuous, he begins his prayer. His rich voice

*It is evident that this parable was not addressed to Pharisees but to disciples.

echoes resonantly through the temple. "God, I thank thee", he begins with apparent reverence; but it is evident that this approach is only a means to his own glorification: "I thank thee that I am not as other men are, extortioners, unjust, adulterers". He looks around him complacently. His eye rests upon the humble figure of a publican, almost hidden in the shadows, a figure pathetic in its self-effacement, head bowed, hands beating on breast in an agony of penitence—"Nor even as this publican". He relates his virtues, "I fast twice a week, I give tithes of all I possess". In his abundant righteousness he condescends to offer more than God desires, but he is entirely oblivious that the very things he offered were designed to emphasize his poverty and need. His prayer concluded, he makes his slow, self-satisfied, important way from the temple. He has had his reward. He has prayed with himself. His words have echoed round the temple and have reached his ears again, bringing a complacent smile to his lips. But God has not heard his words. He is listening to the heart-broken cry of the publican: "Lord, be merciful to me, a sinner". Though he stood afar off in the shadows of the temple, he was near to God. He was learning that God resists the proud but gives grace to the humble. And learning this, peace was gently flowing into his heart. He went back to his house justified. "Every one", said Jesus, "that exalteth himself shall be abased, and he that humbleth himself shall be exalted."

It was singularly appropriate at this time that parents should bring their children to him to be blessed. Their simple trust made a satisfying contrast to the sufficiency of man. But the disciples knew how tired Jesus was. They also *thought* they knew that he was preoccupied with sterner problems. Such an interruption was therefore undesirable. They discouraged the mothers, rebuking their eagerness, dismissing their children. How little they understood him! Can we not see the tired eyes light up with joy, the stern lines on his face softened? Gladly he took them into his arms, and blessed them. Surrounded by happy children and contented mothers, he looked at his disciples, "Suffer little children to come unto me, and forbid them not, for of such is the kingdom of heaven. Verily I say unto you, Whosoever shall not receive the kingdom of God as a little child shall in no wise enter therein".

2

HE WENT AWAY SORROWFUL

WHILST Jesus was happily engaged with the mothers and children, a young man stood watching him. He was rich in possessions and good works. In spite of his youth he had become the ruler of the local synagogue. The more he heard of Jesus, the more convinced he was that, in spite of his religious fervour, there was something important missing in his own life. He was a scribe who had the virtue of sincerity; he was therefore susceptible to the warnings he had just heard.

As Jesus moved away from the little ones, leaving happy smiles and peaceful hearts behind him, the young man ran towards him, and forgetting his own prestige as a scribe, kneeled at his feet. "Good Master, what shall I do that I may inherit eternal life?"

Always sensitive to the spirit of a man's approach, Jesus laid hold of this form of address which had in it just a suggestion of flattery. The young man had many opportunities for perceiving the goodness of God in the Scriptures, but his knowledge of Jesus was only a few hours old. "Why callest thou me good? There is none good save one, that is God." Then Jesus directed him back to the things he knew so well. "If thou wilt enter into life, keep the commandments." Here was the point at which the pilgrimage must begin. To love God and keep His commandments will always be the whole duty of man.

The young ruler listened as Jesus recounted the commandments he knew so well. Long before he had finished speaking the reply was ready, "All these have I kept from my youth up". Had he sat with the multitude on the slopes overlooking the lake of Galilee a year ago, and heard the Sermon on the Mount, he would not have answered so confidently. In a moment Jesus would show him how wrong he was in his artless assurance. But he was sincere. Although he thought he was keeping the commandments he also knew in his heart that something was missing, and that knowledge had brought him to Jesus. Now it prompted him, in the face of the answer he had received to ask, "What lack I yet?"

Looking at him, Jesus saw an earnest and genuine young man, unsullied by the complacency of his kind, aspiring after righteousness with the fresh vigour of youth, humble in his search. Beholding him, Jesus loved him. There *was* indeed one thing lacking. And lacking it the young ruler lacked everything. By one act he could supply the deficiency and prove beyond doubt that he did love God with all his heart, and his neighbour as himself. If he failed then he would show how he had erred (albeit unconsciously) when he said he had kept the commandments from his youth.

"One thing thou lackest: go thy way, sell whatsoever thou hast, and give to the poor, and thou shalt have treasure in heaven, and come, take up the cross, and follow me." By this simple test you can prove all! Become poor and show that you are prepared to serve God and not mammon, and that you do indeed love your neighbours as you love yourself.

Ah, here was the true test for him—the difference between the formal observance of the commands of God, and the real translation of them into the terms of everyday living, involving sacrifice. Jesus had shown him why, in spite of his steady obedience to God's laws, he had knelt at his feet feeling his insufficiency. Now the issue was inescapable. He professed to love God; he had great possessions. To test his loyalty to God his riches must go.

He looked at Jesus; it was hard to disobey him. He thought of his treasures, his estates, his servants; it was harder still to obey. He turned away. He went back to the gods he had chosen. And Jesus, though he loved him, watched him go. How gladly the young man would have served him on any other terms! If only the sacrifice he demanded had not been so great! Perhaps as he went slowly away, he looked back longing to see some gesture of compromise. But he would only see sorrow and love on the face of the one who so dearly wished that the choice might have been different.

This is not an incident we can easily dismiss. Its challenge must recur throughout our lives. Other things besides great possessions come to us and cause our loyalty to God to relapse into formal worship. Externally everything is normal, but in our hearts we know that there is one thing we lack, one sacrifice we must make; one cherished friendship, ambition or acquisition must go. We make the decision in our Master's presence, knowing that he is watching us. There is tender love in his eyes, but no sign of compromise. We hear his voice: "If you will be perfect, give it up, and you shall have treasure in heaven. And come and follow me". There can be no following without sacrifice. That we may receive the word of life, Jesus pronounces the sentence of death upon those burdens which make it so hard for us to follow him.

The disciples must not miss this lesson as they watched the young man go back to his pathetic treasures and his shallow worship. "Verily I say unto you", Jesus said turning to them, "that a rich man shall hardly enter into the kingdom of heaven." The disciples looked at him in astonishment. He made his words plainer: "Children, how hard is it for them that trust in riches to enter into the kingdom of God! It is easier for a camel to go through the eye of a needle, than for a rich man to enter into the kingdom of God."

These words of Jesus covered not only the rich but the poor also. The rich man glorying in his riches is far from the Kingdom of God, but the poor man trusting in his hard-earned pittance is no nearer. Indeed the poor man may clutch his few pounds more tightly than a rich man his thousands. The emphasis in each is upon the same thing. Our trust must not be centred upon riches, great or small, or upon honour, or men, but upon God.

The disciples realized that his words included them. They asked him, greatly astonished, "Who then can be saved?" "With man", he answered, it is impossible, but not with God, for with God all things are possible." No man in his own strength can attain unto the salvation that God has prepared through grace. But the work of grace is made more difficult when men's eyes are diverted from it to the glittering but temporary treasures of the world.

In the sequel to this incident there is a sad commentary upon the limitations of the disciples. They should have been grateful that by the call of Jesus it had been possible for them to forsake everything and follow him and thus be more ready for God's grace. Peter however (and perhaps he was speaking for several others) thought not of God's grace but of his own sacrifice. "Behold, we have forsaken all and followed thee What shall we have therefore?" He had watched the rich young ruler fail where he had succeeded. What is to be the compensation for his sacrifice? He had failed to learn the lesson of the parable which Jesus so recently told him of the servant's duty to his master; the lesson that when we have done

271

all, we are still unprofitable servants, waiting upon the goodness of God. The young man's question, "What lack I yet?" would have been more worthy of Peter's lips than his own, "What shall we have therefore?"

But Jesus was content to acknowledge the renunciation. "Ye which have followed me, in the regeneration when the Son of man shall sit in the throne of his glory, ye also shall sit upon twelve thrones, judging the twelve tribes of Israel. And every one that hath forsaken houses, or brethren, or sisters, or father, or mother, or wife, or children, or lands, for my sake, shall receive an hundredfold, and shall inherit everlasting life."

Even in this life, divine compensations far outweigh a disciple's sacrifice. Though he suffer persecution, so deep will be his fellowship with his brethren that the cumulative blessings and possessions of all will be enjoyed by each. And in the Kingdom, when the earth is renewed in holiness and glory, they will share in the righteousness of God's beneficent reign. "But", said Jesus, reminding Peter of the danger of presumption, "many that are first shall be last, and the last shall be first." He made the warning clearer by telling them the parable of the husbandman who hired labourers to work in his vineyard early in the morning, and at the third, sixth, ninth, and eleventh hours. At the end of the day he gave to each the same reward for his labours. This caused criticism among those who had borne the heat and burden of the day, but the husbandman justified his action. "Is thine eye evil because mine is good?"

Taken in its context the lesson is that the work done, whether for one hour or twenty, bears little relation to the payment at the end of the day. The disciples fishing on the lake were idle in the market place in the sight of God, until they were called to His service. Once in the vineyard their reward was out of all proportion to their work. Peter's "What shall we have therefore?" assumed a relationship between the things they had left and the reward they had earned. No such relationship can ever exist. Paul brought home the lesson of the parable in a brief sentence, "By grace ye are saved, and that not of yourselves, it is the gift of God".

3

"ZACCHAEUS, MAKE HASTE AND COME DOWN"

JESUS turned from the mountains of Judea towards Jerusalem. Apart from a few nights in adjacent Bethany, he would not leave the city again. The disciples watched him as he took the road towards the south. There was a kingly majesty in his bearing that checked their impulse to go beside him. They let him walk on ahead. A purposefulness about him amazed and frightened them. They dare not speak. Walking steadily behind the silent figure, sometimes losing sight of him on a bend in the road, or over a shoulder of rock, they left him to his thoughts. But they found him waiting for them in some quiet place, sheltered from the burning sun, and when they were settled and refreshed, he opened his heart to them, unfolding the complete picture of the events that were to transpire within a week in Jerusalem. When he had first spoken to them of these things, he had told them only that he must suffer many things and be killed, and rise again the third day. On the next occasion he had added the terrible truth of his betrayal. But now he revealed the whole picture.

"Behold, we go up to Jerusalem; and the Son of man shall be delivered unto the chief priests, and unto the scribes, and they shall condemn him to death, and shall deliver him to the Gentiles. And they shall mock him, and shall scourge him, and shall spit upon him, and shall kill him: and the third day he shall rise again."

The disciples listened, but did not understand. Confused between their conception of the Messiah and this awful picture of suffering and death, they could not find a perspective. The changed trend in the teaching of Jesus, and the growing atmosphere of impending crisis had had its effect upon them. In spite of all that he was telling them they persisted in entertaining hopes of immediate glory. But surely the beloved John would understand! No, not even John.

The journey continued in silence. They met, possibly by arrangement, a company of pilgrims from Galilee.* There

---

*The alternative that Salome had been with them in the hill country of Ephraim seems unlikely.

was a happy reunion as James and John saw their mother again. News of the resurrection of Lazarus and the nearness of the Passover had apparently persuaded Salome that the time for the manifestation of the Messiah was imminent. It seems possible that, like Mary, she had lost her husband, Zebedee, and with the unselfishness of a true mother, all that she now desired was the best that her Master could give for her sons. Her interest did not displease James and John. Their growing intimacy with Jesus during the past months had its less pleasing side. It had been revealed by their high-handed rebuke of the one who cast out devils in their Master's name, and their imperious request that they should be allowed to call fire down from heaven upon the inhospitable Samaritans.

Now the mother and her two sons thought to settle for all time the vexed question of who should be the greatest in the coming Kingdom. Jesus had spoken only a few hours before of the Son of Man sitting on the throne of his glory, and of the exaltation of the apostles to twelve thrones. But this was not enough to satisfy them.

The two disciples were hesitant to speak out. They had seen their Master turn on Peter; they had already suffered a stern rebuke themselves. They could not be sure now what he would say. But Salome, with less knowledge of his spirit and with warm love towards her sons, approached him and worshipping, made her request. "Grant that these my two sons may sit, one on thy right hand, and the other on the left, in thy Kingdom."*

No time could have been less opportune for this request. James and John had watched Jesus earlier in the day with fear in their hearts, as he started towards Jerusalem: they had listened as he spoke of his impending sufferings. Even if they could not understand the purport of what he said, they should surely have seen the preoccupation of their Lord, and been full of solicitude towards him as they pondered his words. Yet the petition for all its pride was wanting in neither faith nor loyalty. They had asked to share his glory. Did they realize that the glory lay in the sacrifice?

With loving patience Jesus considered this joint request. He turned not to the mother, but to the disciples. "Ye know not what ye ask." His mind contemplated the path of dark-

---

*Mark represents the two disciples as asking the question, but in view of Matthew's more detailed record, there can he no doubt that Salome asked it with her sons' full concurrence and active participation.

ness and suffering that lay immediately before him, the deep waters which would pass over his soul, the conflict, the desolation of spirit. The way to the side of the King of glory was the way of the man of sorrows. "Are ye able to drink of the cup that I shall drink of; and to be baptized with the baptism that I am baptized with?" They cannot truly know. They will be better able to answer when they have been through the experiences of the next few days. Then, realizing something of the fellowship of his sufferings, they may be able to answer, "Not in our own strength, but with thine, O Lord!" But now, encouraged rather than dejected by words which seem to offer them hope, their hearts prompt the answer, "We are able". You shall. And it will indeed be the road to glory. "But to sit on my right hand and on my left is not mine to give, but it shall be given to them for whom it is prepared of my Father."

It is hardly surprising that the other ten, having heard this conversation, were deeply upset. They were indignant with their brethren not, it is to be feared, because they had ignored the feelings of their Master, but because they had sought a privilege they themselves dearly wanted. Jesus called them to him and spoke to them of the true nature of apostleship. They must not seek exaltation for the purpose of domination. The principle upon which apostleship is based is not so; true greatness can only be found in humility, and serving one another is the only qualification for rulership. There is no other way. They must follow their Lord. He was taking that path. "The Son of man came not to be ministered unto, but to minister, and to give his life a ransom for many."

As they journeyed southwards more and more pilgrims joined them. They neared Jericho. News of his coming went on before him. A few miles north of the Dead Sea and some fifteen miles north-east of Jerusalem, Jericho was a beautiful town. Over eight hundred feet below sea level, it was always hot, but luxurious plants, palms and flowers grew in its stately gardens. Herod the Great had spent money there lavishly. He had built its walls flanked by four great towers, and its amphitheatre. His son, Archelaus, had built its palace and laid out its rose gardens. Away across the salt waters of the Dead Sea, the hills of Moab made a purple background. It was a city of life and romance, colour and fragrance; a centre for both priest and taxgatherer; a busy market on the great highway from Egypt to Arabia and Damascus.

The news spread that Jesus was on his way to Jerusalem for the Passover. Bethany was only twelve miles away.

Everyone had heard of the raising of Lazarus, and the decision of the Sanhedrin which followed. The Lord would have to pass through an avenue of eager, curious people.

One of Jericho's richest citizens was anxious to see Jesus. Zacchaeus was the chief of the taxgatherers for that region. Was it merely curiosity which brought him to see this friend of publicans and sinners? It seems more likely that he was a rather lonely man in spite of his money. The powerful priestly element would keep him out of the social life of the city; the common people despised and shunned him. Probably, looking back on his life and the source of his wealth, he felt some sympathy with men's hostile attitude towards him. His conscience was at work. The more he heard of Jesus of Nazareth (and he had probably heard much) the more convinced he became that here was a man who would understand this estrangement of spirit and encourage these faint stirrings of contrition.

But the road by which Jesus must come was crowded, and Zacchaeus was small of stature. He tried to push forward, but someone recognized him and the word went quickly round. There were dark scowls followed by angry cries, and he backed away. He heard the shouts which heralded the approach of Jesus. He must see him. Jesus was nearly level with him now, and the crowds were closing in behind. Something seemed to impel him; it had become imperative for him to see this rabbi. He broke into a run keeping well ahead. A large sycomore tree spread its branches across the road. He saw in it the answer. Without hesitation, but not without effort, he climbed it, until, astride one of its limbs, he was able to peer between the leaves at the road below. He could see Jesus now quite clearly, surrounded by his disciples, hemmed in by the seething crowds. Now he was below him. He had stopped! He was looking up into the tree! With a sense of unreality he heard his name. "Zacchaeus, make haste and come down, for to-day I must abide in thy house." With a great joy in his heart he scrambled back along the branch and down to the ground. He knew in his heart that a great change was about to come into his life. He who had seen Nathanael under the fig tree, had seen Zacchaeus in the sycomore tree. If with all our heart we truly seek him, we shall surely find him—and be found of him. Christ can so easily be hidden by the crowds that press around him, the indifferent, the curious, the hostile, the patronizing crowds. Our desire to

"And he sendeth forth two of his disciples, and saith unto them, Go ye into the city, and there shall meet you a man bearing a pitcher of water: follow him." (Mark 14:13)

"… they bring him unto the place Golgotha, which is, being interpreted, The place of a skull." (Mark 15:22)

"… they came and took up his corpse, and laid it in a tomb." (Mark 6:29)

see him and a sense of need, must be great enough to lead us to climb into the sycomore tree. The urgent and imperative nature of Christ's words is full of meaning. He must *"Make haste"*; Jesus was only passing through the city, in a last journey. He must dine with him: it was the inevitable consummation for the sinner who had found the Saviour, and the Saviour who had found the sinner.

What transpired during those short, precious hours, we do not know. But we know the result. Zacchaeus stood at the door as Jesus was about to leave him. "Behold, Lord", he vowed, "the half of my goods I give to the poor, and if I have taken anything from any man by false accusation, I restore him fourfold." Claims would soon be coming in from the people who stood listening to this promise. But Jesus was satisfied that he would make it good. The unceremonious scrambling up the tree was not the only humble thing Zacchaeus had done that day. His Saviour left him with a parting blessing, "This day is salvation come to this house; forsomuch as he also is a son of Abraham. For the Son of man is come to seek and to save that which was lost".

4

"SHE HATH DONE WHAT SHE COULD"

THOSE who witnessed the Lord's parting exchanges with Zacchaeus must have been intrigued by the attitude which Jesus adopted towards the man who, because he was chief of the publicans, was also in their eyes the chief of sinners. They were impressed by the transformation that had taken place, emphasized as it was by a practical demonstration of goodwill which could not be gainsaid.

Before he left, Jesus disillusioned the people's minds concerning the coming Passover. They knew that a crisis was imminent. Either Christ would manifest himself or the Jewish leaders would arrest him. To them it was simply a question of power—the conventional power of the Jews against the miraculous power of Jesus. Most of them had great hopes that Jesus was on his way to Jerusalem to overcome the opposition and establish the Kingdom of God. He therefore told them the parable of the pounds, emphasizing the need for the king to go into a far country to receive his kingdom and to return. He used the parable also to stress the obligations of the citizens of the Kingdom during the King's absence, warning them by the picture of the man who wrapped his pound in a napkin against the dangers of indifference and neglect. The Kingdom of God was not so easy a conquest as they believed. The King of Israel had not simply to march upon Jerusalem with the power he had already manifested, overcome the religious and military obstacles and bring in an era of national glory and prosperity. Nor were the subjects of the Kingdom to enjoy so facile a victory. The King must go to Jerusalem to suffer and die before he could return from the far country to receive his inheritance: the subjects must earn their right to be children of that Kingdom, by good and faithful service to their absent King.

As Jesus left the city, two blind men sat begging by the roadside.* Hearing the commotion around them, one of them,

---

*Without more information it seems almost impossible to solve the question of the blind men who were healed at Jericho. Several ingenious but unconvincing attempts at reconciliation have been made. For our purpose we have mentioned only the healing of Bartimaeus and his blind companion as Jesus left Jericho.

Bartimaeus by name, enquired who it was who passed that way. There can be little doubt that they had heard of Jesus and knew something of his healing power. Their voices rose above the noise of the tumult, "Thou son of David, have mercy on us". So loudly and persistently did they cry that many in the crowd rebuked them. This only encouraged them to louder shouts. Jesus was going away from them; and with him would go for ever their hope of sight. Their heart-rending cries rose more stridently. He must not go. He must hear and pause to help. Jesus stood still. He whose ears were always sensitive to the cry of need had doubtless heard their first urgent call. Why did he prolong their agony of doubt? For their own sakes? For those who stood by? It may be for disciples in the days to come, that realizing the darkness of life without him, they might come to feel the urgency and fervour of these men at the walls of Jericho. "Have mercy on us, O Lord, thou son of David."

After what must have seemed an interminable suspense their hoarse cries were silenced. "Be of good cheer, rise, he calleth thee." With trembling hearts but lively faith the men got to their feet. Bartimaeus flung aside the garment which would hinder his progress, and they were led to Jesus. "Lord", they said in response to his question, "that our eyes may be opened!" Compassionately Jesus touched them, and they received sight. Nor was their faith merely a passing cry of need. They used their new gift faithfully, glorifying God and following Jesus in the way. That Mark records the name and father of one of them suggests that he became a true disciple, and was associated with the apostolic ministry.

Jesus left Jericho and took the road westwards. Already the great pilgrimage to Jerusalem had begun and every highway was crowded. The obvious intention of Christ to be at the Passover this year in spite of the determination of the rulers to arrest him, created the utmost excitement and speculation. It was evident to all that the coming week was to be a momentous one. Many expected Jesus to throw off his cloak of lowliness and reveal himself in the glory of his Messiahship.

Bethany lay on the road from Jericho to Jerusalem, and here Jesus stayed. It was both a convenient headquarters only half an hour's journey from the city, and a tranquil retreat where he could find comfort and peace from the bitter turmoil of the temple. There was hatred in Jerusalem, but warm friendliness in Bethany. He needed this last rest before the darkness engulfed him. It was necessary for him to spend these hours in the company of Lazarus, still quietly pondering the mystery of his great experience; of Martha, supplying his needs now with a new understanding of the meaning of service, and of Mary who said so little but understood so much. We shall never know what Bethany meant to Jesus during those last six days of his earthly life.

In common with all the villages within easy reach of Jerusalem, Bethany was filling quickly with worshippers. Many had come from afar; they had heard of the fame of Jesus; his exploits had been discussed by little groups of Jews as their boats ploughed through the sea towards the coast of Palestine: travellers in caravans passing north-east to Damascus and south-west to Egypt told eager pilgrims of the latest events in Jerusalem. They spoke of the popularity of the prophet who accompanied his words with miraculous power. Bethany held a particular interest. Everyone was anxious to see the man who had lain dead in the tomb for four days. So great was the effect of this miracle that the chief priests were anxious to put Lazarus to death, and would doubtless have done so had they been able to contrive it secretly.

It was Friday when Jesus reached Bethany. With sunset his last earthly Sabbath began. The long hot journey, the incessant clamouring of the crowds, the miracles, above all the city to which he drew nearer with each mile, all these things combined to make the familiar home a haven of peace. After a refreshing sleep Jesus would accompany the little family to the synagogue and then, in response to an invitation, they went on to Simon's house to partake of the Sabbath feast. Simon was known as "the leper". It was probably a title he chose to retain in grateful acknowledgment of his healing; for there can be little doubt that his cure was one of the hundreds of miracles unrecorded in the Gospels.

We imagine Jesus reclining between Simon and Lazarus, two powerful witnesses of the glory of God and the authority of His Son. Martha, true to character, is serving at the table. Mary, holding a small box in her hand, is looking steadfastly at Jesus, indescribable love mingling with sadness and a sense of loss reflected in her face. Sitting at her Master's feet she had learned from his lips of his approaching death. In her heart she *knew* it must be so. She could not attempt to draw him back from the coming ordeal as Peter had done.

Realizing that the end was near, and that the wonderful experiences she had enjoyed with him in her home would soon be but a memory, she was filled with unutterable sadness. Yet it was her love, not her sorrow that triumphed, a love so deep and pure that it must find expression. She had come to bid her Lord farewell. Quickly she came forward now, broke the box of spikenard and poured it gently over her Lord's head. Then kneeling she emptied the ointment on his feet and wiped them with the long tresses of her hair. John, vividly remembering the occasion and understanding its beautiful significance, records that "the house was filled with the odour of the ointment".

Yet its fragrance was not discerned by some of those who were nearest to it. To Judas it was an unwelcome scent; he saw only a flagrant dissipation of wealth he could have put to better use. He kept the common purse, and he was a thief. But he veiled his disappointed treachery in fair garments, and in doing so he deceived some of the disciples who had not the penetrating discernment of their Lord. "Why", he asked, was not this ointment sold for three hundred pence and given to the poor?"

There are many acts of homage that seem to have little practical value, yet they are fragrant, and Jesus understands the loving devotion from which they spring. Sometimes they are criticized because they are intangible; occasionally less worthy motives lie behind the depreciation. No one but Jesus had any right to assess the value of Mary's action. Judas entering into this sacred intimacy was guilty of gross sacrilege. It is a scene which can be re-enacted and contains a lesson that we all must learn. It is fatally easy to pass harsh judgments upon tender expressions of love which we fail to understand.

When Mary and Judas are together in the presence of Jesus how great is the contrast! the one consumed with love, the other filled with hate: the one conscious of none but her Lord, the other of none but himself. Yet Jesus did not destroy the loveliness of the scene by exposing the hate and the selfishness he saw in the heart of Judas.

It is not difficult to understand the feelings of Mary as she heard the harsh words of Iscariot and the murmurings of the disciples. It hurts deeply when our warmest impulses are subjected to cold scrutiny and judgment. She probably doubted now the wisdom of her action. Was Judas right? Should her love for her Lord have been expressed in ministry to the poor of the village?

Looking at her troubled face, Jesus immediately justified her action. She had performed a noble and beautiful work, a work which revealed both her love and her faith. She had indeed ministered to the poor. It is one of the wonders of God's grace that though His Son was rich, he became poor that through his poverty men might attain eternal riches. With moving pathos Jesus explained the difference: the poor will remain to receive the succour of the rich, "But me ye have not always". Only a few days now remain to him. "In that she hath poured this ointment on my body, she did it for my burial." Mark adds the commendation of Jesus in the memorable words, "She hath done what she could". Her Lord was going to his death. There was nothing she could or would do to prevent him from accomplishing his Father's will. All that she could do was to show him the greatness of her faith and the depth of her love. It is all that men can do when faced with the wonder of God's grace in Jesus. Yet how few have earned this glowing tribute!

When much else has been forgotten the fragrance of that room in Simon's house lingers with us still. Wherever the page of the Gospel is turned with reverent fingers as man contemplates the culminating sacrifice of the Saviour's dedicated life, Mary appears quietly on the scene, a picture of deep understanding and deeper love. At the very threshold of our Lord's suffering and death, as we are able to see the magnitude of his love and to realize what we owe to him, we are met by this woman who by a tender act of loving devotion, did what she could. And, meeting her here, we are confronted by the challenge, "What have I done? Have I done what I could?"

5

"THY KING COMETH"

ON the first day of the week the King came to Jerusalem.
He entered the city acclaimed by multitudes grown
delirious with joy and hope. The glad cries of the crowd had
been in his ears from the moment he left Bethany and took
the road that winds over the Mount of Olives from the east.
Arriving at Bethphage he had sent his disciples to fetch him
an ass, and mounting it in lowly dignity the journey had
proceeded. About a mile from Jerusalem he was met by a
surging wave of people, for the most part pilgrims lodging in
the city or camping outside its walls. The news of his coming
had gone before him and they had come forth to meet him.
The air was rent with shouts of triumph. He was being
accorded the welcome of a conqueror.

"Hosanna", they cried, "blessed is he that cometh in the
name of the Lord. Blessed be the kingdom of our father David
that cometh in the name of the Lord. Hosanna in the highest!"

Branches ripped from palm trees, robes quickly pulled
from shoulders, made a pathway for the ass's feet. His enemies
watched in anger and apprehension. They had fallen out
among themselves. "Perceive ye", said some, "how ye prevail
nothing? Behold, the world is gone after him." Some had even
approached him and implored him to stop this madness. But
Jesus had acquiesced in the clamour of the people: "If these
should hold their peace the very stones would cry out".
Unknown to them *their* hour was near. Soon the cries of the
people would support them against him. But for the moment
the provincial Jews were enjoying their short-lived jubilation.
By the evening they would be silent and thoughtful. Yes,
there was evidence of inconsistency in this scene of the victo-
rious King riding into the city, not upon a warhorse followed
by a thousand spears, but upon an ass's colt, surrounded by
undisciplined crowds. Looking more carefully into the rider's
face we discern a man of sorrows rather than a kingly conqueror. A few moments ago breasting the shoulder of Olivet
the city of Jerusalem had suddenly come into full view. Jesus
had brought his ass to a standstill, and the crowds had

become strangely quiet. He had looked long and earnestly at this city, its buildings crowding to its walls, its palaces lofty and imperious looking out over the limestone hills, its temple alone in solitary splendour high above the valley. And as he looked his face had grown troubled. The present faded, forty years sped swiftly by. He saw the city encompassed by a relentless enemy; flames licked hungrily about its dwellings, smoke billowed from its heart and rolled heavily away into the distance. Its beautiful buildings were visibly crumbling as masonry fell under the inexorable attack. His sensitive ear caught the cries of agony and terror; his penetrating eye saw the blood-stained dead and the emaciated bodies of the dying.

Jesus lifted up his voice and called across the valley to this stricken city, gleaming now in the morning sunlight oblivious of those distant clouds, "If thou hadst known, even thou, at least in this thy day, the things that belong unto thy peace! But now they are hid from thine eyes". Jesus saw all too clearly the result of their neglect, and because he saw, he wept. "The days shall come upon thee, that thine enemies shall cast a trench about thee, and compass thee round, and keep thee in on every side, and shall lay thee even with the ground, and thy children within thee; and they shall not leave in thee one stone upon another; because thou knewest not the time of thy visitation."

But now the procession had moved on again, the roaring crowds were sweeping down the slopes of Olivet, crossing the waters of the brook Kidron, and entering through the gate into the city. In the narrow streets the confusion became chaotic and the shouting inarticulate. The inhabitants rushed to their doors, climbed on their roofs, asked again and again "Who is this?" The multitude flung back the answer proudly, "This is Jesus, the prophet of Nazareth of Galilee". Matthew tells us that all the city was moved.

Yet there was an anticlimax to this momentous day. Gradually it became evident that Jesus was not prepared to take advantage of this tumultuous popularity; he was not going to supplement it by his miraculous power and assert his Messiahship. As the day wore on the disappointed crowds grew listless and drifted away. Jesus went into the temple and looked carefully round, observing the evidences that the House of God was still a place of barter and merchandise. As the evening shadows lengthened he turned sorrowfully away from the city, retracing his steps over the Mount of Olives, and turned with the Twelve to the welcome warmth of the home in Bethany.

How Jesus spent the night at Bethany we have no means of telling. We do know that the previous day had been one of intense emotion. We know too that similar experiences had been followed by a night of prayer. He was on his way back to Jerusalem with his disciples before the morning sun had risen over the hills of Moab, and he hungered; this seems to suggest that this night too had been spent on some lonely hill under the starry sky. Moreover the incident that occurred on this short journey to the city showed that his mind was still full of that vision of Jerusalem that had wrung from his lips the cry of mingled pleading and judgment the day before. Dare we lift the veil enough to perceive a night of intercession for his people, as Moses had interceded in the past? Can we see the sequel to the unfinished parable of the barren fig tree, the husbandman pleading with the owner of the vineyard for the preservation of the unfruitful tree for another year; a further opportunity of digging, dunging and careful tending? Is it possible to interpret in his subsequent actions the irrevocable answer of his Father that there can be no reprieve from the sentence Israel has brought upon herself? She will refuse her Messiah; she will pay the inexorable penalty. The scene which Jesus had envisaged from the hill above the city will move from prophecy into reality and pass on into history, taking its place in the great purpose of God.

In some sheltered spot by the roadside a fig tree attracted the attention of Jesus, as it must have drawn the wondering eyes of many travellers on their way to the Passover. At that time of the year fig trees were normally without either fruit or leaves. The sight suited his purpose well for it presented him with the opportunity of giving a practical illustration of the parable of the barren fig tree, and of completing a picture which had been left in abeyance. The time of figs was not yet; they appeared before the leaves. Here was a fig tree which made great boast of itself, challenging those who passed by to behold from the richness of its foliage, the succulence of its fruit. Yet, accepting the invitation, the hungry wayfarer was doomed to disappointment, for in spite of its lofty pretensions this tree was no better than the other trees. Its fault lay not so much in its barrenness as in its empty promises. No more penetrating picture of Israel can be imagined than that afforded by this sheltered tree with its abundance of green leaves stirring gently in the morning air. Nor can we confine the picture to natural Israel. It must ever be a challenge to Israel after the spirit also. The richness of the promise must be supported by the abundance of the fruit.

The disciples were startled to hear their Master addressing the fig tree as though it were an animate being: "Let no fruit grow on thee henceforward for ever". Night had probably fallen before they passed the spot on their return to Bethany, and it was not until the following morning that they saw the effect of these words of Jesus. Then they looked with amazement upon the withered tree; its stark branches raised in unavailing gesticulation to the heavens. "Master", cried Peter, "behold the fig tree which thou cursedst is withered away." Yet for the time the lesson was lost upon them. They would see this incident in its true light later on, and then they would understand. There were those who would live to witness the final rebellion of an overburdened nation, and see the withering effect of the military might of Rome. But for the moment they saw only the power of Christ upon the fig tree and were impressed by the deed and not the motive. Jesus, knowing that the time of understanding would come, forebore to correct the mistaken emphasis. He told them again as he had told them often before that such works of power were the result of perfect faith; and with the smallest faith they could overcome the greatest obstacles.

With his thoughts upon the people rather than upon himself, Jesus continued his early morning journey to the city. Yesterday it had been late afternoon when he went into the temple, the business for the day was over; but this time he found the commercial traffic in full spate, preparing for the lucrative business of the approaching feast. As he had done nearly three years before he swept through the Court of the Gentiles turning out all those who bought and sold; he sent the coins scattering across the stone pavement as he turned over the money changers' tables. His voice rang out clearly above the muffled curses and the scurrying footsteps, "Is it not written, My house shall be called a house of prayer? But ye have made it a den of thieves."

When the ungodly and ambitious had been ejected from the temple courts they were replaced by those who were in true need of the sanctuary of God. The blind and the lame came to him and he healed them. He had other visitors too. Those who falsely called themselves the children of God were removed, and the children he loved came to fill their place. Echoing the shouts they had heard all about them yesterday, they cried, "Hosanna to the Son of David!" And when those temple officials saw these things they were sore displeased, "Hearest thou what these say?" "Yea", he replied, "have ye never read, Out of the mouth of babes and sucklings thou hast perfected praise?"

For the second time that morning the Lord had stood before a fig tree, luxuriant in its outward adornments. The morning sun shone on its stately columns; its priests were resplendent in their ornate robes. It was a picture breathtaking in its beauty and promise. But it was barren. In purging the temple the second time his words were of judgment rather than entreaty, and soon the external splendour would fade before the savage onslaught of Rome.

Once more Jesus left the city and returned to the seclusion of Bethany.

6

"BY WHAT AUTHORITY?"

THE third day of Passover week marked the end of Christ's public work. It was a day full of incident, and when it was over Jesus had left the temple for the last time. The atmosphere, already tense and expectant, was mounting with each passing hour.

It was on his way from Bethany this Tuesday morning that the disciples had been startled by the withered fig tree and had received their lesson on the power of faith. The little company continued the journey into Jerusalem and proceeded to the temple where Jesus began once more to teach. But not for long. He was quickly interrupted. Yesterday the Pharisees and Sadducees had watched him in impotent rage as he had for the second time cleansed the temple. They would dearly have loved to have sent the officers to arrest him. But a measure that had failed palpably on a previous occasion was even more likely to fail now. Nor had they been able to oppose him themselves. Their personal courage was totally inadequate to withstand his moral and spiritual strength. They could only stand aside in awe as he swept through them with unapproachable majesty. During the hours of darkness they marshalled their forces. Scribes, Pharisees, Sadducees, Herodians, bitter enemies in so many phases of life and thought, combined in an unholy alliance against him. They drew near now, united in the single determination to destroy him. There were two ways open to them. Either they could break his power over the people and thus safely take him, or they could lure him into making some obviously seditious statement which would make his arrest inevitable. They had carefully chosen their spokesmen, men versed in the laws of polemics and skilled in the cut and thrust of controversy. It was a planned campaign: each issue subtly designed to entrap, powerful reserves waiting to be thrown into the conflict in the event of failure.

To many a pilgrim who saw Jesus for the first time the scene must have presented an incongruous contrast as the lordly aristocrats of the temple, resplendent in their official garments, bore down upon the quiet figure in his homespun robe. The exchanges could surely have but one ending. It was altogether too one-sided. What chance of survival had the Galilean against the prestige and wisdom represented here! But there were many who knew better, and waited eagerly for the attack.

"By what authority doest thou these things? And who gave thee this authority to do these things?" It was a strong opening. After the cleansing of the temple at the outset of his ministry the question had been, "What sign showest thou unto us, seeing thou doest these things?" For three years the Messiah had given them abundant signs of his authority. But they had been wilfully blind. Now they did not ask for signs but for authority. A rabbi was not entitled to teach without the consent of the Sanhedrin. Indeed there was a form of ordination by which a teacher, having first been steeped in the tradition of the elders, was recruited into the service of temple and synagogue as a scribe and rabbi. No such consent had been obtained by Christ, yet not only had he taught openly in the temple, but he had criticized its ministers and abused its practices.

Jesus met this searching question with another, promising to answer theirs when they had answered his: yet his question was in effect both an answer to theirs and an exposure of their crafty motive. "The baptism of John, was it from heaven or of men? Answer me." In appealing to John, Christ appealed to one whom all men accounted a prophet, to one, moreover, whose whole mission was to reveal the identity of Jesus as the Christ. Here was indeed the authority for his work. Jesus challenged them to state their views on the prophet's message. To acknowledge John was to acknowledge Christ: this they obviously were not prepared to do. Yet to condemn the ministry of John was equally impossible in view of the unshakable conviction of the people concerning him. Their only escape lay in an abject confession of their ignorance, a confession which could have deceived nobody, and only emphasized the decisiveness of their defeat. "Neither", said Jesus, "do I tell you by what authority I do these things."

Pressing home the victory he had so easily won from this imposing attack, Jesus by a series of parables demonstrated to them their neglect of the charge God had committed to them, and their ingratitude to Him for the privileges they enjoyed.

A certain man who had two sons asked the first to go and work in his vineyard. He refused, but later he repented and went. When the second was similarly instructed he promised willingly enough, but did not go. It was a simple story and there was only one answer to the question Jesus put to his accusers, "Whether of them twain did the will of his father ?" "The first", they answered shortly. "Verily I say unto you", replied Jesus, looking with sadness rather than anger upon the group of ecclesiastics round him, "the publicans and the harlots go into the kingdom of God before you." The people crowding round him looked horrified. The rulers drew in their breath sharply and turned pale with anger, their eyes changed from hostility to hatred.

Yet Jesus spoke only the truth. The Jews were divided into those who sought righteousness by the law and those who completely ignored the demands of God. When true righteousness was revealed from heaven in the person of Christ, it was the moral and spiritual outcasts who recognized and received it. The ministers of ceremonial righteousness had found so much personal satisfaction in the dignity and power which their office brought that they rejected the righteousness which is by faith.

For the first time Jesus confronted his enemies with the fact of their conspiracy against his life. In the parable of the wicked husbandman he showed them this coming rejection in the wider perspective of the purpose of God. He came as the Son of God in direct line with the prophets sent by His Father to His people down the centuries, seeking the legitimate fruits of His vineyard. In the true character of their faithless ancestors the present husbandmen were in no mood to reverence the Son. As long as they could pay lip service to God and enjoy the fruits of the vineyard themselves they were content. Any attempt to change these favourable conditions, from whatever source it might come, must be effectively suppressed. This man had come with formidable claims; he had done many wonderful works; but he was contesting their power and authority. He must go. They had made Beelzebub serve their purpose in dismissing his miracles: it remained now for them to break his hold over the people and put him out of the way.

Such was the power of Christ's teaching that as he unfolded the parable to them they were visibly impressed. They found themselves reluctantly yet spontaneously answering the question he put to them, "When the lord of the vineyard cometh, what will he do unto those husbandmen?" Their answer came, "He will miserably destroy those wicked men, and will let out his vineyard unto other husbandmen which shall render him the fruits of their seasons."

Without hesitation Jesus brought home the indictment with deadly precision, leaving them condemned by their own judgment: "Therefore I say unto you, the kingdom of God shall be taken from you, and given to a nation bringing forth the fruits thereof". Not since the prophet Nathan had pointed an accusing finger at David, condemning him with the dramatic revelation, "Thou art the man", had men stood so nakedly self-confessed as did these rulers of Israel in the temple on this third morning of the Passover week. Unhappily they had none of the humility and contrition of David and their reaction was in its way as characteristic as his. They sought to lay hands on him, but feared the people.

It was open warfare now. There could be no retreat. It had to be fought out until victory was achieved by one side or the other. So far there could be no doubt which way the battle swayed. The spears of the priests buckled against the breast-plate of righteousness. Their duplicity was no match for his simple honesty. He no longer withstood their onslaught; he carried the war relentlessly into their own camp. The time of pleading was over. Now he exposed them before all the people, laying bare the poverty and iniquity that lay beneath those bright robes and pious practices.

He told them another parable. A king made a great marriage feast for his son and sent his servants to call the guests.* But those who had been invited made light of it and would not come. Not only did they insult the king by casting his favours back in his face, but they maltreated those whom he sent to remind them of their privilege. As Jesus spoke we imagine the vision of Jerusalem appearing once more before his eyes. "When the king heard thereof he was wroth, and he sent forth his armies and destroyed those murderers and burned up their city." But the king's son will have his wedding. Other guests will sit at the table and enjoy the feast. The servants went into the highways to bid them come. Their poverty, their toil-stained clothes, their ignorance of courtly ways matter not one whit, for they will be washed, and the king will furnish them with robes. Yet this gracious invitation must not be lightly esteemed, and one who spurns to wear the wedding garment will enjoy neither the richness of the

---

*This is not to be confused with the Parable of the Great Supper (Luke 14:6). Careful reading will show many interesting and significant differences.

BOOK SEVEN: TOWARDS CALVARY

banquet nor the fellowship of the king's son, but will be cast into outer darkness: "for", concluded Jesus in words which rebuke any facile optimism, "many are called, but few are chosen".

The first phase of the battle was over. The attempt to break Christ's hold over the people had proved an abysmal failure. It had ended in their own disgrace. The Pharisees looked significantly at one another, and then slowly withdrew to consider how they might change the direction of their attack and gain their end by entangling him in his speech.

7

"TO CAESAR ... AND TO GOD"

THERE seems no end to the perversity of the human spirit. No setback was great enough to do more than cause a momentary lull in the attack on Jesus while forces were reformed and sent back into the battle with steady persistence. The Herodians and Pharisees were strange bedfellows, the former anxious to compromise with Rome, the latter intensely nationalistic; yet both considered an alliance necessary to secure the downfall of one whom they deemed a greater danger to their aspirations than they were to each other.

They came to him now, affecting a reverence and humility they were far from feeling. A few of the onlookers may have been deceived by their false demeanour and fair words; Jesus certainly was not. "Master", they said, "we know that thou art true and teachest the way of God in truth, neither carest thou for any man, for thou regardest not the person of men. Tell us therefore, what thinkest thou? Is it lawful to give tribute unto Caesar or not?" This question coming from a group of Pharisees and Herodians lent a certain air of genuineness to the scene. It gave the impression that this had become (as indeed it was) a matter of argument between them upon which they sought the arbitration of Jesus. It was palpably a trap; yet it was not an easy question to answer. A direct affirmative or a direct negative would be fatal: the one would instantly undermine his claims as Israel's Messiah and rob him of the support of the people, the other would immediately expose him to a charge of treason. They waited anxiously for the answer, the crowd watched expectantly. The words of the Psalmist truly reflected the mind of Jesus during these hours of conflict, "The wicked have waited for me to destroy me, but I will consider thy testimonies ... O how love I thy law, it is my meditation all the day. Thou through thy commandments hast made me wiser than mine enemies."

The expectant hush was broken by the quiet voice of Jesus, "Why tempt ye me, ye hypocrites? Show me the tribute money". With a foreboding of the impending frustration they offered him a denarius stamped with the head of the Roman, emperor.* "Whose is this image and superscription?" "Caesar's." "Render therefore unto Caesar the things that are Caesar's, and unto God the things that are God's."

The men marvelled at his answer and went away sobered by his wisdom. But his words were so much more than the astute evasion of a verbal trap. It is an answer which has come down the years to successive generations resolving the problem of divided loyalty. The kingdom of God is not of this world and secular claims only find their place after the claims of God have been met. If we interpret the demands of the state in the light of this word of Jesus we shall have few practical problems on issue even in these complex days.

It was not long before Jesus was interrupted once more. This time a group of Sadducees approached him. During his whole ministry the Sadducees had only once come into open conflict with him. At the close of the Galilean ministry they had joined a deputation of Pharisees to demand a sign from heaven. For the most part they chose to consider his activities beneath their contempt. Now that he had carried the war into their midst they were stung to action and determined to suppress him. But in common with the other enemies of Jesus their methods were limited by the loyalty of the multitudes, and so they in their turn sought first to bring ridicule upon him as a necessary preliminary to his arrest and destruction. They propounded to him a problem which they smugly thought made ludicrous the whole conception of the Resurrection. A man with six brothers died, and in accordance with the conditions of the law each of the brothers married his widow in turn, and pre-deceased her without issue. In the resurrection whose wife should she be?

It was a materialistic quibble well suited to the minds of the worldly Sadducees. But Jesus refused to be drawn into a frivolous dispute. He turned to them with sobering earnestness and answered their question with solemn majestic words. It is an incident which affords a wonderful lesson for all those who are confronted with such cavils in their efforts to preach the Gospel. "Ye do greatly err, not knowing the Scriptures nor the power of God."

Because the Sadducees only accepted the authority of the Pentateuch, Jesus confined his answer to the first two books

---

*Such coins were uncommon in Palestine. Out of deference to Jewish prejudice the Romans issued a special coinage for the Jew, which had no images impressed upon it. But Roman coins came into circulation from other territories, especially at the Passover.

of Scripture. He spoke of their great progenitors, the patriarchs in whom they boasted, Moses who gave them their laws. It may be true that these early books contained no direct references to the Resurrection, but Jesus swept them beyond the scope of their critical polemics and revealed the postulates that were implicit in the written revelation. God is not the God of the dead but of the living. His promises and His covenants are not broken by the human incidence of death. So Moses testifies to the fact of resurrection, and those who show the obedience of the faithful men of God will be accounted worthy to attain the resurrection. They neither marry nor are given in marriage but are as the angels.

The Sadducees, impressed no doubt by this solemn and beautiful revelation and by the authority by which Jesus had spoken, had nothing more to say. But their resolve was not impaired. They were men of action rather than words. They left him with the astonished multitudes.

Presently a scribe approached him. He was a man who though sceptical had been impressed by the answers Jesus had given to his enemies, and he tested Christ with a question frequently heard in rabbinical discussions, on the relative importance of the moral and ceremonial commandments. "Master", he asked, "which is the greatest commandment in the law?" Without hesitation Jesus answered simply, "Thou shalt love the Lord thy God with all thy heart and with all thy strength and with all thy mind. This is the first commandment. And the second is like unto it, Thou shalt love thy neighbour as thyself. On these two commandments hang all the law and the prophets".

As he looked into the face of Jesus and listened to these confident words the law and the prophets became suddenly alive and personal to this man. "Well, Master", he answered, "thou hast said the truth." Reiterating the words of Jesus he seemed almost to be thinking aloud as he concluded, "And to love him with all the heart ... and to love his neighbour as himself, is more than all whole burnt offerings and sacrifices".

Jesus knew the power of his word over that man who had come to try him, and encouraging, as he always did, the first glimmer of humble recognition in a man, he spurred him on with words that would never be forgotten, "Thou art not far from the kingdom of God". Many times we too long to have that encouragement. Yet to see with this lawyer the full scope of our calling, and to recognize humbly that it is satisfied in

the love we bear to God and to each other, and not in the
meticulous observance of religious conventions, is to have our
feet firmly placed on the road to the Kingdom.

The scene had completely changed. There was little self-
confidence left in the bearing of those who had come to expose
the Galilean teacher to ridicule. So great was his mastery
that Jesus could easily have done with them whatsoever he
listed, stooping to their own guile, heaping disgrace upon
them and bringing forth ribald laughter from the crowds. Yet
that would have been thoroughly out of character. Instead
Jesus had elevated the whole battleground and charged the
occasion with solemnity. He had treated none of their questions lightly, but had drawn from them lessons of the utmost
worth. Responding to this atmosphere they were completely
in his power: they dared not ask him any more questions.

It was his turn now to ask the Pharisees a question. There
was no subtlety in it. It concerned their conception of Israel's
Messiah. "Whose son is he?" "David's", they answered without hesitation. Yes, they were right, yet it was only half an
answer. Why does David, speaking under the influence of the
Spirit, call him Lord? Only because he was the Son of God. It
was in their ignorance of the deeper conception of the
Messiah that they failed.

Not only in their questions but in their inability to answer,
they showed their limitations. It was this ignorance combined
with their self-importance which was responsible for their
determination to destroy their Messiah. Nothing could shake
their resolve, and so it was that the Christ must leave his
Father's House and these multitudes he had come to save. In
a few years this temple would be a mass of rubble and these
people of God would lie bleeding and dying in its dust. The
destroyers and murderers stood round him frustrated in
their attempts to humiliate him but undeterred in their
resolve to accomplish his end.

His farewell to Israel marked the opening of the floodgates
of his wrath against those who were responsible for the rejection of her Messiah and the terrible judgments which that
rejection would bring. The pent-up emotions of the last three
years, restrained as long as there was hope of repentance,
burst now in a storm against the blindness and hypocrisy
that had passed beyond appeal.

These scribes of the Pharisees had assumed Moses' seat.
Jesus told the disciples and the multitudes to accept their

teaching but avoid their spirit and their actions. They carefully secure burdens on men's backs but do nothing to help them to carry them. There is no love in their works, only the desire to impress their fellows. He paused to warn his disciples against those first fatal steps which led to such devastating hypocrisy. "Be ye not called rabbi, for one is your master, even Christ, and all ye are brethren ... He that is greatest among you shall be your servant."

As Jesus continued his charge against the scribes his language became more intense. He denounced their sin and hypocrisy in eight specific accusations and eight woes which find strange but significant contrast with the eight blessings of the Beatitudes. As Moses pronounced the blessings and the curses from Ebal and Gerizim so the greater prophet proclaimed the blessings of the Kingdom from the hills of Galilee, and the tragic price of rejection from the heights of Zion.

He accused them of shutting out the Kingdom of God both from themselves and those whom they influenced. Their long prayers sheltered the grossest forms of selfishness. They made feverish efforts to secure a proselyte but, converting him at last, they only succeeded in entangling him in the toils in which they had enmeshed themselves. They were blind guides. They reached absurd limits in their exaction of tithes, yet were unconcerned with the far greater matters of judgment, mercy and faith. With a sudden flash of humour he drew a picture of them straining a gnat out of their glass of wine to avoid pollution, but swallowing a great hairy camel which takes its place. He denounced them for the veneer of holiness and purity which appeared beautiful but hid "dead men's bones and all uncleanness". Finally he turned to their practice of building imposing memorials for the prophets their fathers had killed and thus endeavouring to escape any suggestion of guilt. Their very action condemned them as the children of the murderers, and now, on the point of killing him to whom the prophets had given their united witness, they were about to fill the measure of their fathers.

Then Israel's Messiah became a prophet indeed, and the men who listened grew troubled at his words; in their hearts they knew that nothing could prevent their fulfilment. Their selfish lust would not be sated even by the death of Christ himself; his servants would meet a like fate at their hands! But it would be required of this generation. Nothing would save them from the damnation of hell.

He looked round upon the people he loved, upon the temple which was his Father's house, upon the city which was God's footstool. He was filled with a great longing and a deep compassion. "O Jerusalem, Jerusalem", he cried, "thou that killest the prophets, and stonest them that are sent unto thee, how often would I have gathered thy children together, even as a hen gathereth her chickens under her wings, and ye would not! Behold, your house is left unto you desolate. For I say unto you, Ye shall not see me henceforth, till ye shall say, Blessed is he that cometh in the name of the Lord."

8

"WE WOULD SEE JESUS"

SPENT by the intensity of his rebuke of Israel's rulers, Jesus passed from the courts and ascended the steps which led to the temple itself. Sinking down on the topmost step with his disciples around him he was able to look out across the Court of the Women, its vast colonnades enclosing an area where fifteen thousand worshippers could assemble. The time of sacrifice was over, but many remained to view with wonder the beautiful buildings or engage in private devotion and offering. Spaced round the columned terraces were the great trumpet-shaped offertory boxes, allocated to their several purposes.

With that lively interest in men which is such a clearly delineated characteristic in the Gospels, Jesus watched the people approaching the treasury-boxes to cast in their offerings. He saw lordly men make their ostentatious gifts; he watched rich men give of their superfluity; he noticed others who came quietly past and gave cheerfully with an obvious sense of privilege. But one figure held his attention. She was alone and in mourning. It was painfully evident from her appearance that she was among the desperately poor. Almost afraid to mingle with the other worshippers, she paused for a moment, and then went purposefully forward and dropped into the treasury the two mites which represented the smallest offering legally acceptable. Her gift presented to God, she went her way and was lost in the crowd.

After the relentless conflict of the last few hours this was a refreshing sight. Jesus turned to his disciples: "Verily I say unto you, this poor widow hath cast more in than all they that have cast into the treasury, for all they did cast in of their abundance; but she of her want did cast in all that she had, even all her living".

The woman went to her lonely home and her meagre fare oblivious of the one who had watched her. To have known that her two mites had been singled out would have covered her with confusion; had she suspected that she had been contrasted favourably with the wealthy and the great she would never have understood. But her humble gift, like Mary's precious perfume, has shed its fragrance down the years.

It is easy to make offerings to the Lord which cost us little or nothing. The poor woman's meagre gift was the greatest of all because it was so real a sacrifice. In the light of Christ's judgment there are probably few of us who have given much. There may be some of us who have never really given anything. But there are those who have. Many mites have since been added to the two that fell into the temple treasury; offerings rich in their meagreness because they represented all the giver had to give. For the most part those gifts have remained unnoticed amid the welter of more obvious givings; where they are discovered they are sometimes scorned. But there is an unseen watcher who sees and knows, and in the fulness of time those children of the Kingdom whose poverty has excluded them from so many material blessings will be welcomed by the One who became poor that they might be rich.

Before Jesus left the temple a company of Greeks sought an audience with him through Philip. We know little about these men, but it seems that they were not proselytes but heathens who were not allowed to pass beyond the Court of the Gentiles in their search for Jesus. Many such came to Jerusalem at the time of Passover inspired by differing motives. Whatever may have been the reason for the request, these men assumed an almost prophetic character, foreshadowing the longings of successive generations of Gentiles from every corner of the earth. "Sir, we would see Jesus."

Philip, once more lacking in decisiveness, spoke to Andrew, and together they approached Jesus. Whether the desire was satisfied we do not know. We see the effect upon the Lord. To him it was symbolic. As the Jews were about to slay him, the Gentiles travelling from afar desire to come to him. Their call will one day be answered. "Verily, verily, I say unto you, Except a corn of wheat fall into the ground and die, it abideth alone: but if it die, it bringeth forth much fruit."

The hour had come for the Son of man to be glorified. He was about to seal in his blood the claims he had made to the world, and the promises he had given to his disciples, and in doing so to show them by his death that he that hateth his life in this world shall keep it unto life eternal.

Yet even as he spoke the darkness of the coming hours entered into his soul. All that was human in him cried out against the terrible ordeal that was about to assail his young

300

glowing manhood and sweep him to an untimely grave. Even whilst our heart weeps in loving sympathy, we are grateful for this revealing outburst. "Now is my soul troubled, and what shall I say? Father, save me from this hour."

Yet his spiritual resources were sufficient. In an instant they asserted themselves, putting aside the natural desires of his heart. "But for this cause came I to this hour. Father, glorify thy Name."

With the declaration of submission to the will of God came the answering call from his Father, bringing with it comfort and strength. "I have both glorified it, and will glorify it again."

The people heard the voice but could not distinguish the message; some said it thundered, others more discerning, that an angel had spoken to him. But Jesus said the voice was for them rather than for him. His Father could have communicated encouragement through the silences into his heart. But now the whole world stood at the bar of judgment. The events of the next hours would determine its destiny. Yet it was already determined. The last three years had shown that although the Messiah had come to his own, his own had received him not. The final tragedy was the last inevitable act in the drama of renunciation.

Once more his thoughts soared above the hatred which was bringing him to his death, and returned to the glory of his Father's purpose. "And I, if I be lifted up, will draw all men unto me."

He made a last appeal to his countrymen. "Yet a little while is the light with you ... Walk while ye have the light ... While ye have the light believe in the light that ye may be the children of light."

Nor can we believe that he spoke in vain. For even now his enemies were only prevented from taking him by the loyalty of those who hung upon his words. At night when their protection was removed he stayed arrest by his retirement to Bethany and to the Mount of Olives. The Lamb of God would not be slain before the Passover, nor before the sacred communion of the upper room.

The contrast between the feelings of Jesus as he left the temple for the last time and the thoughts of the disciples throws a poignant light upon the darkened minds of the Twelve. In that light we are able to discern something of the loneliness of the Saviour. To him the stately building must have spoken of the obstinacy and pride of man blinded by his own self-sufficiency to the grace of God, and oblivious of his impending doom. Its imposing strength was full of menace for him. It filled him not with fear but with sadness. Its ministers were about to enjoy their triumph, the triumph of a form of godliness that denied the power: the triumph of man's selfishness, hypocrisy and greed. But it was to be a bloody victory. Generations yet unborn would reap banishment, persecution and despair.

But as the disciples looked up at its commanding beauty and watched the evening sun gilding its colonnades, they had very different thoughts. They were filled only with awe at its strength and rejoiced in its magnificence. "Master", they said, "see what manner of stones and what buildings are here!"

Gently Jesus led them from the danger of being deceived by the imposing nature of material things. "Seest thou these great buildings? There shall not be left one stone upon another that shall not be thrown down."

As the evening shadows lengthened they made their way out to the Mount of Olives. Perplexed and humbled by his answer they asked him a twofold question, "Tell us, when shall these things be? And what shall be the sign of thy coming and the end of the world?"

In what has become known as the Olivet prophecy, Jesus answered these two questions. In these years we have naturally made use of it as evidence of the nearness of our Lord's return. Such emphasis may tend to divert us from its more urgent personal message. Jesus set forth conditions attending the end of both the Jewish and the Gentile dispensations, but the greater part of his words is devoted to the hearts and minds of the disciples. For them it is full of warning and encouragement. Jesus confessed that neither he nor the angels knew the exact time or season of his return. In a sense it was not an important question. Many children of the Kingdom would live and die outside its orbit. Our lives must not be absorbed with speculation but with preparation.

Jesus spoke to the Twelve of events shortly to come to pass. They must not be deceived or deterred by false Christs arising amongst them; he spoke of coming turmoil and bloodshed, to be preceded by their own persecution and suffering. They must not waver under trial; it would be a testimony that they were following their Lord. He turned to their second question and told them of the distress which would overtake the whole earth before his return, of the tumultuous roaring of peoples which we have grown to know so well, the eclipse of kings, the frantic strivings of statesmen to find solutions to situations from which there would be no way out. He spoke of the terror of the inhabitants of the earth as they recognized the relentless menace of powers they were unable to control.

"And then shall they see the Son of man coming in a cloud with power and great glory. And when these things begin to come to pass", he said, raising his eyes above the tensely listening disciples and addressing us over the centuries, "then look up, and lift up your heads, for your redemption draweth nigh."

And now his discourse turns from the world with its cares and troubles, and Jesus speaks only to his own. He speaks of the dangers lurking in these difficult days for them. They would be like the days before the Flood when men lived only for themselves and were preoccupied with the cares of this life. "Watch ye therefore and pray always that ye may be accounted worthy to escape all these things that shall come to pass, and to stand before the Son of man."

He told them the parable of the Ten Virgins, leaving with them the sober vision of the closed door and the echo of the sentence which barred for ever from the joys of the Kingdom: "Verily I say unto you, I know you not".

He told them the parable of the Talents with its emphasis not upon ability but upon zeal. He drew for them a picture of the Kingdom taken from their own familiar scene. As the shepherd divided the sheep from the goats at the end of the day, so when the Son of Man comes in his glory he separates the righteous from the wicked. The separation will be determined by works. To the righteous he will say, "Come, ye blessed of my Father, inherit the kingdom prepared for you from the foundation of the world. For I was an hungered, and ye gave me meat: I was thirsty, and ye gave me drink: I was a stranger, and ye took me in: naked, and ye clothed me: I was sick, and ye visited me: in prison, and ye came unto me".

The righteous will answer, "When did we all these things?" "Inasmuch", their Lord will reply, "as ye have done it unto one of the least of these my brethren, ye have done it unto me."

To the wicked he will say, "Depart from me, ye cursed" Their refusal of that ministering love for their brethren had made their protestations of love for their Lord empty professions. "These", Jesus concluded, "shall go away into everlasting punishment, but the righteous unto life eternal."

This picture which Jesus painted does not imply that good works are a substitute for faith and belief: those qualities are postulated already. But it demonstrates the tragic futility of a belief which fails to respond to the stimulus of men's need. However great our knowledge of God's word, however penetrating our discernment of Christ's gospel of the Kingdom, it will only serve to condemn us if it fails to inspire an active response in following him who came not to be ministered unto but to minister. Christ alone will be the judge of that. There are many wonderful works done in his name; there are many eloquent testimonies given. They are often necessary and their motive often pure. But they are the most dangerous form of service because, being seen of men, there is great danger that they may carry with them their own reward. Under the stimulus of man's approbation it is easy for the motive to lose something of its dedication. The cup of cold water is not so susceptible to that danger. It does not move multitudes; it just brings sunlight into some obscure life. It warms the heart of one of Christ's little ones who has been trembling in the coldness of the world's exposure. It turns poverty into riches, imprisonment into freedom, sickness into health. Whether the ministration is physical or spiritual it matters not; the disciple follows one who healed both body and soul. Succour given in the spirit of Jesus radiates beyond the body and fills the heart, preparing it for the spiritual blessings which are waiting to follow.

9

LOVE TO THE UTTERMOST

THE difficulties of the Sanhedrin were eased by a visit from one of the Twelve. While Jesus was teaching in the city Judas slipped away, presented himself before the chief priests and promised to help them to arrest his Master. It was probably an impulsive rather than a deliberate visit, but it marked the first active move in a dreadful conflict which had been raging in his soul for the last few months.

Efforts have been made to find excuses for the treachery of Judas, to show that his true motive was to force Christ's hand and make him assert his Messiahship. But it is impossible to relieve the blackness of his deed or find any other verdict than that which stares starkly from the written word. Many months before, when the disciples protested their loyalty amid the general disaffection, Jesus had said, "Have I not chosen you twelve, and one of you is a devil?" The Judas emerging from the Gospels is an ambitious man who was drawn to the simple company because he believed fervently that Christ was the Messiah of Israel, and expected material advantages from his association. He was unscrupulous and was not above stealing from the common purse. The months passed without any effort by Jesus to advance his claims, and Judas became restless. When for the second time Jesus rejected the efforts of the people to make him king, and spoke of surrender to his enemies, and of suffering and death at their hands, the baffled man of Kerioth felt he had been cheated. But it was impossible even for a man like him to be in the company of Jesus without being given a vision of life and character beside which his selfish ambitions looked tawdry and filled him with shame. Herein lay the conflict. It is familiar ground; the flesh or the Spirit; the world or the Christ. It was near enough to all the apostles to bring the question trembling uncertainly on their lips, "Lord, is it I?"

But before the evil in Judas should triumph Jesus had some precious hours to spend with the Twelve. It was of the utmost importance that they should not be disturbed, so he prepared secretly. It is not unlikely that Judas, with his base design in view, had prompted the disciples' question, "Where wilt thou that we prepare for thee to eat the Passover?" Peter and John, two of the most loyal disciples, were sent from Bethany to Jerusalem to make arrangements for the Passover feast. But lest by a hasty word they should betray the meeting place to Judas they were left in ignorance to be guided to it by a man carrying a pitcher of water. It would not be difficult for them to find their guide, for women were the pitcher bearers in Palestine. In the large upper room the two apostles made ready. The lamb was purchased, taken to the temple to be killed by the priests, carried back and prepared; the bread, wine and bitter herbs were brought, the simple furnishings arranged, and all was in readiness.

In the evening Jesus left his loved ones in Bethany for the last time. The shadows of Gethsemane were gathering about him, the cross was already growing heavy on his shoulders, the sweat was forming on his brow. Mary watched him move slowly away over the shoulder of the hill. Her love would tell her much. Something of his burden was communicated to her as she bravely smiled her answer to his last farewell. She watched him go with an anguish too great for tears. But when he had gone the smile would fade and her eyes would reveal something of the pain and loneliness that was in her heart. The cruelty and lust of man which was so soon to be directed against the love of God revealed in Jesus, pierced also the heart of the one who loved. And it has done ever since. No true disciple of Jesus can pass through the coming hours without the sword piercing his own soul also. Circumstances were to prevent Mary of Bethany from ministering to her Lord at his tomb, but she had performed her ministry while he lived. It had been a beautiful service of devotion and though the hours to come were to be darkened by an agony of suffering, the resurrection morn was awaiting, and with it the glory of a risen Lord. And so we leave Mary at the door of her little home in Bethany. She does not appear again in the Gospel record. We leave her reluctantly, thankful for the warmth of her devotion and the fragrance of her example. We leave her in the confidence that if we love and serve our Lord in her spirit we shall meet her in the day when the Lord shall stand on the Mount of Olives and minister not only to his people but to the need of all the world.

But now the Lamb of God was going into the city for the Passover. After this week the work of the priests would be finished, the law would be at an end, the righteousness of God would be revealed in Christ, and through him believing men and women would find salvation.

Passing over the Mount of Olives busy now with pilgrims erecting their temporary dwellings for the feast, they made their way into the city. Even now the disciples could not resist the temptation to compete for places at the table, and Jesus was compelled to rebuke them. But the Saviour's mind was filled with the realization that his hour had come. He saw for a moment beyond the degradation which was awaiting him to the hour when, his great work of redemption complete, he would enter the glory of his Father's presence. And, looking upon these men who amid much frailty and waywardness had been loyal companions through the shadowy paths of the last three years, his heart welled up in unspeakable love. "Having loved his own which were in the world, he loved them to the uttermost."

The picture we have of Jesus as he faced these last hours fills us with awe and gratitude. At no time in his life does his character shine in a more radiant light. Around him was hatred and disaffection, in his very midst was treachery, before him lay torture and a lingering death. He was only thirty three. To all outward appearances his mission had been a failure; he had roused the nation only to disappoint it. Now his hour had come, and with the complete dedication which had marked his life, he went forward unfalteringly to his death.

The disciples' unseemly quarrel for precedence at the table gave their Master the opportunity both to administer the most gracious rebuke and to reveal the nature of his Father's love. He rose from the table, wrapped a towel around him, and, taking a bowl of water, proceeded to wash the feet of the Twelve. Human nature combines with history to demand that power must be in natural opposition to humility and servitude. In revealing His love to man God shows how false such a conception is. He sends His Son for the salvation of man. We look for a revelation of glory and power; we find a man of sorrows and acquainted with grief. We look for a conscience stricken people bowing in reverence before his majesty, but we see the Baptist lifting him from the flowing waters of the Jordan. We wait for the fiery judgment of Heaven upon a faithless people, but we see the gentle touch of healing and hear the contented cries of little children. We look for the denunciation of the traitor, but we see the Saviour kneeling at his feet with water and towel.

One by one the disciples submitted to his ministration and, submitting, learned the nature of their vocation. Judas felt the cool hands of Jesus on his feet, feet stained by the dust of the road which led to the high priest's house. But the moment passed and with it went the last opportunity to repent of the evil deed that was in his heart. Only Peter protested. Gently Jesus showed his impulsive disciple that before he could do anything for his Lord, he must suffer his Lord to minister to him, and cleanse the impurities from his robust but earthly heart. We have to learn that too, and learning it may cry with more impulsiveness than wisdom, "Not my feet only, Lord".

As he so often did, Jesus explained to the disciples the significance of his action. "Ye call me Master and Lord. If I then, your Lord and Master, have washed your feet, ye ought also to wash one another's feet." We cannot minister until we have been ministered unto by our Lord: but when we have received his ministry ours becomes imperative: the love that has poured forth from him into our lives is too great to remain there without flowing forth also into the lives of others.

But it was at this point that Jesus felt the full impact of the treachery of Judas. He was about to be betrayed by a familiar friend; one who had shared the hardships and joys of his ministry, who had been a constant witness of his healing touch and his divine power over Nature. In spite of all that he had seen and heard, in spite of what he *knew* in his heart, a handful of silver coins was enough to settle the conflict between good and evil. Now, the very presence of Judas was an oppressing burden. It filled the room: an ominous darkness which formed an effective barrier between Jesus and his disciples, preventing that intimate communion to which he had called them at this hour. The crisis must come. Jesus was troubled in spirit. The concentrated venom of men which he had endured during these last weeks had left him unmoved, but the treachery of one of his own was more painful than anything his enemies could inflict.

They had returned now to the table and reclined with Jesus in their midst. John was on his right, Judas on his left.* Suddenly the Lord spoke. "Verily, verily, I say unto you

*A thoughtful reading of the Gospel accounts seems to indicate the position of Judas. Especially compare John 13:23–27 and Matthew 26:25.

that one of you shall betray me." To eleven of the disciples this was a dreadful shock. To the twelfth it was a moment of awful apprehension. It was inconceivable to the others that anything but complete devotion and love could be in all their hearts. John reveals a tendency we all recognize, when he says, "The disciples looked one on another, doubting of whom he spake". Faced with an accusation we tend to look at our brethren. Gradually the full import of Jesus' words was perceived and the sorrow of Jesus enveloped them. They no longer sought to penetrate the secret of their brother's soul but looked anxiously into their own. One by one they asked him, "Lord, is it I?" Dreading exposure, yet knowing that to remain silent would be to condemn himself, Judas asked the fateful question. But Jesus saved him by an answer which he alone heard. "Thou hast said." Peter was roused from his shocked surprise by the realization that if the traitor was in the room he could be effectively dealt with before he could perpetrate his treachery. He made signs to John to ask who it should be. "He it is to whom I shall give a sop when I have dipped it." Only John heard these words, and only John watched with awful fascination as Jesus quietly offered the sop to Judas. With a deeper understanding than Peter, John remained silent. In that moment Judas knew there could be no turning back. His feet had already begun to slip on the brink of the precipice down which he was to plunge headlong. "That thou doest, do quickly." Judas rose from the table, walked to the door, and under the protecting silence of the Master he was betraying, and the awe-stricken John, he went out: and it was night.

With the departure of Judas the dark cloud of oppression cleared. Jesus devoted himself to his disciples, and all his love for them and his care for their welfare flowed forth unchecked. For a short hour the grim events of the morrow were forgotten and the blessings of all that he was to accomplish were enjoyed. "Now is the Son of man glorified, and God is glorified in him."

10

"WITH DESIRE I HAVE DESIRED ..."

THERE was darkness outside, impenetrable and full of menace. Judas had gone into the darkness. Even now he stood before Caiaphas. All the indecision had gone from him as he told something which brought a gleam of satisfaction into the High Priest's eyes.

But there was light in the Upper Room. With the departure of the traitor the dark shadows had gone, and the disciples felt the warmth and intimacy of their Master's love.

While they were eating Jesus took a loaf from the table before him and broke it in his hands. He offered up a prayer of thankfulness and consecration, then passed a morsel to each of his disciples. "Take, eat, this is my body. Do this in remembrance of me." In wondering silence and with a profound sense of awe they ate the bread. When they had finished Jesus took a cup of wine. Again his head bowed in prayer. He passed it to them to drink one by one. They heard his words, "Drink ye all of it. For this is my blood of the new covenant which is shed for many for the remission of sins. But I say unto you, I will not drink henceforth of this fruit of the vine until that day when I drink it new with you in my Father's kingdom".

There was a solemnity about these moments which must have kept the disciples silent. They would sense the sanctity of something too great to understand, but they would feel a sudden sense of new fellowship with their Lord. These rough, uncultured men felt their hearts bursting with an emotion they had never felt before—emotion that kept their eyes lowered. Jesus looked from one to another; he knew their hearts and his spirit flowed out to them with a love he had not hitherto revealed. For the first time he addressed them as his "little children".

What the disciples could not know is that even whilst he encompassed them in this simple memorial, his eyes were lifted beyond them down the years that were yet to be; towards disciples gathered in caves with Roman soldiers dogging their steps; towards men and women dying in the mountains with his Name upon their lips; towards a faithful remnant struggling to keep the faith in a closing age of folly and darkness. He saw countless disciples down the years and over the world, humble disciples who lived and died unknown. He saw them living out their little lives with their hopes and their fears, their struggles and their failures, their prayers and their victories. He came quietly to them with his invitation, "With desire I have desired to eat this passover with you before I suffer". And in humble earnestness had come their answer, "With desire we desire to meet at thy table, Lord". And so obediently they came, they remembered, they loved, they went back to their tasks inspired by his presence, resolved to struggle on. Eventually they died, faithful to the end, not having received the promise but having seen it afar off.

The time was getting very near now. A few brief hours stood between the disciples and the temple police. Jesus reminded them of this inevitable separation and spoke the words of comfort and instruction which have been preserved for us in the Gospel of John. He began by giving them the new commandment to love one another. His departure from their midst must be the signal not to grieve but to march. The love they had to manifest to one another was new because it was to be "as I have loved you". Such love had never been revealed before, but now it must be perpetuated in the lives of the disciples.

It was too much for Peter to let his Lord go without a struggle. "Lord", he said, "whither goest thou?" "Whither I go", Jesus answered, "thou canst not follow me now, but thou shalt follow me afterwards." We have to turn back to Luke's account to continue the conversation. "Simon, Simon", Jesus said tenderly, reverting to his old name, "Behold, Satan hath desired to have you that he may sift you as wheat. But I have prayed for thee that thy faith fail not: and when thou art converted, strengthen thy brethren." Judas was not to be the only victim of the power of evil. Peter, in spite of his confidence, was about to fall. But his Lord had prayed for him and he would emerge from this greatest lesson of his life, blinded by scalding tears, but with a faith he had never known before. It was necessary for Peter to fail at the point of his greatest human strength—his loyalty to his Lord. He had to learn that his confidence must be in God, not in his own virtue; that of himself he could do nothing; only in Christ were all things possible. It is a lesson we all need: sometimes,

like Peter, we only learn it through a mist of tears and with
hearts burdened by remorse. But we have the sustaining
knowledge that our Lord has prayed for us, and that when we
have "turned again" we shall have the sympathy and the
experience to strengthen our brethren.

But Peter was in no mood to receive these words or accept
the conditions. His love was too strong to allow his Lord to go
alone. The mocking and the scourging he had so little understood on the road to Jerusalem were taking shape in his
mind: he felt instinctively that they were near and he desired
fervently to share them. "Lord", he cried, "Why cannot I
follow thee now? I will lay down my life for thy sake." And
how sincerely he meant it! Will you, Simon? "Verily, verily, I
say unto thee, the cock shall not crow until thou hast denied
me thrice."

But, "let not your heart be troubled", Jesus pleaded; "ye
believe in God, believe also in me." The poignancy is often
lost by the artificial division of the chapter in the middle of
the conversation. But Peter *was* troubled. He was unnaturally silent throughout the discussion which ensued, nor had he
anything to say in the city streets or during the walk to the
garden on the Mount of Olives. It is not without significance
that the next time he appears in the narrative we find him
trying to convince his Lord, and possibly himself, of his
loyalty by an effort to kill the high priest's servant.

Jesus turned from Peter's particular difficulties to the
needs of all the disciples. First in the upper room and later
outside we find the one who was about to suffer indescribable
agony of mind and body concerned only with the need to sus-
tain those who were about to desert him. He told them of the
reason for his going away. It was to prepare "abiding places"
in the house of God. He spoke of his relationship with his
Father, and revealed himself as the manifestation of his
Father's character. He confronted Philip with a challenge we
do well to accept, "Have I been so long time with you, and yet
hast thou not known me, Philip?" He gave them the promise
of a new privilege in prayer. He was about to become their
mediator, and they were to make their petitions known to
God in his name. Then he spoke to them of the coming of the
Comforter, the Holy Spirit which would dwell with them,
bringing to their minds all that the Lord had done and said.
He promised that he would manifest himself to them in
words which have encouraged the aspirations of disciples
ever since. "If a man love me he will keep my words, and my

Father will love him, and we will come unto him and make our abode with him." Probably each disciple in moments of supreme dedication experienced the fulfilment of that promise. Nor is it beyond our reach. With sustained prayer and steady dedication there may come a rare moment of spiritual ecstasy when we know the promise has been fulfilled, and life is transformed for us.

Finally Jesus bequeathed to them his peace: not the shallow cessation from strife which is all that the world can give, but the deep abiding quietude of spirit which finds its source in complete trust in God: a peace which remains undisturbed by the stresses of life; a peace that is sustained in prayer, and fed by the knowledge that all things, whether good or evil, are working together for good.

The hearts of the eleven remaining apostles, troubled by the disclosure of treachery and the terrors of the morrow, grew calm in the serene presence and perfect love of their Lord. The paschal supper which had closed the old covenant and introduced the new, was concluded with a hymn.* Then the little company arose and went out into the darkened streets.

There were still many things to say, and in some quiet corner under the shadow of the city wall Jesus continued his words of comfort and exhortation. "I am the Vine, ye are the branches ... As my Father hath loved me, so I have loved you; continue ye in my love." To peace he added the gift of joy. "These things have I spoken unto you that my joy might remain in you, and that your joy might be full." All was to find its climax in the love which would be fully revealed before the sun had set again over the western hills of Judea. "Greater love hath no man than this, that a man lay down his life for his friends." He spoke to them of the new intimacy they had attained. They were no longer servants but friends. And because they were friends they would be compelled to endure the persecution which had been his lot. He sensed the consternation on their set faces and reminded them again both of the Comforter and of his own return. Moved by his words the disciples expressed their confidence in him. "Do ye now believe?" Jesus answered them, knowing the fear and cowardice of the coming hours; "Behold, the hour cometh, yea, is now come, that ye shall be scattered every man to his

---

*Psalms 113–118 were always sung on this occasion. "They sang", included Jesus. It is the only occasion on which we are invited to think of him as singing.

own, and shall leave me alone." But he remembered that amid all this weakness and fickleness of man there was One who would never leave nor forsake him. "Yet I am not alone, because the Father is with me."

If they could not see his face, they could hear the sound of victory in his voice as he gave them a final assurance before he went forward to his death. "These things have I spoken unto you that ye might have peace. In the world ye shall have tribulation; but be of good cheer; I have overcome the world."

Before he left the shadow of the city wall and crossed the Kedron, Jesus had one further mission to complete. He desired finally to dedicate himself to his Father's will and to commit his loved ones to his Father's keeping. He lifted up his eyes to Heaven and gave expression to the holy utterance recorded in the seventeenth chapter of John. It is a prayer to meditate upon with deep humility and gratitude. "Father, the hour is come: glorify thy Son that thy Son may also glorify thee ... I have finished the work which thou gavest me to do." His exalted thoughts turned towards his disciples. They belonged to God, but the Father had given them to His Son to be perfected and sanctified, and now, his work completed, he once more committed them to the love and care of God. "Sanctify them through thy truth: thy word is truth." He implored his Father that they might enter into that holy relationship which marked their perfect union. "I in them, and thou in me, that they may be made perfect in one; and that the world may know that thou hast sent me, and hast loved them as thou hast loved me." He prayed for the consummation of his Father's purpose, that they might be with him and behold his glory.

We feel the earnest pleading of his prayer as he leaves them tenderly and confidently in his Father's keeping, as he goes away from them to face the full impact of men's malice and wickedness. "O righteous Father, the world hath not known thee: but I have known thee, and these have known that thou hast sent me. And I have declared unto them thy name, and will declare it: that the love wherewith thou hast loved me may be in them, and I in them."

11

GETHSEMANE

IN the light of the paschal moon Jesus led his disciples from the city of shadows across the waters of Kedron to the darkness of Gethsemane. It was a familiar spot. When circumstances had made it difficult to reach Bethany it had been their shelter for the night. But on this night it was different. The joy and confidence with which he had encouraged his disciples was ebbing as he looked back at the walled city with its flickering lights, concentrating for a moment upon its gates, and then pressed forward again towards the olive trees. He left most of his disciples on the fringe of the garden, and called his three beloved friends to follow him as he penetrated further among the trees. Finally he stopped. He spoke in a voice more troubled than they had ever known. "My soul is exceeding sorrowful, even unto death; tarry ye here and watch." They saw him go forward about a stone's cast and throw himself suddenly down among the gnarled roots of the olive trees in an abandonment of grief and prayer.

"Oh my Father, if it be possible, let this cup pass from me."

We must ever look upon this prostrate form of our beloved Lord from the distance which separated him from his three disciples. We could not approach nearer if we would. Yet he desired his loved ones to witness the price he paid, that they might learn as much as the human heart can stand and the human mind conceive; that learning this they might love more fervently, and loving, be his disciples indeed, bound to him by the fellowship of his sufferings.

With sad and reverent hearts we seek the cause of this desolation of spirit. Fear of death—even the excruciating death he knew awaited him, was surely not a prominent factor. The one who touched the leper's scaly flesh, who stood on the bulwarks of the storm-tossed boat, who fearlessly faced enemies armed to kill him, did not fear the wrath of man. There was little that was physical in his human cry for release from the cup that was now pressed to his lips. It was

mental and spiritual. The Psalms which reveal so faithfully
the spirit of Jesus lead us into Gethsemane.

Let us go there now, and turning our eyes from that dejected form, read the words of Psalm 69—

"Save me, O God;
For the waters are come in unto my soul.
I sink in deep mire, where there is no standing:
I am come into deep waters, where the floods over-
flow me.
I am weary with my crying; my throat is dried:
Mine eyes fail while I wait for my God.
They that hate me without a cause are more than the
hairs of mine head:
They that would cut me off; being mine enemies
wrongfully, are mighty:
Then I restored that which I took not away ...

Because for thy sake I have borne reproach;
Shame hath covered my face.
I am become a stranger unto my brethren,
And an alien unto my mother's children ...

But as for me, my prayer is unto thee, O Lord, in an
acceptable time:
O God, in the multitude of thy mercy,
Answer me in the truth of thy salvation.
Deliver me out of the mire, and let me not sink:
Let me be delivered from them that hate me, and out
of the deep waters.
Let not the waterflood overwhelm me,
Neither let the deep swallow me up:
And let not the pit shut her mouth upon me.
Answer me, O Lord; for thy loving kindness is good:
According to the multitude of thy tender mercies turn
thou unto me.
And hide not thy face from thy servant;
For I am in distress; answer me speedily.
Reproach hath broken my heart; and I am full of
heaviness:
And I looked for some to take pity, but there was
none;
And for comforters, but I found none."

We lift our eyes from the page, look again at the bowed form in the fitful light, and enter a little further into that dreadful hour.

There are those who point out the increased sensitiveness of Christ to physical suffering; but have we realized his sensitiveness to sin? He lived in the presence of his Father, in an atmosphere of holiness and light. He went down to the shame and ignominy of a criminal's death. His pure mind had to face all the degradation of mockery, exposure and crucifixion. He was made sin for us, who knew no sin. And because he was bearing the sin of the world and accepting the curse of the tree, he must be alone, forsaken not only by the people he had come to save, not only by those who were about to leave him and flee, but above all, by the One from the light of Whose countenance he had never departed. He knew that the terrible cry of Psalm 22 would be wrung from his lonely, aching heart. Already the horror of great darkness was upon him. The Lord was laying upon him the iniquity of us all. Bearing iniquity was a desolating experience. It was here, not on the morrow in Jerusalem, that our Saviour was undergoing the ordeal of his trial. All that happened to him afterwards would be physical. This was his hour. This was his victory. "Nevertheless not my will, but thine, be done."

After a timeless interval he rose to his feet and groped his way towards his friends. But weariness had triumphed over their love. They had slept as the dreadful conflict swayed between life and death. He had been alone indeed. There had been no human hand to grip, no eye to witness, no heart to share the agony of this loneliness. "Could ye not watch with me one hour?" Yet even in the darkness of that hour, with the hurt tearing into his soul, his thought was for them. "Watch ye and pray that ye enter not into temptation."

For a fleeting moment his features relaxed as he saw their tired, pitiable faces looking stupidly up to his. "The spirit indeed is willing, but the flesh is weak." And then he left them once more and the conflict was renewed in all its agony. Sweat formed on his brow and fell like drops of blood to the ground. Once more the cry of submission answered the call for release. The conflict went on. The disciples were still asleep when he reached them. For the third time he joined issue with the protesting forces of his will. This time he found he was not alone, an angel of God stood with him, and with the angel the vision of the glory that was to be accomplished.

317

He found new strength in the presence of the heavenly messenger and with his final victory came a peace which did not desert him until the last moments on the cross.

The conflict was over. Jesus went back to his exhausted disciples. All the trouble and pain had gone from his voice but they were too tired to notice. "Sleep on now, and take your rest: it is enough, the hour is come: behold, the Son of man is betrayed into the hand of sinners. We can see him looking down at the sleeping men. He knew that their Gethsemane would come to-morrow: terror, sorrow, and dreadful remorse. But they would emerge, and their love would take hold of his once more, and they would never forget.

Lights flickered among the trees of the garden, there was the sound of men's feet, and an occasional oath rose above a muffled background of voices. Jesus woke his disciples for the last time, "Rise up, let us go, he that betrayeth me is at hand".

They met in the garden, the two companies: Jesus with his eleven disciples; Judas with the temple soldiers. The leaping flames of the torches gave an atmosphere of unreality to the scene, casting unfamiliar shadows on familiar faces. But the features of Judas were unmistakable. The veneer had gone, the concentrated evil remained. He came forward to perpetrate his final and unforgivable outrage. "Hail, Master!" he cried, and kissed him. With more grace than we can find in our hearts at the memory of it, Jesus spoke to him, "Friend, wherefore art thou come? Betrayest thou the Son of man with a kiss?" Before Judas could answer Jesus turned to the men who had come with him, "Whom seek ye?" "Jesus of Nazareth", was the reply. "I am he", Jesus answered simply. But the effect was dramatic. Awed by his majesty and his purity, they drew back and fell to the ground.

Such was his command over his enemies. He kept it to the end. Through the hours of questioning, the indignities, the final torture, he was always their master. His victory over himself had been won; now he could triumph over the wickedness of man.

But his victories were on his own battlefield, not on theirs. They would win their own hollow conquests. He was seized by rough hands. His thoughts turned to his disciples, "Let these go their way", he commanded, and no man turned to hinder them. But Peter, his love and anger surging to the surface, took the sword which earlier his Lord had treated with contempt, and raising it aloft brought it down with murderous intent. The wild blow succeeded only in severing the ear of the High Priest's servant. Immediately Jesus stepped forward and freed himself from his bonds to perform his last miracle of healing. This was not the allegiance he desired. "Put up again thy sword into his place for all they that take the sword shall perish with the sword." He had come to bring deliverance not to seek it. Peter had seen a moment before what power Christ wielded over these men if he chose to use it: that power could instantly be supplemented by twelve legions of angels.

Once more Jesus addressed himself to his captors. Why this darkness and treachery? Each day during the Passover week he had been in their midst. They knew the answer. His arrest had been contrived to outwit the people, particularly those who came from the hills of Galilee. It had to be done secretly and urgently—even now Caiaphas was waiting impatiently in the city. They moved forward with him tied with cords in their midst.

The disciples saw it, they realized he was going to submit: his death was inevitable, the Kingdom was not to be. Their courage evaporated, fear gripped them. With a last searching look they turned and fled from the garden, stumbling over the loose boulders of Olivet, and left him alone with his enemies.

12

BEFORE CAIAPHAS

THE trial of Jesus was in fact no trial at all. It was judicial murder. There was a pretence of justice, and with difficulties developing and precious time running out, even that was thrown to the winds. The arrest was illegal: only voluntary witnesses were allowed to bring a wrongdoer to the Sanhedrin. The time of trial was illegal; no capital cases were allowed to be tried after sunset. The cross-questioning and challenge of his judge was illegal; he should have been acquitted immediately; the evidence of the witnesses had failed.

But Jesus was arrested by conspiracy, tried by enemies, testified against by hired witnesses. Time was the great factor, time, and a suitable charge which would allow Pilate to confirm the death sentence. He must be condemned before the multitudes of worshippers realized what had happened. Evil was abroad that night—evil concentrated and unrelieved. This was their hour, and the power of darkness.

They took him to Annas first. The father-in-law of Caiaphas was fabulously wealthy; the temple offerings had flowed into his coffers for many years. They had helped him to live comfortably, not only in personal opulence, but also in the security afforded by judicious financial arrangement with highly placed Romans. Though he was no longer the official High Priest, he kept the title as did five of his sons, and he was still the generally acknowledged head of the Sanhedrin and therefore of the nation. Probably Annas was anxious for a meeting with this man who had constituted such a threat to his position and privileges. The hearing also had the advantage of leaving Caiaphas free to summon as many sympathetic members of the Sanhedrin as possible at the earliest moment.

Annas had little success with his captive. He asked him about his teaching, and with more sinister motive, about his disciples. quietly Jesus directed him to those who had heard him. "I spoke openly to the world, I ever taught in the synagogue and in the temple ... Why askest thou me? Ask them which heard me."

The first blow fell on his cheek, struck by the rough hand of a temple guard. It was the first of many which would disfigure those noble features until he was marred more than any man. Jesus turned to the officer, "If I have spoken evil, bear witness of the evil: but if well, why smitest thou me?"

Meanwhile two of the disciples had rallied from their headlong flight in the garden: Peter, who after the first distracted rush remembered his loyalty, and John who remembered his love. They had stood together watching the company below, marking its course by the light of the distant torches. Then they had followed afar off: along the rocky valley of the Kedron under the shadow of the walls, up the steps which led from the private gate near the pool of Siloam to the Upper City. They had stood before the palace gate. John was known there and had little difficulty in securing admittance. Then a quiet word to the maid who kept the door, and Peter was inside. Here they parted, John to find out where they had taken his Lord, and stay near him, Peter to mingle with the servants and soldiers in the courtyard below. For although it was now long past midnight there would be no sleep in the palace that night.

It was cold out in the open court, and the soldiers lit a fire to warm themselves. It was growing cold inside the heart of the disciple. He was in the midst of his enemies; his Lord was somewhere in that vast building a captive with cords round his wrists. There was nothing he could do here. Men were looking at him suspiciously: that maid who had let him in had peered intently into his bearded face. She was looking at him now. He tried to assume indifference, but he was a poor actor. He had never been in a situation like this before, he was nervous and restless: there was a strange unreality about it all. The reaction of the past hours was setting in, and he was tired—so tired, yet never had he felt farther from sleep. Was he going mad?

The woman was at his side now watching him curiously. He started suddenly at the sound of her voice. "And thou also wast with Jesus of Nazareth." Simon looked at her, and at the enquiring faces turned towards him in the flickering firelight. He was terribly afraid. He became almost incoherent, "I know not, neither understand I what thou sayest". Somewhere a cock crew. It should have been a warning, but Simon, moving away into the shadows, did not hear.

The dawn was breaking on that fateful morning in Jerusalem, when Caiaphas had finally collected the majority of the Sanhedrin. Jesus, still tightly bound, was brought before the assembly and the trial began. Its purpose was not to try him but to find a suitable charge with which he could be taken to Pilate to confirm the death sentence.

The proceedings began with a succession of false witnesses who gave evidence against him. This was so ill-prepared and the discrepancies so gross that to formulate a charge appeared impossible. The complete silence and calm dignity of Christ contributed to this effect. Looking at him, many of the Sanhedrin must have felt they were being judged by their captive. Two witnesses came forward who either remembered or had been reminded of words which he had spoken three years before. "This man said, I am able to destroy the temple of God, and to build it in three days." Here was evidence which could have been used to secure the death sentence. Both sacrilege and sorcery were capital offences. Yet Caiaphas needed more; what would Pilate care about sorcery or sacrilege? There must be a more dangerous charge than that. The time was going and nothing was emerging; in a few hours the Passover pilgrims would be filling the streets and flocking into the temple courts looking for the prophet from Galilee. The High Priest was face to face with the possibility of losing his prisoner. The strained atmosphere was heightened by the silence and detachment of the man who was the subject of all this confusion. It was a battle of character. Caiaphas, High Priest of Israel, was feeling the strain. He turned suddenly upon Jesus, "Answerest thou nothing? What is it which these witness against thee ?" But Jesus remained silent, completely master of the situation, and the tension increased.

It was then that Caiaphas in his desperation saw the answer; a simple answer which, had he seen it before would have saved him this humiliation. It was illegal, but what was one further illegality when justice was thrown to the winds! He rose and faced Jesus, raising his right hand: his voice rang out clearly in the abruptly hushed court, "I adjure thee by the living God, that thou tell us whether thou be the Christ, the Son of God."

Christ well knew the effect of this summons before he spoke. To remain silent now would be to frustrate his enemies, but he could not remain silent. His words were as majestic as his silence had been.

"Thou hast said: nevertheless I say unto you, Hereafter shall ye see the Son of man sitting on the right hand of power, and coming in the clouds of heaven."

The trial was over, the tension had gone. Gloating over his victory, Caiaphas controlled his features: he looked stern and sad as he rent his clothes. "He hath spoken blasphemy: what further need have we of witnesses? Behold, now ye have heard his blasphemy. What think ye?" And they answered as he knew they would answer, "He is worthy of death."

With their verdict Caiaphas completed his case. Now he had the weapon he needed to make the death sentence effective. Already he was thinking of the case he would bring before Pilate, a case so strong that if difficulties were raised the Procurator would find himself in a more desperate situation than he had ever known in all his compromising passages with the Jews. The Messiah of Israel was a king, and a king in a country subjugated by Rome was a threat to Caesar: to ignore that threat was to be guilty of treason. Caiaphas felt he had good grounds for satisfaction.

Jesus was led from the presence of the Sanhedrin through the courtyard past the waiting Peter to the soldiers' quarters to be subjected to the vileness and cruelty of man. He had passed through his greatest spiritual crisis in the garden, now the physical crisis was upon him. We shudder before the indignities he suffered. Our hearts cry out in protest as we see him covered with blood and spittle. We want to dissociate ourselves for ever from those animal natures that mocked him and lashed him and held him down in chains. But from time to time we must summon our courage and look steadfastly upon the scene. It will tell us of his love; it will show us that it is possible to put him again to an open shame.

Peter had not left the palace. He was standing miserably near the porch gripped by indecision, fear and exhaustion. One of the maids was talking to a group nearby: they were talking of the exciting events of the night, of the unprecedented summons of the Sanhedrin in the first light of dawn; of the possible outcome of the trial. Peter's misery was written plainly on his face and the maid understood. "This fellow", she said, "was also with Jesus of Nazareth." Peter turned wildly round and faced her, "I know not the man".

The minutes went on interminably; witnesses came and went. There was still nothing to show how things were going in the council chamber—nothing but gossip and speculation. A group of men passed; with them was a kinsman of Malchus: he paused opposite Peter and looked at him more carefully. Then he spoke: "Did I not see thee in the garden with him?"

BOOK SEVEN: TOWARDS CALVARY

In that moment Peter fell headlong, "Man, I know not what thou sayest." But his rough northern burr had betrayed him. "Surely thou art one of them, for thou art a Galilean, and thy speech agreeth thereto." Peter the disciple became Simon the fisherman. He began to curse and to swear to emphasize his abjuration: "I know not the man", he cried again and again. A cock crew loudly.

And then he saw his Lord.

If Jesus had looked angry Peter might have borne it. But there was no anger, only pain and love. Blinded by scalding tears he rushed out.

13

BEFORE PILATE

PETER was not the only wretched man to leave the High Priest's house that morning. Judas had returned from the garden with the Lord he had betrayed. While Peter had waited in the courtyard Judas was probably lurking in the servant's quarters. It was a very different Judas, facing for the first time the enormity of his crime. The fruits of triumph had turned to ashes in his mouth: his ears rang with the words of the Master he had betrayed; again and again he met that look which had sent him reeling backwards. Never had that dark soul been nearer repentance. It may have been that he was somewhere near the place where they brought Jesus to be maltreated: that he had heard the cruel jibes, the mocking laughter, the whine of the lash, the thud of the blows. It is almost certain that a cold sweat broke out on his forehead, remorse and despair clutched at his heart. Better indeed that he had never been born!

There is nothing Judas can now do to stop the events his treachery has begun, nothing to ease the burden of his soul. How long he remained there we do not know. It was probably several hours before his tortured mind showed him something he could do. The silver coins weighing heavily in the pocket of his tunic had lost their charm. He would give them back to the priests. People made way before the wild-eyed figure rushing distractedly through the streets towards the temple. He found the priests talking excitedly of the quickly moving events. "I have sinned", he cried, "I have betrayed innocent blood." Pathetically he offered them the silver coins. They looked at him with amused contempt. "What is that to us? See thou to that." He flung the money across the marble pavement and fled, obsessed now with the thought of death. It was probably on some tree in the ground bought by his ill-gotten gains that he tied his girdle around his throat and swung out over the rocky gorge; swung until the girdle broke under his weight and he crashed down to the boulders of Gehenna.

If we are to understand the bewildering attitude of Pilate early on that Friday morning it is important that we give careful thought to the probable events which went on behind the scenes. We are only given an occasional clue to them in the Gospels but each of the clues is most significant.* Several hours had elapsed between the departure of Judas from the upper room, and the arrest in the garden. These hours had been busy ones for Caiaphas. It would have been easy for him to have sent Judas back to the house in Jerusalem immediately and arrested Jesus there. But it was by no means as simple as it seemed. If the High Priest was to take advantage of the information that Christ was in their midst and was speaking openly of his death, he must have everything carefully arranged before he could arrest him, so that by the time the multitudes were astir it would be too late for them to intervene. If he was unable to make those arrangements he must leave Jesus alone until after the feast, for it would be impossible to hold him prisoner in Jerusalem for seven days without inciting rebellion. Everything hinged upon the attitude of the Roman Procurator. Caiaphas had no doubt that the majority of the Sanhedrists would play their part, but that would be useless if Pilate refused to ratify the death sentence. It is almost certain, therefore, that after carefully considering the information Judas had given him, the High Priest paid a surprise visit to Pilate. He made the request that he was most anxious to get the Roman's confirmation of the death sentence in a case of great importance. It is not difficult to see the arguments he would use: this man was a political prisoner and a menace to the peace: he had information of his present whereabouts and could arrest him immediately: but to imprison him would cause the gravest risk of rebellion at such a time: the only hope was to try him, confirm the sentence, and crucify him before the people could intervene.

Pilate would probably feel that this was a straightforward case and would be willing to co-operate. He might have felt too that the situation gave him a good opportunity of easing the tension that existed between the Roman citadel and the temple. For Pilate's stubborn nature and lack of diplomacy had caused unpleasant incidents in the past which had not improved his standing in Rome.

---

*We are largely indebted for this reconstruction to Frank Morison, who has carefully examined these events in *Who moved the stone?*

Caiaphas probably returned through the dark streets of Jerusalem very well satisfied and ready to send the company of temple guards with Judas to the garden. But both Caiaphas and Pilate had reckoned without two important factors; the one was the bearing of the prisoner, the other was Claudia Procula, Pilate's wife.

So it was that early on the Passover morning the company moved away from the house of Caiaphas with Jesus in the midst bound with chains. The Praetorium, situated in the magnificent palace of Herod, was only a quarter of a mile away, and in a short time they were passing through the spacious gardens and standing outside the portals of the building. The leaders of the Jews were bringing their Messiah to a Gentile for permission to put him to death. They were drinking to the full the cup of wickedness. Little did they realize that they were leading their nation to its own crucifixion. History has never produced a more terrible hour. They committed Jesus to the Roman guards and waited outside for him to be returned with the necessary authority for his crucifixion. To have gone themselves into the judgment hall would have meant defilement.

Meanwhile Pilate had been early astir and was ready. Although he was willing to accede to the wishes of Caiaphas, he dare not lay himself open to the charge that he had not even interviewed the prisoner. He sat down in the judgment seat. The man who stood before him was lacerated and bruised and covered with blood; his clothes were filthy and torn. Yet looking at him Pilate knew he could not keep his midnight promise. He would have to examine the case. There is no record of any interchange of words at this first meeting but it is most likely that one took place, and what Pilate heard would confirm his decision. John, who gives us by far the most detailed description of the Roman trial, tells us that, leaving Jesus in the judgment hall, Pilate went out to the Jewish leaders at the gate of the Praetorium. By now a multitude had assembled, but most would be from the residence of the High Priest and from the courts of the temple—men who knew what was afoot and waited eagerly for developments. There were probably some worshippers too, on the outskirts of the crowd, drawn from their beds by the commotion which was developing round Herod's palace.

Pilate's first question brought consternation to the Jews. There is nothing in the narrative to indicate the presence of

327

Annas or Caiaphas, so apparently confident were they of the arrangement they had made. The Governor's question showed in a moment that he was not prepared to implement his promise. Roman trial took the prescribed form of an accusation, a cross-examination and a defence. Pilate now demanded the formal accusation. "What accusation bring ye against this man?"

At first sight it would appear that the answer of the Sanhedrists was simply insolent, but in the light of what had probably happened it seems rather the result of their dismay and bewilderment: "If this man were not an evil doer we would not have brought him unto thee". There was an insinuation in Pilate's reply which could not be missed by those who had attended the shameful proceedings in the High Priest's house, for Pilate could see that for envy they had delivered him up: "Take him yourselves and judge him according to your law".

But after the first shock the keener minds were facing the new situation. "It is not lawful", they said, "for us to put any man to death." Then they quickly formulated the charge: "We found this man perverting our nation, and forbidding to give tribute to Caesar, and saying that he himself is Christ, a king".

This was a charge which Pilate had to investigate. He left them, returned to his judgment seat and called Jesus to him. It may have been at this point that the messenger came from his wife, Claudia Procula. It is probable that Pilate had discussed with her the strange visit of the High Priest. She had retired to rest thinking about Jesus, and had had a vivid dream concerning him which filled her with foreboding. Rising, she would go to her husband's apartments only to find that he had already gone to the judgment hall. Immediately she sent an urgent message to him, "Have thou nothing to do with that righteous man: for I have suffered many things this day in a dream because of him". These words would stiffen Pilate's determination that justice should be done. John records the interrogation.

"Art thou the King of the Jews?

"Sayest thou this thing of thyself or did others tell it thee of me?

"Am I a Jew? Thine own nation and the chief priests have delivered thee unto me: what hast thou done?

"My kingdom is not of this world: if my kingdom were of this world then would my servants fight, that I should not be delivered to the Jews: but now is my kingdom not from hence.

328

"Art thou a king then?

"Thou sayest that I am a king. To this end was I born, and for this cause came I into the world, that I should bear witness unto the truth. Every one that is of the truth heareth my voice.

"What is truth ?"

It was a solemn moment, but Pilate could not know that he was standing his trial before the King of all the earth. His mind was made up. The Roman trial was over. He went to the Jews with the verdict, "I find in him no fault at all".

The verdict was greeted with a howl of rage. Hostile cries rose from all quarters; the people, incited by the priests, joined in the commotion. Pilate wavered, and was lost. He caught the word "Galilee". Was the prisoner a Galilean? When he found that he was, he took the opportunity to temporize. He would send him to the adjacent building to be tried by Herod. He perceived that it would also have the advantage of improving his somewhat unhappy relations with Herod. It was a fatal mistake. From that moment Pilate had become a tool of the priests, and no struggling would save him now. Under their pressure he had re-opened a trial that was judicially over.

Pleasure seeking and irresponsible, sceptical yet superstitious, Herod Antipas, "that fox"—as Jesus had described him—was devoid of all finer qualities. He had become debauched, surrounded by flatterers who shared his vices. Reports had reached him about Jesus for a long time, and he was delighted at last to see him; but only because he was anxious to witness his miraculous power. Now he leaned back in his throne and plied him with questions.

But there was no reply from the figure standing before him. The silence became painful. Some Jews who had followed began to accuse him. But Herod had lost interest in his legal obligations. He was piqued by the situation. A king: then he would make him a king! They put on him a resplendent robe, they mocked him, and disported themselves until they tired of their jest. Then they sent him back to Pilate. Wearily Jesus retraced his steps to the Praetorium. It was many hours since he had slept.

Pilate must have watched his return with a sinking heart. But his duty was clear. Herod's attitude, base as it was, confirmed Pilate's verdict. Once more he faced the Jews, their numbers swelling with the passing hours. "I have examined him before you", he declared, "and have found no fault in this man touching those things whereof ye accuse him. No, nor yet Herod: for I sent you to him, and lo, nothing worthy of death is done to him. I will therefore chastise him, and release him."

But it was too late now. Pilate had shown his weakness. They refused to accept his verdict: the clamour grew more insistent. Other elements had arrived to demand that a prisoner be released to them: it was a Passover concession reluctantly yielded by the Romans, riotously acclaimed by the Jews. This time Pilate welcomed it. How little he knew the people! How pitiable his resolution looked as he retreated step by step before their wrath! "Ye have a custom that I should release unto you one at the Passover: will ye therefore that I release unto you the King of the Jews?"

"Not this man", they cried, "but Barabbas." Barabbas was a notorious rebel and murderer.

Pilate gave way before them once more. He gave Jesus up to the soldiers to be scourged. Again the suffering Saviour of men was subjected to the unrestrained brutality of men. When it was over they fetched a thorn bush, plaited it roughly into a crown and crushed it on his head: they draped a purple robe over his bleeding form, and hailed him as their king.

They brought him back to Pilate, and Pilate, looking at him, felt a surge of pity in his hardened soul. He led him out for the people to see, "Behold the man!"

And men have beheld and wept. And from him they have slowly turned their gaze upon those who judged him, those who clamoured for his affliction and death, those who smote him with the palms of their hands.

There was no pity in the Jews. "Crucify him, crucify him", they cried. Pilate was almost beaten. "Take ye him", he shouted, "and crucify him, I find no fault in him." The words of a man distraught; they could not crucify him. "We have a law", persisted the Jews, "and by our law he ought to die, because he made himself the Son of God." Pilate trembled. There had been something about this man which had strangely affected him from the first. The calm, almost unearthly dignity had persisted through all these terrible punishments. He brought him back from the raging crowds to the silence of the judgment hall. "Whence art thou?" he asked. But Jesus remained silent. "Speakest thou not unto me?" Pilate demanded. "Knowest thou not that I have power to crucify thee and power to release thee?" He had already demonstrated his power! "Thou couldst have no power at all against me", Jesus replied, "except it were given thee from above, therefore he that delivered me unto thee hath the greater sin."

Shaken, Pilate went out to make a last great effort to save him. He was met by a storm of menacing shouts. Then he heard something which changed the whole outlook. Perhaps Caiaphas, hearing of the difficulties that had developed, had inspired it. "If thou let this man go thou art not Caesar's friend: whosoever maketh himself a king speaketh against Caesar." Pilate realized now that he was personally involved. He was no longer a judge but a fellow prisoner, and he could only save himself by sacrificing Christ. The alternative did not come into his mind.

"Shall I crucify your king?"

"We have no king but Caesar."

In a pathetic attempt to absolve himself from the crime his weakness had sanctioned he called for water, and washed his hands in the presence of the multitude, crying, "I am innocent of the blood of this just person". But the stain of sin cannot be so easily removed.

"His blood be upon us and upon our children", cried the triumphant Jews. It was a terrible prophecy.

They led Jesus away to his death.

14

THE PLACE OF A SKULL

EARLY Christians refused to look at representations of
Christ on the cross because they had seen men crucified.
Our heart fails and our pen falters as we force ourselves to
look at the events of the next six hours. It is a sight too terrible
to gaze upon for long: yet to refuse to look at him steadily for
a few moments before we wait for the first day of the week, is
to deny ourselves the consolation of his love. We cannot linger
in the shadow of the cross, but we must approach, lift our
reluctant eyes steadfastly to his, and pass on our way with
bleeding but strengthened hearts determined that for us,
that sacrifice shall not be in vain.

They had taken off the blood-soaked robe of purple. His
own familiar garments were clinging to his raw flesh as they
led him out bowed under his cross. Two criminals had joined
him groaning under the weight of their grim burdens. It was
about ten in the morning and the whole city was astir. Roman
soldiers in glittering armour forced a way through the milling
crowds: they led him through the city gate towards Golgotha.

He staggered under his load. Exhausted by lack of food
and sleep, and by the agony of the heavy wood on his
butchered flesh, he sank to the ground. The soldiers untied
the cords that bound the cross to his back. Simon of Cyrene
had probably never heard of Jesus of Nazareth. But he never
forgot that laboured walk to Calvary. There is every reason to
believe that he continued to bear that cross for the rest of his
life and that his two sons also became Christians.

There was pity as well as hatred. A great company, mostly
women, wailed and lamented. Their cries reached him above
the agony of his body. His own suffering was forgotten in his
anticipation of theirs. "Weep not for me, but weep for yourselves and your children."

The awful moment came when the procession halted and
the crosses were lowered to the ground. The searing pain of
nails in hands and feet: the jolt as the uprights fell into the
appointed holes: the torture of overcharged veins taking the

weight of the sagging body: the excruciating anguish of every movement: the thirst growing more intolerable every minute.

Above him they nailed a board with the triple-tongued inscription, "This is Jesus, the King of the Jews".

The chief priests were not yet content. They must lift the cup of triumph again and again to their cruel lips. They must gloat and rave and taunt. "He saved others", they cried, "let him save himself." "Let Christ the King of Israel descend now from the cross that we may see and believe."

Wave after wave of sin and hatred flowed up to him on the cross. His love fought its last battle and prevailed. Hanging on the cross he vindicated his promise to his disciples, "Be of good cheer, I have overcome the world". His love poured forth to meet this hate, "Father, forgive them, they know not what they do".

The two malefactors cursed and railed on him. It was the terrible language of fear and agony. As the hours passed one thief grew silent and watched him. What he saw brought wonder into his pain-dimmed eyes. His memory slowly awoke, faded in a cloud of anguish, was willed again to life. Jesus of Nazareth! Faith was born; it flourished in this fertile soil of pain and blood: faith in a sea of hatred and doubt. Slowly he turned to silence his cursing comrade. "Dost thou not fear God, seeing thou art in the same condemnation? And we indeed justly; for we receive the due reward of our deeds; but this man hath done nothing amiss." Not smooth words: words gasped out between spells of excruciating pain. "Lord, remember me when thou comest into thy kingdom." It was easy to believe on him in Galilee surrounded by the evidence of his power. But at the mercy of his enemies, tortured and dying—here was faith indeed. He was still the Light of the World, the Good Shepherd, the Lord of Life, he was King who would come in his Kingdom. "Thou shalt be with me in Paradise."

Roman soldiers who knew not what they said, took up the cry against him. They took his garments and shared them between them by lot.

He was dying quickly—mercifully. Many lingered two or three days. The heavens were darkening. His love had one more ministry to perform. His eyes glazed with pain and approaching death sought out and focused two familiar faces—faces that reflected the suffering of his own.

"Woman, behold thy son."

"Behold, thy mother."

Two hearts sought each other in growing darkness; a heart bleeding from a sword thrust found strength in the kinship of a disciple who loved; a heart breaking with grief found solace in a solemn trust. "From that hour that disciple took her into his own home."

The unearthly gloom deepened into blackness. The Son of God bowed his head to meet the darkest moments of his life: the hour from which he had shrunk in Gethsemane, pleading for release. For the first time he was alone: bearing in his body the sin of the world. We dare not probe into this mystery of his suffering. Suddenly a great cry burst from him, a cry harsh and unnatural, a cry of utter abandonment: "Eloi, Eloi, lama sabachthani?"

As the ninth hour drew near his greatest victory was accomplished. He emerged from the horror of desolation to find only the agony remained—a welcome agony for it had in it once more the assurance of his Father's love.

The words of the Psalm he had learned as a boy, and had prepared throughout his life to fulfil, came to him in his dying moments. "I thirst."

There were those who risked the jibes of their comrades to minister to his need with the rough wine of the soldiers.

And then God's love was consummated in His Son. "It is finished."

He met his death with his Father's name on his lips "Father, into Thy hand I commend my spirit." His head sank forward on his breast.

The earth shuddered at the death of Jesus Christ. The rocks were rent; the buildings of Jerusalem trembled. In the temple that was no longer the House of God, a heavy veil that separated the Holy Place from the Sanctuary was rent from the top to the bottom. Graves were opened, and three days later, long dead saints were seen in the city.

The Centurion, in charge of the Roman soldiers gathered under each cross, had watched the closing scene. He had doubtless seen many such dreadful sights, but he had never seen a man die like this. And now as the earth trembled under him, and the shattered rocks hurtled down the hillsides, he turned his eyes to the darkened sky. "Truly this was the Son of God."

The Sabbath was drawing near: it would come with sunset. The Jews asked Pilate's consent to break the prisoners' legs so that they could be removed. It was customary to do this with hammers as a final torture to compensate for the merciful release of the spear thrust which followed.

But Jesus was already dead. That indignity would bring no response from the silent form. Yet the Roman spear was raised and thrust deep into his side. Water and blood flowed forth. Reproach had broken his heart.

Afar off women watched and wept.

A rich man came to Pilate begging the body of Jesus. Joseph of Arimathaea had not been summoned to the council: he was known to be a secret disciple: he was a good man and waited for the Kingdom of God. Nicodemus joined him. Their fatal nervousness had robbed them of their opportunity of serving the living Christ, but they have earned our love and gratitude for their tender concern for his body. Slowly the cross was lowered, the cruel nails were drawn out. The body was wrapped reverently in a white linen cloth and carried to the garden tomb: there it was more carefully prepared with myrrh and aloes. Gently they laid him to rest.

And Mary Magdalene and another Mary, less well known to us, but beloved of God, beheld where he was laid.

BOOK SEVEN: TOWARDS CALVARY

Book Eight

THE PRINCE OF LIFE

1

THE THIRD DAY

GUILTY consciences drove on the priests and rulers to one more act. When the earth trembled under their feet, and all nature rebelled against their wickedness, fear crept into their souls. They remembered his claim to be the Son of God. They knew that but for their lies, their threats and their hatred that still form would not have hung upon the cross. They also recalled his prophecy of the third day.

Although it was now the Sabbath the chief priests joined with the Pharisees in seeking yet another audience with Pilate. By now the Procurator was in a mood of cold anger. He knew how against all his better instincts he had been reduced to pitiable weakness by these malevolent schemers. Claudia Procula had been hard to convince that he had had no alternative but to ignore her urgent message. It had been some little consolation to be able to refuse their request to alter the inscription on the cross. Here was another opportunity to assert himself. "Sir", they said, "we remember that that deceiver said while he was yet alive, After three days I will rise again. Command that the sepulchre be made sure until the third day, lest the disciples come by night and steal him away, and say to the people, He is risen from the dead: so that the last error", they concluded with the utmost significance, "shall be worse than the first."

"Ye have a watch", Pilate told them harshly. "Go your way, make it as sure as ye can."

But there was little danger of the disciples making any attempt to revive Christianity by any spectacular or desperate effort. They were too despondent and full of grief. Looking back upon the event, we are sustained in the tragedy of Christ's death by the certain knowledge of his resurrection. But the disciples were not looking backwards as we are. They

337

should have been ready for it, but they were not. There was indeed a faint glimmer of hope, but it was so uncertain that when it was given every reason to burst into flame by a message from the garden tomb, it did not stir. John tells us that as yet they knew not that he must rise again from the dead!

If there was little faith, there was much love. So many Marys linger in the garden! Mary Magdalene was always a little in front. She would never forget. Her hands were aching to minister to her Lord. She had spent a busy Sabbath preparing sweet spices for anointing him. She rose in the darkness of the morning, met Mary the mother of James, Salome, and probably also Joanna, and together they made their way through the deserted streets of Jerusalem, and passing under the arched gate, reached the garden as the sun was beginning to rise over the eastern hills. The problem they discussed was the weight of the stone that Mary had watched being rolled into place on the Friday evening. Their united strength impelled by so much love would not nearly suffice.

In the garden Mary Magdalene seems to have run on ahead, urged by the desire to reach her Lord. She noticed at once that the stone was rolled away: looking quickly inside she found the tomb was empty. Without pausing for any explanation she ran back to find Peter and John. Breathlessly she told her news: they had taken the Lord from the sepulchre.

Meanwhile the other women had hurried on to the tomb with fast-beating hearts, to be met by an angel who calmed them with words of comfort and joy. "Fear not ye: for I know that ye seek Jesus that was crucified. He is not here for he is risen as he said. Come, see the place where the Lord lay."

Early as the women had been they were not the first at the tomb that morning. Terrified by a great earthquake, the guard looked toward the tomb. The stone was rolled away. Upon it sat an angel of God whose countenance was like lightning. They became as dead. As feeling returned they stole away to the city to tell the priests.

The tomb was empty. The Lord had risen indeed. The Father had given assurance unto all men. Every one who came to the Father through him would behold the "working of his mighty power, which he wrought in Christ, when he raised him from the dead, and set him at his own right hand in heavenly places, far above all principality, and power, and might, and dominion, and every name that is named, not only in this world, but also in that which is to come". Each one of us must stand, our heads bowed, before the empty grave. "I am he that liveth and was dead, and behold I am alive for evermore." "Thou art worthy", we cry, "to take the book and to open the seals thereof: for thou wast slain, and hast redeemed us to God by thy blood out of every kindred, and tongue and nation." But it will be our lives not our lips which will give to our Heavenly Father our acknowledgment of His unspeakable gift.

The women, filled with fear and great joy, went eagerly to tell the disciples as they were instructed, and to inform them that Jesus would go before them into Galilee. But their progress was suddenly halted by Jesus, standing in the way. His voice reached their wondering ears: "All hail". They came forward and, falling at his feet, they worshipped him.

We have no means of knowing what had happened to Peter after he had rushed blindly from the High Priest's house. Possibly Peter himself scarcely knew. He may have gone back to Gethsemane to prostrate himself as his Lord had done, finding some ease for his overburdened heart in the fellowship of suffering. He probably knew little of the events of the next dreadful day: his one desire would be to be alone. When eventually he returned to the temporary abode in Jerusalem it may have been to learn the unspoken truth from the tragic form of Mary lying collapsed on the couch, and the haggard face of the disciple Jesus loved. John could not know that Peter was bearing the greater load, but probably during the long hours of the Sabbath that followed, Peter unburdened his aching heart and learned the blessedness of an understanding friend. They had retired to rest at last—this mother who had lost her son, these disciples who had lost their Lord. But night was a sleepless eternity full of bewilderment and grief.

It was still early when an insistent knocking aroused them, and they opened the door to receive Mary Magdalene, a distracted Mary who told them the tomb was empty, her Lord had gone. Forthwith we see the two disciples hurrying through the city streets. But it was a long way and John was younger. Peter arrived breathless to see John outside, peering uncertainly into the darkened sepulchre: but Peter, because he was Peter, pushed past John and went inside. He saw the grave clothes lying folded, and the head cloth neatly placed on one side. But it was John and not Peter who suddenly *knew*. There was nothing they could do now but wait.

They went thoughtfully back to Jerusalem to tell the sorrowing mother.

Mary Magdalene was irresistibly drawn to the garden. She
had followed more slowly and now she was alone at the
empty tomb, weeping because even the last loving ministration was denied her. This time the sepulchre was not empty;
two angels sat, one at the head and the other at the foot of
the place where Jesus had lain. "Woman, why weepest thou?"
"Because", she cried, "they have taken away my Lord, and I
know not where they have laid him."

Even as she spoke she became conscious of someone standing near her. She thought it was the gardener.

"Woman, why weepest thou? What seekest thou?" Mary
saw a possible answer to the mystery; she had a sudden hope
that she would yet find her Lord's body and kneeling before
it, minister tenderly with her spices and her love. "Sir", she
sobbed pathetically, "if thou hast borne him hence, tell me
where thou hast laid him, and I will take him away."

"Mary."

It was enough. It was the voice that had called her from
the darkness of despair in the hills of Galilee. Was ever
devotion more joyously surprised!

"Rabboni."

She fell at his feet to worship, but gently he stayed her.
"Touch me not, for I am not yet ascended to my Father: but
go to my brethren and say unto them, I ascend unto my
Father and your Father, and to my God, and your God."
Whatever theological significance the words may have, Mary
was to learn that Jesus was about to receive the perfection of
nature involved in ascent to God. The personal contacts of the
past were nearly over: he would not be with them in bodily
form to which they could cling as hitherto. But henceforth he
will be always with them, though eye cannot see nor hand
touch him.

We have special need of that lesson too. During the sacred
moments of the Breaking of Bread we have his assurance
that, though we cannot see him, he is with us. Sometimes we
meet him there, and we *know* we have met him. With the
passing years we should grow ever more conscious of his
nearness: not only in moments of remembrance, in times of
great sorrow or temptation, but through all the experiences
of our life.

The woman who loved so dearly and had been rewarded so
richly went to deliver her glad message to the disciples.

2

"PEACE BE UNTO YOU"

TO the thoughtful mind the greatest argument for the resurrection of Christ must always be the fact that Christianity rose with its founder. Nothing but Resurrection can explain the transformation of the men we saw running in panic from Gethsemane into the fearless evangelists of the Acts of the Apostles. These cowed, despondent men stood forth in the city they dreaded and faced rulers and people alike, indicting them for slaying their Lord, announcing his resurrection, and baptizing thousands of repentant Jews who trembled at their words. Before they had been in mortal fear of arrest; now they were to go forth boldly facing imprisonment, persecution and death, and they were to go forth gloriously, counting it joy to suffer shame for his sake.

The source of that transformation lies in the events which followed this first day of the week. When the women brought the message, the disciples dismissed it as an idle tale. Even the priests were less sceptical; they bribed the guards to keep the true facts to themselves and spread the story that the disciples had stolen the body of Jesus.

But that afternoon the cycle of events continued which brought final conviction. Two disciples had left the western gate of Jerusalem and were walking along the road which led to the village of Emmaus, seven miles away. One of them was Cleopas, the other we do not know. They walked slowly because their hearts were heavy; their sad faces reflected the subject of their conversation as they left the bare limestone hills to descend into the verdant valley towards the village. It may have been at the crossroads that they first saw the stranger drawing near, travelling in their direction. It was Jesus, but they did not recognize him. How often does Jesus walk with us unrecognized when our hearts are full?

"What manner of communications are these that ye have one to another, as ye walk and are sad?"

It seemed impossible to the disciples that even a pilgrim in Jerusalem could not know of the terrible events of the past two days. But he questioned them further, and there was something about him that encouraged them to unburden their hearts. They told him of Jesus, of his mighty words and works, and of his ignominious death at the hands of the rulers. They explained that it was the third day since these things happened, and significance lay in the tidings of certain women that the sepulchre was empty, since they remembered some words of Jesus about rising the third day. They added: "We trusted it had been he who should have redeemed Israel".

The stranger had listened patiently. Now he turned to chide them for their lack of discernment. In the tragic happenings of the last days they had completely lost their perspective. But there was encouragement in his rebuke. "O foolish ones, and slow of heart to believe all that the prophets have spoken! Ought not Christ to have suffered these things, and to enter into his glory?" And he began with Moses, and showed them in all the Scriptures the things concerning himself. In growing wonder those disciples watched the features of the Messiah of Israel emerge from the pages of the Scripture they thought they knew.

With glowing hearts and eyes they drank in his words, and before they realized it they had reached Emmaus. He made as though he would have continued his journey, and indeed would have done so had not their earnest desire for him to remain constrained him. They found good reason to keep him in their midst. "It is evening", they said, "and the day is far spent."

As they sat at the table with him, he took and blessed the bread and gave it to them. And in the Breaking of Bread he was made known to them. May it be our prayer each first day that our Lord will reveal himself to us. With their recognition he had gone and they were alone, learning the lesson Jesus had taught Mary Magdalene in the garden.

In spite of the lateness of the hour and the dangers of the road, the two disciples returned that same hour to Jerusalem to tell the disciples the wondrous news. They found them assembled together, full of awe and excitement. Jesus had appeared to Peter. He had come to him alone. A moving personal crisis lies hidden behind that simple record.

They were discussing these amazing events behind locked doors, because they were in danger of arrest. It was impossible to guess at the next step the priests would take, but it was reasonable to expect that the disciples would be involved in it.

Suddenly they were aware of Jesus in their midst. His familiar voice was soothing their tremulous hearts. But they were not easily calmed: the mode of his appearance encouraged their belief that it was a spirit. To convince them that though he was no longer confined to the limitations of mortal life, he was indeed the Christ, he showed them the marks of the nails in his hands and his feet, inviting them to handle him and assure themselves of his reality. He demonstrated the relationship that remained between them by eating fish and honey. John shows by his understatement the inability of words to describe the feelings of the apostles: "Then were the disciples glad when they saw the Lord".

Having fully convinced them, he delivered to them their commission. "Peace be unto you", he said again, "as my Father has sent me, even so send I you." From their joy of heart at the revelation that their Lord was alive to die no more was to flow their apostolic ministry. "He that believeth on me", Jesus had said before his death, "the works that I do shall he do also: and greater works than these shall he do, because I go unto my Father." Their work was to be greater in scope and in time than could be his, but it was only effective because it issued from his infinitely greater work of redemption. So it was that, breathing upon them the Holy Spirit, an earnest of the Pentecostal fire, they were able, by their divine commission, to remit or retain the sins of men. The prerogative must always remain with God, but the call to forgiveness and salvation would come from the Spirit-energized work of the Apostles.

One disciple was absent when Christ came to them on that first day of the week. It was Thomas. However much the others tried to convince him of the appearance of the Lord to them, he would not believe. "Except I shall see in his hands the print of the nails, and put my finger into the print of the nails, and thrust my hand into his side, I shall not believe." It was not that Thomas did not want to believe. He did. He was a man of little imagination but deep loyalty. It was Thomas who had seen nothing but death in Jerusalem, yet urged the disciples to go to die with their Lord. But to protect himself now from the bitterness of disillusionment, he demanded irrefutable evidence. He, above all the apostles, needed the lesson of faith in things not seen.

So it was that after a week of doubt and insistence, Thomas was with the other ten. The circumstances were similar. The doors were locked when Jesus again appeared in their midst. He turned to Thomas. He invited him to ascer-

343

tain for himself that he was the Lord by the tests he had demanded. But Thomas no longer needed them. He *knew* it was the Lord. "My Lord, and my God."

Thomas received the lesson he required and we can be grateful for his doubting when we hear the words of his Lord, and accept them ourselves in what has finely been called "the last and greatest of the Beatitudes": "Blessed are they that have not seen, yet have believed". Peter may have had this dramatic meeting in mind when he addressed those who, like us, had not had the great experience of beholding him to whom their life was dedicated. "Whom having not seen, ye love; in whom, though now ye see him not, yet believing, ye rejoice with joy unspeakable and full of glory." These words describe our heavenly vocation, but they are not without their challenge. We certainly have not seen him. Do we love him with all our hearts? Do we believe with the conviction of the worshipping Thomas?

"These things", John said, "are written that ye might believe that Jesus is the Christ, the Son of God, and that believing, ye might have life through his name."

3

ASCENSION

IN obedience to the command of their risen Lord the apostles left Jerusalem and journeyed north to Galilee. How long ago it was, or so it would seem to them, since they had seen these green slopes alight with gloriously hued anemones, this beloved lake shining under the blue skies. How delightful to enjoy the warm embraces of their families, the hearty salutations of their friends; to gaze at their boats once again. The whole countryside was full of hallowed memories—the spot where that poor woman had been healed, the little bay where he had taught the people from the boat, over there on that distant curve of the hill the slopes where the five thousand had sat down to eat. And to make all these things truly blessed, the knowledge that their Lord was risen and was alive for evermore.

How long they waited in this happy setting for the coming of their Lord we do not know; but it would probably not be many days before Peter had a great urge to feel the swell of the sea under his feet again. It was the most natural thing in the world for Peter, watching the evening shadows darken the distant shore, to say to his companions, "I go afishing". Nor is it difficult to see the other six responding to his mood. Through the dark hours of the night they laboured, Peter thrilling at the response of the boat to his experienced hand; at the sight of the familiar fishing grounds indicated by the landmarks silhouetted against the evening sky; at the sound of the nets splashing into the inky waters. Yet it was a fruitless night, and when the dawn glowed from the eastern hills there were no fish in the nets or in the boat.

They were a hundred yards from the shore when they saw a figure on the beach indistinct in the hazy light. A voice carried clearly over the water to them, "Children, have you any meat?" It was a casual question, and they had no suspicion. "No", they called back. "Cast the net on the right side of the ship, and ye shall find." Still they suspected nothing: they pulled in their nets, dragged them across the boat and dropped them over the other side. Immediately the sea was boiling with fish. John suddenly looked up from his work to stare intently across the water. This experience had touched a chord of memory. What he saw convinced him. It was no other. He called Peter over to him. "It is the Lord!" Peter's response was immediate: it can only be truly explained by those unrecorded moments when Jesus had appeared to him alone: it was the action of a man who was conscious of a blessed forgiveness. He could not wait for the clumsy boat to be manoeuvred to the shore, but flinging on his coat he dived into the sea and swam quickly in. The others made haste to land the catch, pulling the heavy laden net in with the dinghy. Peter ran up the beach towards the Lord, and found him standing near a fire of coals. Did Peter remember the last brazier at which he had warmed himself? It was a thoughtful provision for cold and tired disciples, but it was also a challenge. They found that Jesus had food prepared for them, but he asked them to bring the fish they had caught. They counted a hundred and fifty three. "Come and dine." So they gathered round him, each one of them knowing, none daring to ask.

This incident teems with lessons. Toiling after their own inclinations was toiling in the darkness, toiling for nothing. But in the light of morning in the presence of their Lord and under his instructions, the nets were full. The Lord speaks sometimes in an unfamiliar voice, but when we obey we recognize him because of the results of our labours. The meal that we eat, he has prepared, yet the results of our own toil are added to it, though without his instructions and our obedience those results would not have been possible.

There was in the incident too, a gentle reminder to the disciples that their fishing grounds must change once more: not the smiling waters of Galilee but the towns and villages of Judea, and eventually, all the world, until that day when the net is full and the fish are counted, and the final feast is prepared.

Peter has not yet fully atoned for his faithlessness. Yet it is to prepare him for the future and not to punish him for the past that this ordeal comes to him. Now he is in the presence of the Lord, the disciples are his witnesses, the brazier of coal burns at his side.

He has still to reclaim his right to be the Rock man. "Simon, son of Jonas, lovest thou me more than these?" Do you love me with that love which I have shown to you? and is your love greater than the love of these other disciples? You, Peter, who so confidently cried, "Though all men, Lord, yet not I"?

Ah! Peter is not the confident man he was a few short weeks ago. He cannot say, "Yea, Lord". He cannot measure his love against that of his fellows. But he can with deep sincerity say, "Thou knowest that I am thy friend". "Feed my lambs." The ordeal was not over. Three times Jesus had warned him, three times Peter had failed, and now three times Jesus renewed his commission. "Simon, son of Jonas, lovest thou me?" "Yea, Lord, thou knowest that I am thy friend." "Tend my sheep."

"Simon, son of Jonas, art thou even my friend?" Peter's heart was bursting with grief that Jesus should question even his friendship. In his distress he appealed to his Lord's own discernment of him. "Here I stand, Lord; look right into my soul. You know all things, you know that I am your friend." "Feed my sheep."

It was a painful but revealing ordeal. Peter would never forget, nor would any of the six disciples who watched. We should not forget. Love for our Lord is the indispensable quality for service. With that qualification we feed the sheep, holding the hand of the feeble, strengthening the faint-hearted, rebuking the wayward, instructing the simple: leading the flock over mountain and through desert ever nearer to the sheepfold. Protestations, however vigorous, are not enough: the fire of coals is in our midst.

Jesus turned again to Peter. "Verily, verily, I say unto thee"—an affirmation used in a terrible setting the last time it was addressed to him—"when thou wast young, thou girdest thyself, and walkest whither thou wouldst, but when thou shalt be old thou shalt stretch forth thy hands, and another shall gird thee; and carry thee whither thou wouldst not." So Jesus showed Peter the end of his pilgrimage. From the natural point of view it was a sad picture, but to Peter it was a glorious one. It showed him faithful to the end, following his Lord even to the bitterness of the cross itself. Because we know Peter, we know that, looking steadfastly at that picture, he was content.

He looked at John, the disciple Jesus loved. "What shall this man do?" Gently Jesus showed him that his vocation was to follow obediently, not to speculate upon the road another pilgrim takes. John had a work still to do after Peter had glorified God in his death; and it was not until that work was faithfully done that he followed Peter, resting in hope of the glorious day when his Lord shall return to consummate his Father's purpose.

On a mountain in Galilee, Jesus appeared again to the eleven. On another occasion Paul tells us that more than five hundred met him. He commissioned the Twelve to go forth in his name, teaching all nations and baptizing those who believed. Though they would not see him, he would be with them in their labours: "Lo! I am with you alway, even unto the end of the world".

Finally the day came when they saw their Lord for the last time. He led them out as he had so often done before to the Mount of Olives. They climbed over the brow of the hill until the city was lost to view and Bethany lay before them across the valley. He commanded them to wait in Jerusalem until they should be endued with power from on high. He lifted up his hands and blessed them.

And as he blessed them, he was taken up from them until a cloud received him from their sight. They watched fascinated, his words of blessing still in their ears. And then Two stood by them in glistening garments.

"Ye men of Galilee, why stand ye gazing up into heaven? This same Jesus, which is taken up from you into heaven, shall so come in like manner as ye have seen him go into heaven."

They had learned their lesson; they knew that although the heavens had received him, he was with them still. With great joy in their hearts they returned to Jerusalem to offer their lives in his service.

Two thousand years later we find ourselves in their place, the disciples of Jesus: loving the Lord they loved, serving the Lord they served. The world has changed strangely since their time, but the Gospel has not changed, nor has the commission. Where they failed, we find ourselves slipping. In the fountain of their strength we find the source of ours: the words of love that sustained and comforted them bring us peace and joy. As throughout their troubled lives they looked beyond to the final glory, so we echo their words, "Even so, come, Lord Jesus". And while we work and watch and pray, we hear, as they did, the words of our Lord, "Lo, I am with you alway, even unto the end of the world".

SUBJECT INDEX

curing of ten lepers: 266
Bartimaeus receives sight: 279
the withered fig tree: 286
replaces the ear of Malchus: 319
the last: 346
MOSES
at transfiguration: 205
MOUNT OF TRANSFIGURATION
its locality: 204
MOUNT OLIVET
Christ repairs there to pray: 221
the place of ascension: 348

N

NAIN
the widow's son restored: 140
NATHANAEL
visited hy Philip: 52
his confession: 52
NAZARETH
the return of the holy family to: 10
its appearance: 11
revisited: 80, 169
rejects Jesus 82
NICODEMUS
visits Jesus: 62, 63
takes a stand against the
Pharisees: 220
begs the body of Jesus: 335

O

OLIVET
the prophecy: 302

P

PALESTINE
short of food: 30
PARABLES
the sower: 156
wheat and tares: 156
mustard: 156
leaven: 156
dragnet: 157
good Samaritan: 236
friend at midnight: 238
the rich fool: 241
the barren fig tree: 243, 247
the great supper: 255
lost sheep, lost coin, lost son: 257
the prodigal son: 258
rich man and Lazarus: 260
Pharisee and publican: 268
labourers in the vineyard: 272
of the pounds: 278
pound wrapped in a napkin: 278
of the two sons: 290
of the marriage feast: 291
the ten virgins: 303
the talents: 303
sheep and the goats: 303

PEOPLE
thought the Kingdom of God
imminent: 278
PETER
called: 51
invited to walk on the sea: 180
his affirmation "Thou art the
Christ": 201
Christ's church founded on his
confession: 201
objects to Christ's death: 203
"We have left all and followed
thee": 271
and John seek a room for the
last passover: 309
"I will lay down my life for
thee": 312
uses his sword: 319
his denial of Christ: 321, 323
remembered his loyalty: 321
in the palace with John: 321
his testing time: 321
visits the tomb: 339
Sees his risen Lord: 342
"I go a-fishing": 345
Sees his Lord again: 346
"Simon, son of Jonas, lovest
thou me?": 346
received the command "Feed my
sheep": 347
PHARISEES
their puerilites and hypocrisy:
35, 196
PHARISEES AND SADDUCEES
seek a sign: 194
their leaven: 195, 196
PHILIP
called: 51
visits Nathanael: 52
probably visited by Caiaphas: 326
his weakness at the tribunal: 329
PILATE'S WIFE
Claudia Procula: 327
her message: 328
POLITICS
political excitement in Judea: 27
PRAYER
Jesus rises early and seeks a
solitary place to pray: 90
spent the night in, before
choosing the twelve: 113
Jesus taught his disciples to
pray: 132, 238
Christ's request to the Father: 301
Christ prays on the cross: 333
PUBLICANS
hated: 102